Antisemitism

Antisemitism

■ ■ ■

The Longest Hatred

Robert S. Wistrich

■

Pantheon Books   New York

Pour Dany
L'amour vaincra

All rights reserved under International and Pan-American Copyright
Conventions. Published in the United States by Pantheon Books, a
division of Random House, Inc., New York.
Originally published in Great Britain
by Methuen London in 1991.

Grateful acknowledgment is made to Bat Ye'or for permission to reprint
material from her published lecture, *Oriental Jewry and the Dhimmi Image
in Contemporary Arab Nationalism* (Geneva, 1979, p. 3), given at Jews
College, London on September 5, 1978 (Chairman: Sir Harold Wilson).
Reference is also made to her works *The Dhimmi: Jews and Christians
under Islam*, New Jersey, London and Toronto, 1985 as well as her most
recent publication *Les Chretientes d'Orient entre Jihad et Dhimmitude:
VIIe-XXe siecle*, Paris, 1991.

Library of Congress Cataloging-in-Publication Data

Wistrich, Robert S., 1945–
Antisemitism : the longest hatred / Robert S. Wistrich.
p.   cm.
Includes bibliographical references and index.
ISBN 0-679-40946-7
1. Antisemitism.   I. Title.
DS145.W55   1992
909'.04924—dc20   91–53083

Manufactured in the United States of America
First American Edition

Contents

List of Illustrations

The publishers are grateful to the following for permission to reproduce the illustrations. All possible care has been taken to trace and acknowledge the sources of illustrations. If any errors have accidentally occurred, however, we shall be happy upon notification to correct them in any future editions of this book.

The Ancient Art and Architecture Collection: 1a; *Encyclopaedia Judaica* (Jerusalem, 1985): 1b; Bibliothèque Nationale, Paris: 2a; Archive Dr Tim Gidal: 2b, 8a (*Puck*, Leipzig, 1876), 8b, 11a; Beth Hatefutsoth, University of Tel-Aviv: 3a; Professor Moshe Lazar: 3b, 7b; Offentliche Kunstsammlung, Basel (Hieronymus Hess, 1829): 4a; Bildarchiv Foto Marburg, Marburg (Lucas Cranach the Younger, 1560): 4b; Museum der Stadt, Worms: 5a; Historisches Museum, Frankfurt au Main: 5b, 10a; Anne Frank Foundation, Amsterdam: 6, 16b; Eduard Fuchs, *Die Juden in der Karikatur* (Munich, 1921): 7a, 9a, 9b; The Hulton-Deutsch Collection: 9c, 11b, 12c, 13a, 15b; Norman Cohn, *Warrant for Genocide: The Myth of the World Jewish Conspiracy and the Protocols of the Elders of Zion* London, 1967): 10b; Wiener Library, London: 12a, 12b; Popperfoto: 13b, 14b; ANP-foto, Amsterdam: 14a, 16a; Stern Syndication: 15a; David King Collection: 17, 18b; Jewish National and University Library, Jerusalem: 18a; School of Slavonic and East European Studies, University of London: 19a; Simon Wiesenthal Center Archives, Los Angeles, Ca: 19b, 21b, 22c, 23a; Katz Pictures: 19c; Associated Press: 20a, 20b; Embassy of Israel, The Hague: 21a; Judith Vogt, *Historien om et image Antisemitisme og Antizionisme i Karikaturer* (Oslo, 1978): 22a, 22b; *Der Spiegel:* 23b; Frank Spooner Pictures (Esais Baitel): 24.

Author's Note

This work originated out of a major three-part television documentary series, *The Longest Hatred*, first shown on Thames Television. Rex Bloomstein, the director and producer of the series, is a prominent TV documentary film-maker whose work includes *Traitors to Hitler*, *Auschwitz and the Allies*, *The Gathering*, and *Jewish Humour – American Style*. I had the privilege of collaborating closely with Rex Bloomstein in the making of the film, and gratefully acknowledge his encouragement, advice, and valuable help in facilitating the writing of this book accompanying the series.

RW

Acknowledgements

Written to accompany the Thames Television series on antisemitism, *The Longest Hatred*, with which I have been closely associated as historical adviser, this book's origins go back much further to my long-standing concern with the nature of antisemitism, which already found expression in several of my earlier articles and books. Although there have been a number of important scholarly books published on this subject during the past twenty years, they have been mainly confined to a particular aspect of the problem, to a single country or to a definite period of history, whether ancient, medieval or modern. What has been lacking is a comprehensive *overview* of the phenomenon by an individual author which would trace the entire history of antisemitism from its beginnings until the present day, in a form accessible to the non-specialist reader.

My decision to embark upon this difficult enterprise was not taken on a sudden impulse. It was given crucial encouragement by Simon Wiesenthal, who first proposed, five years ago, that I examine the history of the link between antisemitism and anti-Zionism. With his forceful personality and persuasiveness he convinced me (not that I needed much convincing) of the urgency of this task. His support was reinforced by a grant from the Vidal Sassoon International Centre for the Study of Antisemitism at the Hebrew University of Jerusalem. I am grateful to the Centre and its Director, Dr Shmuel Almog (whose own important work in this field and courteous advice I greatly value), for their patience.

Acknowledgements

My initial research, without which this book could never have been written, was undertaken at a number of archives and libraries whose assistance I am happy to acknowledge. They include the National Library, the Central Zionist Archives and the Archives of the History of the Jewish People in Jerusalem; the Wiener Library in Tel Aviv and London; the Bibliothèque Nationale, the Archives of the Alliance Israélite Universelle and the Centre de Documentation Juive in Paris; the Centre de Documentation Moyen-Orient, Geneva; the Austrian National Library in Vienna; the Public Record Office, the British Library, University College Library and the Institute of Jewish Affairs in London; St Antony's Middle East Centre in Oxford and the Kressel Archive in Yarnton; Harvard University Library, Boston; the Archives of the American Jewish Committee, New York; the Library of Congress, Washington, DC; and the Simon Wiesenthal Center, Los Angeles.

What appears in this book is a highly condensed and concentrated version of this research, aimed at the interested general reader without encumbering him or her with an unnecessarily massive scholarly apparatus or an overly dry, academic approach. Nevertheless, I have tried to avoid any oversimplification by sticking to a *historical* method that emphasises the continuities in antisemitism even though the central thrust of the book is an analysis of its *contemporary* manifestations. I have been aided in walking this tightrope of interlocking past and present by my own pedagogical experience in teaching related courses at the Hebrew University and abroad.

The book would not have taken its present form without the encouragement of my friend and colleague Rex Bloomstein, who invited me a year ago to collaborate with him on making a three-hour television documentary on the topic, which proved to be an immensely challenging, if exhausting, project. This involved countless interviews, travel to many countries, the viewing and discussion of films, videos, transcripts, reports, surveys and recent scholarly research relevant to the topic. Rex Bloomstein not only gave me full access to this valuable raw material but, with his inexorable enthusiasm for the subject, helped to provide a new focus for my own concerns. Working on this project brought home to me in a peculiarly graphic way the *immediacy* of the resurgence of antisemitism. I hope that this will be reflected in my text, which seeks to combine scholarly rquirements with a certain freshness of approach.

I have acknowledged in the notes the many intellectual debts I owe to specific individuals with whom I have shared ideas or crossed swords in argument over different aspects of this subject. I should like, however, to take this opportunity to thank those most immediately helpful to the completion of this project under the special pressures of a television schedule. My thanks, therefore, go to Loyce Blackmur, Teresa Cherfas, Mirelle Harris, David Hudson-Millman and Sophie Levey of the Nucleus television production team; Roger Bolton of Thames Television for his perceptive observations; Michael May, Director of the Institute of Jewish Affairs for his discreet and valued assistance; Sara Drake of Thames Television and Anne Mansbridge of Methuen for their encouragement and belief that the task could be accomplished despite a punishing schedule; my mother for looking after me during an extended stay in London; and above all my wife, Daniella, for her wonderful patience and unfailing support.

Hopefully, this book will encourage the general reader, whether puzzled, bewildered, intrigued or simply outraged at the persistence of antisemitism, to delve still further into this painful, often shocking, yet perennially fascinating subject.

Robert S. Wistrich
London
January 1991

Introduction

'Antisemitism' is a problematic term, first invented in the 1870s by the German journalist Wilhelm Marr to describe the 'non-confessional' hatred of Jews and Judaism which he and others like him advocated. The movement which began at that time in Germany and soon spread to neighbouring Austria, Hungary, France and Russia was a self-conscious reaction to the emancipation of the Jews and their entry into non-Jewish society. In that sense it appeared to be a novel phenomenon, since, as the early antisemites were at pains to stress, they were not opposed to Jews on *religious* grounds but claimed to be motivated by social, economic, political or 'racial' considerations.

Religious hostility in late nineteenth-century Europe was regarded by many intellectuals as something medieval, obscurantist and backward. There was clearly a need to establish a new paradigm for anti-Jewishness which sounded more neutral, objective, 'scientific' and in keeping with the liberal, enlightened *Zeitgeist*. After all, Jews by virtue of their emancipation had become *equal* citizens before the law in European societies which, formally at least, had abandoned discrimination based on religious differences. Antisemitism which grounded itself in racial and ethnic feelings provided a way around this problem. By focusing attention on allegedly permanent, unchanging characteristics of the Jews as a social and national group (which depicted them as being fundamentally 'alien' to their fellow citizens) the antisemites hoped to delegitimise Jewish equality. They sought to restore the

xv

social boundaries which had begun to disappear in Europe and they ultimately expected to return the Jews to their earlier pre-emancipated status.

'Antisemitism' – a term which came into general use as part of this politically motivated anti-Jewish campaign of the 1880s – was never directed against 'Semites' as such. The term 'Semitic' derived from the Biblical Shem, one of Noah's three sons, and designated a group of cognate languages including Hebrew, Arabic, Aramaic, Babylonian, Assyrian and Ethiopic, rather than an ethnic or racial group. Similarly, the contrasting term 'Aryan' or 'Indo-European', which became popular at this time, referred originally to the Indian branch of the Indo-European languages. Strictly speaking, 'Aryans' were people speaking Sanskrit and related languages who had invaded India in pre-historic times and subjugated its indigenous inhabitants. Indians and Iranians were 'Aryans' but Germans and North Europeans certainly were *not*, any more than European Jews, who no longer spoke Hebrew, could be meaningfully described as 'Semites'.

Nevertheless, in the late nineteenth century this pseudo-scientific nonsense became eminently respectable even among the European intellectual élites, so that the distinction between 'Aryan' and 'Semite' was easily grafted on to the much older distinction between Christian and Jew. As a result, for the last hundred years, the illogical term 'antisemitism', which never really meant hatred of 'Semites' (for example, Arabs) at all, but rather hatred of Jews, has come to be accepted in general usage as denoting *all* forms of hostility towards Jews and Judaism throughout history.

There is clearly a danger in using antisemitism in this overly generalised way, extending it to all times and places regardless of specific circumstances, differences between historical epochs and cultures, or other factors that might give the term more specificity and critical sharpness. Antisemitism is *not* a natural, metahistorical or a metaphysical phenomenon whose essence has remained unchanged throughout all its manifestations over the centuries. Nor is it an intrinsic part of the psychic structure of Gentiles, a kind of microbe or virus which invariably attacks non-Jews, provoking the 'eternal hatred' for the 'eternal people'. Such a theory, which has some roots in the Jewish tradition ('Esau hates Jacob', the legacy of Amalek, etc.) and was adopted by early Zionists in Eastern Europe such as Pinsker, Lilienblum and Sokolow, is quite unhistorical.

It ignores the fact that Jews have often been welcomed by the surrounding society; that their equality of status and integration was accepted as a binding legal and social principle in many countries during the modern period; and it crucially forgets that Jewish participation in cultural, scientific, economic and political life since the Western Enlightenment has in many respects been a remarkable success story. If antisemitism had really been a 'hereditary disease of the Gentiles', or been based on an instinctive racial aversion to Jews (as antisemites sometimes claim), such a development would have been impossible. Admittedly, there has also been a backlash to Jewish integration, influence or success at some points in time – whether in first-century Alexandria and Rome, in medieval Muslim or Christian Spain, in fin-de-siècle Paris and Vienna or in Weimar Germany – but this pattern has definite historical causes and has nothing to do with any theory of innate Gentile antisemitism.

Any empirically valid discussion of antisemitism or hatred of Jews must, in my opinion, first of all come to terms with the problem of its historical continuity and development. This necessarily leads us back to the Hellenistic era, when a widespread Jewish Diaspora first emerged which was quite distinctive in the ancient world. Not only were the Jews the only monotheistic minority in this pagan world, bearers of a doctrine of election which claimed that Judaism was the sole truth, the supreme ethical teaching; not only did they persist in their historic existence as a separate social and religious group; not only did they refuse even to intermingle with the

Gentiles because of their own dietary laws, Sabbath observance and prohibition on intermarriage; above all, this unique Diasporic nation which had set itself apart asserted spiritual supremacy over the polytheistic majority.

There is nothing surprising in the fact that such special characteristics and claims could provoke the hostility or resentment which one finds in Greek and Latin literature. To some extent this pre-Christian antisemitism looks like the normal, xenophobic prejudice which has prevailed between ethno-religious groups during virtually every period of history. But such a plausible conclusion ignores the *unique* character of the Jewish Diaspora, its unusual social cohesion, compactness and religiously sanctioned exclusiveness. This does not mean that the cause of antisemitism lay in the Jews themselves, but it can help us to understand how the peculiar brand of social hostility which we call by this name first arose as *one* possible response (there were of course others, ranging from admiration to indifference) to the reality of Jewish exclusiveness.

Pagan anti-Jewishness is important because it provided fertile soil for its Christian heirs, and it also reminds us that there was a significant form of hostility to Jews in Antiquity which *preceded* the birth of Christianity. Not a few early Christians had, for example, absorbed this Jew-hatred as a consequence of their pagan upbringing. Nevertheless, it is undeniable that Christianity would appear on the stage of history as a *negation* of Judaism in a much deeper sense than its pagan predecessors; that its theological polemics against Judaism were to be vital to its own identity far more than was the case for any other religion or culture. No other religion, indeed, makes the accusation that Christianity has made against the Jews, that they are literally the *murderers* of God. No other religion has so consistently attributed to them a universal, cosmic quality of evil, depicting them as children of the Devil, followers of Antichrist or as the 'synagogue of Satan'. The fantasies concerning Jews which were developed in medieval Christendom, about their plotting to destroy Christianity, poison wells, desecrate the host, massacre Christian children or establish their world dominion, represent a qualitative leap compared with anything put forward by their pagan precursors. Such charges, beginning with deicide, are peculiarly *Christian*, though in the twentieth century they have been taken up by Islam as well as by secular political religions such as Nazism or Bolshevism which have exploited the fiction of a Jewish world conspiracy.

Thus it is evident that Christian anti-Judaism and anti-semitism did add a wholly new theological and *metaphysical* dimension to antisemitism which was absent in its pagan forerunners and quite distinct from the stigmatising or persecution of other minority groups. The pervasive influence of Christianity (from the fourth century AD), on government, culture and society led to the marginalisation of the Jews and their institutionalised oppression. The Christian theology which had usurped the Divine Promises to the Jews and proclaimed the Church as God's Chosen Elect, cast Israel in the role of God's forsaken, rejected and abandoned people – condemned to wandering and exile.

In the writings of the Church Fathers the negation of the Jews' religious and cultural values became a central motif. An overwhelmingly negative stereotype of the 'deicide people' was transmitted through theological writings, the sermons of the clergy, the mystery and Passion plays, folklore, ballads and the plastic arts. This hostile collective stereotype of a Jewish people bearing the mark of Cain, a nation of Christ-killers and infidels in league with the Devil, became deeply embedded in the Western psyche following the massacres of Jews during the Crusades. During the next few centuries, new and even more irrational myths were added, that of the Jew as a ritual murderer, desecrator of the Host wafer, an agent of Antichrist, usurer, sorcerer and vampire. As Christianity spread among all the peoples of Europe, this devastating image crystallised until it was an integral part of European and Western culture, a fact which more than any other accounts for the pervasiveness of antisemitism to this day.

Jew-hatred no longer required any connection with real human relationships, indeed it no longer needed the presence of Jews at all. The stereotype had acquired a cultural dynamic of its own, as in medieval England after the expulsion of 1290, in Spain after the mass Jewish exodus of 1492, or in the 'Judaising' persecutions of Muscovite Russia. Even today, in post-Holocaust societies like Poland, Austria or Rumania where there are very few Jews left, one finds a similar phenomenon of 'antisemitism without Jews'. Nothing could make clearer the fallacy that antisemitism can be simplistically viewed as a 'natural' or even a 'pathological' response to a *concrete* Jewish presence, to Jewish activities, behaviour or traditions.

The common denominator in all these societies is of course the impact of the Christian legacy and its translation over centuries into legalised discrimination, Jewish servitude, ghettoisation and the narrow economic specialisation of Jewry. Even where Jews converted in large numbers, as in late medieval Spain, the descendants of the converts were regarded with hostility and suspicion, leading to the Inquisition and 'purity of blood' statutes that pointed the way to modern racial antisemitism. Not even the rise of humanism during the Renaissance and Reformation could successfully throw off the impact of the medieval image of the Jew. A reformer like Erasmus never dreamed of applying his humanist teachings on toleration to the Jews, who simply remained beyond the pale as far as he was concerned. Martin Luther, for his part, reiterated all the medieval myths about Jews, reinforcing rather than undermining them with an apocalyptic fury and vehemence all his own. Thus Luther's assault on the Papacy and the whole fabric of the Catholic Church, instead of liberating the Jews made his Protestant followers more suspicious of them. Had they not refused to convert even after the great German Reformer had revealed to them the pure, unadulterated word of God? Were they not secretly encouraging the 'Judaising' Christian sects in Central Europe? Were not the stubborn Jews in league with the Muslim Turks and perhaps even with Rome in seeking to destroy the new Church from within?

If the Reformation failed to bring any diminution of antisemitism, the eighteenth-century Enlightenment offered, at least on the face of things, a more promising prospect. There were Enlightenment writers who condemned the persecution of Jews as a way of attacking Christian intolerance. Their anti-clericalism and concern for universal principles of human rights led them to a new conception of the status of the Jews, which found expression in the French Revolution of 1789. The Jews were not to be emancipated as a community but as *individual* human beings, the assumption being that, once oppression was removed, their distinctive group identity would disappear. There was no sympathy among the French revolutionaries for Judaism as such, which was generally viewed in Voltairean terms as a barbarous superstition.

The Enlightenment and the French Revolution demonstrated that anti-Judaism and antisemitism did not require a specifically Christian source of inspiration and could even be animated by anti-Christian sentiments. Enlightened Europeans and their radical successors in the nineteenth century, on the Left as well as the Right, were nevertheless still influenced by Christian stereotypes when they attacked Judaism or denounced the 'Jewish' origins of Christianity. Even wholly secularised antisemites like Voltaire, Bruno Bauer, Richard Wagner and Eugen Dühring always assumed that Christianity was a superior religion to Judaism and did not hesitate to draw on Christian teachings to reinforce their own cultural or racist perspectives. They inherited the pervasiveness of the Christian antagonism to Jewry while no longer believing in its scheme of salvation, which had still retained an overriding commitment to the conversion of the Jews. This development opened up a dangerous situation whose demonic possibilities only became fully apparent with the rise of Nazism. For although Christianity had provided the seedbed on which Nazi racialist doctrines concerning the Jews could flourish, the Church still provided the Jews with an exit. If a Jew converted he was saved. There was no need for the extermination of the Jews because they had their place, even if it was a subordinate and degraded one, in the Christian world-order.

The Nazis took over all the negative anti-Jewish stereotypes in Christianity but they removed the escape clause. There was no longer any way in which even fully assimilated or baptised Jews could flee from the sentence of death which had been passed by the inexorable laws of race. In that sense, the 'Final Solution', the purification of a world that was deemed corrupt and evil because of the very existence of the Jews, went beyond even the most radical Christian solution to the 'Jewish Question'. Hitler and Nazism grew out of a Christian European culture, but that does not mean that Auschwitz was pre-programmed in the logic of Christianity. Indeed, one could argue that the decline of religious belief by removing all moral restraints actually intensified the anti-semitism which had been incubated for centuries under its protective shield. If anything, this released an even more virulent Germanic strain of the same virus which ultimately turned on Christianity itself as one of the prime symptoms of the so-called 'Judaisation' of Western civilisation.

Antisemitism did not disappear with the Holocaust any more than it has been eradicated by secular universalist ideologies like Soviet Communism or indeed Zionism, which proposed to 'normalise' the Jewish status by creating an independent nation-state in Israel. The image of the Jew as an outsider, a nonconformist, an anomaly and an irritant has survived the rise and fall of all the secular ideologies of the nineteenth and twentieth centuries. Antisemitism, too, has adapted itself to the post-war situation of Jewry, transformed by the creation of Israel, by the Cold War and by the response of the Arab and Islamic world to the challenge of a non-Muslim, non-Arabic-speaking Jewish state in its midst.

These new factors have, if anything, heightened the usefulness of antisemitism as a weapon that can be exploited for the most protean purposes. Fundamentally irrational myths like *The Protocols of the Elders of Zion* have found a new lease on life in the post-war era and are still widely believed in the Arab world seventy years after their definitive exposure as a forgery. As Hitler put it in *Mein Kampf* in 1924: 'The *Frankfurter Zeitung* repeats again and again that the *Protocols* are forgeries. This alone is evidence of their authenticity.' Much the same might be said today by certain Arab nationalists, Islamic fundamentalists, Russian antisemites or European and American neo-Nazis. A tissue of lies they may be, but in terms of their effect the *Protocols* might just as well have been true. For wherever there is a will to believe, events can be made to fit even into the paranoid vision of the Jewish world conspiracy, with its geo-political centre in Zion and its secret affiliates supposedly operating throughout the globe.

The modern antisemitic imagination has been coloured for over a century by gloomy, apocalyptic prophecies of the coming victory of the omnipotent Jew. A demonic, mythical creature whose undeviating will to destroy the Gentiles is assumed to lie behind all the negative processes of change and provides a seductively simplistic explanation for a world out of joint – whether it be fear of pollution by alien, 'inferior' races; the *angst* provoked by class struggle, ethnic and religious conflict, the levelling tendencies of mass society; the hatred of capitalism or of Communism, of modern urban civilisation or of liberal, pluralist democracy; the belief in sinister occult forces (freemasons, Jews, etc.) working to undermine order, hierarchy, authority and tradition; or else the fear of a spiritual vacuum induced by the decline of Christianity or Islam in a world of rapid modernisation and social change. The same delirious causality, developed during the Christian Middle Ages, appears to haunt the modern antisemitic discourse. The principle of evil is not in ourselves. It comes from the outside, from the insidious 'other', it is the product of conspiracy and of devilish forces whose incarnation is the mythical Jew.

A century ago, it might be Edouard Drumont's cryptic formula, 'All comes from the Jew, all returns to the Jew', Wilhelm Marr's prophecy of *Finis Germaniae* or Houston Chamberlain's vision of Teutons and Jews locked in a relentless battle of Destiny. Fifty years ago it was Hitler's either-or polarisation of the struggle for world hegemony between 'Aryans' and 'Semites'; followed in 1952 by the dying Stalin's vision of 'rootless cosmopolitans' and Jewish 'poisoners' in the service of Wall Street capitalism and Western intelligence services (the Doctors' Plot); then came the post-Stalin imagery of the 'world Zionist corporation' with its octopus-like tentacles reaching out to subvert the 'socialist camp' and forestall Third World national liberation movements; more recently we have seen the efforts of Arab dictators or Islamic theocrats (Qaddafi, Saddam Hussein, Khomeini, etc.) to unite the Muslim masses against the deadly threat of a Zionist-imperialist 'cancer', said to be threatening to extirpate their existence.

In all these cases we find across the cultural and political divides an astonishingly similar conspiracy theory of history, society and politics, integrated into a closed system of belief and salvationist politics whose eschatological drive is always directed against the Jews. This is a murky apocalyptic fantasy-world, imbued with sadistic visions and coloured at times by occult sectarianism, permeated with notions of retributive punishment on a cosmic scale if the implacable enemy is not eradicated in time. Yet this negative millenarianism, with its vision of the satanic, ubiquitous, immoral and all-powerful Jews or scheming Zionists, is often harnessed to a cold, calculating political agenda, turning antisemitism into a crucial lever of mass mobilisation and totalitarian control. Did not Hitler tell Hermann Rauschning that it was from the *Protocols* that he had learned the methods of 'political intrigue, the technique of conspiracy, revolutionary subversion, as well as prevarication, deception and organization'?

Any attempt to analyse the resurgence of antisemitism in so many parts of the globe, less than fifty years after the Holocaust, must come to grips with this miasma of nightmarish paranoia, millennial fantasy, homicidal hatred and sheer political cynicism. It must always take into account the special and peculiar Christian hatred of the Jew that ultimately derives from the ambiguous origins of Christianity and its obsession with the non-recognition by the Jewish people of Christ as the true Messiah. It has to take cognisance of the seething hatreds unleashed in a radicalised Islam, not only against Israel and Zionism, but also against Judaism and the Jews, whose history is now being vilified by some Muslims in a fashion previously unknown. It has to deal with the unraveling of the Messianic vision of Communism in Central and Eastern Europe which has generated a revival of 'national' and 'Christian' values against the intangible cabal of 'cosmopolitan' and 'godless' conspirators, still allegedly striving for world domination. This free-floating antisemitism, for which the actual presence of Jews is almost immaterial, thrives on archetypal fears, anxieties and reflexes that seem to defy any rational analysis.

More alarming still is the advanced state of decay within the Communist heartland of the Soviet Union, where the ground appears to be burning under the feet of the still substantial Jewish minority. Trapped in a crossfire of nationalist hysteria, ethnic conflicts, mass deprivation and the possibility of civil war as internal centrifugal forces undermine the arthritic colossus of Communist power, Soviet Jewry is fleeing *en masse* to the Jewish homeland of Israel. Not even the Scud missiles of the Iraqi dictator can stay the exodus from the bleak despair of the 'socialist' fatherland, to which Soviet Jews had once given their life-blood and intellectual energies.

In the light of these momentous transformations and the continuing threat of antisemitism, the historian might well be tempted to question the value of rational analysis and the applicability of the normal tools of his trade. Is this phenomenon really susceptible to the rules of logic and historical evidence? Is antisemitism ultimately explicable any more than we can explain the mystery of Jewish survival and the tenacious clinging to a vocation and an identity that has exacted so high a price in trials and tribulations over the centuries? Is there really anything new in the endless accusations that have echoed across the centuries from Haman to Hitler? Is there any meaning to be extracted from the myths, the stereotypes, the fantasies and obsessions that have characterised the antisemitic discourse for more than two millennia? Is there any answer to the agonising question of why this people has been subjected to such a seemingly unending catalogue of persecution and discrimination?

The historian cannot in my view give any definitive reply to these questions. What he can do is to provide as lucid an account as possible of the path along which different anti-Jewish traditions have been transmitted. He can examine their continuities and metamorphoses according to changing conditions; he must try to illuminate the mechanisms and consequences of antisemitism in different social, cultural and political contexts. While recognising the astonishing longevity and persistence of the phenomenon, the similarity and even repetitiveness of much of the antisemitic discourse, he must also be alive to its adaptability to new circumstances and its constant capacity for renewal. There is no universal key to the understanding of antisemitism, nor should it be seen as a completely intractable phenomenon of equal intensity at different times and in different places. The historian may be ultimately unable to explain the 'why' of this extraordinarily complex phenomenon, but if he can demonstrate 'how' it came to develop into what we are witnessing today, then that, too, is a measure of progress.

Part 1

∎ ∎ ∎

∎

From The Cross
to the Swastika

1

■ ■ ■

Pagan Roots of Antisemitism

The relative importance of antisemitism in pagan Antiquity has long been a source of contention and disagreement among historians. Not only are the sources and documentation often fragmentary and the uncertainties manifold but the term itself – in so far as it evokes an irrational, deeply rooted hatred of Jews more typical of the Middle Ages or of the modern world – may be misleading when applied to Antiquity. Certainly, racial antagonism of the kind presupposed by the modern concept of 'antisemitism' pioneered in the nineteenth century does not appear to have existed in the ancient world. Nor does religious hostility of the type exemplified by the Christian Middle Ages (and to a lesser extent by Islam) seem to have been a decisive factor.[1] Economic grievances against the wealth of the Jews or against their middleman role were also far less significant in Antiquity than they would become in later periods, though one may assume that human greed was, even then, an element in hatred of Jews at the popular level. Nevertheless, many of the arguments that belong to the arsenal of medieval and modern antisemites had already surfaced in the Hellenistic and Roman literature about Jews, demonstrating the longevity and persistence of the phenomenon itself.[2]

The emergence of antisemitism in history must, however, be distinguished from the 'normal' kinds of territorial conflict or hostilities between rival powers that have always characterised human history, including that of the Jews in their own homeland. Only after the beginning of their Dispersion, especially in the third century BC, do we find responses to the

3

Jewish Diaspora in the Hellenistic world which reflect through the prism of antisemitic discourse the uniqueness of the phenomenon which it represented. At the simplest level this uniqueness was exemplified by the very persistence of the Jews in their historic existence as a distinct social and religious group in exile. Instead of intermingling with Gentiles and assimilating into the dominant Hellenistic culture, they insisted on preserving their own monotheistic religion, their dietary laws, their separate life-style and above all their self-conscious pride in their special vocation as a people covenanted by God.

Something of the murderous resentment which this attitude could provoke may well be preserved in the Biblical Book of Esther. This quintessentially Diasporic tale probably reflects Hellenistic reactions to the Jews in the second century BC rather than the realities of the Persian Empire four centuries earlier. What is particularly interesting is the discourse of Haman, the archetypal persecutor of Jews, whose name is forever execrated by the stamping of feet and shaking of children's rattles in the synagogues during the Festival of Purim: for Haman, enraged that the Jew Mordechai 'bowed not, nor did him reverence', sought to destroy all the Jews in the Persian Kingdom, arguing that they persisted in observing their own laws, refusing to commingle or to worship either the imperial authority or the national gods.

The archetypal story recorded in the Book of Esther reminds us that for many Jews (and not only the orthodox) anti-semitism is perceived as being virtually coextensive with the history of the Jewish nation. For orthodoxy this is symbolised by an ancient *midrash* in which it is said that the Lord offered the nations of the world the Torah (the religious commandments) which each of them rejected for a different reason. So the Torah was given on Mount Sinai to the Jews instead and hatred of Israel (*Sin'at Yisrael* in the Hebrew root) was simultaneously given to all the nations. According to this meta-historical explanation, which presupposes that the very

4

existence of the Jewish people and its religious vocation arouses Gentile hatred ('Esau hates Jacob' or the 'eternal hatred for the Eternal People' in its secular variation), antisemitism is fated to exist until the end of time.[3] One might indeed go back to the Exodus from Egypt and see in Pharaoh's decree to kill the Israelite first-born male children an antisemitic act. But such an approach, however appealing it may be to the advocates of the thesis of 'eternal antisemitism', tends to replace history with myth and is contradicted by much of the Jewish experience from Antiquity through to modern times.[4]

What is, however, significant is that the story of the Exodus was malevolently rebutted as early as the third century BC by Manetho, an Egyptian priest who was one of the first antisemitic polemicists of Antiquity. His hostile account, repeated by the Alexandrian Apion (who synthesised the Egyptian and Greek brands of antisemitism), presented the Hebrews as a race of lepers who had been cast out of Egypt in the days of Moses.[5] Already in Alexandria, in the three centuries before the Christian era, one finds a seedbed of pagan antisemitism in which accusations which would echo across the centuries are rehearsed by the Graeco-Egyptian intelligentsia of the age. Jewish civilisation is depicted as sterile, having produced nothing useful or great; the Jews are a superstitious, 'godless' people who worship an ass's head in their Temple in Jerusalem; once a year they kidnap a Gentile Greek, who is fattened in order to be eaten by their deity in his Holy of Holies (the first ritual murder charge against Jews known to history). Above all the Jews are exclusivist, their separatism is an expression of misanthropy and hatred of the gods.

These are charges that Apion would carry with him from Alexandria to Rome where they would recur in the writings of some of the great names of Latin literature: Seneca, Juvenal and the historian Cornelius Tacitus. Echoes of this antisemitism can be found, too, in the entourage of Antiochus

Sidetes, the Seleucid ruler who had besieged Jerusalem in 133 BC. His advisers reminded him of the concentrated assault on Judaism by his predecessor Antiochus Epiphanes (175-164 BC) who had sacrificed a swine on the altar at Jerusalem and sprinkled its juices over the Torah statutes that he regarded as inimical to humanity. They even counselled Antiochus Sidetes to completely destroy the Jewish people, since it alone refused to associate with other peoples.[6]

In Alexandria itself, the most advanced point of the Hellenised world outside Greece, the Jews, who represented almost 40 per cent of the city's population, had been in socio-political competition with the Hellenised Egyptians. This was the background to the popular antisemitism that exploded into a veritable pogrom in the year AD 38 at a time when Caligula was Emperor in Rome. The Jews were accused of being unpatriotic and even of manifesting dual loyalties on the occasion of a visit to Alexandria by the Jewish King Agrippa I. But the real cause was the long-standing resentment at their position of privilege, their wealth and their power, whipped up by professional agitators and abetted by the inaction of the Roman governor Flaccus. Again in AD 66 Alexandria erupted following news of the Judean revolt against the Romans, and once more the target of hostility was the equal rights and the special religious privileges granted to the Jews.[7] The question which was raised here was not in itself 'antisemitic' – namely, if the Jews wished to be Alexandrian citizens why did they not worship the same gods as everybody else? But the scale and severity of the riots clearly pointed to the depth of popular hatred for Jews and Judaism.

Vulgar and intellectual antisemitism in the Hellenistic world could constantly draw on the fact that no other nation apart from the Jews so consistently refused to acknowledge the gods of its neighbours, partake in their sacrifices and send gifts to their temples, let alone eat, drink or intermarry with them. As if to compound the insult, these 'haters of mankind' claimed superiority over the 'heathen' in the religious sphere and were engaged in a vast and rather successful proselytising campaign. As with much of the Roman antisemitism which developed in the first century AD the Graeco-Egyptian anti-Jewish literature, epitomised by intellectuals like Apion, Lysimachus and Chaeromon (an Egyptian priest, Stoic philosopher and one of Nero's instructors) was partly a reaction to this intensive Jewish campaign of conversion.[8]

Hence, the other face of antisemitism in the Graeco-Roman world was undoubtedly the sheer power of attraction exerted on the pagan mind by Judaism as a transcendent monotheistic faith and rational code of ethics. Apart from those who loathed Judaism or were indifferent to it, there were also growing numbers who did fully embrace it as converts or else engaged in Judaising practices. Only thus can one explain how Jews came to number some ten million (10-12 per cent of the total population) in the Roman Empire at the beginning of the Christian era. Roman government attitudes to this large and influential community, while often punctuated by persecution and soured by the Jewish revolts (in Palestine and beyond) against Roman rule, were more often characterised by tolerance and even alliance with the Jews.[9]

Admittedly, both Titus and Vespasian refused the honorary titles of 'Judaicus' following their victory in Judea (no doubt because of the negative connotations linked to it) and the Emperor Hadrian, a zealous Helleniser, sought to eradicate Judaism for good by erecting a pagan city, Aelia Capitolina, in Jerusalem. But neither Titus nor perhaps even Hadrian were motivated by a rabid hatred of Jews as such, but rather by the brutal logic of imperial repression directed against a rebellious foe. Although the Jews were the only subjects of the Empire to erupt three times into revolt (not only in Judea but also in the great Diaspora revolt of AD 115–17), and although Hadrian did in fact ban circumcision and other Jewish observances after the Bar-Kochba rising (AD 132–5), the policy of toleration was not fundamentally reversed.

Already under Julius Caesar (100–44 BC) Jews had been

showered with privileges and Cicero in his famous plea *Pro Flacco* (59 BC) observed how numerous they were in Rome, 'their clannishness, their influence in the assemblies'. Naturally such privileges, and the success of the Jews in winning converts to their religion, provoked the envy of their pagan neighbours. Judaism was indeed given exceptional status in the Roman Empire – Jews were, for example, exempt from having to follow many external acts of the Roman cult and they were permitted to observe their Sabbath without hindrance.

Nevertheless, a vehement antisemitism did develop in Rome, especially in the late first century AD, which repeated some of the scurrilous accusations made in the Greek anti-Jewish literature produced in Alexandria, while adding some new motifs of its own. Some Latin authors, like the philosopher Seneca (who died in 65 BC), were angered by the great influence which radically distinctive Jewish customs such as the Sabbath (merely a day of idleness to his jaundiced eye) had attained in Rome.[10] Opposed in general to the spread of oriental cults to the Roman world, Seneca depicted Judaism as a particularly harmful superstition and a humiliating example of how 'the vanquished [the Jews] had imposed their laws upon the victors [the Romans]'. The great rhetorician Quintillian shared Seneca's negative view of the Jewish *superstitio*, as did many of the leading satirists in Rome, above all Juvenal. He openly detested the Greek and oriental atmosphere which had begun to permeate Rome, and the attraction which Judaism had come to exert on Roman youth. Juvenal, like other satirical contemporaries, emphasised the allegedly misanthropic character of the Jews, deriding circumcision and the dietary laws as barbaric and anti-Roman.[11]

However, it was the historian Tacitus, in his *Histories* (composed in the first decade of the second century AD), who represents the apogee of pagan Roman literary antisemitism of the highbrow kind. Like Juvenal he focuses on the misanthropy of the Jews, their separation and isolation from the Gentiles: 'But toward every other people they feel only hatred and enmity. They sit apart at meals, and they sleep apart, and although as a race they are prone to lust, they abstain from intercourse with foreign women; yet among themselves nothing is unlawful.'[12]

For Tacitus, Judaism supposedly encourages disdain of the gods, the abjuring of the fatherland; it means forgetting parents, brothers and children. Of all enslaved peoples, the Jews are the most contemptible and loathsome, their customs are both sordid and absurd.[13] Tacitus concludes that 'all that we hold sacred is profane to them; all that is licit to them is impure to us'. But it is clear that, as with Seneca and Juvenal, what especially troubles Tacitus is the spreading of Judaism, its penetration into various levels of Roman society, including even the upper ranks of men and women in the senatorial class. Pagan Judaising was in their eyes a threat to the traditional warrior virtues and life-pattern of Rome, a major symptom of its corruption and decadence. It was subversive of the self-confident 'Romanism' of the establishment when even the Emperor Domitian's cousin Flavius Clemens and his wife Flavia were convicted of 'atheism' (which in the context meant Judaism or 'drifting into Jewish ways') in AD 95. Among the masses, too, according to the Jewish historian Josephus, 'there is not one city, Greek or barbarian, nor a single nation, to which our custom abstaining from work on the seventh day has not spread, and where fasts and the lighting of lamps and many of our prohibitions in the matter of food are not observed.'[14] Even if we allow for some probable exaggeration in this description, there can be no doubt that Judaism and Jewish proselytism did exercise an important influence on Romans of the first century. It was above all this appeal which explains the upper-class antisemitism in some Roman literary circles.[15] But ambivalence rather than deep hostility remains in most cases the more characteristic pagan Roman attitude towards Judaism.

For example, the Emperor Julian, who came to power in AD

360, venerated the 'very great and powerful god' of the Jews even as he echoes the classical pagan objections to Judaism: that their Torah was in parts barbarous and ruthless, that they had been slavish throughout their history, that they were alien or that they had made no original contribution to philosophy or science. Yet Julian was also attracted to certain aspects of Judaism, he announced a plan to rebuild the Jewish Temple in Jerusalem and on a number of occasions contrasted the god-fearing Hebrews very favourably with the Christians.[16]

Such examples were by no means uncommon among pagans who generally respected the great antiquity of Judaism as against Christianity – which to more sceptical minds appeared as a *parvenu* religion and one which was, moreover, intellectually much less convincing. Thus the notion that Gentiles brought with them a deep-seated antisemitism from the pagan world into Christianity would be difficult to sustain. At the same time it is undeniable that pre-Christian anti-semitism was a social, cultural and political reality, centuries before the birth of Jesus.

During the Hellenistic and Roman periods Jews did, for instance, encounter hostility from governments, though they were also supported and protected at various times by the Persians, by Alexander the Great, by the Ptolemies, the Seleucids and the Romans. They were at moments of intense crisis the victims of mob violence, especially in Alexandria, but at the same time Judaism also had a certain appeal to the masses, especially in the late Roman world. Intellectuals, while never being uniformly hostile to Judaism or fully articulating an antisemitic ideology, were however frequently antagonistic to the Jews for their alleged intolerance, their missionary zeal, their seditiousness, their credulity and above all their exclusivity.[17] This separatism led, as we have seen, to the most serious charge that the pagan world brought against the Jews and Judaism – namely that they hated the gods and the rest of mankind. For some Hellenes, thoroughly convinced of their own superiority over the non-Greek world, Judaic separatism must have seemed like an intolerable affront by a culturally backward people to the unity of Hellenic civilisation. The fact, moreover, that Hebraic monotheism insisted on its own 'chosenness' and cultivated a sense of moral superiority over Gentiles aggravated the feelings of resentment.

Many Romans shared this Hellenistic repugnance against Jewish exclusiveness and lack of respect for what was esteemed by the rest of humanity. But the patrician antisemites among them went further, for they began to fear Judaism as a source of subversion, the doctrine of a mere rabble, which in turn was swaying their own lower classes with new anti-Roman ideas. The long-standing refusal of Jews to accept the imperial cult and to deify the state could only reinforce such sentiments. By the end of the first century AD all the libels in the older Greek antisemitic literature could be found in Rome, depicting the Jews as degenerate outcasts, hated by the gods and men.[18] Christianity would eventually take over many of these pagan conceptions, which had become well-established by the time it appeared on the scene. For example, the pagan repugnance against circumcision, the rejection of the Jewish dietary laws and the Sabbath, the notion that Jews do not show reverence to the beliefs of others (though Christianity itself was almost as exclusivist and intolerant of paganism as its Judaic forerunner) were all features that Christianity could and did turn against Judaism. Christians could undoubtedly draw on a pre-existing strand of Judeophobia in the classical world, though without the original and far more vehement hostility to Judaism which Christianity itself brought forth it is rather unlikely that pagan antisemitism would have sustained itself. In comparison with the Christian charge of deicide (the killing of God's only Son, a divine being whom He had sent to redeem the world), pagan enmity might appear almost trivial – it simply never required the kind of religious and theological basis which was so central to its Christian heir. Indeed, for many pagans Christianity itself was at least as offensive as Judaism (if not more so) in its social separateness and religious exclusivism.

Furthermore, pagan attitudes were never motivated by the sibling rivalry between Judaism and Christianity as two antagonistic monotheisms sharing a common Holy Book (the Hebrew Scriptures) and a similar set of symbolic references. There was an important sense in which the legitimacy of Christianity came to depend on its successful usurpation of the Jewish heritage and its attempted demonstration that Judaism had betrayed the divine message which had originally been granted to it.[19] Christians claimed to represent the *true* Israel, to be chosen by God in place of the blinded and obdurate Jews who had gone astray. Pagan antisemitism, on the other hand, remained essentially cultural rather than theological or racist, never developing the dynamic of institutionalised discrimination, stigmatisation and humiliation of the Jews which would be the historic legacy of Christianity.

2

■ ■ ■

Church and Synagogue

There is an inner contradiction at the heart of Christianity diagnosed at the beginning of this century by the Chief Rabbi of Vienna, Moritz Güdemann, which may help to illuminate the paradox of Christian antisemitism. Güdemann wrote in 1907: 'The Christian kneels before the image of the Jew, wrings his hands before the image of a Jewess; his Apostles, Festivals, and Psalms are Jewish. Only a few are able to come to terms with this contradiction – most free themselves by antisemitism. Obliged to revere a Jew as God, they wreak vengeance upon the rest of the Jews by treating them as devils.'[1]

Jesus was born, lived and died as a Jew in first-century Roman Palestine. He never conceived nor dreamed of a Christian Church. His father, mother, brothers and first disciples were all Jews, so that early Christianity can be said to have been essentially a rebellious Jewish sect that emerged out of the matrix of Judaism and had to define itself against the mother religion. Jesus, according to Christian teaching and theology, was also the Son of God, sent by the Father into this sinful world in order to atone for the original sin of mankind. He was sent, naturally enough, to the Jewish people, for they were the historic people of Abraham, Moses and the Prophets with whom God had chosen to make his original Covenant. But Jesus, the glorious Messiah, who, according to the Christian theological interpretation of the Hebrew Scriptures, had come to redeem the world, died ingloriously on the cross – crucified by the Roman occupying power – most probably as a

13

troublesome Jewish agitator. However, the story of the death of Jesus as told in the New Testament systematically shifts responsibility for his crucifixion from the Romans to his own people, the Jews.

The first gospels, which were written after the Jewish revolt of AD 70 against Roman rule in Palestine, operate this fateful shift, partly for political reasons in order not to antagonise the Romans and partly to affirm the identity of a Christian movement that had arisen out of Judaism and was seeking to mark itself off from its origins. In the gospels we are offered, for example, the highly improbable spectacle of the Roman governor of Palestine, Pilate, offering to release Jesus (in whom he can find no guilt) in exchange for a common criminal, Barabbas, but being unable to do so because of the large, mocking crowds of Jews who are baying for Jesus's blood. In the New Testament (especially in the Gospel of John) not only are the Jews responsible for the death of Jesus the Messiah, but his crucifixion is presented as the logical consequence of their relentless, murderous hostility towards him. Throughout his ministry, the Jewish leaders have been antagonistic towards Jesus, refusing to believe in his divinity so that their betrayal of him to the Romans is no longer surprising. The consequences of this Christian myth were, however, incalculable, for by killing the Son of God, the Jews were deemed to have become an accursed people, their Temple was destroyed (as Jesus had prophesied in the Gospels) and they were condemned to permanent exile and wandering. Henceforth, it is the Christian Church which takes on the mantle of the new Israel and becomes the recipient of the Divine Promises to Abraham. As Hyam Maccoby has put it: 'All the blessings of the Old Testament were regarded as applying to the Christian Church, while all the curses were allotted exclusively to the Jews: a neat division.'[2]

The personality most responsible for the detaching of Jesus from his Jewish background, for the shifting of guilt for the Crucifixion from the Romans to the Jews and for their stigmatisation as a God-rejected people was Paul, the true founder of Christianity. According to St Paul in *Thessalonians*, '. . . the Jews, who killed the Lord Jesus and the prophets and drove us out, the Jews who are heedless of God's will and enemies of their fellow-men, [are] hindering us from speaking to the Gentiles to lead them to salvation. All this time they have been making up the full measure of their guilt, and now retribution has overtaken them for good and all.'[3] Here we can see that not only are the Jews solely responsible for Christ's death, but that this horrendous act is in tune with their earlier alleged murders of the prophets, with their hatred of mankind (an echo of pagan antisemitism) and with their disobedience towards God.

Equally, however, it must be noted that St Paul, though he sees himself as Christ's apostle to the Gentiles, is himself an Israelite and in his Epistle to the Romans he maintains that the Jews are 'still beloved for the sake of their forefathers'.[4] Yet it is this same Paul who insists that salvation is only possible through faith in the risen Christ, which has come to supersede the Torah. Outward observance of the commandments, obedience merely to the Law and good works are no longer the path to redemption. On the contrary, they are a dispensation of death, they belong to the cursed sphere of the old, carnal Adam which separates mankind from the true, spiritual light of Christ, the aeon of the newly risen eschatological man. Baptism symbolises this new spiritual principle in contrast to the external and by now irrelevant mark of circumcision. It is solely faith and inward obedience to Christ which abrogate the Law – itself the sign of an inferior, this-worldly and therefore superseded Judaism. Indeed, in Paul's dualistic vision (which provides the root for centuries of mystical Christian anti-semitism) the Gentile Christians – though only grafted on to the stem of Israel – become the true elect of God. Spiritual man transcends carnal man just as the gathered-in-Gentiles within the Church transcend the old Mosaic Covenant. The Old Testament is now merely a witness to the coming of Christ –

the real and ultimate Revelation. In Paul's doctrine Judaism has been absolutely superseded and no longer has any intrinsic validity.[5] The conversion of the Jews is, however, necessary as part of the last act in the economy of salvation which will allow the final ingathering of the elect.

In the Gospel of John, the hostile resonance of the term 'the Jews', as an embodiment of everything that resists and rejects the light, is even more explicit, as is the portrayal of the malice of the Jewish authorities who persistently seek to kill the Messenger of God. John insists that Jesus is crucified by the Jews under Jewish Law and thereby corroborates the core of the deicide charge concerning the ultimate religious crime of murdering God's own essence and self-expression. The reason why 'the Jews' wilfully seek to kill Christ is that they themselves are not of God but of the Devil; indeed they incarnate a hostile principle in the world. Thus we have already in the New Testament a theological form of diabolising the Jews which will later be expanded by the Church Fathers.[6]

Their anti-Jewish theories build upon the accusations in the gospels and also reflect the rivalry with Judaism for proselytes as the new faith spread into pagan circles. Early Christian religious fervour and Judeophobia become fused in the effort to prove that the young Church was the real heir of the divine promise and that 'Israel according to the flesh' (to use the Pauline language) had been outcast. In the third and fourth centuries AD, the Greek fathers of the Church, like Gregory of Nyssa and St John Chrysostom, who operated in areas where there was a large and influential Jewish population, were especially vehement in their anti-Jewish invectives. Chrysostom, for instance, tells his flock in fourth-century Antioch that wherever the Christ-killers gather

> the cross is ridiculed, God blasphemed, the father unacknowledged, the son insulted, the grace of the Spirit rejected. . . . If the Jewish rites are holy and venerable, our way of life must be false. But if our way

is true, as indeed it is, theirs is fraudulent. I am not
speaking of the Scriptures. Far from it! For they lead one
to Christ. I am speaking of their present impiety and
madness.[7]

Chrysostom's diatribes, which reproached Jews with dissolute
living, extravagance and gluttony as well as the supreme crime
of deicide, were clearly designed to discourage Gentiles from
continuing to frequent their Jewish neighbours.[8] They reflect
the deep-seated fear of the Church Fathers about the powerful
impact of sermon and worship in the synagogue, which
ultimately culminated in an absolute prohibition by the
Church on Jewish proselytism in any form.

But the calumny of the 'carnal', 'lewd' and materialistic
Jews in this early Christian literature would have more far-
reaching consequences down the centuries. It led to the
creation of a monstrous, inhuman stereotype constructed out
of theological abstractions and divorced completely from the
real, concrete Jews of everyday life. Church Fathers like St
John Chrysostom, St Ambrose, St Jerome and St Augustine
(second only to St Paul as a Christian authority for the Western
world) had by the end of the fourth century AD crystallised a
demonic image of the Jew who combined superhuman
malevolence with total spiritual blindness. Expanding on the
Gospel of John, they portrayed the Jews as embodying Satan's
synagogue, as the sons of darkness. This was an image that
would be developed over more than a millennium in countless
sermons, in medieval drama, literature and the visual arts.[9]

The monkish, ascetic St Jerome, embittered by the spectacle
of successful missionising in Antioch by the large Jewish
population, denounced the synagogue in these terms: 'If you
call it a brothel, a den of vice, the Devil's refuge, Satan's
fortress, a place to deprave the soul . . . you are still saying less
than it deserves.'[10] St Jerome, who had grown up in Rome but
after various travels spent the last thirty-five years of his life in
Bethlehem surrounded by Jews, was in many ways the

prototype of that deeply neurotic, monastic kind of intellectual Christian in whom antisemitism and hatred of women coalesce. A morbid fear of all sexuality (which was identified with lust, filth and licentiousness), the unrestrained invective against women and the downgrading of marriage to mere procreation were of a kind with the projection of all the repressed 'sinful' (i.e. sexual) impulses onto the 'carnal' Jew. In sharp contrast to the more relaxed, naturalistic attitude of Judaism in sexual matters, love was portrayed by the Church Fathers as virginal, manly, asexual. Following the lead of St Paul, marriage and sex were negatively associated with sinful humanity and with the Old Testament. The Christian, however, was to follow the Gospel, for Christ was a man living without sex. Hence virginity became the Christian ideal while Judaism was linked to the sexual lusts of a wicked, carnal world. In this context, it seems significant that ascetic monks were so frequently in the forefront of Jew-baiting in succeeding centuries – during the Crusades in the Rhineland, in medieval Spain and in Reformation Germany (to name only a few instances) – suggesting a possible link between intensely repressed sexuality, misogyny and antisemitism.

The dualistic conceptions of flesh and spirit, body and soul, earthly and heavenly, sensual and intellectual which St Paul had bequeathed to the Christian Church reached their apogee in the writings of St Augustine, the immensely influential North African Church Father who lived at the end of the fourth century AD. His teachings had a dogmatic importance of the first order for the policy of the Popes and secular Christian rulers of the Middle Ages with regard to the Jews. They served to underline that the Church had become the new chosen people, replacing the old Israel which had betrayed the true message of God – which it should, of course, have been the first to acknowledge. St Augustine even likened the Jewish people to Cain, the first criminal recorded in biblical history, who had murdered his own brother and merited death but instead had been condemned to wander unhappily ever after. The Torah is the mark of Cain of the deicide people, who have mis-interpreted their own Scriptures and continue to live in blindness and error. The Jews might deserve to be eradicated for their crime, but St Augustine prefers that they be preserved as 'witnesses' to Christian truth until the end of time, when they will turn to Christ at the Last Judgement.[11]

The Augustinian theology reinforced the notion of the Jews as a wandering, homeless, rejected and accursed people who were incurably carnal, blind to spiritual meaning, perfidious, faithless and apostate. Their crime, being one of cosmic proportions, merited permanent exile and subordination to Christianity. Israel, the older son, must be made to 'serve' the Church, the younger son, which is the true heir and rightful owner of the Divine Promises enunciated in the Old Testament. In St Augustine's *Contra Judaeos* not only Cain, but also Hagar, Ishmael and Esau, symbolise the Jews who have been rejected, whereas their contrasting pairs, Abel, Sarah, Isaac and Jacob, prefigure the election of the Church.[12] Thus the biblical heroes of the Old Testament are detached from Jewish history and turned into a proof of the permanent and irrevocable reprobation of Israel, whose evil nature will never change. The blinded and dejected synagogue is left with the empty vessel of the Law, while the beautiful, triumphant *Ecclesia* – as depicted on medieval cathedrals – radiates only truth and light.

This theology is for the first time institutionalised in the fourth century AD, when Christianity becomes the official religion of the Roman Empire. Ancient privileges previously granted to Jews are withdrawn, rabbinical jurisdiction is abolished or greatly restricted, and proselytism becomes punishable by death – as indeed are sexual relations with Christian women. Jews were henceforth to be excluded from pursuing military careers or holding high office. Thus the inferiorisation of Jewish legal status became an inexorable consequence of the growing power and influence of the Church on the imperial government. The *Codex Theodosianus*

(AD 438) clearly reflects the spirit and sometimes even the letter of the Church councils, denigrating Judaism as a 'wicked sect' and Jews as 'abominable' while Christianity is referred to as a 'venerable religion'.[13] The Justinian Code in the first half of the sixth century encroached on Jewish rights still further, virtually stripping Judaism of any legal protection, banning the Mishnah, closing synagogues in North Africa and decreeing that those who disbelieved in the Resurrection or the Last Judgement be put to death. Jews were in effect at the mercy of the ruler, increasingly excluded from normal life and reduced to a restricted number of occupations.

Popular outbreaks of violence (including some Jewish assaults on Christians) also occurred in the first centuries of the Christian era. In AD 388 in Mesopotamia, a Christian mob led by a bishop burned the local synagogues. Their action was defended by St Ambrose, who vehemently reproached the Emperor Theodosius for ordering it to be rebuilt and successfully prevented this from happening. In Rome, in other parts of Italy, in Antioch, in Edessa, even in Africa, synagogues were also destroyed or converted into churches and Jews occasionally massacred.

Justinian's oppressive legislation provoked Jews to take their revenge on Christians at Caeserea in 556, and at the beginning of the seventh century to kill many Christians in Antioch. They aided the Persian invaders in bringing about the fall of Byzantine Jerusalem in AD 614, helping them to lay waste to Christian homes and churches. Jews also welcomed the armies of Islam in the same century for similar reasons, as they advanced upon the Christian orthodox world. In AD 711, when the Visigothic Kingdom in Spain was overrun, the Jews were especially jubilant, for only a century earlier they had been given an ultimatum of baptism or exile by its Christian rulers. Under King Erwig (680–87), for example, draconian anti-Jewish laws were passed, whose driving force had been the Archbishop of Toledo.

The anti-Jewish measures of the Spanish Visigothic Church

targeted in particular the compulsorily baptised Jews, suspected of secretly belonging to the old faith.[14] They had to swear to renounce their obstinate 'unbelief' and the deep-rooted 'aberrations of our forefathers', to avoid all contact with their former co-religionists and to repudiate all Jewish customs and ceremonies on pain of death. Thus, already in Visigothic Spain the Jews were victims of forced baptism and at the same time objects of deep suspicion as converts. Even infants were not spared, for as decreed by the Seventeenth Council of Toledo in 694, all Jewish children above the age of six were to be reared as Christians.

In the Frankish Kingdom forced conversion was also periodically perpetrated, notably by King Dagobert (629–39), though there was an undeniable improvement in the Jewish status under Charlemagne and even more under his son Louis the Pious (814–40).[15] The Carolingian state gave the Jews equal juridical rights and positions of trust; they were granted special letters of protection and the murder of a Jew was heavily penalised. As merchants and traders in luxury products from the Orient, Jews were well regarded and in medicine they enjoyed the highest reputation. For the Church this lack of distinction between the faithful and the 'infidel' was anathema, and St Agobard (779–840), Archbishop of Lyons, launched a counter-offensive reviving all the invectives of the Church Fathers in his onslaught against the 'Judaising' of the Carolingian Empire. (A father confessor of the Emperor Louis did actually convert to Judaism, a fact which had alarmed many Churchmen).

Agobard, who was a leading ecclesiastical reformer and a highly educated man, openly feared that the fragile Christianity of the Frankish Kingdom, still under the influence of pagan superstition, would be no intellectual match for Judaism. He was, moreover, alarmed at the possibility of Jewish missionary efforts and at the imperial protection granted to the Jews, falling back defensively on the segregationist policy advocated by the Church Fathers. Agobard's nightmare, shared by so many generations of medieval Churchmen, was that the common, ordinary people might actually listen to the Jews and be convinced that they 'possess a purer and truer faith than our own', that perhaps they were the chosen people of God after all. A sharp line had therefore to be drawn which would prevent any fraternising between the Christians and Jews, between the sons of light and the sons of darkness. It was unseemly, Agobard wrote, 'that the Church of Christ, who should be conducted immaculate and unblemished to her heavenly bridegroom, be defiled by contact with the unclean senile and corrupt synagogue'.[16] It was, he claimed, like seating a virgin at the table alongside a whore. Were not the Jews descendants of the sinners of Sodom and Gomorrah? Had not their own prophets branded them for all time as 'a sinful, useless race', or in the words of John the Baptist as a 'generation of vipers'?

Nevertheless, the period between 430 and 1096 (the date of the First Crusade) is considered by specialists on Jewish–Christian relations in the West to be better than that which preceded it and most certainly than that which would follow. There was some hostility and violence, but with the exception of Visigothic Spain it was not persistent. Jews obtained a prominent role in trading, particularly from the eighth century onwards, but were not yet identified with usury. They appeared to be reasonably well integrated, especially under Charlemagne and his successors, in the 'barbarian' societies in which they lived. Even some popes, like Gregory the Great, adopted a more balanced policy based on a qualified respect for Judaism though they shared many of the fourth-century stereotypes of the Church Fathers and still worked zealously to convert the Jews to Christianity.

Theological anti-Judaism remained, however, an ever-present reality around which the view that the Jews were wicked and despicable could always revive, and which justified the curbing of Jewish rights.[17] The continuing refusal of the Synagogue to accept the doctrines of the Church, its insistence on pursuing its own vocation and the obsessive need to defend both Church and state against Jewish proselytism (even though it was outlawed) further exacerbated Christian antisemitism. But this was essentially legislative and juridical rather than economic or populist in character before the Crusades, with actual persecution remaining rather sporadic except for Spain. Jews, it must be remembered, were the only non-Christian group of any significance permitted to practise their faith in early medieval Europe, which placed them in a unique category. They could lead a tolerated, though limited existence within Christendom, even if the fabric of this 'toleration' was exceedingly fragile. After all, each Easter Sunday with its celebration of the Resurrection – a major drama in the Christian calendar and liturgy – awakened once more the image of Jews as malevolent Christ-killers.

The decisive turning-point for the worse came, however, with the First Crusade (1096), which led to massacres hitherto unprecedented in the history of Jewish–Christian relations. The bands of crusaders who set out to recapture the Holy Sepulchre in Jerusalem (where Jesus had reputedly died) from Muslim invaders, were mainly recruited from the lower strata of society in northern Europe. On their way to the Holy Land they attacked the Jewish quarters of French and German towns, claiming that they were wreaking vengeance first of all against the enemies of Christ in their own backyard, those who had crucified him on the Cross. Most of the besieged Jews they encountered preferred collective suicide in sanctification of their faith (*kiddush ha-shem*) to the forced conversion which the crusaders offered them. Between a quarter to a third of the Jewish population in Germany and Northern France (about 10,000 people) were killed in the first six months of 1096 alone, mainly as a result of mob actions, reinforced by religious fanaticism. Massacres took place in Rouen, in Lorraine, throughout the Rhine valley, in towns along the Danube and in Bohemia, climaxing with the slaughter of Jews (along with Muslims) at the end of their journey in Jerusalem (1099). The leader of the First Crusade, Godfrey Bouillon, who had sworn to avenge the blood of Christ on Israel and 'leave no single member of the Jewish race alive', burnt the synagogue of Jerusalem to the ground, with all the Jews inside.

The massacres left a deep scar on the Jewish psyche, and remembrance of the martyrdom they inspired became a fixed part of the synagogue service.[18] But they appeared to exacerbate popular hostility towards the Jews and to provoke a further decline in their status by embedding the notion of Christ-killers more firmly in the mass consciousness and by demonstrating that this was indeed a defenceless population. For though emperors, kings, bishops, popes and local authorities might at times defend the Jews, popular crusading zeal, whipped up by demagogic preachers and reinforced by a desire to annul debts to Jewish moneylenders, ensured that Jewish miseries would continue. The Second Crusade (1146), like its successors, led to renewed anti-Jewish excesses with fatalities, though less severe than the first, still running into many hundreds. Not only popular attitudes but also the theological scapegoating of the Jews seemed to harden in the wake of these criminal actions. The influential Abbot of Cluny, the Venerable Peter, actually suggested that Jews should finance the Crusades from their own money; he wrote to Louis VII (1120–80) that they must be punished severely for, more than the Muslims, they defiled Christianity and mercilessly exploited Christians. Echoing the Augustinian theology, he concluded that they should not be put to the sword but 'like Cain the fratricide, they should be made to suffer fearful torments and prepared for greater ignominy, for an existence worse than death'.[19]

The medieval historian Gavin Langmuir has noted that one of the most significant aspects of the Crusades was the renewed hostility it demonstrated among Christians to the phenomenon of Jewish disbelief and the ways in which it encouraged the social degradation of Jews to be used to confirm Christian belief. Jews, he points out, were a real threat to those Christians whose sense of identity had been upset by massive social dislocation or by their own intellectual doubts. Holy war gave such people a sense of integration in their lives that could be reinforced by focusing on those responsible for the death of Christ, who stubbornly rejected the beliefs of Christianity, even to the point of martyrdom. Punishing the Jews for their disbelief by degrading their legal status and making them pariahs in European society was becoming a way of silencing any latent doubts about the meaning of the central symbols, particularly transubstantiation, of Christian faith.[20]

The Augustinian doctrine that 'the Jew is the slave of the Christian' was soon embedded in canon law and confirmed by the Third Lateran Council (1179). Even the great medieval philosopher St Thomas Aquinas (1125–74) affirmed the legitimacy of holding the Jews in 'perpetual servitude' for their crimes, while urging that they not be deprived of those things necessary for sustaining life. At the beginning of the thirteenth century, Pope Innocent III (1198–1216) was even more emphatic about the need for 'the blasphemers of the Christian name' to be 'forced into the servitude of which they made themselves deserving when they raised their sacrilegious hands against Him who had come to confer true liberty upon them, thus calling down His blood upon themselves and their children'. Innocent III also believed, like St Augustine before him, that the Jews must be preserved as 'wanderers' upon the earth until they acknowledged their crime and called on the name of Jesus Christ as Lord and Saviour.[21]

The canonical legislation of the Church would fully institutionalise by the thirteenth century the reprobate status of the Jew and the doctrine of *Servitus Judaeorum* (the 'perpetual servitude of the Jews').[22] The Jews had to be subordinate to Christians, they could exercise no position of authority and Christian society had to be rigidly protected from 'contamination' through living, eating or engaging in sexual relations with them. The Fourth Lateran Council (1215) codified this will to segregate the Jews by requiring them to wear distinguishing dress – a conical hat in the Germanic lands and a

25

'Jew badge' (usually a yellow disc sewn into the clothing, whose colour symbolised Judas's betrayal of Christ for gold pieces) in the Latin countries. The effects of the badge were to make the Jews more visible and vulnerable to attack, reducing their ability to travel freely.

Other canonical restrictions, all intended to display publicly the superiority of Christianity and the inferior status of Judaism, including the ruling that Jews could not enter churches or walk in the streets on holy days, that they could not work on Sundays and that their synagogues must remain lowly and miserable buildings. In addition to all these humiliating restrictions, the Talmud now came under attack for the first time as a symbol of Jewish 'blaspheming' against the Christian faith. Ironically, it was a converted Jew, Nicholas Donin who first denounced the Talmud to the Pope in the thirteenth century, which led to its investigation and burning in Paris at the request of the Church. The realisation that the Talmud was a major source of Judaism in the centuries after Christ, and that it contained some anti-Christian statements, had come very belatedly and as a considerable shock to many Christians. Henceforth, the image of the mysterious Talmudic Jew, plotting and blaspheming against Christianity, would be added to the existing antisemitic armoury and enjoy widespread popularity down into the twentieth century.[23]

Another central stereotype which came to shape Christian attitudes towards Jews and Judaism in this period was that of the usurer. The Jews, prohibited from landowning, constantly constricted in trade and excluded from the guilds, had increasingly gravitated towards moneylending, especially as the Church forbade Christians to take usury from co-religionists. The financial vacuum that was created encouraged the secular authorities, especially in medieval England and France, to make use of Jews as moneylenders. As royal usurers they were to a certain extent protected and granted some privileges, but at the same time they were also vulnerable to the greed of the princes, the reproval of the

Church and the hatred of the indebted poor. The Jews, already stigmatised as infidels and deicides, soon found themselves depicted as alien 'bloodsuckers', a potent source of socio-economic antisemitism in the more agrarian societies of Europe for centuries to come.[24] As economic instruments of the royal power, entirely dependent on the kings for their rights of residence, they could be squeezed whenever this suited the rulers, their property confiscated and debts to them revoked, or else they could be conveniently sacrificed as pawns to popular anger. This is what happened to the Jews of medieval England under Edward I, who carried out with the overwhelming support of public opinion the expulsion of all the Jews of his kingdom in 1290, after he had first milked them dry.[25] The image of the moneylending Jew would, however, survive the four centuries when Jews were absent from British shores. In England, as on the Continent, priests and friars continued to remind their flocks that usurers were invented by the Devil. The Jew was Satan's partner in all his financial dealings, fleecing poor Christians without mercy through this devilish practice.

Although the moneylending Jew was in fact performing an essential economic function in medieval society, the status of usury as a deadly sin simply accentuated his role as a vulnerable scapegoat and execrated outsider. Jews became associated in the popular mind with banking, money, exchange and the parasitical exploitation of a land-based Christian peasantry which formed the backbone of the European nations. This essentially medieval stereotype of the Jew as the standard-bearer of the money-economy and in a later period the personification of modern capitalism would play a fateful role in the history of European antisemitism. In the Middle Ages, however, it was only one weapon among many in the ideological warfare waged by the Church against the Synagogue. As the European masses became more exposed to a Christian theology that emphasised the role of the Jews as murderers of Christ, new and more irrational accusations emerged, like desecrating the host, poisoning the wells and ritual murder, which would have an even more devastating effect on the position of Jewry. The restraints which the medieval Church had still exercised in an earlier period in tolerating Jews as long as they were passive and subservient came to be challenged by irrational, primitive scapegoating and fantastic beliefs.

It was indeed striking that at the very historical moment when the Catholic Church and Christian state reached the peak of its power, the Jewish people were to be plunged into new depths of oppression and misery by the scourge of antisemitic hysteria. As the Catholic historian Edward Flannery has written, the era of Innocent III and Henry II, Gregory VII and Henry VI, of Thomas Aquinas and Dante, of St Francis of Assisi and of Notre Dame Cathedral, was also 'the age of anti-Jewish hecatombs, expulsions, calumnious myths, auto-da-fé, of the badge, the ghetto and many other hardships visited upon the Jews'.[26]

3

. . .

The Medieval Legacy

The antisemitism of the later Middle Ages took over most of the elements of earlier Christian anti-Judaism virtually unchanged. But by 1350, especially in northern Europe, it had added a litany of new and terrifyingly irrational charges which led many Christians to believe that Jews engaged in ritual murder, host profanation, had caused the Black Death by poisoning wells and were generally conspiring to overthrow Christendom. The deliberate unbelievers were now stereotyped as usurers, bribers, secret killers, sorcerers, magicians and oppressors of the poor. It had become much easier to think of the Jews as somehow less than human; they had become 'a symbol to express repressed fantasies about crucifixion and cannibalism, repressed doubts about the real presence of Christ in the Eucharist, and unbearable fears of the bubonic bacillus that imperceptibly invaded people's bodies'.[1]

As amply evidenced in medieval art, Jews were portrayed as agents of Satan with evil faces, horns and a tail, invariably striking grotesque poses. Sometimes the Devil might be seen in painting or sculpture as riding on the back of a Jew; sometimes he appeared with dark, bulging eyes and a goatee or in the guise of a seductive woman to underline the lechery that was traditionally attributed to Jews. Logic, too, as the art of the Devil, could be easily associated with Talmudic Jews seeking to entrap innocent believers and entice them away from their Christian faith. The Devil motif was important to medieval Christianity as a symbol of all the temptations of this evil world, especially those that embodied the forces of heresy and rebellion against God.[2] Its linkage with Jews, whether in the visual arts, literature, passion plays, sermons or folk legends, offered a way of explaining why Jews had so stubbornly and arrogantly rejected Jesus. By depicting the Jew as embodying the will of Satan, medieval Christendom would inaugurate an inexorable process of dehumanisation.

The apocalyptic fantasy of the Antichrist, a man who would lead the armies of the Devil against those of Christ, provided a popular, millenarian underpinning to the association of Jews with satanic forces. A doctrine with roots in the New Testament, but never officially embraced by the Church because of its tendency to encourage dangerous millennial hopes, it postulated that both Antichrist and his main supporters would be Jews. This demonic Jewish parody of Jesus, conversant with all the black arts, would resurrect the Temple in Jerusalem and briefly rule over a world Jewish Empire before being vanquished by Christ at the head of his armies, who would put an end to the reign of the Devil for ever.[3] The entire Jewish people would be annihilated in this apocalyptic battle at the end of days. The popular Antichrist myth, which had contributed to the massacres of Jews at the time of the Crusades, already seems to herald the millenarian doctrines of Nazism with Hitler in the role of a secular Germanic Christ come to execute a 'Final Solution' against the source of all evil, the Jews.

The fantasy of ritual murder was another, no less pernicious medieval superstition which would encourage the most virulent Jew-hatred in subsequent centuries. Invented in Norwich, England in 1144 following the murder of a Christian boy just before Easter, who would later be venerated as medieval Europe's first child martyr, this crime was attributed without any evidence to local Jews.[4] They were accused of crucifying him in mockery of the passion of Jesus, and the fantasy gained acceptance because people wanted a local saint to work miracle cures and the Norwich clergy realised that his shrine would enhance the city's standing on the pilgrim route.

Similar accusations soon spread across England and to the Continent, so that by 1255, when 'Little St Hugh of Lincoln' became England's most famous child-saint, the ritual murder myth was firmly established.

The accusation that Jews abduct Christian children in order to re-enact the Crucifixion of Jesus at Easter-time seems to have been connected with fantasies arising out of the notion that the Christ-child was actually present in the wafers of the Eucharist. Guilt feelings associated with the act of cutting up and eating a small child, must have preoccupied Christian believers in the twelfth century at an unconscious level and would have been easier to handle once they were projected onto Jews.[5] The allegation that Jews used the blood of the murdered Christian child by mixing it with their *matzot* (unleavened bread) during the Passover added a further, even more sinister, dimension to the ritual slaughter myth.

Among the more outlandish assumptions that underlay the blood libel was the notion that Jewish men menstruated and therefore required Christian blood to replenish themselves, or alternatively that they needed to make up for the blood they lost through circumcision. This blood fantasy, utterly alien to anything in Judaism (which as the dietary laws make plain, abhors the shedding of blood and insists on its removal from food) seems to reflect European myths and folklore about bloodsucking demons and vampires.[6] Such primitive notions, when amalgamated with the older identification of Jews with 'the Church of Satan', could only induce fear, loathing and horror, providing a pretext for pogroms and massacres down into our own century. They reinforced hostile theological stereotypes with the delusions of the unbridled popular imagination, to provide an image of the Jews as pathologically malevolent and cruel.

Another allegation which appeared in the thirteenth century and revolved around the Easter–Passover festivals was the desecration of host wafers by Jews. This slander arose out of the dogma of transubstantiation (whereby Christ's flesh and blood become present in the consecrated host and wine), which had been confirmed at the Fourth Lateran Council of 1215. The cult of the Eucharist had now acquired a concrete character and by 1264 the new feast of Corpus Christi had become official for the whole Church. Yet doubts about whether Christ's body and blood were really present in the bread and wine of the Eucharist clearly persisted.[9] At the end of the thirteenth century, after they had already been expelled from England and France, Jews were suddenly accused of deliberately mutilating and torturing the transubstantiated body of Christ by profaning the host wafers. As in the ritual murder charge, Jews were assumed to be compulsively repeating their original cruelty towards Christ. However irrational (since the charge absurdly assumed that Jews believed in one of the most problematic of all Christian dogmas), this fantasy was widely accepted and spread rapidly through Central Europe. Many Jews were slaughtered in the name of this wholly mythic belief and many shrines established for the allegedly desecrated hosts. Not until the rise of Protestantism did this particular medieval superstition cease its ravages.[8]

The Black Death which raged in Europe between 1347 and 1360 added yet another deadly accusation against the Jews – that of poisoning wells in order to wipe out Christians and establish their domination of the world.[9] There is no doubt that the masses believed this charge, since Jews were massacred in their thousands despite papal prohibition and despite the fact that the official Church rejected the libel. While religious fervour undoubtedly played a role in the well-poisoning accusations (which were sometimes accompanied by the blood libel) there were also social and economic factors at work. The fourteenth century was a period of intense social conflict and major upheavals in the cities of Germany, in which craft guilds fought the city authorities. The masses who set out to kill the Jews were often indebted craftsmen who regarded the moneylending Jews as servants of the merchants

32

and the patrician urban leadership with whom they were in conflict.

The struggle that developed was more over the exploitation of the Jews and their possessions by the royal exchequer, the city councils or the lower-class mobs in revolt, than over any religious issue.[10] Greed for Jewish property rather than religious zealotry motivated the killers, except in the case of the flagellant bands (considered by the Church as sectarians and heretics), whose numbers had greatly increased during the Black Death and who undoubtedly whipped up popular passions. What was most ominous, however, was the way in which the well-poisoning hysteria provoked a new charge against Jewry which suggested that they were engaged in a generalised conspiracy against the Christian world, in order to take revenge on their subjugators. This powerful libel, which led to the destruction of many Jewish communities in medieval Germany, would also become a central theme in the repertoire of modern antisemitism.[11]

The myths of popular demonology were not endorsed, but on the contrary frequently combated by the ecclesiastical and also the lay authorities. The Papacy and the Church as a whole, while rejecting any notion of Jewish equality with Christians, did seek to protect certain basic rights of Jews. The Papacy forbade forced baptism and condemned violence against Jews, interference with Jewish festivals or desecration of Jewish cemeteries; it also repudiated the allegations that Jews committed ritual murder or poisoned wells.[12] On the other hand, as we have seen, at the Fourth Lateran Council a distinctive dress (the Jew badge) was imposed upon Jews for the first time in Christian lands, one of the many restrictions which marked off the Jew from his social environment and turned him into a social pariah. The popes consistently condemned the Talmud and deplored Jewish obstinacy in refusing to acknowledge Jesus Christ as their saviour. The Papal legislation was designed to reinforce the inferiority and 'perpetual servitude' of Judaism so that Jews could bear witness to Christian truth, but it was not intended to completely eliminate the Jews from Christian society as long as they lived peacefully and did not infringe the laws. This blend of limited tolerance and restrictive legislation was ultimately aimed, of course, at the conversion of the Jews. Not until the mid-sixteenth century under Pope Paul IV were Jews living under Papal jurisdiction to be enclosed behind ghetto walls in the mistaken belief that such severe measures would accelerate their large-scale conversion.[13]

The most implacable religious adversaries of the Jews in the late Middle Ages were not the Popes but the mendicant Franciscan and Dominican orders.[14] Particularly vituperative was the Italian Franciscan reformer St John of Capistrano, a fiery, ascetic preacher who zealously denounced heretics and Jews all over Europe. This fifteenth-century inquisitor terrorised the Jews wherever he went, threatening with hell-fire those who dared to associate with them in any way. In Breslau he personally supervised the torture of Jews accused of host-desecration, extracting confessions from them for these and other imagined ritual crimes.[15] John of Capistrano also successfully put an end to the privileges enjoyed by the Polish Jewry under Casimir IV, in a country which served at that time as a haven for Jews fleeing from persecution elsewhere.

Another Italian anti-Jewish Franciscan preacher, St Bernardinus of Feltre, who once described himself as a dog who 'barks for Christ' against the Jews, has often been linked to the Trent episode which gave a renewed impetus to ritual murder charges in Europe. After his preaching a series of Easter sermons in Trent (northern Italy) in 1473, the local Jews were accused of having murdered a three-year-old Christian boy called Simon, whose body had been found in the Adige river. Jews were arrested, tried and confessed under torture, and by the end of the affair all the Jews of Trent (except a handful who were baptised) had been burnt. Simon of Trent became the object of a cult, which in this instance was approved by the Pope.[16]

In Spain, Dominican friars like Vincente Ferrer led the doctrinal assault against the Jews, who enjoyed a privileged position until the completion of the Christian *reconquista* at the end of the fifteenth century. Under a succession of tolerant Spanish kings, Jews had become well integrated, excelling in commercial and intellectual pursuits and growing in prosperity, prestige and creativity. They were showered with honours and favours by royal benevolence, acting as ministers, councillors and physicians to the kings of Castile and Aragon. The rise of some Jews to great eminence at court, and their role in financial affairs, aroused the envy of the nobility and the populace as well as the ire of the Church, who saw the prominence of Spanish Jewry as an insult to the true faith. At the end of the fourteenth century the preaching of the Archdeacon of Seville, Fernando Martinez, against Jewish wealth and false Jewish doctrines set in train a wave of bloody persecutions.[17] In 1391 the mob broke into the Jewish quarter of Seville and massacred 4,000 Jews. The carnage spread to other parts of Spain and within three months about 50,000 Jews were dead and many more had been baptised. Those who remained Jews became the object of renewed missionary efforts, not least by converted Jews like the former Rabbi of Burgos, Solomon Levi, who became a much revered and powerful bishop under his Christian name of Pablo de Santa Maria. Like some other *conversos*, he did not hesitate to malign Judaism and to advocate anti-Jewish legislation as a way of fighting heresy and bringing Jews to the true faith. He even justified the persecutions of 1391 as part of the providential plan for Christian redemption.[18]

Equally dedicated to the conversion of the Jews was the Dominican preacher St Vincente Ferrer, who brought about some 35,000 baptisms between 1411 and 1412 alone. Though he supported the oppressive legislation of 1414 and the setting-up of the first compulsory Spanish ghettos, he opposed violence against Jews and criticised the disdain of the 'old' Spanish Christians for the new converts to the Church. But the phenomenon of crypto-Judaism (the secret practice of Judaism), while outwardly observing Christianity, was a source of constant friction, especially as the *conversos* began to penetrate the upper ranks of the Spanish universities, the judiciary, the professions and even the Church. By the mid-fifteenth century popular anger against the *conversos* (frequently referred to by the derogatory name of *marranos* or pigs) was rampant, born of envy and resentment against their alleged duplicity. Anti-*converso* feeling was feeding a new kind of antisemitism which held that Jewish blood was a hereditary taint which could not be eradicated by baptism. This was the origin of Spanish racism, the first of its kind in Europe to be directed against the 'bad blood' (*mala sangre*) of the Jews and to become veritably obsessed with the issue of blood purity (*limpieza de sangre*). Statutes based on this criterion were eventually legislated to bar the entry of 'New Christians' to certain guilds and to certain military and religious orders.

It was the failure of the Inquisition to stamp out crypto-Judaism, despite elaborate regulations, that focused attention back on those Jews who had never abandoned their ancestral faith and still maintained links with the *conversos*. The fanatical Torquemada, Inquisitor General since 1483, became convinced that only by expelling *all* Jews who had retained their Jewish faith from Spain could he stamp out the phenomenon of crypto-Judaism. The fatal decree was issued by Ferdinand and Isabella, the rulers of a newly united Spain, on 2 January 1492, shortly after the fall of Granada, the last stronghold of Muslim Spain. A preliminary blood libel trial in La Guardia, in which *marranos* were accused of profaning the host and of carrying out a ritual murder, provided the pretext.[19]

Ironically enough, the expulsion of all Jews from the Spanish Kingdom on 31 March 1492 did not solve the 'Jewish question' or bring Spanish antisemitism to an end. 'New Christians' of Jewish origin continued to be regarded with hostility and hatred as a separate caste, altogether distinct from 'old', pure Christians who could boast a noble lineage. The same stereotypes were applied to the 'New Christians' as had been directed against their ancestors, since Jewish blood was assumed to be irrevocably 'polluted'. Occupations associated with the 'New Christians', such as business, finance, medicine or intellectual activity, were looked down upon with contempt. 'New Christians', for centuries after the expulsion, were seen as a foreign body in Spanish society which threatened its integrity.[20] The obsession with blood purity and the racist fervour which in some respects anticipated that of Nazi Germany helped bring about the decline of Spain through demographic impoverishment and contempt for the productive and commercial occupations. Jews also suffered from the consequences of the Counter-Reformation in other regions of Europe which remained Catholic, where ecclesiastical usages and canon law were now more strictly applied towards them. The kind of segregation resulting from the introduction of ghettos in the second half of the sixteenth century, first in Italy and then in the Habsburg Empire, was intended to punitively demonstrate the error of Judaism. Pope Paul IV's *Cum nimis absurdum* decree, establishing the first ghetto in Rome in 1555 (which lasted until Italian unification in 1870), insisted that as long as Jews 'persist in their errors they are made to feel and see that they are slaves and the Christians free men through Jesus Christ our God and Lord.'[21]

Segregation and repression, it was hoped, would break the back of the stubborn Jewish resistance to conversion and root out any social fraternising which could obscure the legal status of the Jews as 'slaves'. By the end of the sixteenth century all Jews had been removed from the Papal State except for those living in the ghettos of Rome, Ancona and Avignon. This harsh policy must also be seen against the background of belief in an approaching 'end of days' which made the reform of Church and society seem more urgent. Rather than leading to a more tolerant attitude towards Jews, this strengthened the drive to create a more closed and protected Christian society (among both Catholics and Protestants) which sought to eliminate all forms of heresy. Radical reform of the Church in the turmoil of the fifteenth and sixteenth centuries came to mean the eradication of the 'enemy within', which included Jews, heretics and all the followers of Antichrist. The vision of a mass conversion of the Jews was now subordinated among many Christians to the apocalyptic expectations of the coming of Antichrist, sent to gather in his obstinate Jewish followers for the purpose of destroying the Church. The revival of such beliefs, which identified the Jews with Antichrist, even among sophisticated theologians, helped raise the temperature of anti-Jewish agitation in the later Middle Ages.[22]

It was above all in Germany, where the Jews had never been completely expelled, that the chimeric medieval fantasies concerning the Jews retained their force and were barely affected by the rise of Protestantism. Unlike the relative tolerance towards Jews shown by Calvinists in Holland, England and France, German Lutheranism would only reinforce the medieval tradition of antisemitism, already deeply rooted in German culture. As far as Jews were concerned, Martin Luther (1483–1546), instead of being a forerunner of the Enlightenment, was essentially a medieval man who gave a new legitimacy and power to antisemitism. In contrast to the Calvinists, Luther insisted that God's Covenant with the Jews had been definitely revoked and replaced by a new Covenant. For Luther there was no good Jew except a converted Jew or, as he put it in the epilogue to a sermon of February 1546: if the Jews are willing to convert and abandon their blasphemy and crime, 'then we will be glad to forgive them: if not, we should not tolerate and suffer them'.[23] Driven by his vision of the approaching 'end of days' and the need for a closed, protected Christian society, Luther wanted to force the issue between integration or expulsion. Either the Jews accept salvation by baptism or they must be expelled.

Initially, the young Luther had hoped that Jews could be won to his new Protestant faith, stripped of 'popery' and the corrupt practices of the Roman Catholic Church. In his pamphlet of 1523, *Jesus Christ was born a Jew*, Luther had denounced the papists for dealing with Jews, as if they were dogs rather than human beings.

> If the Apostles, who were also Jews, had dealt with us
> Gentiles as we Gentiles deal with the Jews there would
> never have been a Christian among the Gentiles . . . we
> in our turn ought to treat the Jews in a brotherly
> manner in order that we might convert some of them
> . . . we are but Gentiles, while the Jews are of the
> lineage of Christ. We are aliens and in-laws; they are
> blood relatives, cousins and brothers of our Lord.[24]

But the Jews did not meet Luther's expectations. Worse still, he became greatly concerned with the reportedly successful 'Judaising' counter-offensive of the 1530s, leading to the conversion of the Sabbatarians.

In 1543 he published a tract, *Concerning the Jews and their Lies*, which depicted the Jews as poisoners, ritual murderers, usurers, as devils incarnate and parasites on Christian society – a veritable *summum* of medieval hatred which contains some of the most violent language in the history of antisemitism:

> First, their synagogues or churches should be set on
> fire, and whatever does not burn up should be covered
> or spread over with dirt so that no one may ever be able
> to see a cinder or stone of it. And this ought to be done
> for the honour of God and of Christianity in order that
> God may see that we are Christians, and that we have
> not wittingly tolerated or approved of such public lying,
> cursing and blaspheming of His Son and His
> Christians. . . . Secondly, their homes should likewise
> be broken down and destroyed. For they perpetrate the
> same things there that they do in their synagogues. For
> this reason they ought to be put under one roof or in a
> stable, like gypsies, in order that they may realise that

they are not masters in our land, as they boast, but miserable captives, as they complain of us incessantly before God with bitter wailing. Thirdly, they should be deprived of their prayerbooks and Talmuds in which such idolatry, lies, cursing and blasphemy are taught. Fourthly, their rabbis must be forbidden under threat of death to teach any more. . . . Fifthly, passport and travelling privileges should be absolutely forbidden to the Jews. For they have no business in the rural districts since they are not nobles, nor officials, nor merchants, nor the like. Let them stay at home. Sixthly, they ought to be stopped from usury. All their cash and valuables of silver and gold ought to be taken from them and put aside for safekeeping. For this reason, as said before, everything that they possess they stole and robbed from us through their usury, for they have no other means of support. . . . Such evilly acquired money is cursed, unless, with God's blessing, it is put to some good and necessary use. . . . Seventhly, let the young and strong Jews and Jewesses be given the flail, the axe, the hoe, the spade, the distaff and spindle and let them earn their bread by the sweat of their noses as is enjoined upon Adam's children. For it is not proper that they should want us cursed *Goyyim* to work in the sweat of our brow and that they, pious crew, idle away their days at the fireside in laziness, feasting and display. And in addition to this, they boast impiously that they have become masters of the Christians at our expense. We ought to drive the rascally lazy bones out of our system. If, however, we are afraid that they might harm us personally, or our wives, children, servants, cattle etc, when they serve us or work for us – since it is surely to be presumed that such noble lords of the world and poisonous bitter worms are not accustomed to any work and would very unwillingly humble themselves to such a degree among the cursed *Goyyim* – then let us apply the same cleverness [expulsion] as the other nations, such as France, Spain, Bohemia, etc. and settle with them for that which they have extorted usuriously from us, and after having divided it up fairly let us drive them out of the country for all time. For, as has been said, God's rage is so great against them that they only become worse and worse through mild mercy, and not much better through severe mercy. Therefore away with them. . . . To sum up, dear princes and nobles who have Jews in your domains, if this advice of mine does not suit you, then find a better one so that you and we may be free of this insufferable devlish burden – the Jews.[25]

This outpouring of hate reflected Luther's conviction that it was harder to convert the Jews than Satan himself. Luther's antisemitism was not yet racial, it was still constructed in the framework of apocalyptic prophecy with Jews being seen (along with the Pope in Rome and the infidel Turk) as 'the storm troops of the devil's forces'.[26] Luther, in his struggle for a reformed Church on the brink of collapse, had become obsessed with the legions of Antichrist at the gates. The blaspheming, stubborn Jews were an integral part of this diabolical alliance against Christendom from within and without, standing under the aegis of the Antichrist. In his warnings against the danger of the Jewish 'infection' and his polemical vituperation against rabbinical lies and distortions of the Bible, what predominates is the hatred of Judaism as a legalistic religion which threatens the evangelical Church. Law and gospel remain deadly enemies. the contest is one between God and the Devil, Christ and the Antichrist.

Luther rejected the Calvinist teaching of 'salvation through works' (a 'Jewish faith') in favour of justification by faith alone. He vehemently opposed the Roman Church's legalism with its focus on ceremonial and priestly mediation as being spiritually bankrupt. 'Because the Papists, like the Jews, insist that anyone wishing to be saved must observe their ceremonies, they will perish like the Jews.'[27] The 'Judaic' heresy within the Church, which sought to approach God through ceremonial law, had to be uprooted and the Jews themselves expelled so that they no longer contaminate Christians with their blaspheming heresies. No wonder that many Jews, who had originally welcomed Luther's Reform as heralding a new era, came to see in the German monk a modern Haman, seeking to annihilate them by harsh measures and forced conversions.[28]

The German Reformation, under Luther's guidance, therefore led in a very unfavourable direction for Jews, when compared with parallel developments in English, Dutch or Swiss Protestantism.[29] The seed of hatred sown by Luther would reach its horrible climax in the Third Reich, when German Protestants showed themselves to be particularly receptive to Nazi antisemitism.[30]

4

■ ■ ■

Modern Secular Anti-Judaism

With the decline of religious faith in post-medieval European society the traditional theological hostility towards the 'deicide' people became less relevant, especially to intellectuals who identified with the sceptical temper of the Age of Enlightenment. At first sight, the rise of rationalist thinking in the seventeenth and eighteenth centuries appeared to be a positive development for Jews, for it attacked the foundations of the Christian religion and the unified Christian state which had excluded or oppressed Jews for reasons of creed. It was partly from the rationalist assumptions of the German Enlightenment that the Habsburg Emperor Joseph II derived his Toleration edicts of the 1780s; that Moses Mendelsohn felt empowered to build a bridge between traditional Jewish and modern German cultures; that his friend Gotthold Lessing immortalised a more positive image of the Jew in his famous play, *Nathan the Wise*. Without the philosophy of the Enlightenment, the Prussian bureaucrat Christian Wilhelm Döhm would never have written his tract *'Über die bürgerliche Verbesserung der Juden'* ('Concerning the Civic Amelioration of the Jews') in 1781, an indictment of the responsibility of the Christian world for the degradation of the Jews.

In France, during the same period, enlightened Gentiles like the Abbé Grégoire, Count Mirabeau and the revolutionary Maximilien Robespierre, argued along similar lines in urging the emancipation of the Jews as part of the overthrow of the *ancien régime* with its feudal privileges, social inequalities and injustices. The Declaration of the Rights of Man by the French

revolutionaries in 1789 and the granting of equal civic rights to
the Jews two years later was indeed a triumph of the liberal
rationalist credo which had been born out of the Enlightenment.

There was, however, a darker, more complex and ambivalent strand in rationalist thought about the Jews and Judaism
which first surfaced in English deism of the late seventeenth
and early eighteenth centuries. Here, for the first time, radical
thinkers who put forward the notion of 'natural religion' as an
alternative to the 'revealed' truths of Christianity, critically
examined Judaism from a rationalist standpoint. The para-
doxical result 'was a denial of all religious value to Judaism,
which was presented as an obscurantist prejudice hostile to
human reason. The extreme language of the English deists and
the French materialists of the eighteenth century in their
attacks on Jews and Judaism revived the hostility towards
Jews and renewed the force of the old negative stereotypes.'[1]
For the English deists and French materialists, the Old
Testament was no less obnoxious than the Gospel, the
Synagogue no less offensive to reason than the Church, and
rabbis as much imposters as priests.[2] Indeed, those rationalists
who were sworn enemies of the Church were often disposed
to see the source of its intolerance, fanaticism and superstition
in the Hebrew Bible and the teachings of Judaism.

Their return to the sources of classical Antiquity for inspiration, if anything reinforced this inimical disposition to
Judaism. For in the writings of the French Encyclopaedists one
can find clear traces of early Graeco-Roman literary antisemitism, whose ideas and phraseology passed into the
mainstream of Enlightenment thinking. Thus pagan, pre-
Christian antisemitism was grafted on to the stem of medieval
Christian stereotypes of the Jew and would pass over into the
post-Christian rationalist anti-Judaism of the eighteenth and
nineteenth centuries. As the historian Arthur Hertzberg has
written, 'the vital link, the man who skipped over the
Christian centuries and provided a new, international, secular,

anti-Jewish rhetoric in the name of European culture rather than religion was Voltaire'.[3]

Instead of disappearing with the Enlightenment, anti-semitism simply found a new guise, one which no longer blamed the Jews for the crucifixion of Christ but held them responsible for all the crimes and perversities committed in the name of monotheistic religion; the Jews were no longer guilty of rejecting Christian belief but were judged to be inherently perverse, and their 'fossilised' religion to be an obstacle to human progress. In the arch-sceptic Voltaire the resulting image of the Jew is one of utter scorn and contempt. The Old Testament is ridiculed and calumnied as a compendium of cannibalism, folly and error. The Jews were caricatured as 'the most imbecile people on the face of the earth', as 'obtuse, cruel and absurd', the heirs of a history that was both 'disgusting and abominable'.[4] In his entry *'Juifs'*, written for the *Dictionnaire Philosophique*, Voltaire echoes the familiar litany of insults drawn from classical pagan antisemitism. 'In short, we find in them only an ignorant and barbarous people, who have long united the most sordid avarice with the most detestable superstition and the most invincible hatred for every people by whom they are tolerated and enriched.'[5] Not only did Voltaire repeat the pagan canard that Jews were the 'enemies of mankind', but he even justified the long history of persecutions and massacres to which they had been subjected.[6]

These diatribes cannot be convincingly explained by Voltaire's personal psychology or by disappointments that arose out of business dealings with individual Jews. For they were largely shared by other prominent thinkers of the French Enlightenment like Diderot, the atheist Baron d'Holbach (for whom the Jews were also the vilest nation on earth) and to a lesser degree by Jean-Jacques Rousseau. Rather, they should be seen as a philosophical expression of the crisis of religious belief, in which a war conducted against the very roots of the Christian faith led logically to an assault on its Jewish origins. Conducted in the name of progress, renewal and freedom of thought, it paradoxically perpetuated the hostile historical image of Judaism handed down by the Christian culture on which these philosophical sceptics and radicals had been nourished.[7]

In post-revolutionary France the impact of this tradition can clearly be seen in the thinking of the great French historian Jules Michelet, especially after the spiritual crisis which he underwent in the early 1840s. Henceforth, he began to level sharp criticism against the Judeo-Christian enslavement to an arbitrary, capricious God who bestowed his favours without justice or reason. Naturally, Michelet rejected completely the notion that Israel had been chosen by God as an exclusivist principle which discriminated against those who had not been chosen. More significantly, he objected to the fact that the choice had fallen on so undeserving an object as the small, scattered and weak Jewish people – whose horizons were limited and whose stubborn particularism was anathema to his own universalist credo. For Michelet, Judaism was utterly lacking in grandeur or noble ideals; it had always supported reaction and above all its historical connection with Christianity made it viscerally repugnant to him.[8]

The influential French scholar Ernest Renan, though by no means an antisemite or accepting all of Michelet's conclusions, did agree that it was Israel which had brought forth Christianity and 'the conversion of the world to monotheism'. At the same time he decried the exclusivist tendencies and fanaticism of the Jewish intellect, character-traits which had become 'a stumbling block in the march of humanity after having been the cause of its great progress'.[9] Renan saw in this exclusivism and self-imposed isolation of the Jews, exacerbated by the teachings of the Talmud and by an ingrained complex of superiority, the ultimate cause of the detestation with which they were widely regarded. The intolerance of the Jews was a function of their monotheism but it was also, in his view, a trait of the 'Semitic peoples' in general, including Arabs.

In the 1850s Renan, along with the German scholar Christian Lassen, would be one of the first thinkers in Europe to popularise the racial concept of 'Semites' in contrast to the Indo-Europeans or 'Aryans', whom he placed at the top of the ladder of human civilisation.[10] Renan argued that Semites lacked creative ability, a sense of discipline and the capacity for independent political organisation. The 'Semitic' race, so he claimed, had 'no mythology, no epic, no science, no philosophy, no fiction, no plastic arts, no civic life; there is no complexity, nor nuance; an exclusive sense of uniformity'.[11] Nor surprisingly after this catalogue of negative qualities, Renan could only conclude that Semites 'represented an inferior combination of human nature'.[12] Renan attributed all of these 'Semitic' faults to the ancient Hebrews as well, who were of a narrow horizon, essentially primitive, and whose limited creativity was ultimately confined to their simple, religious conceptions. His view of contemporary Jews was a little more nuanced but still riddled with antisemitic clichés emphasising their egoism, clannishness, worship of Mammon and their leading role in modern revolutionary movements. Yet in spite of his racist outlook, Renan never drew the practical conclusions from his theories that French and German antisemites were wont to do, clearly opposing any political manipulation of the racial principle towards the end of his life. He openly admitted that his concept of a 'Semitic' race was basically erroneous, that it could not be meaningfully applied to modern assimilated Jews and that national identity was based on voluntary choice, not on racial determinism.[13]

But Renan's antithesis between 'Aryans' and 'Semites' found a ready echo in nineteenth-century France, where it was adopted by a number of leading socialist writers who used it to bolster their radical antipathy to Jews and Judaism. This was most obviously apparent in the Blanquist movement, a militantly atheist, anticlerical and 'patriotic' wing of French socialism whose rallying-cry was *Ni Dieu, Ni Maître*.[14] From Renan and the Count de Gobineau they adapted the notion of

'Semitism' as intrinsically inferior to the 'Aryan' genius of Greece and Rome, which alone had created the foundations of modern civilisation.[15] The Semitic Deity of the Old Testament was depicted in the spirit of Voltaire as a murderous, hypocritical and exploiting Moloch-God who devoured his children and encouraged the cult of human sacrifice. This blood-lust, which biblical Judaism had transmitted to Christianity, found its culmination in the wage-slavery of modern capitalism which had reduced the masses to a state of helotry. The mercantile 'Semitic' spirit of exploitation had triumphed under capitalism over the 'Aryan' love of nature, respect for the family, and the pagan ideals of beauty, harmony, liberty and fraternity.

According to the Blanquist revolutionary, Gustave Tridon, in his *Du Molochisme Juif* (1884) the 'Semites' represented the negative pole of humanity; they were 'the evil genius of the world', the 'shadow in the picture of civilisation', the enemies of 'Aryan' humanity.[16] Since intolerance was 'the Semitic legacy to our world' it was 'the aim of the Indo-Aryan race' and a revolutionary duty 'to fight the Semitic spirit' in modern society. Similar ideas were disseminated in the leading journal of the French Left, *La Revue Socialiste*, during the 1880s by respected socialists like Albert Regnard and Benoît Malon. Hence it is not surprising that the high priest of modern French antisemitism, Edouard Drumont, should write in 1889: 'Of all the revolutionaries, only the Blanquists have had the courage to refer to the Aryan race and to proclaim that race's superiority.'[17] He paid a similar compliment to other French socialist forerunners like Charles Fourier, Alphonse Toussenel and Pierre-Joseph Proudhon, whose visceral antisemitism drew on diverse and often contradictory strands of anti-capitalism, Enlightenment anticlericalism and Catholic anti-modernism.[18]

In Germany the secular, anti-Christian strand of Judeophobia emerged over half a century later than in France, reflecting the more backward social and political development of the fragmented German states. It was first manifest in the late 1830s among the free-thinking, radical Young Hegelians, whose critique of Judaism owed more to Voltaire and the French materialists than it did to the philosophy of Hegel on which they claimed to draw.[19] The Young Hegelians saw themselves as engaged in an assault on the religious foundations of the authoritarian Christian state in Prussia – one which Karl Marx, himself a product of this school of thought, praised as 'the greatest achievement of German philsophy'.[20] At the same time, their abstract philosophising on Jews and Judaism was part of an ongoing debate in German society over Jewish emancipation which would not be resolved for several decades.[21]

Although the Young Hegelians were atheistic radicals who spoke in the name of freedom and progress, they abandoned the historical premises of Hegel and the German Enlightenment which had still granted Judaism a respectable position on the ladder of human development. Ignoring the actual evolution of Germans and Jews since the eighteenth century and the effects which Christian persecution had exercised on Jewish society, they traced all the flaws in Judaism to an allegedly immutable essence. This was most obviously apparent in the polemical tract of Bruno Bauer, 'Die Judenfrage' ('The Jewish Question'), written in 1843 from a radical anti-Christian standpoint which nonetheless opposed Jewish emancipation. Like Voltaire before him, Bauer depicted Judaism as a fossilised religion, based on superstition and obscurantism, whose diety was cruel, vengeful, stubborn and egotistical. He had been created in the image of his own 'chosen people', reflecting the egoistic national spirit of the Jews, their exclusivism and hatred of all other peoples. Insulated behind the walls of their Torah (religious law), the Jewish people had pursued their ahistorical, 'chimerical' existence, indifferent to the development of modern civilisation. As a result of their fanatical separatism and stubborn particularism, they had contributed nothing to the German struggle for liberation and had not even begun the radical critique of Judaism which would have been the indispensable first step to their emancipation. As long as the Jews remained enclosed in their narrow-minded 'Jewish essence' there could be no question of granting them civic equality. Nor could the Christian state in Prussia, which by its very essence was based on religious prejudice, exclusivism and privilege, be expected to emancipate German Jewry.[22]

Bruno Bauer's radical critique of Judaism was largely accepted by his Young Hegelian contemporaries, including the philosopher Ludwig Feuerbach and the founder of 'scientific socialism', Karl Marx. Like Bauer, Feuerbach linked monotheism with Jewish 'egoism', unfavourably contrasting its practical utilitarianism with pagan curiosity and openness towards nature. Judaism was reduced in his analysis to a theoretically narrow, ethnocentric and positivist religion based on the satisfaction of private needs and devoid of any ethical content. Another German radical, Georg Friedrich Daumer, was more vitriolic, writing to Feuerbach in 1842 about 'the cannibalism in the Talmud', human blood being drunk on Purim and the 'bloody mysteries of the Rabbanites [sic] and Talmudists, the Sabbatians who border on Christianity, and the Hassidic sects who are so numerous in Slavic lands'.[23] He promised Feuerbach 'unbelievable' information about the ritual murder practised by fanatical Jewish sects, to which, he suggested, Jesus Christ himself had belonged. Daumer, whose main target was Christianity, described 'the idea of the human victim sacrificed to God' as its central notion and argued that its whole history from the Crucifixion to the Inquisition was one long chain of ritual murders. Daumer's study, *Die Geheimnisse des christlichen Altertums* (1847), was hailed by Karl Marx as 'the last blow to Christianity' and as a sign that 'the old society is approaching its end and that the structure of falsehood and prejudice is collapsing'.

Like his Young Hegelian contemporaries, Karl Marx's

critique of Judaism was part of a wider assault on organised religion and the foundations of Christian society. For him, as for Feuerbach, Judaism was a purely worldly religion which embodied 'actual contempt for and practical degradation of nature', not to speak of its 'contempt for art, for history, for man as an end in hmself'.[24] In the Marxian myth of the worldly Jew, money was 'the jealous god of Israel before whom no other god may stand'. In Christian bourgeois society, 'the god of the Jews has been secularised and become the god of the world. Exchange is the true god of the Jew. His god is nothing more than illusory exchange.'[25] Thus Marx linked together 'the practical spirit of Judaism' with both Christianity and the economic structure of bourgeois society, which was constantly producing 'empirical Jews' from within its bowels. Though himself born a Jew (his family had converted to Lutheranism when he was six) and in favour of Jewish emancipation as a tactical weapon to undermine the semi-absolutist Prussian Christian state, Marx never disguised his repugnance towards Jews and Judaism.[26]

His polemical answer to Bruno Bauer, '*Zur Judenfrage*' ('On the Jewish Question') published in 1844, for all its anti-Christian rhetoric, faithfully reproduces the deeply rooted anti-Jewish mythology of that bourgeois Christian society he was seeking to overthrow. Like Bruno Bauer, he argued that, despite their lack of political rights, the German Jews had already emancipated themselves 'in a Jewish manner' through their control of high finance. Like other radicals and socialists in the nineteenth and twentieth centuries, he singled out the Rothschilds and other Jewish banking houses for particular odium. The economic power of the House of Rothschild, citizens of five different countries, prominent everywhere and in close collaboration with different governments, would become one of the most potent symbols for the fantasy of a shadowy Jewish world government and an obsession with antisemites of the Right and Left for generations.[27]

Marx himself stopped short of full-fledged antisemitism but in his own way reinforced the negative stereotype of the Jew as the personification of modern capitalism, which would later be adapted by the Nazis and their imitators. In 1844 he could write that 'the practical dominance of Judaism over the Christian world has reached its unambiguous normal expression in North America', while in Europe 'the practical spirit of the Jews has become the practical spirit of the Christian peoples'.[28] Judaism for the young Marx was 'a universal and *contemporary anti-social* element which has reached its present peak through a historical development in whose harmful aspects the Jews eagerly collaborated, a peak at which it will inevitably disintegrate'. Since huckstering was for Marx the cold, egoistic heart of the Jewish religion and the symbol of human self-alienation, it was only logical that 'emancipation from *haggling* and *money*, from practical, real Judaism would be the self-emancipation of our time'.[29] Marx's messianic solution to the 'Jewish question', which already pointed to his imminent conversion to Communism, involved the complete overthrow of a society based on the cash-nexus. In the new society, where money no longer played any role, the Jews and Judaism, based as they were on the 'chimerical nationality of the merchant', would automatically disappear. 'As soon as society succeeds in destroying the *empirical* essence of Judaism – buying and selling, and its presuppositions – the Jew will become *impossible*, because his consciousness will no longer have an object. . . . The *social* emancipation of Jewry is the *emancipation of society from Judaism.*'[30]

Whatever the interpretation one gives to these words, the implementation of Marx's vision of Communism in the USSR in the name of 'human emancipation' would cause untold suffering, not only to Jews and other national or religious minorities but also to millions of ordinary Russians. Although Marx never opposed Jewish emancipation as such (unlike Bruno Bauer, who later became a virulent racist antisemite[31] and Prussian conservative) his writings on religion were used in the Soviet Union to legitimise fanatical atheistic campaigns, and in the post-war period to justify the most vulgar anti-semitic propaganda. At the same time, the fact that the founder of Communism was himself born a Jew made him the arch-symbol of Jewish revolutionary subversion for the conservative and radical Right all over the world. Modern antisemitism seized on the prominent role which 'non-Jewish Jews' like Marx played in Socialist, Communist and other radical movements to construct a new myth of the Jew as the 'rootless cosmopolitan' enemy of all national values, religious traditions, social cohesion and bourgeois morality. In post-1918 Germany, in particular, the high visibility of Jews in the revolutionary movement was a key element in the revival of antisemitism on the Right, and a similar backlash occurred elsewhere in Europe which has not yet played itself out. Even the Holocaust itself can be seen on one level as a macabre consummation within National Socialist demonology of the myth of 'Jewish' Communism that begins with Marx.

Paradoxically, therefore, it might be said that the criticism and radical protest directed against modern society, which began with a fierce critique of its Christian foundations, in the long run reinforced and even intensified hostility towards Jews. Antisemitism, far from being weakened by the decline of Christian belief, revived in an age of secularisation, of modernisation and rapid social change. New ideologies rose up, which adopted their own brand of secularised anti-Judaism and antisemitism to suit the new age.[32] Liberals and free-thinkers attacked the intolerance and ahistorical rigidity of Judaism or the isolationist particularism of the Jews; Socialists condemned Jews as the embodiment of the 'capitalist spirit'; nationalists and racists deplored the 'alien' origins and allegedly 'Semitic' character of their Jewish minorities; while conservatives pointed to Jews as a source of permanent unrest and revolutionary subversion in European society.

5
■ ■ ■

Antisemitism in Central Europe

The role which Jews played in the German-speaking culture of
Central Europe from the middle of the nineteenth century
until the rise of Hitler was unprecedented in its scale and
quality. Indeed it is difficult to imagine the culture of
modernity without the contributions of Marx, Freud, Einstein,
Kafka, Mahler, Schoenberg, Wittgenstein and many others
whose parents or grandparents had only recently been
emancipated from life in the ghettos of Central Europe.
Without the German-Jewish 'symbiosis' there would have
been no great cultural peaks like fin-de-siècle Vienna or Berlin
during the Weimar Republic. Paradoxically, the Jews became
victims of their very success in penetrating and remoulding the
agenda and the cultural axes of modernity in Central Europe.
Identified by conservative and radical reactionary forces with
the credo of liberalism or Marxism – with being standard-
bearers of Western ideals of freedom, equality and social
democracy – they were fated to be the first victims of the great
counter-revolutionary backlash which culminated in National
Socialism.

So deeply were Jews implicated in reshaping the culture,
economy and politics of societies like Germany and Austria
whose democratic traditions were weak and whose own
national identity was insecure, that the antisemitism which
developed in Central Europe assumed a uniquely racial and
extremist quality. Racial antisemitism, grafted on to an older
and still powerful Christian legacy of hate, served here to
uproot at its very core the modern dream of assimilation,

replacing it first with segregation, then expulsion and finally mass extermination of the Jews.

Already in 1819, post-Napoleonic Germany, shaken by economic crisis and political upheaval, had experienced the anti-Jewish outbreaks known as the 'Hep! Hep!' riots (a derogatory rallying cry against Jews). The goal of the agitation was to return the Jews to their previous ghetto status, following their entry into certain occupations – such as the civil service and the legal profession – which had been made possible by the Napoleonic conquest of Germany. Not only the mob but also the 'educated' burgher classes, university professors like Friedrich Rühs and Jakob Fries, and student leaders, railed against acceptance of Jewish civic equality within a Christian state. A new kind of 'Teutomania' came into being, rejecting the ideals of the French Revolution as 'alien' to Germany, adopting a mystical cult of the German nation as an *Urvolk* ('natural folk'), deploring the commercialisation of urban life and attacking the Jews as despoilers of the German people (*Volksausplünderer*).[1] Throughout the nineteenth century German antisemitism would feed on this explosive ideological mix of romanticism, anti-capitalism, *völkisch* nationalism and hatred of Western liberal democracy.

Even radical intellectuals in Germany during the first half of the nineteenth century – like the Young Hegelians, Arnold Ruge, Bruno Bauer and Karl Marx – made, as we have seen, their own distinctive contribution to the subsequent emergence of a secular, anti-Christian antisemitism. They condemned the 'fossilised', antihistorical character of Judaism, its religious separatism and its 'exploitative' character, which, according to the radical Hegelians, had permeated bourgeois Christian society with a Judaic ethos. This depiction of Judaism as something alien and inferior which has nevertheless succeeded in 'Judaising' European society and culture finds its apogee in Richard Wagner's antisemitic tract, '*Das Judentum in der Musik*' (1850). Drawing on both the radical Hegelian and romantic nationalist traditions, Wagner identifies the 'spirit of Judaism' with that of modernity – understood not as progress but as an expression of decadence and artistic decline.[2] As it was for the young Marx in the economic arena, so for Wagner, 'liberation from Jewry' becomes the goal of redemption in the creative sphere.

But the great composer, one of the most influential anti-semites of the modern age, goes much further than his contemporaries in his backlash against Jewry and the 'abstract rationalism' which underpins their emancipation. For Jewry's entry into modern society is perceived by Wagner as the infiltration of a wholly alien and antagonistic group whose success symbolises the spiritual and creative crisis of German and European culture. The Jews represent the 'evil conscience of our modern civilisation' or, to quote another phrase much repeated by the Nazis, 'the plastic demon of the decline of mankind'. They embodied the corrupt, money-making principle of the new bourgeois world which Wagner held responsible for its artistic decay.[3] The modern, educated, assimilated Jew is depicted by Wagner, already in 1850, as 'the most heartless of all human beings', alien and apathetic in the midst of a society he does not understand, whose history and evolution are indifferent to him. The Jew, wholly divorced from the *Volksgeist* ('spirit of the race'), has no passion, no soul, no 'inner capacity for life', no true music or poetry. He is a cold, loveless, purely cerebral being. Contemporary German-Jewish artists like the composers Felix Mendelssohn and Meyerbeer, the poet Heinrich Heine or the radical writer Ludwig Boerne, are dismissed as arid, sarcastic and self-negating in their life and work.[4] The only redemption from this sterility lies in the 'going under' of Jewry, its complete dissolution and disappearance.

Wagner's essentially racist vision of Jewry would have a profound influence on German and Austrian antisemites, including the English-born Houston S. Chamberlain, Lanz von Liebenfels and above all on Adolf Hitler himself. Richard Wagner gave to German antisemitism a metaphysical pseudo-profundity, an aesthetic rationale rooted in the pagan world of classical Greece and a mythical quality which also finds expression in some of his operatic works as well as in his writings. The later Wagner, influenced by the racist philosophy of the French diplomat and historian Comte de Gobineau, is already a theorist of blood purity and the need to cleanse European civilisation from the spiritual and physical pollution of the Jews. In 1881 he writes to Ludwig II of Bavaria: 'I hold the Jewish race to be the born enemy of pure humanity and everything noble in it. It is certain that it is running us Germans to the ground, and I am perhaps the last German who knows how to hold himself upright in the face of Judaism, which already rules everything.'[5]

It was in the late 1870s, in the decade immediately following formal Jewish emancipation in both Germany and Austria, that such ideas became commonplace and served as the basis for organised political antisemitism in Germany. It was the stock market collapse of 1873 in Vienna and then Berlin which provided the trigger by provoking an economic crisis which adversely affected the lower middle classes. It was against this background that radical German journalists like Otto Glagau and Wilhelm Marr wrote popular antisemitic tracts, and Prussian conservative publicists lashed out against the rule of the National Liberals ('Manchesterism' as it was often called), of Jewish financiers and of the German Jewish-liberal press.[6] Both Glagau and Marr suggested that 'the social question is nothing but the Jewish question' and the latter sought in 1879 to create an Antisemitic League – the first of its kind in Europe. His highly pessimistic book *The Victory of Judaism over Germanism* (1879), which put forward the thesis that 'Germanism' was lost, since the Jews were already constructing their Jerusalem on the ruins of the new Germany, went through several editions and aroused extensive press comment.[7]

Far more effective than Marr, however, was the Lutheran court-preacher Adolf Stoecker, who in 1879 organised Berlin's first genuine antisemitic movement. Stoecker's bitter critique of Judaism and of modern German Jewry's 'domination' of the press and the stock exchange combined traditional Lutheran theology with an anticapitalist appeal designed to win over the working-class to Throne and Altar. Although Stoecker's Christian-Social Party failed in this objective, he remained one of the main propagators of a modern political antisemitism founded on Christian ideology in the Second German Reich.[8] His Catholic counterpart in Vienna, Karl von Vogelsang (an ex-Protestant German expatriate) who founded the conservative newspaper *Das Vaterland* in the 1870s, played a similar role in laying the ideological-political foundations of Austrian antisemitism. Here, too, the assault on the Jews derived from a sharp critique of the Liberal hegemony and capitalistic exploitation of labour, combined with fear of secularising trends in modern society and the resulting decline of Christian belief.

Racial antisemites like Eugen Dühring (a Berlin philosopher and economist), Theodor Fritsch and the Hessian peasant leader Otto Boeckel took an even more intransigent, uncompromising view of the threat posed by emancipated Jewry to German society.[9] Moreover, they regarded Christianity as itself part of the problem since it was a 'Semitic' religion which had imposed the 'alien yoke' of the Old and New Testaments on the Germanic race, thereby inhibiting and distorting its natural instincts, its strength, virility and heroic virtues. This racist trend of antisemitism had considerable appeal to university students in Germany and Austria, who in the early 1880s already began to exclude Jews from membership in their fraternities (*Burschenschaften*). In an age of formal equality when Jews had emerged as dangerous competitors in the liberal professions, especially journalism, medicine and law, racism had obvious attractions. It provided a way of reconstructing the social boundaries that had fallen with the ghetto walls – replacing them with new biological criteria based on blood and descent. In a secular, scientific and positivist age, 'race' distinctions still had a certain objective, neutral quality to them and seemed more persuasive to many pseudo-intellectuals than outdated Christian theological concepts in which they no longer believed. Above all, the notion of race had a certain finality to it, suggesting that negative Jewish qualities were fixed and unchanging – hence not amenable to assimilation, conversion or any other attempts at social integration.

Anti-Jewish stereotypes had, of course, preceded racial thinking by centuries and existed quite independently of the emergence of this new ideology in the late nineteenth century. One could, like Paul de Lagarde, one of Germany's most prominent Orientalists and Bible scholars, radically negate Jewish existence without espousing racism.[10] De Lagarde, in calling for a Germanic Christianity which would completely eradicate its 'Jewish' components, was one of the few nineteenth-century intellectuals to openly favour expulsion or imply approval for the physical destruction of German Jewry.

More influential at the time was the conservative nationalist historian, Heinrich von Treitschke, who had welcomed the Berlin antisemitic movement in 1879 with the famous slogan 'The Jews are our misfortune' ('Die Juden sind unser Unglück').[11] Von Treitschke gave academic legitimacy and respectability to what had hitherto seemed to be a rather disreputable, vulgar street movement. His demand for the total, unconditional surrender by German Jews of any distinctive Jewish identity did not openly employ racial arguments, but he did suggest that they remained an 'alien' element in the German population who were largely to blame for the antisemitic response which their emancipation had aroused. Von Treitschke, like other Prussian conservatives, especially detested the 'progressive' role which German Jews had played in promoting liberal ideas, radicalism and Social Democracy. Already in the Second Reich it had become fashionable to blame Jews for the policies of National Liberalism (Lasker,

Bamberger), for stock-exchange capitalism (Rothschild, Bleichröder) and for revolutionary Marxism (Marx, Lassalle, Rosa Luxemburg). But what concerned the mandarin class in particular was their sense of Jews intruding into, subverting and ultimately controlling German intellectual and cultural life. This fear was rationalised as a desire to defend the semi-feudal, organic and 'idealist' values of Germandom against the vulgar 'materialism' with which Jews were supposedly corrupting the new capitalistic Germany. One finds such anxieties echoed across the political spectrum from radical economists like Werner Sombart to conservative monarchists like Houston S. Chamberlain.[12]

It was rare to find a German intellectual like Friedrich Nietzsche, who not only admired the Jews for their spiritual mastery and grandeur, while detesting 'the stupidity, crudity and pettiness of German nationalism', but vehemently dissociated himself from the 'damnable German antisemitism, this poisonous boil of *névrose nationale*'.[13] The German philosopher who took an axe to the Christian religion (he was also highly critical of the Jewish 'slave rebellion in morals') deplored 'these latest speculators in idealism, the anti-Semites, who today roll their eyes in a Christian-Aryan bourgeois manner and exhaust one's patience by trying to rouse up all the horned-beast elements in the people'.[14] The problem was essentially a digestive one, for the German type, so Nietzsche believed, was 'still weak and indefinite, so it could easily be blurred or extinguished by the stronger race'. He had no doubt that the Jews were indeed 'the strongest, toughest, and purest race now living in Europe', who could gain mastery over it if they so wished.[15] Yet, as Nietzsche stressed, they desired nothing but accommodation and absorption, to put an end to their centuries of wandering – to which purpose the German philosopher suggested that 'it might be useful and fair to expel the antisemitic screamers from the country'.[16]

The German antisemites in Nietzsche's day never constituted a major threat to the established social and political order.

Their organisations were too divided among themselves, too limited in their electoral appeal and lacking in charismatic political leaders to obtain more than an ephemeral success at the polls. At the peak of their appeal during the Second Reich there were sixteen antisemitic deputies sitting in the Imperial Parliament – half of them from Hesse.[17] On the eve of the First World War party political antisemitism was clearly declining, but it would be very misleading to measure the impact of anti-Jewish feelings by such a narrow criterion. The influential Conservative Party adopted an openly anti-Jewish paragraph in its Tivoli Programme of 1892 and the ideologically affiliated Agrarian League (Bund der Landwirte) was a powerful ultra-conservative and antisemitic pressure group.[18]

If purely antisemitic rabble-rousers like Otto Boeckel, Hermann Ahlwardt and Liebermann von Sonnenberg were ultimately unsuccessful, this was not so true of right-wing, imperialist lobbies like the Pan-Germanic League (Alldeutscher Verband), the Deutschnationaler Handlungs-gehilfenverband (a white-collar trade union), the Akademischer Turnerbund (a gymnastics club) or the Verein Deutscher Studenten – an antisemitic students' movement. The impact of such lobbies and interest-groups, imbued with an antiliberal, *völkisch*-national and antisemitic outlook, was considerably greater than that of ephemeral anti-Jewish political parties which rose and fell in accordance with the vagaries of the economy and the political system as a whole.[19] Moreover, as we have seen, organised antisemitism, which had first emerged in Germany after 1873, had a strong underpinning in cultural and religious stereotypes that remained entrenched in almost all sectors of the population. Once this potential was activated by the effects of defeat in the First World War, by inflation, massive economic depression, chronic political instability and the rise of a powerful mass movement of the Right, German antisemitism was rapidly transformed into a formidable political force.

Before 1914 it was, however, in German Austria and above

all in Vienna that antisemitism first displayed its vote-catching efficacy. The Jews of Vienna, who formed about 8 per cent of the population, were heavily over-represented in the liberal professions, especially journalism, law and medicine – half of the students in the medical faculty in 1910 were Jewish. The Jews dominated the liberal educated class in fin-de-siècle Vienna and, even more than in Germany at that time, they seemed to be the creators, the critics, the impresarios and managers of German high culture. For Stefan Zweig they contributed nine-tenths of everything important in Viennese culture – an exaggeration, no doubt, but one containing enough truth to arouse the rage of the Austrian antisemites from Lueger to Hitler who denounced the 'Judaisation' of the press, art, literature and the theatre. The challenging innovations of Viennese Jews in psychoanalysis (Freud, Adler, Reich), in music (Mahler, Schoenberg), in literature, criticism and philosophy (Schnitzler, Salten, Beer-Hoffmann, Kraus) simply intensified the resentment of many Catholic Austrians.[20] Anti-Jewish theologians like August Rohling, author of the notorious *Der Talmudjude*, and Joseph Deckert railed against a 'Semitic' conspiracy of powerful Jews who aimed at the subversion of the Catholic faith and even practised, so they alleged, ritual murder as part of their hatred of Gentiles and insatiable drive for domination in Austria.[21] Antisemitic politicians like Schneider, Gregorig, Pattai, Lueger and Schoenerer disseminated these and other baseless slanders to a mass audience.

To some extent this fin-de-siècle Austrian antisemitism was a displaced reaction against the liberal capitalism which threatened those declining social strata – especially the Viennese artisans – with economic decline into the proletariat. Jewish industrialists and bankers as well as migrant pedlars from Galicia were seen as two sides of the same threat posed by capitalist modernisation to the traditional way of life of the lower middle classes. While the multi-national Habsburg state valued the contribution made by Jewish enterprise to building up the railroads, financing the coalmines, pioneering sugar-refining, establishing the beer industry, developing the iron and steel industry, the banking system and the metropolitan press, ordinary Austrians resented the dizzying ascent of the Jews in wealth and social status within one generation. It was all too easy and convenient to ascribe this success story to money-grabbing 'materialism', dishonesty in business dealings or to a malevolent conspiracy to subjugate and oppress the Catholic majority.

The immensely popular resonance of anticapitalist antisemitism among the Viennese found its best expression in the spectacular career of Karl Lueger, the first democratic politician to triumph anywhere in Europe on an explicitly anti-Jewish platform.[22] Elected Mayor of Vienna in 1897, at the head of the Christian-Social Party, he retained power until his death in 1910 and was the first political role-model for the young Adolf Hitler, who admired him as 'the greatest German *Bürgermeister* of all times.' Lueger's attack on the Jews was a central part of his general assault on Liberal political hegemony in city politics and later of his defence of bourgeois class interests against the rising Social Democrats – most of whose intellectual leadership was Jewish, beginning with its founder Victor Adler. Lueger denounced Jewish influence in Hungary (coining the abusive term 'Judeo-Magyars'), in Austrian banking, industry and commerce, in the Viennese Press, in medicine and the liberal professions. His Christian-Social party called openly for segregation in the school system (though this was never implemented), for banning the immigration of foreign Jews and for the restriction of Jewish influence in public life. Although officially Catholic in its discourse, the party had prominent agitators in its ranks, including Schneider, Gregorig and priests like Father Deckert and Joseph Scheicher, whose populist antisemitism was as incendiary as that of any beer-swilling Pan-German racists. After his election to office in 1897 Lueger himself was more covert in his anti-Jewish rhetoric, limited as he was by Franz

Joseph's imperial authority, which upheld the equality of all religious faiths and of all Austrian citizens before the law. Nevertheless, Lueger did not disown the more extremist Jew-baiters in his movement and did on occasion resort to racist remarks as well as carrying on surreptitious discrimination against Jewish employees of the municipality.[23]

Although himself the holder of an academic degree, Dr Lueger did not hesitate to indulge in the crass anti-intellectualism so often directed by the more plebeian members of his party against Jews, free thinkers or socialists. Thus he frequently denigrated the universities and medical schools for being 'Jew-infested' strongholds of atheism, free thinking, revolutionary subversion and the undermining of Christian morality. At the time of the 1905 Russian revolution, he threatened the Jewish community that if they supported the Social Democrats a pogrom could result. 'I warn the Jews most expressly; for the same thing could perhaps happen as in Russia. We in Vienna are not anti-Semites [sic!], we are certainly not inclined to murder and violence. But if the Jews should threaten our fatherland, then we will show no mercy.'[24]

The Christian-Social Party, he declared on another occasion, was determined that the 'Christian *Volk*' and not the alien Jews should be masters in their own house. His movement advocated 'Christian solidarity' accompanied by an economic boycott of Jewish businesses to achieve this end, though such calls were rarely observed. It constantly campaigned against the *Verjudung* ('Judaisation') of Austrian culture, though here too it met with little practical success. But it was more effective in implanting antisemitism in the hearts and minds of the younger generation, in making its discourse respectable and normal in public life, in linking it with a traditional, sentimental, religiously oriented Austrian Catholic patriotism.[25]

Lueger's conservative antisemitism was not incompatible with the toleration of baptised Jews or collaboration with wealthy, powerful Jewish capitalists whom the municipality needed to help fund its more ambitious projects for modernising Vienna. This pragmatic, opportunist approach had always been typical of Lueger's politics and it did not change after he had embraced antisemitism as an integral part of his platform and ideology. He understood the value of antisemitism as a tactical weapon for attaining power but also recognised, unlike many of his rivals and his more extreme supporters, its limits once in office. His 'war against the Jews' was carried out within the framework of a conciliatory, supranational Habsburg dynasty which deplored antisemitism as the politics of the street; mass violence within this *Rechtsstaat* (a state based on law) was rare, except in moments of crisis in Hungary, Galicia or Bohemia. There were no major economic crises such as characterised the post-1918 era in Austria. Nor were there any pogroms in Habsburg Vienna despite the hysterical diatribes of the more rabid Austrian antisemites. Viennese Jews were not stripped of their civil rights; there was no expropriation of Jewish wealth and, for all the anxiety and insecurity which antisemitism aroused, Jews continued to make a brilliant contribution to German-Austrian culture.

Nevertheless, Austrian antisemitism – that of Lueger and of his great rival, the Pan-German Georg von Schoenerer – provided the first model for Adolf Hitler's own war against the Jews, demonstrating to him its possibilities as a method of mobilising the masses against a single, highly visible and vulnerable enemy. It was in pre-war Vienna that the young Hitler would discover the 'Jewish Question' and begin to link it inexorably with capitalism, Marxism and the struggle for existence of the German nation. From Austrian Pan-Germanism Hitler took the biological, racist foundation of his world-view, and from Lueger he would learn how to use antisemitism as a political tool.[26]

6
...

Hitler's 'Final Solution'

The 'Final Solution' of the European 'Jewish question' was the direct outcome of the ideology and policies adopted by Adolf Hitler as head of the German Nazi State. Already in his first written political statement, dated 16 September 1919, the future leader of the Third Reich advocated a so-called 'rational' systematic antisemitism that would aim at the elimination by the German state of the Jews altogether.[1] Insistently, in his early speeches in Bavaria in the 1920s, he referred to the Jews as being made in the image of the Devil, as a universal form of 'racial tuberculosis' or a subhuman species of vermin whose 'eradication root and branch' was a matter of life and death for Germany and mankind as a whole.[2] In 1922 he declared that if he gained power 'the annihilation of the Jews will be my first and foremost task', and spoke of public hangings that would go on 'until the last Jew in Munich is obliterated' and all of Germany would be cleansed.[3] The 'Jewish question', he consistently emphasised, was an encounter of cosmic significance between two antagonistic races fighting for world domination. No neutrality and no quarter could be given in this either-or struggle, for Jews did not merely represent one danger among others, but rather the totality of evils confronting 'Aryan' civilisation, and their eradication was the condition for its future development.

Adolf Hitler, as an Austrian-born Catholic educated in Linz, who had arrived in Munich before the First World War, was the heir of an age-old tradition of Christian antisemitism which had become transmuted into biological racism, especially in the German-speaking world of Central Europe. The secular political faith of National Socialism which he propagated borrowed its motifs freely from Christian liturgy, from the hierarchical structure of the Catholic Church and the demonological view of Judaism as a satanic force which had its roots in the Middle Ages.[4] In his early years as a political agitator in Bavaria he frequently played on the deicidal myth and on his own messianic role as a militant Germanic saviour bearing a sword rather than a crown of thorns, who would drive the Jewish capitalists from the Temple of the Lord. 'The task which Christ began but did not finish', he told a Munich audience in 1926, 'I will complete.'[5] In *Mein Kampf* he had written, two years earlier, that 'in defending myself against the Jews I am acting for the Lord'.[6] Without the irrational beliefs inculcated by centuries of Christian dogma – reinforced by xenophobic, nationalist and Germanic racial mythology – Hitler's antisemitism and the echo which it found throughout Europe would have been inconceivable.

At the same time it must be recognised that there were elements in Nazi antisemitism that turned against the Christian doctrines which had incubated it for centuries. Already in his Vienna days the young Hitler had rejected the traditional Catholic view that 'a splash of baptismal water' could redeem the biological 'taint' of Jewry, and dismissed any attempt to separate *Geist* ('spirit') from race. In conversations with Dietrich Eckart in the early 1920s he reproached Martin Luther for having translated the Bible into German, thereby inadvertently helping to permeate the German people with a 'Jewish spirit'. Since the Jews were the physical incarnation of the very principle of evil, only a radical solution which involved their elimination as a race could cure the 'inner Judaisation (*Verjudung*) of our people'.[7] For Hitler and the Nazis, in contrast to the traditional teachings of Christianity, no spiritual redemption of the Jews was possible – their racial characteristics were eternal and unchanging. Jewish influence meant the triumph of antinature over nature, of disease over health, of intellect over instinct. This mystical, biological and naturalistic racism was later to be used to sanction final measures against *all* Jews, whatever their social background, beliefs or political convictions.

Unlike the Christian Churches, who had never officially condoned the slaughter of Jews but had generally been content to degrade, stigmatise or marginalise them, the Nazis were driven with terrifying literalness to institutionalise their irrational belief in an unchanging, satanic Jewish 'essence' which was supposedly rooted in physical characteristics. In order to demonstrate the reality of their myth of 'Aryan' racial superiority (which would be irrevocably tainted by miscegenation or physical contact with Jews) they committed themselves to the total eradication of Jewry as a people. In the process, Nazism itself became contaminated with a profound Christophobia, decrying Christianity as a 'Semitic' religion which was emasculating the healthy, heroic and warrior virtues of the German people with its preaching of the virtues of humility, compassion, charity and love.

In his wartime *Table Talk*, Hitler spoke of the Jew as having 'fraudulently introduced Christianity into the ancient world – in order to ruin it – reopening the same breach in modern times, this time taking as his pretext the social question'. Christianity was now compared with Bolshevism (its 'illegitimate child'), St Paul with Karl Marx, and the equality of all believers before God was reviled as a sinister doctrine of subversion of the Roman Empire.[8] The official philosopher of the Nazi movement, Alfred Rosenberg, had gone even further in his *Myth of the Twentieth Century* (1934), branding Christianity as an effeminate, race-destroying dogma invented by Jews which was sapping the pristine Germanic values of honour, freedom, independence and virility.[9] Hitler's closest aide, Martin Bormann, was also undoubtedly sincere when he defined National Socialist doctrine in November 1944 as 'anti-Jewish *in excelsis*, for it is both anti-Communist and anti-Christian'.[10]

But the Nazi leaders, except for Rosenberg, were generally careful to restrain their Christophobia in public and, whatever their private feelings, it did not stop them from exploiting the rich armoury of Christian myths of the Jew as Satan, Antichrist, sorcerer, usurer and ritual murderer for their own political ends. Even though they had secularised and radicalised what was an essentially religious stereotype, by continuing to use a long-familiar language about the diabolical Jew, they could guarantee themselves the collaboration of the Christian Churches and of millions of ordinary laymen throughout Europe. In this way they successfully subverted Christianity from within, even as they replaced it with a pseudo-scientific, irrational ideology based on blood and soil, race and destiny, the worship by the *Herrenvolk* ('master race') of its own eternal renewal.[11] It was a world-view whose forerunners went back to early German romanticism, to Richard Wagner, Houston Chamberlain, Paul de Lagarde, German *völkisch* prophets and Austrian occultist racists like Lanz von Liebenfels from the turn of the century – for all of whom Judaism had embodied the antithesis of both pagan and Christian-Germanic values.

Hitler's radical antisemitism could not, however, have attained the resonance it did without the operation of other, more mundane factors in German politics. The collapse of the Hohenzollern Monarchy, the defeat in the First World War and the abortive revolutions in Munich and Berlin which occurred in 1918 and 1919, created a counter-revolutionary mood of rare violence in the newly formed Weimar Republic. The fact that many of the leaders of the suppressed revolutions were Jews (Kurt Eisner, Eugen Leviné, Ernst Toller, Erich Mühsam, Gustav Landauer, Rosa Luxemburg, etc.) was undoubtedly a crucial factor in intensifying German antisemitism against the background of national trauma and humiliation.[12] Although Hitler's own Judeophobia predated this trauma, it offered him and the German radical Right a uniquely favourable context for claiming that the so-called 'November criminals' were part of a Jewish world conspiracy.

69

That German Jews were for the most part intensely patriotic members of the respectable middle class and voted for the liberals rather than Social Democrats or Communists was immaterial to the myth-makers; for the Nazis and the German conservative Right had no difficulty in portraying November 1918 as a 'stock exchange' revolution serving Jewish financial interests and not those of ordinary German workers. Both capitalism and Marxism were depicted as part of the same international conspiracy to enslave Germany to the will of the vengeful Allied victors, responsible for inflicting massive war reparations on the German people.[13] The Jews symbolically represented these foreign powers – they allegedly controlled big capital, international finance, the bourgeois parties, the organised labour movement, parliamentary democracy and all those sinister forces working to undermine the authority of the state and national independence. Above all, the successful revolution which had occurred in Soviet Russia was depicted as a prelude to the future 'Bolshevisation' of Germany and the beginning of the last stage in world Jewry's coming bid for global hegemony.[14]

This organic linkage of anti-Communism with antisemitism ensured in the long run the support of the traditional élites in German society for Hitler's political programme. By connecting his racist obsessions with a far-reaching plan for smashing organised labour, restructuring Germany along authoritarian lines, ensuring *Lebensraum* ('living space') to the East and the destruction of Soviet Russia as the bastion of international Communism, Hitler guaranteed his broader appeal to the Conservatives and disorientated middle classes as well as to the unemployed masses. In contrast to so many of his racist predecessors and contemporaries, he recognised that pathological antisemitism mixed with Social Darwinism or the 'Aryan' myth could not on its own make deep inroads into German public opinion. Militant anti-Communism and an uncompromising assault on parliamentary democracy as a source of internal weakness and disorder provided, by

1a Relief from the Arch of Titus in Rome, commemorating the victory over the Jews in AD 70. Spoils carried in the triumphal procession include a seven-branched candelabrum, known as a *menorah*.

1b Paul arguing with the Jews, a traditional Christian portrayal of the New versus the Old Testament.

2a Bible illustration from the time of the Crusader persecutions, showing two Jews, identifiable by their hats, being put to the sword.

2b Statues on the façade of Strasbourg Cathedral portraying Church and blind-folded Synagogue holding a broken staff and the Tablets of the Law. Such statues appear on many medieval cathedrals.

3a This German woodcut depicts the alleged ritual murder in 1473 of Simon of Trent, later declared a saint. This anti-Jewish accusation was maintained by the Church until about 1950.

3b The six children of Regensburg, alleged victims of ritual murder.

4a A compulsory
conversion sermon in
Rome, customary for
centuries.

4b Martin Luther
holding a Hebrew book.

5a A sixteenth-century painting showing a German Jewess wearing the obligatory Jew-badge on her outer garment.

5b The Frankfurt *Judensau*, a seventeenth-century broadsheet engraving. Satanic figures and pigs were particularly common in antisemitic imagery.

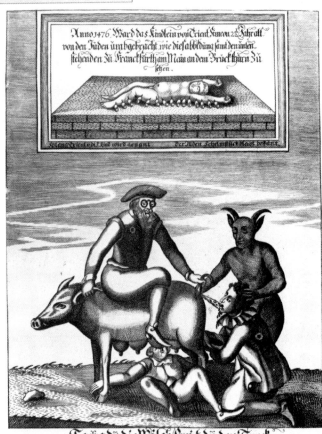

Plünderung der Iudengaſſen zu Franckfurt am Main den 22 Auguſtj 1614. Nach Mittag vmb 5 uhr vor
den Handtwercks geſellen angefangen, vnd die gantze Nacht durch Continuirt, da dan ein Bürger
vnd 2 Iuden gar todt plieben, vil aber beiderſeits beſchedigt worden, hiſz ihn entlich
s als ſie bis in die helfft der gaſſen komen f von der Bürgerſchafft gentlich abge-
wehrt worden.

6 The plundering of the
Judengasse, the Frankfurt
ghetto, in 1614. Immediately
afterwards the Jews were
driven out of Frankfurt.

7a 'Jewish greed.'
Manchester, 1773.

7b 'Solomon amusing himself with
two attractive Christian girls.'
This drawing by Thomas Rowlandson (c.1800)
illustrates the stereotype
of the lecherous Jew.

8a Wagner triumphant, pulled by Tristan and Isolde, with Wagner-obsessed Jews following in his train.

8b Caricature of a German Jewish capitalist from the satirical journal *Simplicissimus*, 1907.

contrast, a powerful rallying-cry at a time when the German and European middle classes were increasingly deserting liberal solutions to their problems. Hitler understood that the widespread identification of Jews with world revolution and avant-garde cultural modernism offered him a way to capitalise on these German bourgeois anxieties by focusing them on a single scapegoat; at the same time it also enabled him to present National Socialism as the guardian of authentic European civilisation.[15] The irrational dynamic of Nazism and its uncompromising exterminatory drive towards Jews could be masked by its posture as a militant mass movement fighting against the Marxist danger and for a genuine national revival, along the lines of Italian fascism or other radical right-wing movements in Europe.

The racist antisemitism of the Nazis, with its phantasmagoric view of the Jews as a deadly bacillus and 'poisoner' of the nations, did not initially infect large masses of Germans, but through zealous propaganda (extended for over a decade before the seizure of power in 1933) it undoubtedly affected public attitudes. After 1933 such antisemitic doctrines became moreover, an official article of faith, the policy of the ruling Nazi Party and state institutions, one of the ideological pillars of what was to be the German 'New Order' for Europe.[16]

The Nazis now felt free to implement their antisemitic programme, step by step, through a series of stages from legal discrimination, expropriation, forced emigration and then ghettoisation to the mass extermination undertaken during the Second World War. Before the 'Crystal Night' pogrom of November 1938, they concentrated on removing all Jews from public office and German cultural life. Drastic measures such as the Nuremberg Race Laws of 1935 effectively introduced institutionalised apartheid between Germans and Jews. Through massive indoctrination and newspapers like Julius Streicher's *Der Stürmer* a poisonous brew of antisemitic hatred, sadism and perversity was served up to the German people, warning them against international Jewish machinations and racial defilement through sexual contact with Jews, and zealously encouraging the economic boycott of Jewish businesses.[17] A major objective of this propaganda was to bring about the mass emigration of German Jewry, but this was partly frustrated by the tight quotas imposed by foreign countries on the admission of Jews. Simultaneously, Hitler sought with some success to export his radical antisemitism to neighbouring countries as a weapon of internal subversion and political penetration in East-Central Europe and as a method of psychologically undermining the Western democracies.

His secret memorandum of 1936 for the Four Years' Plan, in which he also expounds on the coming inevitable confrontation with the 'Jewish Enemy' as a part of war preparations against the Soviet Union, sketches out the world-historical perspective in which he had always placed the 'Jewish question'. Bolshevism appears in this context as the last stage in a long historical struggle whose essence and aim was the replacement of the old leadership strata in the Nordic nations by the domination of world Jewry. Marxism, through its victory in Russia, had established 'a forward base for future operations' against which an ideologically divided democratic world was incapable of fighting effectively. Because of its history and geographical position at the heart of the West, Germany alone stood as a barrier against the Jewish-Bolshevik onslaught. Failure in this battle would lead to the 'extermination of the German people' and a 'catastrophic disaster of the European nations, unprecedented in the history of mankind since the fall of the Ancient Empires'.[18] It was precisely this kind of apocalyptic thinking which would influence Hitler's fateful decision to invade the Soviet Union in June 1941. The purpose of that attack was to achieve in one blow what the Nazi leader had always seen as his central political goals – the destruction of European Jewry, the elimination of the citadel of Bolshevism and the creation of German 'living space' in the East.

The pogrom of November 1938 – the most violent public display of antisemitism in modern German history – marked a watershed on Hitler's road to the 'Final Solution'. An orderly, legislative and bureaucratic method of resolving the 'Jewish question' was for the moment abandoned, the seizure of Jewish property and the total exclusion of Jews from the German economy was accelerated and the violence of the SS unleashed without restraint. Every synagogue in Germany was burnt down or demolished, over 30,000 Jewish men were seized and sent to concentration camps, many Jewish businesses destroyed and several hundred Jews murdered or severely wounded. Cruelty, terror and mocking humiliation of Jews in Germany became rampant. A meeting held at Field Marshal Goering's offices in the Reich Air Ministry on 12 November 1938 reveals the degraded, sadistic fantasies that the top Nazi leaders indulged in when discussing their anti-Jewish policy.[19] Propaganda Minister Joseph Goebbels felt that Jews themselves should 'clear away the damaged or burnt synagogues and present the German people with cleared free spaces for their own use';[20] they should be banned from sitting next to Germans in variety shows, cinemas or theatres or from sharing sleeping compartments on trains with Germans; swimming pools, beaches, seaside resorts and forests should be forbidden to them as well as German parks. Above all it was 'necessary that Jews be absolutely excluded from German schools'.[21] Goering, for his part, cynically decided on the one-billion-Mark fine to be imposed on German Jewry 'as a punishment' for the damage inflicted upon them and their property by the Nazis! His closing threat was an ominous one in keeping with other pronouncements by Nazi leaders in 1938–9. 'If the German Reich comes into conflict with foreign powers in the near future, it goes without saying that we in Germany will first of all let it come to a final reckoning of our account with the Jews.'[22]

Hitler's notorious Reichstag speech of 30 January 1939 was even more chilling in its tones of apocalyptic prophecy.

During the time of my struggle for power it was in the first instance the Jewish race which received my prophecies with laughter when I said that I would one day take over the leadership of the State, and with it that of the whole nation, and that I would then among many other things settle the Jewish problem. Their laughter was uproarious, but I think that for some time now they have been laughing on the other side of their face. Today I will once more be a prophet: If the international Jewish financiers in and outside Europe should succeed in plunging the nations once more into a world war, then the result will not be the bolshevisation of the earth, and thus the victory of Jewry, but the annihilation of the Jewish race in Europe![23]

Hitler's threats of extermination were wildly applauded by the Nazi deputies, but the *Kristallnacht* pogrom had shown that the German public as a whole was less than enthusiastic about the plundering of property and burning down of synagogues. The pogrom had not been 'spontaneous' but centrally co-ordinated by the regime, which was well aware of public reservations through its secret 'opinion' reports. As a consequence, future violence against the Jews would be carried out in secrecy and in a more 'orderly' manner. The 'Final Solution' would not adopt the spontaneous pogrom violence of Russian and East European antisemitism but rather be implemented in a methodical manner by the highly organised, bureaucratised state machine of the Third Reich, using the SS and the Wehrmacht as its instruments. They would be helped by thousands of top bureaucrats, by German industrialists, lawyers, doctors, engineers, accountants, bankers, clerks, railway officials and ordinary workers, without whom the trains to Auschwitz would never have run on time.

This machinery of destruction, as historians like Raul Hilberg and sociologists like Zygmunt Bauman have pointed out, reflected the technological and organisational alienation of a bureaucratically organised society such as Nazi Germany, as well as the totalitarian methods of domination perfected by the SS.[24] But massive ideological conditioning was also required in addition to the routinising of operations and the deliberate fragmentation of responsibilities encouraged by a modern technically advanced state, in order to carry out the mass murder of an entire people. Indeed, Nazi antisemitism achieved its greatest success in the complete *depersonalisation* of the Jews, their gradual dehumanisation as a result of ceaseless propaganda and their transformation in the eyes of ordinary Germans first into social pariahs and then into *total* outsiders. In the years before the Second World War, millions of Germans had been systematically taught that Jews were cowards, sexual perverts, corrupt exploiters, dangerous revolutionaries and ultimately subhuman vermin. These stereotypes gained in force the more that Jews were stripped of their civil rights and socially excluded. The terrifying image of a *non-people* seemed paradoxically to gain in credibility the fewer Jews there were in Germany itself. In historian Ian Kershaw's words, 'depersonalisation increased the already existent widespread indifference of German popular opinion and formed a vital stage between the archaic violence of the pogrom and the rationalised "assembly line" annihilation of the death camps'.[25]

The ideological and mythical concepts that underlay the Nazi war against the Jews came to their horrific climax following 'Operation Barbarossa', Hitler's holy war against the Soviet Union in the name of the twisted Cross of the Swastika. The task of mass murder was entrusted first and foremost to the SS under the command of Heinrich Himmler, who saw the 'Final Solution' above all as a *hygienic* measure to ensure the racial purity of the greater Germanic Reich and the New Order in Europe. It was the fulfilment of a moral duty to the German people 'to destroy this people [i.e. the Jews] who wanted to destroy us', an action which he compared to having 'exterminated a bacterium because we do not want in the end to be infected by the bacterium and die of it'.[26] Mass murder was rationalised as an act of apocalyptic 'idealism', of harshness towards oneself in the service of a sacred mission – the creation of a new master race of blue-eyed, blond heroes. The executioners should pride themselves on this great historical achievement, as Himmler told his audience of SS and high police officials in Posen on 6 October 1943 – it was 'a page of glory in our history, which has never been written and never is to be written'.[27] The character traits of the 'ideal' German – uprightness, honesty, cleanliness, purity, strength and above all decency(!) were harnessed by Himmler to the gruesome task commanded by the *Führer* of the German Reich. 'Most of you must know what it means when a hundred corpses are lying side by side, or five hundred or a thousand. To have stuck it out and at the same time – apart from exceptions caused by human weakness – to have remained decent men, that is what has made us hard.'[28]

This kind of perverted masculine idealism was characteristic of the creed of the SS, designed to be the spearhead of a total revaluation of all values along racial lines throughout Europe. Its global and historical mission would never be accomplished without the annihilation of the Jews and of a 'Judaised Europe', with its incurable diseases of a sick and debilitating Christianity and a 'corrupt' Marxism. Both Judaism and Christianity after all had severed man from his organic bond with nature, from the primordial values of blood, soil and race, from the warrior virtues of the tribal, Germanic past. As the educators of the SS never tired of emphasising, the Jews in particular had always been a disruptive 'ferment of decomposition' in all times and places, seeking to undermine the blood consciousness of the host peoples, their racial pride and ethnic integrity. In the words of the Nazi philosopher, Alfred Baeumler in 1943, the Jew represented not only Judaism but *all* the forces against which Nazism was fighting – the legacy of monotheism, Western civilisation, liberalism, rationalism and critical humanism.[29] Thus Judaism was the arch-enemy of the German, the symbol and substance of everything hostile to Germandom and Nazism, the total adversary personified. In contrast to Nazi policy towards other groups, however ruthless or cruel, there could be no Jewish candidates whatsoever for re-Germanisation or assimilation to the Nazi racial ideal.[30] For Hitler's war against the Jews was always conceived as a war of world outlooks (*Weltanschauungskrieg*) for global hegemony between two 'chosen peoples', the Germans and the Jews.

It was this intensely ideological, mystical and deeply irrational character of Hitler's antisemitism, linked to his exceptional political skills and the total power which he exercised as the head of a highly developed military and industrial state, which made the Holocaust possible. In his eschatological world-view, itself a monstrous mutation born out of centuries of Christian diabolising of the Jews, the 'final solution of the Jewish question' was indeed the key to world history, to the future of Germany, of European civilisation and of the white, Aryan race. Antisemitism remained the bedrock of his political credo right until his inglorious end in a besieged and ruined Berlin in April 1945, with 'the thousand-year Reich' going up in flames around him. His last testament charged 'the leaders of the nation and those under them to scrupulous observance of the laws of race and to merciless opposition to the universal poisoner of all peoples, International Jewry'.[31] In its fanatical intransigence this testament represented the apocalyptic nemesis of a bimillennial disease that had been raging intermittently in the heart of Christendom.

7
■ ■ ■

After Auschwitz:
the German Response

The German National Socialists lost the Second World War but through their murder of six million Jewish men, women and children they brought to a tragic end the immensely creative, millennial Ashkenazic culture of Central and East European Jewry. Hitler's demonic racism killed or forced out the most distinctive minority in Germany, leaving in ruins the German-Jewish 'symbiosis' which had done so much to shape the colour, tone and content of modern culture. There are of course, educated, sensitive Germans, capable of seeing beyond the remarkable material prosperity of post-war Germany, who fully comprehend the scale and magnitude of the loss. There are also more ambiguous verdicts like that of the historian Golo Mann, who could write in 1960: 'The astonishing success of the Bonn Republic in the eyes of its own people and thus in the eyes of the outside world, the relative composure that characterises public life in Germany today, has something to do with the fact that the German Jews have fled or were murdered.' The success of post-war Germany's streamlined, acquisitive consumer society has for a long time been bought at the price of an evasive forgetfulness of the massive crimes committed against the Jews – a denial of guilt that began during the war years and even today has scarcely been fully digested. For recent research shows that the common claim that 'the German people did not know' what was being done in its name does not stand up to serious examination and that as long as the Nazis could point to successes during the war, antisemitic propaganda acted as an efficient, socially integrative force.

Only as defeat came closer and news of the mass murder filtered through more widely did the German public begin to throw up the defence mechanisms of wilful ignorance and denial which continue to shape the attitudes of many Germans today.[1]

Opinion polls regularly undertaken since 1946–7 show a disturbing pattern of prejudice that has persisted despite the horrors of Auschwitz and the drastic reduction of German Jewry from its pre-Hitler strength of half a million to some 30,000 Jews in the new united Germany of 1990.[2] In 1947, three-quarters of all Germans considered the Jews to 'belong to a different race than ourselves', and almost as many declared they would not marry a Jew. In October 1948, 41 per cent of Germans still approved the Nazi seizure of power (as late as 1978 over a third held that the Third Reich had not been all that bad); in 1952 a third evaluated Hitler positively and a similar proportion agreed that antisemitism was caused primarily by Jewish characteristics. In the same year, 37 per cent of the population felt that it was better for Germany not to have any Jews (this had declined to 19 per cent by May 1965). Also in 1952, 65 per cent of Germans said that the Nazis had succeeded in spreading aversion to Jews and no less than 88 per cent affirmed that they had no personal responsibility for the mass exterminations. Two-fifths of Germans were against the Allied de-Nazification programme and only a fifth had ever discussed the persecution of the Jews with their children.[3]

These figures retrospectively reveal how few Germans were anti-Nazi during the war years in the sense of opposing the government or helping the Jews, and how many had accepted the Nazi view of the German destiny and the place of the Jews in it. They also testify to the half-hearted nature of American and British de-Nazification programmes after 1946. The Western Allies wanted a strong Germany as a counterweight to the Communist threat from the East and settled for a state in which many of the élites who had been influential in the Third Reich retained their wealth, status and power. Many ex-Nazis were employed by the military government, academics with a Nazi record or German judges who had enforced Nazi law and other former Nazis in the police force, industry, business and the schools retained their positions. Only a tiny handful of Germans were adjudged major offenders by the Allied courts, while the great majority went unpunished.[4]

Only in Communist East Germany was the old order largely destroyed by land reform, the expropriation of the biggest industrial firms and the extensive application of the death penalty to war criminals. Active Nazis were usually barred or dismissed from schools and universities, though those who were not war criminals were admitted into public life.[5] However, by the end of 1952 East Germany was engulfed in the Soviet-inspired tide of antisemitism that affected most of Eastern Europe. Unlike the Federal Republic, it categorically refused to pay reparations to the State of Israel, though Jewish 'victims of fascism' resident on its soil were supported through pensions and other material benefits. The new German 'workers' and peasants' state' based on the Communist 'antifascist' tradition, claimed to have established a new national reality with no ties to the Nazi past. But in the 'socialist paradise', topics like antisemitism, the Jews and the Holocaust remained even more taboo than in the capitalist Federal Republic.[6]

Konrad Adenauer, the Catholic chancellor of West Germany from 1949 to 1963, did acknowledge German crimes against the Jews and the obligation to make 'moral and material amends' even though he tolerated ex-Nazis like Hans Globke (a legal expert who had furthered the Nazi race laws) in prominent positions within his administration. He recognised that to morally rehabilitate and integrate a rump German state in the West required an official policy of 'philosemitism' and friendly relations with Israel.[7] At the same time the Nazi past was repressed as far as possible, while the myth was encouraged that the Federal Republic represented a completely new beginning and that Germans had finally released themselves from the lure of power and greatness. To be sure, post-war Conservatives were no longer avowed antisemites like their predecessors under Weimar or the Third Reich, though their visceral anti-Communism had remained fully intact, permanently fuelled by the Stalinist dictatorship in East Germany. Indeed, a positive attitude to their Jewish *Mitbürger* (fellow citizens) became in their eyes one of the touchstones of the new humanistic, Christian and democratic Germany. But no serious attempt to punish thousands of war criminals or to re-educate the German public (who had in their majority opposed Adenauer's restitution policy) was made. Even the swell of German sympathy for Israel's spectacular victory in the Six-Day War of 1967 remained tinged with ambiguity, with its associations of *Blitzkrieg* and the war-time desert campaigns of Field Marshal Rommel's Afrika Korps. The admiration of the right-wing Springer press for Israel was no doubt genuine but soon produced its own backlash in the form of the anti-American and anti-Zionist rhetoric of the German student revolt.[8]

The German New Left from the late 1960s until today has been strongly conditioned by its reaction against what it has perceived as the artificial, hypocritical 'philosemitism' of the conservative Establishment. The feminist, ecology and peace movements of the last decade, like their 1960s predecessors, have certainly professed to deal more seriously than their elders with the guilt of the Nazi past. In their rhetoric they are earnestly antifascist and antiracist, and claim to be sympathetic to all persecuted minorities. They stress the elements of continuity between the Third Reich and post-war Germany and were the first to argue for removal of the taboos about the 'Jewish question'. The post-war Federal Republic, they hold, could only master its 'abnormal past' by radically unmasking the complacent façade of *Modell-Deutschland*, the dehumanisation and alienation lurking behind the 'economic miracle' of the present.[9]

Paradoxically, however, their antifascism and anticapitalism has increasingly led the Left into the cul-de-sac of a Manichean world-view in which dead Jews (especially of the leftist, 'progressive' variety) are idealised as victims, and those who are very much alive are castigated as victimisers. In the Middle East conflict, this has led parts of the Left to demonise the mythical 'Zionist genocide' of the Palestinian people and adopt an irrationally hostile attitude to Israel as a means of coming to terms with its own feelings of guilt. When refused entry to Israel in 1984 the Green Party Euro MP Brigitte Heinrich declared:

> The genocide of the Jews created the psychological pre-requisites for setting up Israel as an internationally recognised state. The expulsion of the Palestinians is therefore indirectly the result of the Nazi persecution of Jews . . . For the same reason that we – the generation which did not experience National Socialism – do not reject the moral guilt of our people for killing millions of Jews, we cannot keep silent about Israeli expansionist policy, occupation of foreign territories by Israeli troops, the repressive measures in the occupied territories.[10]

Thus, in the name of the German past, Israel is often presented on the Left as a copy of the Third Reich, and the Palestinians as the 'new Jews' of the Middle East. The victims of German history become the Jewish victimisers of new victims – the Palestinians – who in turn are being manipulated to purge a suffocating sense of German guilt. This role reversal, in which Israel's depiction as a criminal, 'terrorist' state is used to free the Germans from their *Judenkomplex*, is equally popular with neo-Nazis and right-wing radicals. The neo-fascists in Germany, as in other Western countries, like to contrast the 'fictive' Holocaust perpetrated by the Germans against Jews with the 'real' Holocaust supposedly inflicted by Israel on the Palestinians.

In recent decades, the Left has also been increasingly keen to end the alleged 'immunity from criticism' that German Jews have enjoyed since Auschwitz. The controversy surrounding the play *Garbage, the City and Death* by the late Rainer Werner Fassbinder (written in 1975 but not staged until ten years later) was a good illustration of this trend, with its implicitly antisemitic portrayal of a rich Jewish speculator who had changed the face of Frankfurt to the detriment of the people. Fassbinder's declared motive was to expose the taboo on discussing Jews, which he felt had created 'a boomerang effect' and provoked hostility towards them.[11] But in his play the 'rich Jew' becomes a symbol of 'the city' with its destruction, anonymity, alienation, decadence, and corruption as well as being the willing instrument of a cynical German capitalist establishment. Sexual and socio-economic stereotypes from the classic antisemitic repertoire abound in his script, and a character in the play revels in imagining how the Jew 'gasps for air in the gas chamber'. In a pathologically antisemitic monologue he rants that the Jew 'drinks our blood and makes out that we are wrong, because he is a Jew and we bear the guilt'.[12] The rich Jew murders a prostitute in a scene that echoes the myth of ritual slaughter, and his ruthless profiteering is motivated as an act of revenge against the city in which his own family was murdered. The play seems to reflect the anxiety of a post-1945 generation burdened by its parents' guilt, projecting its fears on to surviving Jews and ending up in a new tangle of antisemitic stereotypes about 'the Jew', 'Jewish capital' and 'Jewish power'. More disturbing still, was the statement in support of Fassbinder by the principal of the Frankfurt Theatre, Gunther Rühle, that 'the no-hunting season is over', that Jews must once again be subject to criticism.[13] The play was staunchly defended by most of the German left-wing intelligentsia for its anticapitalism and in the name of an absolute right to free speech. The antisemitic mythology which it exuded was trivialised or else dismissed by allusions to Fassbinder's antifascist credentials while it was often hinted that Auschwitz was once again being used to silence legitimate criticism of Jewish behaviour.[14]

This public controversy, which took place at the end of 1985, followed closely on the heels of the Bitburg affair, which exposed the erosion of sensitivity on the political Right to Jewish concerns. Chancellor Kohl had already evoked the 'gift' of his later birth (he was a teenager during the early 1940s) on a visit to Israel, in order to justify the 'normalisation' of Germany's relations with the Jewish world.[15] Now his insistence that President Reagan pay homage to the German war-dead (including the Waffen SS) at Bitburg cemetery provoked an outcry in America, by no means confined to Jews, despite attempts to present the protests as an orchestrated 'Jewish' campaign against Germany. Kohl served notice that the memory of the Holocaust would not be allowed to impinge upon the imperatives of Allied reconciliation. The Second World War was to be seen from the German side as far as possible like any other war. The Nazi regime was not fundamentally different from other totalitarian terror regimes, and crimes committed 'in the name of the German people' could not imply any collective guilt.[16]

Growing resentment at reminders of the Nazi past in the new self-confident and increasingly assertive West Germany now spilled over into open antisemitism. The young Bavarian deputy Hermann Fellner (from the Christian Social Union) attacked Jewish survivors who after years of litigation were still seeking compensation for their slave labour from the giant Flick concern, which had consistently denied any moral or legal obligation. He complained that 'Jews are quick to speak up when they hear the tinkling of money in German cash-registers'. The Mayor of a small town in north-Rhine Westphalia, Graf von Spree, suggested that the only way to solve his budget deficit might be to kill 'a few rich Jews'.[17] The local chairman of the Christian Democratic Youth Union protested against the 'arrogance' of Israel in making 'our democratic constitutional state responsible for the murder of the Jews in the Third Reich'.[18]

With German national sentiment resurfacing, and with the return to 'normalcy' in the 1980s, anti-Jewish prejudice, too, was being articulated more freely and becoming socially respectable in various ways. Public opinion polls showed that many Germans still believed that Jews were 'shrewd and money-grabbing', vindictive and ruthless in exploiting Germany's Nazi past for financial benefit; that they exercised too much influence at an international level; that they did not forgive or forget.[19] According to the researcher Werner Bergman, some six to seven million Germans could be classified as being antisemitic, with around two million of that number classified as hard-core antisemites. The only consolation in these figures is that they still represent a decline in anti-Jewish prejudice over the past forty years – with its main pockets concentrated among the older generation, people of low educational attainments and in lower paid jobs. Moreover, this is an 'antisemitism without Jews', no longer based on real social conflicts but rather on abstract stereotypes and un-resolved complexes pertaining to the Holocaust and the 'unmastered' German past.[20]

Racism in general is, however, flourishing, directed mainly against Turkish 'guest-workers' or immigrants from Africa and Asia who have taken advantage of Germany's generous welfare state and prosperity to settle in the country.[21] This immigration problem largely accounted for the spectacular growth of the ultra-conservative Republikaner Party, which in January 1989 won 7.5 per cent of the vote in West Berlin and in June 1989 polled 7.1 per cent in elections to the European Parliament. The 'Germany first' watchword of this party, with its hatred of all foreigners, its attacks on the 'degeneracy' of German political and spiritual culture and with its call for the restoration of the 1937 borders of the old Reich, links it unmistakeably with the pre-war fascist tradition.[22] Led by an ex-Waffen SS soldier, Franz Schonhüber, its antisemitism has been more muted than that of its rivals on the far Right, but this is largely an electoral tactic to give it more respectability.[23]

Both the Republikaner and the more extreme neo-Nazis have won growing support among the disaffected youth of East Germany since the crumbling of the Berlin wall and the collapse of Communism. In Berlin and Leipzig cemeteries have been profaned and on the walls of Dresden one can find slogans like 'Hitler lives!'[24] No doubt the neo-Nazism of skinheads and football rowdies in both East and West has elements of sheer nihilism, the desire to provoke and (in the East) hatred of Communism, that are as least as important as a mindless antisemitism without any first-hand knowledge of or contact with Jews. Yet the recent rise in antisemitic incidents is undeniable and likely to grow as unemployment and economic hardship increase in East Germany.[25]

This is happening, moreover, in a part of Germany where the former Communist government for decades systematically pursued a virulent anti-Zionist propaganda, ostentatiously helped the Arab states and secretly trained Palestinian terrorists. Shortly before its demise, the new Parliament of a reformed East Germany did, however, finally pass a resolution accepting 'responsibility on behalf of the people for the expulsion and murder of Jewish men, women and children'; it even offered political asylum to Jews fleeing a rising tide of antisemitism in the Soviet Union. Moreover, there has in the past few years been an encouraging revival of Jewish life among the tiny Jewish community in East Berlin.[26] At the same time, skinheads running amok have also returned antisemitism to the level of street politics, where it once flourished immediately after the First World War. Nothing could more graphically illustrate the bankruptcy of forty years of antifascist education in what was once the German Democratic Republic.

In the new united Germany the 'Jewish Question' will, however, be essentially bound up with issues relating to the possible redefinition of German identity and the continuing drive to 'normalise' the German past and the present relationship to the Jews against the background of the Holocaust. The current emphasis on the continuities in German history, on legitimate national pride and the calls for an end to self-laceration encourage a relativisation of the 'Shoah' and lead some Germans to see the Jewish victims of Nazi terror as an embarrassing obstacle to creating a healthy new national consciousness. This kind of resentment in turn feeds the urge on both the Right and the Left to finish once and for all with reparations, with reminders of Jewish suffering and German crimes and to enjoy a *Heimat* restored to its old glory. Behind the search for 'normalcy' also lurks the temptation to re-discover the 'evil Jew' in the present, who can retrospectively justify liberation from a poisonous past.

The intellectually sophisticated and humanly understand-able wish to free German history from the traumatic ballast of Nazism in order to reinforce the new German patriotism undoubtedly strikes an emotional chord among many Germans.[27] The danger is that this desire has already led to a marked tendency to deny the singularity of Auschwitz and to exculpate the Germans from their historic responsibilities – a trend that may arguably become one of the main sources of a new cultural antisemitism in a resurgent and reunified Germany.

8

...

The Waldheim Syndrome

Austria has had one of the strongest antisemitic traditions of any country outside of Eastern Europe. Already before the First World War, as we have seen, it was one of the cradles of modern political antisemitism. Karl Lueger (still fondly remembered by many Viennese today) represented the more pragmatic, economic and religiously based variety of popular antisemitism, while the provincial Austro-German middle class and academic intelligentsia were more attracted by the racist antisemitism of the Pan-German movement. The Pan-Germans sought to redefine the Austrian identity in purely German terms and strongly advocated *Anschluss* (Union) or the reintegration of Austria into the German Reich. Their influence grew under the First Austrian Republic, following the trauma of defeat in the First World War and the refusal of the Allies to allow the German rump of the Habsburg Monarchy to unite with Germany. They created the seedbed of Austrian Nazism which gradually absorbed the Pan-German block, seized control of the students' movement and by 1933 was attracting about a fourth of the Austrian electorate.

Both Pan-Germanism and Austrian Nazism thrived on the insecure national identity of the ethnically more hetero-geneous German population in Austria, its lack of self-esteem (which masqueraded behind anti-Slav and antisemitic racism) and the prevailing belief of many Austrians that their small republic had no viable independent existence.[1] As in Eastern Europe, Austria's students led the way in demanding restrictive *numerus clausus* laws in higher education and in initiating violent actions against Jews and socialists. Their ideology was racist, but they were driven above all by an economically motivated fear of Jewish competition and by right-wing radicalism of the Nazi type.[2]

In the 1920s the Pan-German Grossdeutsche Volkspartei affirmed in its official programme that it would 'oppose the Jewish influence in all spheres of public and private life', curtail the immigration of foreign Jews and expel the *Ostjuden* who had come to Vienna during the First World War.[3] This rhetoric was echoed by the Nazis, the mushrooming Anti-Semitic Leagues and the gymnasts' organisations grouped in the Deutscher Turnerbund. The Christian-Social Party also called for a resolute struggle against the 'Jewish peril', and deplored the 'destructive' influence of Austria's 220,000 Jews on cultural and economic life. They were aided by the traditional anti-Judaism of the Catholic Church and there were some priests like Bishop Hudal, for example, who saw no contradiction between Christian teaching and Nazi racialism.[4] The clerical Chancellor of Austria, Ignaz Seipel, following the well-established Luegerite tradition, focused his antisemitism against the Jewish-led Austrian Social Democratic Party which controlled the city administration in Vienna.[5] A similarly 'moderate' antisemitism was also adopted by the quasi-fascist Heimwehr movement, led by Prince Starhemberg, which denounced 'Jewish Marxists' and the 'foreign flat-footed parasites from the East who exploit us', though it officially disapproved of Nazi racial theories.[6]

For a short time during the 1930s the clerico-fascist regimes of Dollfuss (who was murdered by Austrian Nazis) and his successor Schuschnigg sought to stem the Nazi tide, but Hitler's invasion of his former homeland in March 1938 turned the deeply rooted indigenous Austrian antisemitism into a veritable stampede. Huge crowds gathered in Vienna to cheer Hitler, and swastikas appeared everywhere – in the words of Carl Zuckmayer, 'hell itself was let loose'. Pillaging of Jewish property, arrests of Jews and attacks upon them by the previously illegal Austrian SA and SS, as well as by Austrian civilians, became routine.[7] As the *Daily Telegraph* correspondent observed,

> Their favourite sport on that Saturday and Sunday morning was to round up all ranks of Jews, particularly those of the middle classes, in order to make them clean the streets and scrub the pavements that had been decorated with pro-Schuschnigg posters and slogans painted in oil. These were the familiar scenes of Jews scrubbing pavements, with their bare hands, usually accompanied by a jeering mob of Viennese citizens. In many cases, acid was poured on the hands of the Jews . . . The older and feebler who stumbled or collapsed were brutally kicked and beaten . . . From time to time a roar of delight from the crowds would announce . . . 'Work for the Jews at last, work for the Jews!' or 'We thank our Führer for finding work for the Jews'.[8]

This spontaneous outburst of degrading cruelty was followed by legislation legally retiring Jewish civil servants, expelling Jewish pupils from all public educational institutions and 'Aryanising' Jewish enterprises. On 26 April 1938 the *Völkische Beobachter* prophetically stated: 'By 1942 the Jewish element in Vienna must be eliminated and made to disappear. No business, no enterprise must be in Jewish hands by that time, no Jews must have an opportunity of earning money anywhere.'[9] The extension of the *Kristallnacht* pogrom into Austria showed that the Nazis meant what they said; 21 synagogues were burnt down, dozens of prayer-rooms were destroyed, 4,083 Jewish shops were plundered and closed down, 1,950 Jewish homes were ransacked, 7,800 Jews were arrested, 680 committed suicide and 91 were murdered. Indeed, in some areas, Austrian antisemitism was showing itself to be a few steps ahead of Germany in the persecution of

Jews. As the Austrian historian Gerhard Botz has put it, 'Not only were the comparable measures applied earlier in Vienna than in Germany, but they could also count on much broader support among the non-Jewish population. Here, the organisational instruments and procedures could be developed which would later be applied by Eichmann in the "Final Solution".'[10]

Eichmann himself was of Austrian background, like Hitler, Kaltenbrunner, Globocnik, Seyss-Inquart and many others implicated in the mass murder of Jews, including some of the top commanders of the death-camps in Poland. The integration of Austria into the Third Reich provided them with new opportunities to advance in their careers, especially in the extermination apparatus of Greater Germany. Within Austria itself, the explosive antisemitism fuelled by the German invasion – which had surprised the German Nazis by its radical, spontaneous character – also had a pragmatic, opportunistic side.[11] The mass of ordinary Austrians saw a chance to improve their economic situation (housing, jobs, etc.) and social status through the expropriation of the more successful Jews, whom they had long envied and detested. Similar reactions would be manifested in Rumania, Poland, the Baltic States and the Ukraine after the German invasions. The economic motive behind the hatred of the Jews was of course all the stronger in countries where there was an unstable economic situation. In Vienna, in contrast to the German heartland, it did not need to be substantiated by 'theory' since it offered the fulfilment of immediate, concrete desires: the removal of the Jewish competitor in trade, the department-store owner, the doctor, lawyer or academic and the acquisition of scarce housing accommodation. Indeed, Austrian 'Aryanisation' procedures and methods of forced emigration became a model for other parts of the German Reich and for the persecution of Jews elsewhere in Nazi-occupied Europe.

Already by 30 November 1939, 126,445 Jews had been forced to emigrate from Austria as a result of Eichmann's draconian measures. This was followed by a massive deportation policy after the outbreak of war, culminating in the mass murder of about 65,000 Austrian Jews with a mere 5,700 surviving in Vienna by 1945. Official Austrian government policy towards the survivors was far from friendly and was designed through various manoeuvres and delays to avoid paying any financial compensation to Jews. Official, no less than popular, attitudes – as the historian Robert Knight has shown – displayed a whole range of antisemitic stereotypes which were barely affected by the Holocaust.[12]

A false symmetry was established between those ex-Nazis who had temporarily been stripped of their civil rights and Jewish concentration-camp survivors, and any 'special treatment' of Jews was ruled out as a form of 'racism in reverse'. As part of the effort to create a new national identity in post-1945 Austria, everything was done to dissociate the country from the Germans – including, of course, the Austrian contribution to National Socialism. With the support of the Western Allies, Austria could fall back on the myth that it had been the first 'victim' of the Third Reich and repress all public consciousness of its responsibilities in the atrocities against the Jews.[13] The fact that a relatively higher proportion of Austrians had been active members of the Nazi Party (one-tenth of the population) than in Germany and that Austria had supplied three-quarters of all concentration-camp staff was conveniently forgotten. De-Nazification, as in the Federal Republic of Germany, was superficial and by 1949 most of the many ex-Nazis had been re-enfranchised. By no later than 1955 even prominent National Socialists were fully integrated into the political process.[14]

The two dominant political parties, the Socialists and the Catholic Conservatives (ÖVP) as well as the German national camp, which still advocated annexation to Germany, were soon competing for this *Ehemalige* (former Nazi) vote. This readiness to attract ex-Nazi voters led to a conscious playing-down of anti-Nazi traditions. Representatives of the two major parties who had only fulfilled their 'duty' in Wehrmacht uniforms during the Second World War were pushed to the foreground. A former leader of the pre-war Austrian Nazis, Anton Reinthaller, who had become party chairman of Austria's Freedom Party (which continued the Nazi tradition in its personnel) even made possible through a political deal the election of the Conservative chancellor Raab to the Federal Presidency in 1957.[15] Those who had fallen in the uniforms of Greater Germany were honoured on numerous war monuments in Austria and the various veteran soldiers' leagues were allowed to continue their activities undisturbed. Cases against mass murderers of Jews like Franz Murer were thrown out by Austrian courts with even less hesitation than in neighbouring Germany. Only the case of Taras Borodajkewycz, a prominent ex-Nazi who held a chair at the Vienna College of Economics and regularly made antisemitic remarks in his lectures, briefly disturbed the domestic calm. In 1965 his activities provoked anti-Nazi demonstrations and violent right-wing counter-demonstrations which forced his retirement.[16]

The election of a Jewish-born Socialist, Bruno Kreisky, as Austrian Chancellor in 1970, and his immense popularity during the thirteen years that he dominated the political scene, did not fundamentally change Austria's relationship with its Nazi past. Although he had lost his family in the Holocaust, Kreisky remained demonstratively cool to the 8,000 Jews who still lived in Austria and perfectly willing to employ an antisemitic discourse where it could advance his interests, strategically and politically. For the Socialists to win elections in post-war Austria it was essential to have the votes of the older, more antisemitic generation, a point which had not escaped Kreisky's attention. Nevertheless, his decision to take three former Nazis into his first Cabinet, and then his defence of the right-wing Freedom Party leader, Friedrich Peter (who had been an SS *Obersturmbannführer*), with whom he sought to make a coalition in 1975, were shocking examples of his wilful desire to repress and cover up Austria's Nazi past. Peter's patriotic 'duties' had included not only participation in the invasion of the Soviet Union but also the extermination of civilians – especially defenceless Jews – under the pretext of warfare against 'partisans'.[17]

Kreisky did not hesitate to make antisemitic remarks in seeking to discredit Simon Wiesenthal, Austria's lone Nazi-hunter, who had the temerity to expose Peter's wartime role. Much to the delight of German and Austrian neo-Nazis and right-wingers, he branded Wiesenthal a 'Jewish fascist' and a servant of Zionist ideology, which he termed a kind of 'mysterious racism in reverse'. The campaign against Peter, he alleged, had been the work of an international 'Mafia'. Wiesenthal, it was libellously hinted, was himself a former Nazi 'collaborator' whose activities were a stain on Austria, whereas Herr Peter's disclaimers that he had been engaged in illegal acts were accepted without question. 'If the Jews are a people', Kreisky told one Israeli journalist in a moment of fury, 'then they are a lousy people.'[18]

As with his subsequent attacks on Israel's Prime Minister, Menachem Begin, 'a small-town Polish grocer' who epitomised the 'warped mentality of the *Ostjuden*', Kreisky appeared to be echoing the more vicious prejudices of the Viennese back-alleys. The Peter–Wiesenthal–Kreisky affair showed some striking structural similarities with the Waldheim affair ten years later. Both Peter and Waldheim had 'forgotten' important parts of their wartime biography while seeking high political office; both had been defended as patriotic Austrians who had only done their 'duty' in the service of the fatherland; on both occasions international criticism was dismissed as unwarranted interference in Austria's internal affairs and as a Jewish conspiracy – in the first case by Zionists and in the second by the World Jewish Congress – to blacken Austria's good name.[19]

Nevertheless, there was an important difference, for Kurt Waldheim's previous high visibility as Secretary General of the

United Nations and his standing as the official Conservative candidate for the Austrian Presidency made his campaign a matter of great international interest. The revelation that Waldheim had served as a staff officer in the Balkans with a unit that supervised mass deportations of Jews and partisans to death camps scarcely seemed to disturb most Austrians, especially of the older generation, who could identify with a man who had only done his 'duty'. What did anger the 'man in the street' and the political establishment (especially Conservative politicians) was the 'international campaign' against their elected President which provoked an unprecedented backlash of public antisemitism, even for post-war Austria. The reservoir of hostility and prejudice towards Jews which had been consistently demonstrated by public opinion surveys but held in check by official taboos now found an unexpectedly vehement outlet and cathartic release. The widely held beliefs of many Austrians concerning Jewish power and influence seemed suddenly to be vindicated by the campaign of the World Jewish Congress, whose very name echoed the old Nazi myths about the machinations of 'World Jewry'. (A Gallup poll of 1980 had shown that nearly 50 per cent of Austrians either agreed or 'tended to agree' that 'the Jews rule world politics'.)[20]

After 1986 it became once more respectable to claim that international Jews, based on the East Coast of America, had through their control of the world's media deliberately instigated the 'slanders' and defamation of Waldheim. The Secretary General of the People's Party, who had already coined the phrase that 'garbage can campaign',[21] declared that unless the President could be personally shown to have strangled five or six Jews with his own hands he must be considered blameless. He called the World Jewish Congress a dishonourable 'mafia of slanderers' who would stop at nothing to achieve their ends.[22] This was echoed in different words by the Party chairman and later Foreign Minister Alois Mock.[23] The Austrian press, too, condemned the campaign of hatred, supposedly driven by motives of revenge, against Waldheim and Austria. One journalist wrote that 'we are dealing with people who, like so many other Jews, have been psychically severely damaged'.[24] As in many Austrian press comments on the Affair, the actions of individual Jews were taken to be representative of Jewry as a whole or of *'das Ausland'* (the outside world) in general. Austrian patriotism and self-respect demanded repudiation of those who sought to 'destroy' the country by attacking its President. Waldheim himself had set the tone for this defence by telling *Le Monde* in May 1986 that 'the international press is dominated by the World Jewish Congress. This is well-known.'[25]

The Waldheim affair removed previous taboos that had inhibited the open articulation of anti-Jewish prejudice in post-war Austria. Austrian 'antisemitism without Jews' (they constitute only 0.1 per cent of the total population) seemed to be illustrating the truth of Henryk Broder's remark about the Germans: that they will never forgive the Jews for Auschwitz! For it was above all the repression of unavowed guilt feelings about a past that had never been confronted which characterised the Austrian response to the Waldheim affair. The fear of the discovery of war crimes, the anxiety that stolen or 'Aryanised' property might be demanded back, that reparations might have to be paid or that in some other way Jews would seek revenge, had long conditioned the Austrian pattern of guilt-denial. This was easily rationalised by presenting Austrians as the 'victims' of Nazism and the 'tricky', conspiratorial and powerful Jews as its would-be beneficiaries. Antisemitism, it was argued, was in any case the Jews' own fault, for they used unworthy and dishonourable methods – as in the self-aggrandising campaign of world Jewry against Kurt Waldhiem. Catholic antisemitism, too, could be mobilised in the service of time-honoured stereotypical images. Thus the former Vice-Mayor of Linz could write to the President of the World Jewish Congress on 12 May 1987, drawing an analogy between the 'persecution' of Waldheim and the Jews handing

96

over Jesus to the Romans. This was not the only time that criticism of Waldhiem was linked to the deicidal myth of the Christ-killers or that Jewish attitudes were depicted in terms of the Old Testament adage, 'An eye for an eye, a tooth for a tooth', which 'is not our European attitude'.[26]

Such statements by Austrian public figures revealed the ease with which even the most traditional antisemitic prejudices could be activated in Austria and politically mobilised. An opinion poll conducted in January 1989 showed that 10 per cent of all Austrians had hard-core antisemitic attitudes and another 27 per cent exhibited more diffuse anti-Jewish prejudice.[27] Thus more than a third of the population displayed antisemitic tendencies, with the more extreme variety being found among supporters of the Freedom Party, which did well in the 1990 Austrian elections. These figures underline the point that there has never been a sharp break in Austria's antisemitic tradition, even after the Second World War. Its roots are still deeply embedded in the national political culture which preceded Nazism, and at the same time it serves as a way of repressing the unavowed guilt that is linked with Austrian behaviour during the Third Reich. Although less violent and immediately dangerous to Jews than the antisemitism of its neighbours to the East, the Austrian variety has been no less persistent in a more diffuse way. Often expressed through allusions, insinuations and vague innuendos, it is no less insidious in its underlying meaning and when activated by economic or political crises can become openly vicious. The stereotypes live on as part of the local culture, almost as a way of life, in the land that gave birth to Hitler.

Part 2

■ ■ ■

■

Enemies of the People

9
■ ■ ■

Britain: the Limits of Tolerance

As two recent anniversaries have underlined – that of the mass suicide of York Jews in 1190 besieged by a fanatical Christian mob and the expulsion 700 years ago of *all* Britain's Jews by Edward I – medieval England exceeded most of Europe in its mistreatment of Jewry. It led the way in the introduction of the Jew badge ('a badge of shame') around 1220 and in the blood-libel accusation, as well as being the first country to carry out a medieval-style 'final solution' – namely the mass expulsion of Jews – in which it preceded France, Spain and Germany. As a result, the Jews virtually vanished from British shores for nearly 400 years, until their re-admission under Oliver Cromwell in the middle of the seventeenth century. Nevertheless, throughout these four centuries anti-Jewish stereotypes became ingrained in English life through sermons, plays and religious literature. Catholics, Anglicans and even Puritans adopted the demonic medieval image of the Jews as a rejected and despised group, and the word itself carried connotations of scorn and contempt. Jews, along with witches, became scapegoats for the repressed desires of Christian society. As usurers, as agents of the Devil, as heretics, they were always held up by the Church to be a physical threat to both Christians and Christianity.[1]

The stereotypes survived into the Elizabethan era, with Jewish villains becoming popular stage figures of the period. The prosecution of Dr Rodrigo Lopez, a crypto-Jew and personal physician to Elizabeth I, for treason gave a certain topicality to the anti-Jewish prejudices rampant in English society, which flared up as soon as the fact that there were still some Jews in the country was brought out into the open.[2]

Two of the most famous dramatic portrayals of Jews on the Elizabethan stage, Christopher Marlowe's *The Jew of Malta* (1591) and William Shakespeare's *The Merchant of Venice*, illustrate the tenacity of these negative stereotypes. Marlowe's villain, Barabbas, combines medieval images of the Jew as infidel, as sorcerer and poisoner, as a direct descendant of Judas Iscariot in the New Testament, with the more modern notion of a scheming Machiavellian intriguer. However much Marlowe flayed the hypocrisy of Christians, his caricature of the Jew as an unbridled materialist and symbol of evil incarnate is what retains the attention. Shakespeare, too, however masterly his characterisation of Shylock, is depicting an old Jew obsessed with his wealth, his possessions and his 'pound of flesh' – a vengeful figure whose narrow-minded legalism can only arouse horror and contempt. The cruel, usurious Shylock becomes a foil with which to highlight the superiority of Christian values of love, mercy and justice. Despite Shakespeare's skill in humanising certain qualities of the Jew, his portrait served to crystallise and reinforce an antisemitic literary stereotype for centuries to come.[3]

This Shylock image survived the love of the Old Testament and of the Hebrew language fostered by Puritan and Anglican preachers in the seventeenth century, their identification of modern England with ancient Israel and the more positive view of Jews to be found in the millenarian movements that developed out of the Puritan Revolution.[4] English 'philo-semitism' related more to biblical Jews and not so much to their latter-day descendents, whose conversion was generally considered a necessary prelude to the second coming of Jesus. Nevertheless, some Puritans did favour the readmission of Jews to England, which was implemented by Oliver Cromwell in 1656 for a variety of economic, political and religious reasons. By the end of the seventeenth century, despite the persistence of religious prejudice and envy over their commercial success, Jews in England were economically secure, permitted to live in peace and to practise their faith unmolested. They were not restricted to ghettos, and the principle of religious toleration advocated by political philosophers such as John Locke (1632–1704) was widely accepted.

The decline in the authority of the Church, the emphasis on individual freedom and the spirit of emerging capitalism in England ensured that the situation of Jews would be better than anywhere on the Continent, with the possible exception of Holland. The older anti-Jewish attitudes were pushed into the background and in contrast to most of its Continental rivals, no anti-Jewish outbreaks would henceforth be sanctioned by the rulers of England. Moreover, the numbers of Jews were still relatively small – only 25,000 Jews lived in England at the end of the eighteenth century. They were mainly concentrated as merchants, stockbrokers and bankers in the City of London or in other commercial and financial trades.

In the nineteenth century the leading families of Anglo-Jewry – originally Sephardic and later German-born Ashkenazim – became immensely wealthy. Some of these families turned into veritable dynasties, among them the Rothschilds, Montefiores, Goldsmids, Cohens, Jessels, Franklins and Sassoons who came to be known as the 'Cousinhood'.[5] In the age of Victorian liberalism, when Britain emerged as the workshop of the world and enjoyed unrivalled world power, the Jewish grandees aroused relatively little élite prejudice or popular antisemitism. Although Jews played little part in English intellectual or political life (Benjamin Disraeli, converted in his teens, was the great exception to the rule), their disproportionate wealth initially seemed to ease rather than obstruct their acceptance into English life and society.[6] Admittedly, their formal emancipation came much later than in France (the first practising Jew was permitted to sit in the House of Commons only in 1858), but it aroused less overt antisemitism than on the Continent.

The broad consensus favouring religious toleration, social mobility, representative government and free-market capitalism did not provide fertile soil for a Central European type of antimodernist backlash against Jewish emancipation. There was little likelihood of British Jews being negatively depicted as carriers of 'modernity' or bearers of the capitalist ethic in a forward-looking highly industrialised society like that of Victorian England, where entrepreneurial initiative and individualist doctrines of self-help were part of the national ethos. Moreover, until the end of the nineteenth century, the Catholic minority (mainly Irish in origin) were far more frequently the object of rancour and racial or religious prejudice than the Jewish community.

This optimal situation began to change in the 1880s with the arrival of a mass immigration from the Russian Pale of Settlement to London's East End and also to provincial cities like Glasgow, Manchester and Leeds. As a result of this influx the Jewish population of the British Isles, which had been about 36,000 in 1858 and 60,000 in 1880, increased nearly five-fold by the end of the First World War. During the half century from around 1890 to 1940 antisemitism attained a new virulence in Britain which presented a serious challenge to the country's religious tolerance and the liberalism of its political élites. The specific configuration of this antisemitism – less ideological and political than on the Continent but nevertheless widespread – was already apparent in the period between 1881 and 1914. It combined negative stereotypes of poor immigrant Jews with a whole range of 'rich Jew' antisemitism, intellectual racism, Social Darwinism and class snobbery, with vulgar conspiracy theories about Jewish plans for world domination.

The mass influx into the East End at the turn of the century of Yiddish-speaking East European Jews, who were foreign in religion, language, customs and outlook, was undoubtedly the single most potent factor in the new antisemitism.[7] The newcomers were closely identified with the practice of sweated labour, they were said to be dirty in their habits, carriers of disease, clannish, materialistic, prone to various types of crime (many of the same stereotypes are today applied to Asians in London's East End) and disloyal to Britain. Trade unionists claimed that they lowered the wages of English workers, acted as blacklegs to break strikes and did not share the class-consciousness of their British counterparts. Conservative politicians exaggerated the size and flow of the immigration, to paint a picture of England being inundated by foreigners.[8] In 1901 the British Brothers League was formed in the East End; it aimed to restrict this alien immigration and gained substantial popular support. This resulted in some ugly demonstrations and small-scale violence against Jews. The anti-immigration cause was eventually taken over by more respectable parliamentary bodies and culminated in the Aliens Bill passed by a Conservative government in 1905; this drastically restricted Jewish immigration.

'Rich Jew' antisemitism also had its supporters on the British Left, despite the official opposition of the Socialist movement to racial or religious prejudice. Initially directed at the wealthy English Jews of Hampstead, Bayswater or the West End, it exploded during the Boer War (1899–1902) when South African Jewish diamond and gold millionaires (the Barnatos, the Beits, Lionel Phillips, the Albu brothers, etc.) were targeted by the extreme Left and Right.[9] The radicals blamed the outbreak of the war on the 'Jew-Jingo' gang and the 'Jew press', which had supposedly brainwashed the British public into supporting their 'piratical imperialism' in the Transvaal and elsewhere. The leading Marxist newspaper in Britain referred to the 'Jew war in the Transvaal', engineered by a 'Jew clique' around Joseph Chamberlain and Balfour. Jewish press magnates were accused of being 'poisoners of the wells of public information', and Jewish financiers of being the soul of a sinister 'golden international'.[10] The radical antiwar movement, including the distinguished liberal economist John Hobson, the Labour MP John Burns and the Marxist Henry

Hyndman, denounced the cosmopolitan financiers behind 'imperialist Judaism in South Africa', presenting their activities as part of a secret Jewish cabal aiming to seize the gold-rich Boer lands to further the interests of world Jewry.[11] They would have agreed with the labour leader Keir Hardie that modern imperialism was run by 'half a dozen financial houses, many of them Jewish' or with the TUC resolution of September 1900 which condemned the Boer war as designed to 'secure the goldfields of South Africa for cosmopolitan Jews, most of whom had no patriotism and no country'.[12]

A little over a decade later, similar outbursts occurred in response to the Marconi and Indian Silver financial scandals, though here antisemitism was more obviously used as cover for conflicting economic and political interests within the British ruling élite. There was, indeed, a growing feeling on the eve of the First World War that Jews were exercising too much influence over economic policy, the financial markets, the press and public opinion. Even the style and taste of society was affected, for in King Edward VII's inner circle, Jews like the Rothschild and Sassoon brothers or Sir Ernest Cassel (a convert of German-Jewish background) were conspicuous. In politics, too, Jews were becoming increasingly prominent. This aroused the resentment of conservatives, who bemoaned the commercialisation of England, and it fuelled the hatred of antisemites like Arnold White, Joseph Bannister, Hilaire Belloc and the Chesterton brothers, who saw British cultural values as being undermined by cosmopolitan Jewish influence.[13] Although this English cultural antisemitism was less elaborate and sophisticated than its French, German or Russian counterparts, it did have a certain resonance before the impact of the Holocaust began to discredit it in more educated middle-class or literary circles. But before 1914, Belloc and G. K. Chesterton, leading Anglo-Catholic writers and corporatists, freely denounced the 'corrupting' role of Jews in public life, called for their emigration or demotion to the status of aliens, and encouraged a conspiratorial view of Jewish behaviour in general.

In 1919 T. S. Eliot would include these unpleasant lines in his great poem 'Gerontion':

> My house is a decayed house,
> And the Jew squats on the window
> sill, the owner . . .

In the same year, in his notorious 'Burbank with a Baedeker: Bleistein with a Cigar', Eliot wrote:

> The rats are underneath the piles
> The Jew is underneath the lot.[14]

Eliot's genteel, snobbish antisemitism was consistent enough with his Anglican antimodernist outlook, his distaste for free-thinking secularism, commercialism and the rootlessness of modern civilisation.[15] It would be shared by many cultural critics and artists in twentieth-century England, ambivalent about progress, modernity, mass politics, urban values and the legacy of uninhibited Victorian capitalism. Those among them who believed that Jews were aliens, intent on remaining separate, could all too easily slide over into the diffuse and elusively polite antisemitism that tinged much of British life between the wars.

The potentially more dangerous variety of political anti-semitism, spawned during the First World War itself, arose out of the role attributed to Jews in the Russian Revolution. The conservative *Morning Post*, in particular, tended to see in Leon Trotsky and other 'Jewish' Bolsheviks a symbol of world revolutionary upheaval instigated by Jews and Judaism. German and Russian Jews, it was suggested, were engaged in a conspiracy against England and its Empire.[16] The resonance which *The Protocols of the Elders of Zion* initially achieved in Britain (it was eventually exposed by *The Times* as a forgery in 1921) added force to these anxieties.[17] The danger of spreading revolution could be linked with phobias about Jewish immigration, and in some conservative circles was even used as an argument against supporting Zionist aspirations in Palestine – allegedly part of a single world-wide Jewish conspiracy to dominate the world.[18] Indeed, Britain's commitment to sponsor a Jewish national home in Palestine (made in the 1917 Balfour Declaration) helped provoke in Britain between 1918 and 1922 a right-wing anti-Jewish and anti-Zionist campaign of unusual intensity.

This campaign, which opposed British involvement in Palestine and reviled Zionist policies towards the Arabs, spilled over into indiscriminate vilification of Jewish capitalists, Jewish radicals and Jewish interests in general. The emergence of a new Jewish diplomacy encouraged openly antisemitic attacks on the dual loyalties of British Jews who openly defended Zionism or other Jewish national interests abroad. Similarly, the conviction that Jews were instigating revolutionary Communism and encouraging attempts to subvert the British Empire intensified malevolent interpretations of their role in world affairs and allegations about their sinister, occult influence, especially in upper-class establishment circles.[19]

Even after its exposure as a forgery, the 'Protocols of Zion' mythology was kept alive by a number of political outsiders like Captain Henry Hamilton Beamish (founder of the Britons' Publishing Society) and the racial antisemite Arnold Leese, who in 1929 founded the Imperial Fascist League. Beamish had close contacts with the Nazis, while Leese was the most extreme racialist among the inter-war British fascists, accusing the Jews of ritual murder, defaming them as a mongrelised people whose repulsive features were a 'warning to all Aryans' and openly calling for their total segregation or expulsion from Britain.[20] (Leese would have preferred 'to exterminate them by some humane method such as the lethal chamber' but felt that most Britons would reject this drastic solution.)[21]

After 1932 Leese's organisation was thrust to the margins by the rise of Sir Oswald Mosley's British Union of Fascists (BUF)

– far more significant in the quality of its leadership and potential mass appeal. Initially, Jew-baiting was not a part of the movement, but after 1934 Mosley launched an antisemitic campaign which accused the Jews of dragging Britain into a war with Nazi Germany, attacking them as foreigners and as a corrupting force responsible for every social and political evil, especially international Communism.[22] His East End campaigns were deliberately intended to whip up anti-Jewish feelings and, while they failed electorally (in the inter-war years fascist groups won only two local council seats), the BUF was nonetheless the most effective vehicle of antisemitic politics that England had hitherto produced. Although the British government clamped down on Mosley's movement and interned BUF members as security risks during the war against Nazi Germany, they still exercised a subterranean influence on British attitudes towards Jews during the war years.[23]

Paradoxically, popular prejudice against Jews appears to have increased between 1939 and 1945 despite its theoretical incompatibility with liberal democracy and the war against fascism. Although there was no actual violence, Jews were often the butt of insinuations or accusations that they controlled the black market, shirked the war effort, ostentatiously flashed their wealth in seaside resorts or country towns, or were responsible for overcrowding in air-raid shelters. Significantly, the role of the British government was not without ambivalence, often guided by the belief that any drawing of attention to antisemitism might lead to anti-Jewish riots.[24] Antisemitic demands for the internment of alien Jews (fleeing from Nazi persecution) were acceded to, official pronouncements against antisemitism studiously avoided and virtually nothing was done to rescue European Jewry from the Holocaust. Britain's Palestine policy, which closed the gates of the Jewish National Home to all but a trickle of Jewish refugees, was a lamentable example of British officialdom's callous insensitivity to the Jewish plight.[25] The period between

1945 and 1948 would witness rampant antisemitism in the British Army in Palestine, an inhumanly executed policy by Britain's foreign secretary Ernest Bevin towards Holocaust survivors 'illegally' immigrating to what would become Israel, and anti-Jewish riots in several British cities following the execution of two British army sergeants in Palestine by Jewish underground fighters.

It is apparent that negative images of Jews in British society had not only survived the defeat of Nazi Germany but had been temporarily reinforced by the Anglo-Zionist conflict over Palestine. Although conscious antisemitism was never a part of British policy, a mixture of *realpolitik*, an Arabophile tradition in the Foreign and Colonial Offices, bureaucratic closed-mindedness, xenophobia and a casual, non-theoretical prejudice against Jews did affect attitudes and even decision-making.[26] As Harold Nicolson noted in his diary in June 1945: 'Although I loathe antisemitism, I do dislike Jews.'[27] This kind of social dislike, rather than organised, systematic anti-semitism, was a charcteristically British attitude, sometimes tempered by admiration for Jewish achievements, resilience in adversity and ability to withstand persecution.

In post-war Britain, the majority of Jews initially supported the Labour and to a lesser extent, the Communist parties – doubtless aware of the suspicion with which they had been traditionally regarded by the Conservative Party. In 1945 the overwhelming majority of Jewish Members of Parliament represented the Labour Party, and their number continued to increase until they represented over 10 per cent of all Labour MPs in the 1970s. On the other hand, only a handful of Jewish Conservative MPs were elected until the late 1970s. This began to change radically during the last decade as many British Jews were alienated by what they regarded as the influence of the hard Left within the Labour Party, pushing it in an anti-Zionist and (in the eyes of the average Jewish voter) an anti-Jewish direction. At the same time, Anglo-Jewry had, since the 1950s, begun to enjoy unparalleled affluence and to take a prominent role in property development, finance, retailing and the entertainment industry. The impact of Jewish millionaires like Wolfson, Clore, Weinstock, the Grade brothers, Cohen (of Tesco fame) Marks and Sieff, Maxwell, Weidenfeld and many others has been legendary, without provoking any marked antisemitism. In the scientific, cultural and academic élites, the Jewish contribution to post-war British life has also been unprecedented.[28] This process of social, economic and cultural *embourgeoisement* undoubtedly facilitated a steady drift of Anglo-Jewry towards the politics of Thatcherite conservatism. Indeed, never before in its history had the prevailing ethos and values of most middle-class British Jews seemed so congruent with those of the new-style Conservatism. Politically, this was reflected in the prominence of Jewish Ministers like Sir Keith Joseph, Sir Leon Brittan, Nigel Lawson and others in Mrs Thatcher's Cabinets during the 1980s, and in the support which she found in the teachings of Chief Rabbi Jakobovits. Mrs Thatcher's support for Jewish causes (especially that of Soviet Jewry), her friendliness towards Israel and her espousal of traditional Jewish values such as a close family life, self-reliance, hard work and individual initiative was undoubtedly appreciated by many British Jews.

Nevertheless, it would be mistaken to assume that anti-semitism has therefore disappeared from Britain's increasingly multi-racial post-war society. Racism, intolerance and anti-Jewish prejudice continue to exist within a mainstream liberal framework and take multiple forms that may become politic-ally more important in the 1990s. Neo-Nazi and ultra-Right movements stubbornly persist on the shadowy fringes of British politics, calling for the repatriation of all non-white immigrants while espousing the classic Jewish conspiracy theories of the pre-war period. In the late 1970s the National Front enjoyed some modest, temporary successes in London and in the Midlands, and still retains some appeal among unemployed youth.[29] It has espoused the denial of the Holocaust as part of its efforts to rehabilitate the fascist legacy, while combining a sham pro-Palestinian rhetoric with racist bigotry. It publishes the antisemitic hate-sheet *Holocaust News* without having charges pressed against it for claiming that the mass murder of European Jewry never happened. It was a British fascist, Richard Verrall (pseudonym Richard Harwood) who first popularised this wicked myth with his 1974 pamphlet 'Did Six Million Really Die?'. The myth-makers have now been joined by the prolific British historian David Irving – an idol of the so-called Holocaust 'revisionists' in America and Germany – who also denies that the gas chambers ever existed.[30] In other words, Auschwitz was a Jewish deception or, in the words of the American engineering professor Arthur Butz, 'the hoax of the twentieth century'.

The denial of the Holocaust – whether in Britain, France (where it first originated), America or other Western countries – has become an integral part of the revamped antisemitic mythology of a world Jewish conspiracy. But there are other disturbing signs that antisemitism may be growing in contemporary Britain: the recent spate of grave desecrations in Jewish cemeteries, the growth in antisemitic graffiti, the assaults on orthodox Jews in North London and the verbal abuse directed at pupils of the Jewish Free School,[31] the racist and antisemitic slogans heard regularly on the football terraces and the evidence of growing co-operation between organised fascist movements in Britain, Europe and the United States. Although these are for the moment still sporadic and politically marginalised forms of violence, it must be recognised that the revival of nationalism throughout Europe also has its counterparts in Britain. A new, more inward-looking British nationalism that emphasises heritage, kith and kin and the continuities of a millennial English culture will inevitably be less than hospitable to those from a different background.[32]

For the moment it is Asians and blacks who are more usually portrayed by nationalists as representing everything that is alien to British society and culture, but it is in the logic of exclusivist nationalism and of those who advocate a monolithic conception of British culture to regard all minorities with suspicion. Jews were traditionally the favourite targets of this kind of hostility, which became somewhat muted without ever disappearing. In the eyes of militant British nationalists Jews are indeed responsible for the racial tensions in English society and represent the occult, international power that governs world affairs. But even in more respectable British middle-of-the road opinion there exists a latent strain of antisemitism which feels uneasy at Jewish influence in politics, business, the media and cultural life, which finds Jewish particularism distasteful and bridles at the alleged 'dual loyalties' of Anglo-Jewry towards Israel.

British antisemitism in modern times has always been a somewhat elusive, *ad hoc* phenomenon, rather resistant to conventional classifications. It has rarely exploded into mass violence in this century (except for isolated instances in Limerick and South Wales shortly before the First World War and in the East End during the 1930s), but it has been a remarkably persistent undercurrent in British society and culture. Whether this latent anti-Jewish prejudice will stretch the limits of tolerance in Britain's liberal democracy should economic conditions deteriorate, political stability be threatened, religious fundamentalism grow or racial tensions explode, must remain an open question.

10

...

America: Whites, Blacks and Jews

The American Jewish community, generally estimated at around six million in size, is the largest, wealthiest, most influential and politically powerful that has ever existed in Diaspora history.[1] Its contribution in this century to American life has been second to none and it has had the good fortune to operate in what has arguably been the most open and liberal democracy of the Western world since 1945. In American society, especially during the past thirty years, antisemitism – according to the existing social research – has been a peripheral phenomenon, not a part of the mainstream culture or political system. In contrast to the kind of rampant pre-war discrimination against Jews in education, employment, social and public life which was once commonplace, American Jewry appears today not only as an equal and successful part of the larger society, but even as an empowered élite in America. The antisemitism that does exist often seems (particularly to non-Jewish observers) to be at most latent or relatively passive. Certainly there are no explicitly antisemitic political movements which have significantly developed, persisted or made electoral headway in the post-war era. This raises a number of important questions: to what extent does this fact give an accurate picture of contemporary American attitudes to Jews, how much continuity is there to antisemitism in the United States, how far is it different from its European counterparts and what general societal or political causes may extend or limit its present or future course?[2]

One salient feature about America which it shares with

Europe is that it has always been a Christian country, a fact which potentially provides a fertile soil for antisemitism, no less than in most European societies. Moreover, many of its variegated ethnic groups, particularly Catholic Poles or Slovaks, Lutheran Germans or Orthodox Christian Rumanians and Ukrainians, have brought an antisemitic tradition with them to America. The notion of Jews as Christ-killers has therefore been a familiar one in modern America, though significantly less potent than in Eastern Europe. During the 1930s, however, antisemitism of an extremist kind did flourish under a 'Christian' proto-fascist banner. The most striking example of its political potential could be found in the incendiary propaganda of the Catholic radio-priest, Father Charles E. Coughlin, who had an audience of millions.[3] The Christian Front, inspired by his diatribes, organised movements to boycott Jewish businesses in many American cities between 1938 and 1940, physically assaulted Jews and constantly attacked them as 'warmongers' seeking to drag the United States into war with Hitler's Germany. Coughlin appealed especially to American Catholics, who in the 1930s were looking to the political Right for their salvation, identifying Jews with Communism at a time when antisemitic sentiment was already reaching unprecedented heights in America.[4] It was not until 1942 that the American Catholic hierarchy appeared clearly to dissociate itself from the campaigns of Coughlin's followers, which singled out Jews for special condemnation.

There were other Christian clergymen, like Gerald B. Winrod who also espoused a conservative, 'patriotic' anti-semitism in the 1930s. In 1938 Winrod had 110,000 subscribers to his publication *Defender* and received a sizeable vote when he ran for a Senate seat in Kansas and lost. Another self-styled Christian Party, this one openly fascist in its ideology, was William Pelley's Silver Shirts, who in 1933 had 15,000 followers and emitted an unrelenting stream of propaganda against Jews controlling industry, finance and property in America. Pelley was eventually charged with racketeering and received a fifteen-year prison sentence. A more durable antisemite was the Protestant, far-Right demagogue Gerald L. K. Smith, whose *Cross and the Flag* newspaper was replete with attacks on 'organised Jewry' during the Second World War.[5] Yet, even during the period of the great economic depression which briefly produced an antisemitism comparable to some of the worst manifestations in Europe, it never became politically entrenched.

Although Christian theological considerations did colour some of the rhetoric which inspired Hitler's American imitators in the 1930s, it was not their main motivation. This suggests that American Christianity has not been especially hospitable to antisemitism, recognising as it does the multiplicity of sects, the principle of religious pluralism, the separation of Church and state and the importance of equality in matters of religion as central elements in the credo of the Republic. In the United States, the medieval Christian demonology of the Jew has on the whole been rather muted, and even the far more influential notions about the 'Christian character' of America are limited by the fact that there is no *national* Church from which Jews stand apart.[6] Indeed, in America, unlike Europe, Judaism has achieved a significant legitimacy and standing which is equal, at least in theory, to that of Protestantism and Catholicism.

American Jews have also been fortunate that they did not need to be formally emancipated in a New World that was 'born free', without any feudal aristocracy to retard the development of a Calvinist spirit of capitalism. America did not offer fertile soil to the kind of antimodernist backlash against urbanism, commercialism or democratisation so characteristic of antisemitism in France, Germany, Austria, Eastern Europe and Russia. Moreover, Jews in America, unlike their European co-religionists, had never been obliged to gain their livelihoods through 'usury' or a pariah form of capitalism. Modestly prosperous, they could never compete in wealth with the great

Anglo-Saxon industrial and financial tycoons of the Gilded Age – the Carnegies, Rockefellers, Morgans, Vanderbilts and Goulds – though by the end of the nineteenth century they had a few representatives of their own within the financial élite.[7]

The unparalleled mass immigration of Jews from Tsarist Russia to the United States – some three million impoverished, Yiddish-speaking Jews arrived between 1881 and 1924 – did, however, spark off an aggravation of the hitherto rather mild forms of existing antisemitism. With their strange, exotic customs, language and dress, the East European Jews were seen as 'alien' and un-American, as unwelcome competitors on the job market and in some cases as sinister conspirators who controlled 'invisible money powers'. They found themselves shut out of exclusive clubs, salons, fashionable resorts, schools, fraternities or the boards of élite cultural and charitable institutions.[8] The White Anglo-Saxon Protestant establishment (the only version of 'aristocracy' that America has ever known) particularly resented the new Jewish immigrants as pushy, uppity parvenus or else as coming of tainted, inferior stock. A Boston Brahmin like Henry Adams could write in the 1890s of the 'accursed Judaism' of his money-grabbing contemporaries (Jewish or Christian) with the same racist obsessiveness as any European aristocrat. 'The Jew has penetrated to my soul. I see him – or her – everywhere, and everywhere that he – or she – goes there remains a taint in the blood forever.'[9]

From this established upper-class milieu, American racial theories first developed, which culminated in the drastic immigration law of 1924, affirming the superiority of Nordic over Slavic and 'Semitic' races. Although America stopped short of articulating a fully fledged ideological antisemitism or a political movement on Central or East European lines, its receptiveness to racial arguments (against the 'yellow peril' or about blacks) undoubtedly facilitated the adoption of new myths about the Jews. The popularity of works like Madison

Grant's *The Passing of the Great Race* (he was an American counterpart to Houston S. Chamberlain) showed that European racist ideology was making an impact in the United States with distinctly adverse effects for American Jewry.

It was in this climate of opinion that the atrocious lynching of a young Southern Jew, Leo Frank, who was wrongly accused of murdering a Gentile girl, occurred in 1916.[10] Tom Watson, a vitriolic antisemitic and anti-Catholic agitator (he was nonetheless elected to the US Senate in 1920) was one of those Southerners who contributed to the lynching by his relentless accusations that Jews habitually committed ritual murder, and his racist attacks on Jewish and Negro 'licentiousness' and on Jewish fraud. The Frank Affair, which was sparked off by a blood libel, demonstrated the potential for violent antisemitism in America. The activities of the Ku Klux Klan, the best-known of America's nativist organisations and also based in the South, underlined this threat, appealing as it did to a new American xenophobia and hatred of minorities that followed the First World War. Originally anti-black and anti-Catholic, the Klan began between 1915 and 1925 to incite a violent hatred against the alien, unassimilable Jews who were supposedly trying to dominate America.[11]

The foremost advocate of antisemitism in America during the 1920s was, however, undoubtedly the motor-car tycoon Henry Ford, whose weekly *The Dearborn Independent* disseminated *The Protocols of the Elders of Zion* (an antisemitic Russian émigré had convinced Ford of its truth) and systematically defamed American Jews for seven years.[12] Ford had a four-volume reissue of the antisemitic articles in his weekly separately reprinted, under the title *The International Jew* – a work which was highly praised by Adolf Hitler and widely distributed in German translation by his Nazi Party.[13] Eventually Ford retracted in 1927, following a Jewish boycott of his products, but considerable damage had already been done. Ford's paper had depicted the Jews as a universally corrupting influence, responsible for all the evils of 'progress' –

from liberalism, unionism and Bolshevism to Negro jazz music. One can see why Hitler once told an American reporter: 'I regard Heinrich [sic] Ford as my inspiration.'[14]

The 1920s and 1930s witnessed a growing institutionalisation of antisemitism in the United States, already heralded by the 1924 Johnson Bill which had drastically reduced the Jewish immigrant influx in the name of preserving America's 'native stock'. Nine years later, when Hitler came to power in Germany, he could remark with some justice: 'Through its immigration law, America has inhibited the unwelcome influence of such races as it has been unable to tolerate within its midst. Nor is America ready now to open its doors to Jews fleeing from Germany.'[15] The attitudes of the chief State Department official responsible for refugees in the Roosevelt administration, Breckinridge Long, Jr, a paranoid antisemite who regarded all Jews as Communists, demonstrates the extent of American responsibility when it came to the Jewish immigration issue. Nor was this merely isolationist protectionism. Long, after reading *Mein Kampf*, for example, called it 'eloquent in opposition to Jewry and to Jews as exponents of Communism and Chaos'.[16]

Such attitudes were extremely popular in the United States during the late 1930s. Four separate polls in 1938 revealed that between 70 and 85 per cent of the American public opposed increasing the already drastically restrictive quotas to help refugees.[17] American Jewish organisations undoubtedly felt intimidated by such public sentiments and government willingness to adapt its policy to them.

In employment, housing and higher education, too, Jews found themselves discriminated against to an astonishing degree by the kind of quotas more familiar in Eastern Europe. Their representation in élite schools was severely restricted, and the percentage of Jewish students at Columbia and Cornell had dropped to less than 5 per cent by 1940. A negligible number of Jewish medical graduates could find employment in non-Jewish hospitals run by private philanthropy. In fields like dentistry and psychiatry a quota system was openly proposed. With the deepening of the economic crisis, advertisements accepting 'Christians only' could even be found in the *New York Times*, which was owned by Jews. Opinion polls in 1938 showed that popular antipathy was indeed widespread, with 41 per cent agreeing that Jews had 'too much power in the United States', a figure that actually rose to 58 per cent by 1945, despite the war which America was waging against Nazi Germany.[18] Large numbers of Americans evidently thought Jews to be greedy, dishonest and aggressive or tended to blame them for the antisemitic persecution in Europe. During the war years, poll-takers noted that, after the Germans and Japanese, Jews were held to be the greatest menace to American society.[19]

Against this sombre background of socio-economic prejudice and discrimination, the steady decline in American antisemitism during the past forty-five years represents a substantial progress. In part this can be attributed to the remarkably favourable economic and political circumstances of America in the post-war era. Under the conditions of general prosperity and even affluence prevailing in the 1950s and 1960s, when the United States clearly emerged as the world's richest and most powerful nation, the status of Jews also began to improve dramatically. The descendents of immigrants began to enter the white American middle class in large numbers and to gain open access to the universities. By the 1970s and 1980s they were concentrated in the upper ranks of American society as far as income, education and professional success was concerned. Although more often excluded from the highest corporate office or ownership of the biggest firms, Jews no longer felt politically powerless or as defensive as they had done in the 1930s and early 1940s. The establishment of the State of Israel in 1948 and the success of Jewish lobbying efforts on its behalf further reinforced self-confidence, particularly as Americans in general were supportive of the new state and sympathetic to its needs.

Another important factor in the attenuation of American antisemitism was the vigorous struggle by American Jewish organisations in the post-war years against social and educational discrimination. Using all the means available in an open society — legislation, court decisions, education and growing political clout — the major American Jewish defence organisations did largely succeed in removing anti-Jewish discrimination in education, employment and housing, as well as in diminishing the pervasiveness of antisemitic stereotypes.[20] Nevertheless, many American Jews in the 1980s believed that there had been a significant rise in antisemitism, owing partly to resentment about Jewish political power (particularly the way it is used on behalf of Israel) and partly to growing hostility between blacks and the American Jewish community. These issues first came together in the mid-1960s with the emergence of a 'Third World' ideology among militant American blacks, linking their struggle at home with that of non-white peoples abroad, oppressed by European and especially American imperialism. Already in 1964 the black nationalist leader Malcolm X had ventilated his anger at the 'Jews who with the help of Christians in America and Europe drove our Muslim brothers out of their homeland [Palestine], where they had been settled for centuries, and took over the land for themselves'.[21] Malcolm X was to be the first in a long line of militant blacks to suggest that American aid to Israel to pursue its 'aggression' against the Third World was taken from the pockets of black taxpayers; and to portray Jewish businessmen in Harlem as 'colonialists' who exploited the Negroes no less than the Western colonialists had oppressed the peoples of Africa and Asia. After 1967, the anti-Zionist rhetoric of the newly created militant Black Panther Party which adopted this outlook became much more explicit, openly identifying Zionism with 'racism' and fascism.[22]

The long-term effects of this radical Third World ideology were clearly to be seen in the 1984 Presidential election campaign of the Reverend Jesse Jackson, the most charismatic

leader in the American black community, whose pro-
Palestinian and anti-Israel stance upset many American Jews.
Jackson's own private references to American Jews as
'Hymies', and above all his reluctance to distance himself from
the antisemitic black Muslim preacher, Louis Farrakhan (who
had called Hitler a 'great man' and Judaism a 'gutter religion'),
added credence to Jewish fears.[23] According to a 1984 survey,
Jews in America held blacks to be more antisemitic than any of
the other groups named in the poll, including Catholics,
fundamentalist Protestants, big business or the State
Department – though there is no clear-cut evidence at a grassroots level for such an unqualified assumption.[24]

Certainly, the hate-filled tirades of Louis Farrakhan, leader
of the Nation of Islam and a preacher with a considerable
following among black audiences in the great American cities,
has contributed to this image – as has the refusal of many
prominent black spokesmen to criticise him directly.
Farrakhan's antisemitism derived from the black Muslim faith
preached by Elijah Muhammad in the 1950s, which was a part
of his general anti-white stance and call for *separation* from
American white society. (Jews, it should be remembered,
were in the early 1960s still among the strongest white
supporters of the *integrationist* civil rights movement among
blacks.) The older, more traditional black ghetto nationalism
which Farrakhan imbibed in his early days included a well-
entrenched hostility to Jews as landlords and merchants in
certain urban black communities.[25] But since the early 1970s
this has been overlaid with leftist nationalist concepts, Third
Worldism, support for the PLO and the acceptance of interest-
free loans from Colonel Muammar al-Qaddafi of Libya. The
most worrying feature of his popular appearances has been the
chord that they have struck among educated, upwardly
mobile blacks. Nevertheless, research tends to show that the
'silent majority' among blacks (including millions of white-
and blue-collar wage-earners) are far more moderate in their
politics and in their attitudes to Jews and to Israel.

The picture that emerges from the more recent research is that some 37 per cent of blacks as against 20 per cent of whites score as antisemitic, with particular emphasis in the black community on the perceived business power of the Jews. However, this prejudice is not significantly greater than that which blacks hold towards other white groups. Less than half of black antisemites are *more* antisemitic than they are generally anti-white, but antisemitism among blacks does appear to increase where there is economic contact with Jews and 'perceived exploitation' – specifically by Jewish merchants, landlords or employers. Undoubtedly, there are also other social and political resentments arising out of various conflicts of interest – those of blacks moving into positions directly beneath those of Jewish professionals, tensions between parts of the new black middle class and Jewish homeowners, or black anger at Jews opposed to 'affirmative action' for Negroes, which would run counter to their own ethos and economic position. Thus there is an 'objective' basis to black antisemitism rooted in real social conflicts, though this should not be reduced to being a mere derivative of anti-white hostility. Blacks, in contrast to most whites, are today far more likely, for example, to accuse Jewish businessmen of shady practices, of being shrewd and tricky, of engaging in unfair competition or of excessive economic power.[26]

More striking still is the fact that antisemitism among blacks today appears to rise with the educational level, whereas the opposite is true among young white Americans. This increase in antisemitism among college-educated young blacks seems to reflect their politicisation and heightened ideological sensitivity, one which has been sharpened by the black power movements of the past twenty years.[27]

Nevertheless, it is significant that Negroes as a whole emerge as significantly less antisemitic than whites when it comes to supporting discriminatory behaviour. As a persecuted minority themselves, Negroes display more opposition to occupational or social club discrimination against Jews, to laws against Jewish immigration or to antisemitic violence of any kind. Neo-Nazi attacks on Jewish stores or synagogues are usually condemned sharply in the black press as expressions of white racist persecution. Thus, although Negroes are more prone to accept negative economic stereotypes about Jews, they are less likely than whites to approve of discriminatory attitudes or practices.[28]

This pattern coincides with the fact that historically black antisemitism has been less of a threat to American Jews than white racism, despite sporadic outbreaks of Negro violence such as the Harlem riots of 1935 which bore an anti-Jewish character. Does the Farrakhan phenomenon constitute a break in that pattern? Certainly, it is remarkable that white hate-groups and individuals, from the Californian 'Aryan' racist Tom Metzger and the Liberty Lobby founder (and patron of Holocaust denial literature) Willis Carto, to leading neo-Nazis and Klansmen, have all expressed sympathy with Farrakhan. Meetings have taken place between these right-wing racists and left-wing black nationalists without yet leading to a serious alliance of white and black antisemites. The white hate-groups still believe in the racial inferiority of blacks but continue to see the Jews (or the so-called 'Zionist Occupation Government') as the evil controlling-force responsible for America's problems. These white groups do not have a mass audience but they undoubtedly express some of the latent hatreds, phobias and paranoia within the majority population. Like Farrakhan, they too focus on the power of the Jewish lobby, use 'anti-Zionist' code-language, like to attack Hollywood and the 'Jewish' media, or blame sexual immorality and 'secular humanism' on the Jews.

Parts of this message may also find an echo among the far more respectable Christian conservative fundamentalists in America, who despite their support for the State of Israel still seem to consider Jews collectively responsible for shedding the blood of Jesus Christ. Other parts of the white suprematist credo are more openly espoused by Louisiana state representative David Duke, whose own racist, antisemitic and neo-Nazi past did not prevent him from winning a very substantial vote in his recent bid for election to the United States Senate.[29] These are warning signals that the 1990s may prove less hospitable to American Jews than the previous three decades. Nonetheless, the American strain of antisemitism seems distinctly less virulent than its European counterparts. Racist bigotry has a plethora of alternative targets against which to focus its animosities.[30] Jews themselves remain vigilant and determined to defend their rights, and as long as American democratic ideals remain intact they are unlikely to succumb.

11
∎ ∎ ∎

France: from Dreyfus to Le Pen

France was the birthplace of Jewish emancipation in Europe, the home of the Great Revolution and the Declaration of the Rights of Man. At the same time *'la grande nation'* has also been a kind of laboratory of antisemitic concepts, ideas and slogans since the nineteenth century, which have demonstrated remarkable intellectual and political continuity until the present day. The theories of integral nationalism, racism and Catholic antisemitism pioneered more than a hundred years ago by writers like Gougenot des Mousseaux, Arthur de Gobineau, Edouard Drumont, Jules Soury, Maurice Barrès and Charles Maurras find more than an echo in the French New Right, in 'revisionist' circles, among Catholic fundamentalists and above all in Europe's largest fascist movement, Le Front National, led by Jean-Marie Le Pen.

This persistence of antisemitism in a country which was not only the first to emancipate the Jews but also the first to permit them to enter the state structure and the highest levels of administration and politics (there have been more Jewish prime ministers in France than in any other country outside Israel) is at first sight surprising. Jews in France during the past two hundred years have, after all, been one of the most assimilated and best integrated Jewish communities anywhere in the world. Their patriotism and commitment to French republican values have been second to none. Moreover, until the First World War this was a decidedly small Jewish community, numbering between 80,000 and 100,000 at the time of the Dreyfus Affair – the event which gave rise to one of the most violent manifestations of antisemitism in fin-de-siècle Europe. Today, ironically enough, when France has the largest Jewish community in Europe (outside the Soviet Union) – variously estimated at between 550,000 and 700,000, antisemitism is less intense than it was a century ago, though it still remains persistent and potentially dangerous.

Traditionally, political antisemitism in France has been strongest on the nationalist and clerical Right, though it has at times been able to draw support from the Left and to cut across regional, class and other barriers. Although violent anti-Jewish riots broke out in Alsace in 1848, there was no organised antisemitic movement before 1870 – the year Henri Gougenot des Mousseaux published a book denouncing the 'Judaisation of the Christian peoples' through the secret forces of freemasonry and the influence of eighteenth-century liberal rationalism. According to des Mousseaux, international Jewry (directed from Paris by the Alliance Israélite Universelle) was aiming to rule the whole world by promoting the shocktroops of liberalism and secularism against Christianity. This reactionary, antimodernist Catholic refrain was repeated in the Abbé Chabauty's book, *Les Juifs, nos maîtres* (1882) and with much greater success in the best-selling *La France Juive*, published by Edouard Drumont in 1886.[1] Drumont was a skilled journalist who combined Catholic, populist, quasi-socialist and frankly racist motifs in a pot-pourri of scandal, gossip and pointed denunciations of social and political corruption which appealed to a mass audience. By 1889 he had founded an Antisemitic League and in 1892 he began editing the influential daily *La Libre Parole*, which concentrated its hatred against the Jews, the Republic and the parliamentary corruption exposed by the Panama Scandal.[2]

Drumont's central thesis was that the Jews had seized power in France since the Revolution of 1789, that they were successfully subverting French traditions and culture, that they controlled the financial system and were expropriating

127

the French labouring masses. He found much support for these myths among the Catholic clergy, which since the 1870s had found itself in intense conflict with the Republic and was seeking a way to recover its political influence. Antisemitism, by depicting the Jews as a symbol of all the liberal, secular, alien and capitalistic elements seeking to de-Christianise France, provided an ideal, integrating ideology for the dis-orientated clergy, which would later align itself whole-heartedly with the Army in the agitation against Dreyfus.[3] The campaign against the Jews did reflect a fundamental social and religious crisis in French society, one which was exacerbated by modernisation and urbanisation but was still more often expressed in traditional Catholic terms.[4]

In the 1890s a whole range of antisemitic organisations were created in France around such ephemeral figures as the Marquis de Morès, Jacques de Biez, Jules Guérin (who organised a section of his Parisian lower-class supporters into anti-Jewish commandos) and Max Régis. The latter was a naturalised Italian who in 1898 was elected Mayor of Algiers and together with Drumont became a member of the anti-semitic faction in the French Chamber of Deputies. Régis and his hot-headed followers among the French 'colons' carried out anti-Jewish atrocities in Algiers.[5] In 1898, the peak year of the Dreyfus Affair, there were also small-scale antisemitic riots in most of the largest French cities, including Paris, Marseille, Lyon, Nantes, Rennes, Tours, Bordeaux and Clermont-Ferrand. The cry 'Death to the Jews' swept France, and for a few months it appeared as one of the most popular weapons in the arsenal of those in the Army, the Church and ultra-nationalist circles who hoped to overthrow the Republic.

The case of Captain Dreyfus, an Alsatian Jew on the French General Staff who had been wrongly convicted (as it turned out) of selling military secrets to the Germans, now divided French society into two camps – for or against the Republic – and it had also exposed a festering, deep-rooted antisemitism. Not only the lower clergy and many provincial Catholics, but also small traders, businessmen, journalists, army officers and members of the liberal professions voted for antisemitic deputies, read the flourishing antisemitic press, supported boycotts against Jewish shops, demonstrated or even joined the Antisemitic Leagues.[6] Nevertheless, Dreyfus was eventually acquitted in 1906 (he had been pardoned in 1899 following a retrial which again found him guilty with 'extenuating circumstances'!) and, more importantly, the Dreyfusards were victorious in their struggle against the enemies of the Republic. Politicians like Clemenceau and Jean Jaurès, officers like Picquart, writers and intellectuals like Emile Zola, Charles Péguy or Marcel Proust, whatever their personal ambivalence towards Jews, did henceforth oppose antisemitism as a matter of principle once the lines of battle were clearly drawn. The eventual success of the Dreyfusards in routing the opposition appeared therefore to vindicate the 'politics of assimilation' which had prevailed in France since the Revolution.[7]

Antisemitism, though temporarily marginalised, nonetheless remained a vehicle for all kinds of grievances and discontent in French society which would resurface between the wars. Politically heterogeneous, it could appear as both radical and conservative, royalist and republican, anticapitalist and anti-Marxist. Above all, as the founder of integral nationalism and Boulangist deputy Maurice Barrès put it in 1889 – it offered a 'national union' against the alien, cosmopolitan Jews, which cut across the division of social classes.[8]

Barrès, himself one of France's most distinguished writers, was an excellent example of that literary antisemitism of the French intelligentsia which from Paul Bourget in the 1880s to Céline and Jean Giraudoux in the 1930s included many first-rate talents as well as successful, popular writers. The anti-Jewish stereotypes disseminated in French letters exercised a great influence, due to the prestige of their authors and the brilliance of their prose.[9] The depiction of Jews as strangers, intruders, cosmopolitan financiers, as rapacious parasites, unscrupulous *parvenus*, or as base, immoral, cowardly, treacherous and dishonest, abounds in French popular fiction.[10] But even among the most sophisticated writers there is a similar sense of the supposedly unassimilable, corrosive nature of the Jew, his shiftiness, his unpleasantly manipulative qualities and cold, abstract intellectuality. Such images can be found in Maupassant, Zola, Bourget, in famous literary personalities like Edmond de Goncourt, Jules Vallès or Alphonse Daudet or in a far more pathological form in Céline's hysterical calls for the destruction of Jewry in the 1930s. Even so eminent a figure as André Gide expressed the wish that the literature of French Jewish writers appear 'in translation' only so as not to contaminate the purity of the French language. Gide's private thoughts on his close friend, the highly assimilated and quintessentially French socialist intellectual Léon Blum, reveal a similar disdain for his 'foreignness'. For Gide it was 'enough that the virtues of the Jewish race are not French virtues'.[11]

The antisemitism of the intelligentsia, particularly evident among academics, journalists, playwrights, painters and cartoonists (three of the most famous – Willette, Jean Forain and Emmanuel Poiré drew hideously anti-Jewish caricatures) no doubt reflected a mixture of snobbery, envy, prickly national sensitivities and the generally hostile climate of public opinion. In the long run this enmity was probably more dangerous than the snobbish antisemitism of the anti-Republican officer class and the hostility of the lower clergy or of the poor, uneducated peasantry with their atavistic notions of Jews as Devils with horns or as mythical incarnations of Antichrist. For it was intellectuals who formulated the new antisemitism, with its modern, 'scientific' pretensions and racial concepts (Gobineau, Jules Soury, Vacher de Lapouge) or its carefully constructed bureaucratic measures to restrict Jewish immigration and naturalisation, to ban Jews from public employment, to withdraw full citizenship, to restore the ghetto or even to expel Jews from France. This was at the heart of the ideology of Drumont, the high-priest of French antisemitism, and also of Charles Maurras, the founder in 1899 of the Royalist Action Française, which remained a political force in France for the next forty years.[12]

Maurras's *antisémitisme d'État* was above all political – aimed at eradicating the influence of the four *'états confédérés'* within the state whom he believed to have seized the levers of command – the Jews, the Protestants, the freemasons and the *métèques* (foreigners). This purging of alien elements would involve sweeping away the satanic Republic and the evil work of the Revolution in order to restore the strong, homogeneous state of the ancient régime – based on the Roman virtues of order, hierarchy and authority. For the 'Catholic' atheist Maurras (proscribed in Rome during the 1920s but rehabilitated by Pope Pius XII in 1939) antisemitism seemed almost 'providential' as an ideological pillar of his counter-revolutionary world-view. In the 1930s Maurras and his disciples, though overtaken by more dynamic groupings on the French Right, were indeed as radical as any of their rivals in the ferocity of their antisemitism, directed with special hatred towards the Popular Front government of 1936 and its Jewish leader, Léon Blum. Such campaigns, led by the nationalist, antisemitic Right in the 1930s, undoubtedly prepared the ground for the lack of public resistance to the racial policies of the Vichy government (1940–4) and its active participation in the deportation of 100,000 French Jews to their deaths.[13]

The anti-Jewish sensibility of the 1930s claimed to be defending France against the fears of revolutionary change – against the spectre of Bolshevism, of the Popular Front, war with Nazi Germany and the inundation of France by foreigners – especially Jewish refugees. It thrived on a sense of French decadence and weakness, of parliamentary disorder, demographic decline and fears of racial pollution whose symbol and cause was supposedly the Jew, whether assimilated patriot or a recent immigrant from the Polish ghettos. The more radical, younger spokesmen of this fascist antisemitism – Lucien Rebatet, Robert Brasillach, Henry Coston and Darquier de

Pellepoix – were openly racist in their outlook, especially towards the immigrant, refugee Jews. But even a republican like the celebrated dramatist Jean Giraudoux complained in 1939 that France was being swamped by hundreds of thousands of lawless, corrupt, racially inferior Ashkenazi Jews who had escaped from the Polish and Rumanian ghettos. They were, he suggested, 'a constant threat to the spirit of precision, of honesty, of perfection which is that of the French artisan class'.[14] Giraudoux, who at the time headed the Commissariat of Information, declared that he was in full agreement with Hitler 'that a policy only attains its highest level if it is based on race, because this was also the thinking of Colbert and Richelieu'.[15]

Within a year of these remarks, the new French government in Vichy under Marshal Pétain, set up after the defeat by Germany, had already passed its first *Statut des Juifs* eliminating Jews from any important position in the Army, civil service, teaching, journalism, theatre or films. A second statute passed in June 1941 set quotas of 2 and 3 per cent respectively for Jews in most professions and in educational institutions. A month later an Aryanisation Law was adopted, permitting government confiscation of Jewish property. These and other measures of Vichy antisemitic legislation designed to eliminate 'all Jewish influence in national life' were not taken under German pressure but reflected an autonomous racist tradition. As legal measures, they met with open opposition from very few Frenchmen, with the approval of growing numbers and with the indifference of the majority. The judicial system not only facilitated legal persecution but in 1942 it became an instrument of the German policy of systematic deportation. The French police provided critical support in enforcing the anti-Jewish policies of an occupying Nazi power that was desperately short of manpower. Indeed, nowhere in Western Europe did the Nazis receive such substantial assistance, and the strictness of the Vichy racial laws even outdid such traditionally antisemitic allies of Germany as Hungary, Rumania and Slovakia.[16]

There is no doubt that the Pétain regime was backed by a large section of the French population who saw nothing wrong with excluding Jews from all but the most menial jobs, even though their families had lived in France for generations. The racial laws were also approved by the Catholic Church, though in 1942 a handful of Catholic priests supported by Protestant Churchmen, appalled by the brutal application of the round-ups of Jews, helped to bring them to a temporary halt.[17] It must also be said that if 70 per cent of French Jews neverthe-less survived the war, despite the institutional antisemitism and daily vilification in the media which took place on an unprecedented scale, this was a result of the help and protection of many non-Jews in France, as well as of their own escape routes and organisations.

The trauma of Vichy and Hitler's genocide did, however, mark the end of the naïve trust which pre-war French Jewry had felt in the French state, which after 1940 had abandoned the universal principles of the Revolution and betrayed its Jewish population.[18] It was, after all, a French government which had set up permanent concentration and labour camps holding thousands of Jews who died of disease, starvation and neglect even before they reached the death trains; it was French gendarmes who hunted Jews down with the help of detailed race-censuses or forced the old, the sick, mothers and even children of three or four into cattle trucks that took them to Poland. It was also a French administration which stamped identity cards with the word '*Juif*', which tolerated hysterical, unrestrained slander of the Jews in the antisemitic press and which encouraged the isolation and stigmatisation of its Jewish population.

For nearly forty years after the war the complicity and collaboration of official France under Pétain in the German 'Final Solution' was barely acknowledged in official French textbooks.[19] Eminent Frenchmen continued to pretend that Pétain had sought to protect Jews despite his racial legislation and the fanatical antisemites in his entourage. More

133

important still, the French government and judiciary have continued until the present to obstruct the trial of high Vichy officials like Paul Touvier (the Lyon *milice* chief hidden for forty years by the Catholic Church) and Maurice Papon, formerly a Gaullist minister and Paris prefect of police, who during 1942–4 had helped deport Jews from Bordeaux. Perhaps the best-known example of all has been that of Réné Bousquet, a prominent French banker, who in 1942–3, as the young Secretary General of the Vichy police, was responsible for co-ordinating with the Nazis the deportation of Jews from the Free Zone. It is currently a socialist government, and a judiciary with much to answer for concerning its condemnation of Jews during the war, that has been delaying the trial of Réné Bousquet.

Another disturbing phenomenon with echoes of the Vichy past is the renewed personality cult of Marshal Pétain in National Front circles, including the recommendation of his nationalist antisemitic programme at its rallies.[20] Taken together with Le Pen's dismissive reference to the Holocaust and to the deportation of Jews from Vichy France and with the spread of 'revisionist'[21] and also notoriously antisemitic Vichy literature, freely available in the bookshops, the old taboos which for a time made antisemitism itself disreputable in post-war France no longer appear to apply. Already in the 1970s *le mode rétro* in films and literature dealing with the Vichy period, the publication of memoirs by former fascist collaborators like Lucien Rebatet, the rediscovery of Céline, the provocative interview in *L'Express* with unrepentant collaborator Darquier de Pellepoix and the fascination with the German SS were all signs of the potentially seductive influence of a rehabilitated and sanitised fascist legacy. Already at that time, a former Pétain admirer, Alfred Fabre-Luce, accused Jews of seeking to deliberately blacken the record of Vichy, and was given a respectful hearing.[22]

Antisemitism had of course never died in post-war France and popular hostility to Jews was still strong – a 1946 opinion poll showed, for example, that over a third of the French population felt that Jews could never become loyal French citizens. The French philospher Jean-Paul Sartre's moving and brilliant analysis *Réflexions sur la Question Juive* (1946) reflects this climate of opinion. After having provided a devastating portrait of the French antisemite as an inauthentic Manichean, a sadistic mediocrity and 'a criminal in the very depths of his heart', he critically observes the silence of his compatriots about the Jews at the end of the war:

> Today those Jews whom the Germans did not deport or murder are coming back to their homes. Many were among the first members of the Resistance; others had sons or cousins in Leclerc's army. Now all France rejoices and fraternises in the streets. . . . Do we say anything about the Jews? Do we give a thought to those who died in the gas chambers at Lublin? Not a word. Not a line in the newspapers. That is because we must not irritate the anti-Semites. . . . Well-meaning journalists will tell you: 'In the interest of the Jews themselves, it would not do to talk too much about them just now.' For four years French society has lived without them; it is just as well not to emphasise too vigorously the fact that they have reappeared.[23]

This uneasy silence on the Jewish question lasted for about twenty years after the war, with prejudices remaining strong, especially on the Right. In the mid-1950s over half of those identifying themselves with the Right denied that 'Israelites' (the polite French term for Jews) were French like anybody else, in a survey conducted in Paris.[24] This poll was taken at a time when the Jewish Prime Minister, Pierre Mendès-France, was the object of scurrilous antisemitic attacks, whose rhetoric at least was reminiscent of the invective directed at Léon Blum in the 1930s. The lower middle-class, populist movement led by Pierre Poujade, which was on the upswing in this same period, had revived some of the classic themes of French antisemitism.

In 1966 another poll indicated that about 20 per of the French population 'held seriously antisemitic opinions'.[25] Exactly a year later, at a notorious press conference following the Six Day War, French President General Charles de Gaulle referred to Jews as 'an élite people, sure of itself and domineering'. This was the first time a major Western head of state since the Second World War had so openly linked criticism of Israel with a stereotypic image of the Jewish people as a whole. Whatever de Gaulle's intentions, it conjured up the image of Jewish power and domination, an arrogant sense of 'chosenness', and encouraged suspicions about Jewish loyalties. In this public statement – designed to explain France's new, pro-Arab foreign policy – de Gaulle not only implied that Israelis were driven by a 'burning ambition for conquest' but managed to hint that Jews in general may have 'provoked' antisemitism in different times and places by their wealth, influence and propaganda. Moreover, Israeli traits of aggressiveness and 'arrogance' were depicted by de Gaulle as if they were inborn Jewish characteristics.[26]

Not surprisingly, the distinguished French-Jewish political commentator Raymond Aron (at one time a strong supporter of de Gaulle) accused the French President of having once more made antisemitism respectable, of having 'knowingly, voluntarily, opened a new era in Jewish history and perhaps in the history of antisemitism'.[27] In fact, de Gaulle's statement expressed a rather traditional prejudice, deeply rooted in the mentality of the French bourgeoisie – one which had been reactivated by the reorientation of French Middle East policy and by irritation at the pro-Israeli attitudes of most French Jews. The spectre of dual allegiance was henceforth to be periodically brandished not only by the Gaullists but by successive French Presidents, who supported the Arab cause and denounced Jewish lobbying.[28] There can be little doubt that French governmental hostility to Israel and its policies also helped to make the display of domestic antisemitism more open, more nonchalant and more respectable in the 1970s.

On the Left, beginning with Fourier and Proudhon, there was a tradition of socialist antisemitism dating from the nineteenth century – which had been attenuated in the wake of the Dreyfus Affair – but had never entirely disappeared. In the aftermath of the Six Day War a section of the French Left which came to see the 'liberation of Palestine' (and consequent dismantling of the Jewish State) as central to their 'anti-imperialist' crusade began to revive this old antisemitism in a new anti-Zionist form. In contrast to the Right, what bothered them was not so much dual loyalties but the fact that Jews were allegedly acting as the 'accomplices' of Israeli colonialism and Western power structures in their repression of Third World liberation.

The Communist Party, still a force in the 1960s and 1970s, had not only whitewashed Soviet antisemitism, but its own neo-Stalinist hostility to Zionism frequently contained more plebeian anti-Jewish insinuations. The pro-Palestinian discourse of the *gauchiste* sects on French campuses even more often oozed an unadulterated antisemitism. Moreover, the left-wing media in the 1970s pioneered new themes and motifs that lent themselves to anti-Jewish manipulation such as the equation of Zionism with racism and Nazism and the portrayal of Israel as a terrorist state practising 'genocide' against the Palestinians.[29] Left-wing French Catholicism combined some of these themes with a more traditional theological animus and disdain for the expression of Jewish ethnic particularism.[30] By the time of the Lebanon war (1982) a partly familiar yet in some respects novel anti-Jewish discourse was in place that contained Christian, Marxist and Third Worldist elements which contributed to a paroxysm of anti-Zionist hysteria in the French media (*'le fascisme aux couleurs d'Israël'*) which had no counterpart in the rest of the Western media.[31] Another new element adding to this litany of hostility has been the rise of Muslim fundamentalism among the growing North African Arab immigrant community in France. Imbibing the negative Jewish stereotypes of radical Islam along with its visceral enmity to Israel, sections of the Muslim population (despite being the prime target of indigenous white racism) have also contributed to the spread of antisemitism in France.

It is still not clear whether the bomb which killed four people outside a Paris synagogue in the Rue Copernic in 1980 was the work of Palestinian terrorists, their left-wing supporters or neo-Nazi groups. It followed a series of bombings and outrages carried out during the previous year against synagogues, schools and other Jewish or Israeli institutions, provoking acute anguish among most French Jews.[32] Over half the respondents to an opinion poll taken shortly afterwards indicated that they felt that antisemitic feeling in France was 'widespread', though only 10–12 per cent felt that there were too many Jews in France or that they were not 'as French' as other citizens. Nevertheless, there was a definite feeling among Jews in particular that the Giscard d'Estaing government's laxness towards Arab terrorism, its unfriendliness towards Israel and its coolness towards the Jewish community had encouraged a climate of opinion in which such actions could flourish. This was reinforced by the 1982 terrorist assault in the Rue des Rosiers on a Jewish delicatessen which left six dead and twenty-two wounded – an event which further heightened the sense of isolation among many French Jews.[33] Although there was no further repetition of such anti-Jewish violence, throughout the 1980s there was a steady flow of desecrations of Jewish graves throughout France, climaxing with the gruesome incident at Carpentras in Provence on 9 May 1990 which seemed symbolic of the recrudescence of the ugly face of French racism.[34] Vandals damaged or destroyed thirty-four graves, while the corpse of an 81-year-old man was exhumed and impaled upon an umbrella. A rash of similar incidents occurred across the country, provoking a mass demonstration in Paris called by Jewish leaders, which included prominent Christians and Muslims as well as most leading French politicians. President François Mitterrand also answered the call, the first time a French President had joined a street demonstration since the Liberation in 1944.[35]

Conspicuous by his absence was the leader of the ultra-Right Front National, Jean-Marie Le Pen, whose party had polled 14.4. per cent of the vote in the April 1988 presidential elections. Until that point the main target of Le Pen's diatribes had been the more than two million Arabs living in France. His appeal of 'La France aux Français' ('France for the French') was aimed at the defence of the French race or *ethnie* against dilution by immigrants from North Africa, against multiculturalism, Communism and cosmopolitan, universalist ideals. His movement has consistently blamed the high unemployment rate in France on the immigrant workers, denounced laxity in law and order and the contemporary decadence of French culture.[36] Anti-Jewish motifs were also apparent in the Front National propaganda during the 1980s, with prominent Jewish personalities like the former Justice Minister Robert Badinter, the former Minister of Health Simone Veil and the converted Jewish-born Archbishop of Paris, Mgr Lustiger, being specially targeted. Simone Veil, an Auschwitz survivor, was accused, for example, of carrying out a 'genocide' against French babies with her abortion bill.[37]

More recently Le Pen has been increasingly explicit in his attacks against 'L'Internationale Juive' and the alleged Jewish control over the French media. The journals and newspapers of the Front National and the radical Right like *Présent*, *National Hebdo*, *Minute* or *Choc du Mois* support the 'revisionist' (i.e. denial of the Holocaust) theorists; they systematically attack Jewish politicians or journalists (the 'Judeo-cosmopolitan-médiocratie'), insinuate dual loyalties at every opportunity and use the language of the pre-war fascist Right.[38] The cult of Jeanne d'Arc, mixed with that of Pétain and of a monolithic Catholic civilisation allied against the forces of 'anti-France' (Jews, Muslims, homosexuals, leftists and other deviants), recalls the familiar traditions of the counter-revolutionary Right in France from de Bonald and de Maistre through Drumont, Barrès and Maurras to Vichy.

Roman-Marie, the closest lieutenant of Le Pen and one of the first ultra-right deputies elected to the European Parliament, openly espouses the conspiratorial theories of *The Protocols of the Elders of Zion*, blaming Jews for fomenting the Russian Revolution and for being one of the foreign super-powers who are 'colonising' France. More recently he expressed his joy at the declarations of the Polish Primate, Cardinal Glemp, concerning the controversy over the Carmelite nuns at Auschwitz and the control which international Jews exercise over the world media. This imaginary monopoly exercised by Jews over the press, television, radio, international communications and finance has once more become a veritable obsession for the ideologues of the radical Right.[39] The opposition of the mainstream media in France to the Front National is conveniently explained away by this alleged conspiracy.

It would be dangerous to underestimate Le Pen and the most powerful fascist movement in Europe since the Nazi era, one which attracted 4.37 million votes from across the social spectrum in the last presidential elections, eclipsing the Communist Party and emerging as a kind of 'national opposition'. This is a mass movement with a charismatic leader and a hate-filled message that is clearly fascist, racist and antisemitic behind its more respectable patriotic and Catholic veneer. Moreover, unlike Barrès, Maurras and the old French Right, which was more literary, ideological and ineffectual, Le Pen, the ex-paratrooper and street brawler, relies on instinct, force and shameless demagogy to make his impact.[40] Primitive anti-Arab racism provides an invaluable method for channelling real social grievances and discontent, but visceral anti-semitism is probably more central to the hard-core militants of the Front National.

When Le Pen made his notorious remark about the Nazi

Holocaust being 'just a detail in the history of the Second World War' he was clearly testing the waters to see how far the climate was receptive to an antisemitism that is so integral to his followers' vision of a White and Christian Europe.[41] His subsequent attacks on government ministers like Michel Durafour (whom he called *'Durafour-crématoire'*, an offensive, Holocaust-related pun on the word for crematorium in French) and on Lionel Stoleru for having 'dual nationality', revealed that the gloves have come off since 1989.[42] Even Israel, which Le Pen once supported for its hard line against Arabs, has been sharply criticised and the fascist leader has become one of the strongest advocates in France of Saddam Hussein, who he praises as a great 'Arab patriot'.

Other Front National figures, like the film-maker Claude Autant-Lara, until very recently a member of the European Parliament, have also gone public with their antisemitic opinions. In a public speech in 1989 which eventually led to his forced resignation from the Parliament, Autant-Lara slandered Simone Veil, cast doubt on the existence of Auschwitz and claimed that France was in the hands of a left-wing dominated by Jewish internationalists and cosmopolitans. Such views are rampant in a movement where, according to a recent opinion poll, 77 per cent of its members agreed that they hated Jewish people.[43] This is of course considerably higher than the average in the French population as a whole, where, if a 1990 survey is to be believed, 'only' 20 per cent said they disliked Jews and 24 per cent that there were too many Jews in France. No less than 90 per cent said the same about Arabs![44] But for the radical Right, the racism is always *en bloc* – anti-Arab, antisemitic, anti-Israel and also anti-black.

Apart from the growing popularity of 'revisionist' literature in France, most of the themes in Front National literature belong to classic antisemitism: the assertion of ubiquitous Jewish power in banking, the international economy, politics and the media. The Jew is portrayed as a stateless nomad, connected only to the shadowy 'Jewish international conspiracy' which strives to win control over France, Europe and ultimately the world. The influence of this propaganda is once again growing and finding expression on the streets in graffiti, in attacks on synagogues, desecrations of cemeteries, in hate-mail and acts of violence against individual Jews and Jewish or Israeli institutions.

A similar language can be heard among the conservative-Catholic *intégristes* who condemn the Vatican for its doctrinal liberalism and describe their enemies as part of a Judeo–Masonic–Republican conspiracy against the true faith. For an *intégriste* like the Abbé Laguérie, for example, the Archbishop of Paris, Cardinal Lustiger, is only a 'so-called Catholic' whose Judaism 'is always ready to peep out', who is 'more Jewish than Catholic' and who believes that Israel, not Christ, is the Messiah. The *intégristes* share the belief of the Front National that there is a media conspiracy of 'antiracist' organisations manipulated by Jews, who in reality provoke and stir up an anti-French racism in the country. With their traditional Catholic theology of the Jews as a God-rejected people, they provide a religious underpinning to the xenophobic racism of the Front National.[45]

The recent upsurge in French antisemitism cannot therefore be dismissed as an ephemeral or marginal phenomenon. It has to be seen against a wider background of resentment at Third World immigration, at the growth in Muslim fundamentalism within France, at the paralysis of government and of the political parties, worries over unemployment, over a falling birth-rate, a newly unified Germany and economic fears about the European free-for-all in 1992. Many of these anxieties may be irrational, but it has always been easier to displace them on to immigrants and Jews, especially in a country where the ghosts of Dreyfus and of Vichy have never been laid. The myth of 'Jewish power' has for at least a century struck a chord in part of the French population, and with the end of the post-war taboo on open, public antisemitism it is being more vocally expressed. For the moment less popular than the hatred of Arabs, its profile is nonetheless being heightened. As the news editor of Radio Beur (a radio station for Arab immigrants), Abdel Aissou, puts it, the radical Right 'uses racism and antisemitism as a two-stage, rocket. By lighting the first stage, of anti-Arab racism . . . they want to kick the Arabs out of France. . . . But when they attack the Jews they want to wipe them off the map of the world.'[46]

France is not, of course, an antisemitic state, nor is the level of contemporary antisemitism as yet comparable to that of the 1930s. Jews play a very active role in its cultural and political life – indeed there have never been so many Jewish Cabinet ministers and prominent advisers as during President Mitterrand's Presidency of the 1980s.

The Jewish community is the only one among those in the Western democracies to have significantly increased in size since 1939, when it numbered 300,000, to over 600,000 in 1990. Not only is it the largest Jewish community on the European continent, but also, thanks to its majority Sephardic component (over 250,000 North African Jews have settled in France since the mid 1950s), it has a vibrant ethnic and religious identity which is more self-assertive than that of its Ashkenazi brethren before the war and more emotionally attached to Israel. It is both culturally integrated and at the same time vigilant and militant in its self-defence against antisemitism. It has also benefited from the relative toleration of the Socialist government in France for 'the right to be different', though this era may already be fading. Furthermore, given its numbers, its activism, its enterprise and defence of its interests, this is a community which cannot be ignored by the French political establishment. Despite tensions between it and the government over Middle Eastern policy, its objective position has probably never been better.

All the major political parties except for the Front National have publicly opposed antisemitism. There has, moreover, rarely been such a degree of political stability or consensus over the basic republican institutions in France as during the past thirty years; nor so little ideological polarisation between the mainstream Left and Right. The French intelligentsia since the Second World War has no longer thrown up antisemitic writers and ideologues of real talent like Drumont, Barrès, Maurras, Céline, Brasillach and Drieu la Rochelle who could provide a convincing intellectual or aesthetic underpinning to movements like that of Le Pen.

Indeed, France itself has changed since the 1960s beyond recognition, emerging as an industrially modern and technological society, more mobile, European, cosmopolitan and reconciled to the 'spirit of capitalism' than at any earlier period in its history. All these broader societal factors make the prospects for a full and successful Jewish integration seem bright. Nevertheless, the ideological continuity in French antisemitism has shown remarkable persistence, and the power of ancient stereotypes of the Jew nurtured on Catholic, nationalist, populist and racist myths continues to cast its shadow into the 1990s.

12
■ ■ ■

East European Nationalisms

Throughout Eastern Europe between the two world wars the 'Jewish question' and antisemitism became a socio-economic, cultural and political issue of the first importance. Newly created or restructured nation-states like Rumania, Hungary, Czechoslovakia and Poland had to contend with intractable internal and external difficulties, many of them deriving from the ethnic diversity of the region. In all these countries there were substantial Jewish communities whose occupational structure, levels of acculturation and political orientations posed serious problems for mixed-nationality states which had not yet industrialised, which often lacked a fully crystallised 'native' bourgeoisie and whose sometimes fragile national identity was threatened by powerful neighbours to the East and West.

Antisemitism thrived in this environment on the weakness of liberal democratic traditions, the absence of sustained economic growth, the endemic political instability, the consuming fear of Communism felt by traditional ruling élites and on all-pervasive, intolerant chauvinism. In the 1990s, with the collapse of a Communist tyranny that kept these nations in a vice-like grip for forty years, many of the old, pre-war ideologies and political parties have resurfaced with a vengeance. Along with a virulent anti-Communism, reinforced by the bitter experience of four decades, traditional peasant and Christian values wrapped up in populist demagogy have revived. The resurgence of antisemitism in contemporary Eastern Europe – traditionally linked with conservative nationalism, populism and anti-Communism — must be seen against this background.[1]

Rumania is a particularly interesting case, since, with the exception of Tsarist Russia, it alone among European states before the First World War refused to emancipate its Jews.[2] Only in 1919, under Allied pressure, did the Rumanians promise absolute equality to all citizens without distinction of race, religion or language. As a result of the Peace Treaties which brought what was formerly Hungarian Transylvania, Austrian Bukovina and Russian Bessarabia into the Rumanian nation-state, its Jewish community came to number around 750,000 in 1930. This increased the traditional Judeophobia which was part of the general hatred of foreigners in Rumania and the suspicion, especially in Transylvania, that Jews were agents and natural allies of the former Hungarian rulers. Rumanian antisemites were also quick to denounce alleged Jewish domination of the economy, though many Rumanian Jews were in reality extremely poor.

In the 1920s violent antisemitism was mainly the province of university students and of the radically anti-Jewish League of National Christian Defence, led by Professor Alexandru Cuza, which helped foment riots against Jews in Transylvania.[3] The Rumanian students were especially attracted to a militant, xenophobic, anti-Communist brand of antisemitism. The large number of Jewish students, their 'foreign' origin (i.e. as formerly Hungarian, German or Russian citizens) and the general economic insecurity favoured this stance and support for the radical Right in the 1930s. The Iron Guard Movement led by Corneliu Codreanu, a fanatically anti-Communist disciple of Cuza, was strongly influenced by the German Nazi model, proclaiming the 'Jewish question' to be a life-and-death issue for Rumania. By 1937 the third strongest party in the state with 16 per cent of the total vote, the Iron Guard openly called for the destruction of the Jews. The government felt obliged to appease the extremists by itself adopting a programme calling for removal of the Jews from the economy and the universities, for the expulsion of Jews who had entered Rumania after 1918 and other drastic measures.[4] Although King Carol acted against the Iron Guard, by 1939 about a third of Rumanian Jews had been deprived of their citizenship, and under the National Legionary State of Marshal Antonescu established in September 1940, Rumanian Jewry would be terrorised by an openly antisemitic regime. The Iron Guard celebrated its revived power with a bloody pogrom in the Rumanian capital, Bucharest, in January 1941; the majority of Jews in Bukovina and Bessarabia were murdered with alacrity and great cruelty by Rumanian (and German) troops, expelled or sent to concentration camps. But for political reasons (the desire to preserve a modicum of sovereignty in internal affairs and to keep his Western options open) Antonescu did not accede to German pressure to mass murder the Jews of the Regat or of southern Translyvania. As a result more Jews were saved under Rumanian rule during the Holocaust than in any other country of Eastern Europe, despite the strength of indigenous antisemitism and the presence of such a powerful local fascist movement. Out of the 800,000 Jews who lived in Rumania in 1939 385,000 perished during the Holocaust, and the overwhelming majority of those who survived emigrated in the post-war years, mainly to Israel.[5]

Today there are approximately 20,000 Jews left in Rumania, yet with the end of the Ceaucescu era the antisemitism which had been officially suppressed by an authoritarian Communist regime has now returned in force. There are not only desecrations of synagogues and antisemitic graffiti, but also articles in the Rumanian press representing the Jews as Satan or Antichrist, blaming them for having imposed the Communist scourge on post-war Rumania. Remnants of the old fascist Iron Guard have also returned from abroad or revived inside the country. Increasingly, there are efforts to rehabilitate Marshal Antonescu, the nation's wartime fascist leader. The spokesman of the traditionalist National Peasants'

Party, Valentin Gavrielscu, expresses outrage that Rumania's
Prime Minister, Petre Roman, is of Jewish origin – 'a disgrace
to our Revolution', while on the walls of Bucharest one can
find graffiti with a Star of David under pictures of Roman and
Silviu Brucan, the chief ideologist of the ruling National
Salvation Front.[6] These are worrying signs in Rumania's
fragile democracy, where a breakdown of law and order, as the
country's Chief Rabbi Moses Rosen has warned, can mean
pogroms.

Rabbi Rosen's own role under the Ceaucescu regime is itself
a problem, for the Balkan dictator allowed the Jewish community freedom of worship as long as the Chief Rabbi could
assure the Western world that Rumanian Jews lived well
under Communism. The official policy under Ceaucescu had
indeed been two-faced, permitting Rumania's Jews greater
autonomy than that allowed under any other Communist
regime, while tolerating antisemitic writings of a sometimes
virulent nature. Rumania did not break off diplomatic relations with Israel in 1967 and encouraged it to 'buy' Jews from
the Rumanian government for a price depending on the
citizen's value to each state.[7] This policy of semi-independence
from Moscow and the silence on human rights abuses in
Rumania (in which Rabbi Rosen is alleged to have acquiesced)
helped Ceaucescu acquire the economically advantageous
'most favoured nation' status with the United States.

In public opinion, however, resentment was stirred by the
perception that Jews enjoyed better conditions than other
Rumanians or ethnic minorities under the Ceaucescu regime.
For the Jews, already associated by many Rumanians with the
post-war imposition of Communism on their country, such
notions have helped to feed the visceral cultural and religious
antisemitism which is endemic to Rumania.[8] The revival of the
historic pre-war parties for whom Jews and Communism were
always synonymous has exacerbated this trend. Not by chance
has the role of the 'diabolical' Anna Pauker, post-war
Rumania's Stalinist Foreign Minister, with her Jewish back-

ground as the daughter of a Moldavian rabbi, been heavily underlined in the Rumanian press after the downfall of the Ceaucescu dictatorship. Needless to say, the fact that Jews also suffered under the Stalinist terror, along with other Rumanians, is today forgotten in the mood of overheated nationalism and suspicion of all minorities – whether they be Hungarians, Gypsies or Jews.

Hungarian Jewry, in contrast to that of Rumania, was already before 1914 one of the most assimilated Jewries in the world, playing a central role in the economy and cultural life of the nation. From their legal emancipation in 1867 right until the collapse of the Habsburg Empire in 1918, the 'Magyarised' Hungarian Jews, almost a million in number and 5 per cent of the total population of Greater Hungary, enjoyed almost optimal conditions for their development. They were indispensable for preserving Magyar hegemony in outlying areas like Slovakia, Transylvania and the subcarpathian Rus – a role which aroused antisemitic sentiments among the Slovak, Rumanian and German minorities who lived under Hungarian rule. But the ruling aristocratic élite in pre-1918 Hungary, eager to modernise the country and imbued with liberal ideas, welcomed the Jews as partners and encouraged their full integration. The Jews took over the role of the absent Hungarian middle-class, concentrating their talents in industry, business, commerce and the professions – in which they came to play by 1900 an absolutely preponderant part.[9] Interestingly enough, Jewish assimilation and economic success did not produce an antisemitic backlash of comparable intensity in pre-1918 Hungary to that which occurred in either Germany or Austria. Although the Jews were seen as a group apart and suffered some social snobbery at the hands of the ruling élite, the alliance was mutually beneficial and the Hungarian government repressed open antisemitism more firmly than in neighbouring Austria.

Nevertheless, two distinct and temporarily influential antisemitic movements did develop in Old Regime Hungary. The first, which was led by the Liberal deputy Victor von Istoczy, won its greatest success in 1883 when it returned seventeen antisemitic deputies to the Hungarian Parliament, following the agitation and riots that surrounded the notorious Tisza–Eszlar ritual-murder trial a year earlier.[10] But its strong links with the antisemitic movement in Germany made it appear too anti-Magyar to many Hungarians, and it had no clear position on the critical issue of relations with Habsburg Austria. Moreover, the Hungarian government, fearing that attacks on Jews would end with an assault on the great landowners, did everything they could to neutralise its influence. By 1885 the party had begun to break up, and for a decade antisemitism virtually disappeared from the parliamentary arena. In the late 1890s the Catholic People's Party focused its attacks against what it held, in Nathaniel Katzburg's words, to be 'destructive ideas introduced and disseminated by Jews, such as liberalism, socialism, cosmopolitanism and similar currents of thought, regarded as anti-Christian, unpatriotic and alien to the deep-rooted Magyar tradition'.[11] But this type of Catholic antisemitism had nothing like the resonance which Karl Leuger's populist movement achieved in Vienna during the same period, and Jewish assimilation in Hungary proceeded apace.

What transformed antisemitism into a serious political force in Hungary was the catastrophic effects of defeat in the First World War and the Trianon Treaty, as a result of which Hungary lost 60 per cent of its population and 70 per cent of its territory. The demise of the old multi-national state meant that the Hungarian ruling class no longer needed the Jews as 'agents' of Magyarisation in the peripheral regions which it had lost. Moreover, in the harsher economic conditions of post-1918 Hungary, where unemployment was growing, a 'native' Hungarian middle class began to compete with Jews in commerce, industry and the free professions.[12] Discrimination was introduced into the state bureaucracy and a *numerus clausus* law of 1920 restricted Jewish access to the Hungarian universities. Above all, the national trauma and humiliation of

1918 was immediately followed by a Communist coup led by Bela Kun (a Transylvanian Hungarian of Jewish origin) in whose short-lived government 31 out of 49 People's Commissars were Jews.[13] Although the Red Terror did not spare Jewish capitalists or traditional, orthodox Jewry, it was perceived by many Hungarians as anti-Christian and anti-Magyar in its essence, acting under the guidance of a hostile foreign power, the Soviet Union. A venomous antisemitic literature came into existence as a consequence, in which Hungary was depicted as being enslaved to the Jews.

Nationalism in inter-war Hungary increasingly shed its liberal ethos, becoming authoritarian, closed in on itself and hostile to the Jews, though traditional Old Regime politicians like Admiral Horthy and Count Bethlen resisted efforts to revoke Jewish civil rights or damage Jewish financial interests. But in 1932 Gyula Gömbös, a military officer influenced by Nazi racial doctrines, who stood for a 'Christian Hungary' free of Jewish influence, came to power.[14] The Hungarian radical Right continued to grow in influence throughout the decade and by 1938–9 Jewish participation in industry, commerce, banking, law, medicine, government employment and the universities had been drastically reduced. During the Second World War a total of 564,507 Hungarian Jews were killed, despite the fact that the Germans did not begin deportations until May 1944. This ghastly slaughter would not have been possible without the full collaboration of the Hungarian police, gendarmerie, civil servants and other officials. Only the entry of the Red Army in January 1945 saved the remaining 250,000 Jews in Budapest.[15]

As in Poland, antisemitic pogroms occurred almost immediately after the war, in protest against the payment of reparations to Jews who had suffered losses and against alleged black marketing activities. At the same time, Communists of Jewish origin like Mátyas Rákosi (General Secretary of the post-war Hungarian Communist Party) played a key role in the Sovietisation of the country. Rákosi, a faithful ally of Stalin, who had spent the war years in Moscow, dominated the political scene for the next decade. Many of his leading lieutenants were Jews like Ernö Gerö, Mihály Farkas, Zoltán Vas and József Révai, while a disproportionate number of high police officials (including the head of the political police, Major General Gabor Peter) were also of Jewish origin.[16] As in Poland and Rumania, these facts gave some plausibility to the pre-war stereotypes identifying Jews with Communism, and resentment was particularly heightened by the prominence of Jews in the apparatus of repression. Nevertheless, the popular revolution in the streets of Budapest in October 1956 against Stalinist rule did not lead to pogroms or to open expressions of antisemitism on any significant scale – possibly because Jews were also well represented among the anti-Stalinist reform Communists. The new regime of Janos Kádár also avoided using antisemitism as a means to establish its popular legitimacy and did not exclude Jews from positions of responsibility, though it did not parade them in its top leadershp either. A good example of Kádár's balanced policy was his refusal to tolerate the kind of rampant 'anti-Zionist' antisemitism which occurred in the Soviet Union, Poland and Czechoslovakia after 1968. At the same time public discussion of the 'Jewish question' and of Hungarian collaboration during the Holocaust was for a long time virtually suppressed. As a result the 'Jewish question' was never really addressed in Hungary but was simply swept under the carpet.[17]

During the Kádár years, a new antisemitism nevertheless began to grow from below, among a section of the middle classes, vehemently anti-Marxist and opposed to the dissident intellectuals (a high proportion of whom were Jewish) who were regarded as 'alien elements'.[18] Since the collapse of Communist rule it has come more visibly to the surface (as in other East European countries), along with the revival of nationalism, populism and the ideology of the pre-war peasant writers' movement. Some observers have seen residues of this right-wing nationalist antisemitism in the Democratic Forum

Party which won Hungary's parliamentary elections in April 1990.[19] Many of its members are from the minor intelligentsia whose advance was blocked by the Communists, and some harbour a patent resentment of the urbanised Jewish intelligentsia with their international connections – many of whom are prominent in the rival Free Democrats movement. Thus a division which was characteristic of Hungarian history before 1939 – between a cosmopolitan, social democratic, intellectual, Westernised and 'Jewish' Budapest and the more 'national', 'Christian' peasant countryside, has returned to haunt Hungary fifty years later. Nevertheless, life in Hungary for its 80–100,000 remaining Jews (the largest community in Eastern Europe) is more tolerable than in the neighbouring countries, and there has been a resurgence of cultural activity alongside the signs of an increase in popular antisemitism.[20]

In contrast to Hungarian, Rumanian or Polish Jews, their co-religionists in independent pre-war Czechoslovakia had enjoyed a far more congenial environment, relatively free of antisemitism. This had not always been the case, for in Habsburg Austria and Hungarian-ruled Slovakia before 1918, Czechoslovakian Jews had found themselves caught in a crossfire of national conflicts which adversely affected their interests. There had been no Czech-Jewish alliance comparable to that existing in Hungary, and already in the 1840s there had been anti-Jewish riots in Prague directed against Jewish entrepreneurs and protesting against the identification of Bohemian Jews with German language, culture and political aspirations. One of the founders of Czech nationalism, the radical publicist Karel Havlíček-Borovský, described the Jews in 1846 as 'a separate Semitic nation which lives only incidentally in our midst and sometimes understands or speaks our language'.[21] The language issue was indeed of critical importance to nineteenth-century Czech nationalists, who placed great pressure on Jews to abandon German-language schools in Bohemia and Moravia, which were perceived as a thorn in the flesh of the Czech national renaissance. Jewish reluctance to comply was seen as a slap in the face to the Czechs, fighting to assert their national rights against the large German minority in the Czech lands, and against the refusal of the Habsburg State to give them equality with the ruling nations of the Dual Monarchy.

In the 1890s anti-Jewish violence exploded against the Jews in Prague and in parts of the Czech countryside, against a background of intense and bitter conflict with the Germans. This Czech antisemitism had religious and economic facets as well as a nationalist dimension.[22] It culminated in the Hilsner ritual-murder case in Polna (Bohemia), which greatly exacerbated the atmosphere.[23] Although Thomas Masaryk, the future President of Czechoslovakia, denounced this irrational medieval superstition, he was disowned at the time by most of the Czech press.[24] Calls for a boycott of Jewish traders and slogans like 'Buy only from Christians' were encouraged by the lower clergy and by nationalist agitators at the end of the century. In 1899 there were a series of anti-Jewish disturbances in Bohemian and Moravian towns, with widespread assaults on Jewish property.[25]

After 1900 this agitation against Jews subsided, but it revived briefly during the First World War and its aftermath, with allegations against Jewish profiteering and continued resentment at the loyalty of the Jewish community to the Habsburg cause. This mistrust was somewhat mitigated by the support which the Zionist movement and the American Jewish community gave to Masaryk in his bid to win Allied support for Czech independence during the war. Masaryk's warm sympathy for Zionism and his commitment to full Jewish equality in the new Czechoslovak state after 1918 partly reflected his gratitude for this important help. The new Czech leadership, though far from uniformly pro-Jewish, was conscious of the dangers of antisemitism and sought to limit its malignant influence where possible.

It could not, however, prevent the spontaneous eruption of anti-Jewish disturbances in Prague in November 1920[26] (though this was the last such instance in independent Czechoslovakia) or the continuing undercurrent of social and political antisemitism which persisted until the German invasion of 1939. This was especially true in the German-speaking Sudetenland and in the much less developed, agrarian and overwhelmingly Catholic region of Slovakia, where a religious, economic and nationalist antisemitism had already flourished before 1918. Slovaks had especially resented the Jews as instruments of oppressive pre-war Magyar rule and claimed that Jewish store-keepers, merchants and industrialists dominated the local economy.[27] After 1918 they perceived the Jews as agents of Czech domination, and antisemitism became closely linked to the movement for Slovak independence. It was reinforced by the anti-Jewish doctrines of the Roman Catholic Church, which profoundly shaped Slovak nationalism. The clerical, authoritarian ethos of Slovakia in the 1930s was very different from the liberal, tolerant politics that developed in the more industrialised Czech lands under Masaryk's leadership.[28] In March 1939 German troops put an end to the Czech Republic and 277,000 Jews out of a pre-war population of 357,000 were annihilated by the Nazis, some of them with the collaboration of the clerico-fascist Slovak regime.

By 1950 there were fewer than 20,000 Jews left in post-war Czechoslovakia, three-quarters of the Jewish community having emigrated in the wake of the Communist coup. Nevertheless, the General Secretary of the ruling Party was a veteran Communist of Jewish origin, Rudolf Slansky, who together with eleven other leading 'Jewish' Communists would be tried and sentenced to death for alleged crimes against the state in 1952. The charges in this notorious Stalinist show-trial included allegations of collaborating with Western imperialism, with Titoists, Trotskyites and especially with 'Zionists'. The antisemitic tone of the proceedings was unmistakeable and partly orchestrated by Soviet advisers from Moscow. The Czech Communist media openly encouraged this incitement, which reached heights redolent of wartime Nazi-style Judeophobia in occupied Czechoslovakia.[29] This neo-Stalinist and 'anti-Zionist' type of antisemitism, which accused Jews of being a fifth column of subversive intriguers against the socialist fatherland, was repeated in the wake of the Russia invasion of Czechoslovakia and the crushing of the Prague Spring in August 1968. For the next twenty years, until the recent overthrow of Communist rule in Czechoslovakia, the existence of the tiny Jewish community (numbering around 12,000 today) was frozen in a time-warp. Jewish history was systematically distorted, its religious and cultural life destroyed, and for the first time in its thousand-year-old history the Jewish community did not have a rabbi between 1970 and 1984.[30] A politically motivated antisemitism masquerading under the guise of hostility to Israel and to Zionism was allowed free rein and was virtually indistinguishable from that which prevailed in the USSR.

Today, Czech Jews have been liberated from this nightmare and Jewish issues are once more discussed sympathetically and freely in the Czech media. The new President Vaclav Havel appears to be renewing the more liberal pre-war tradition of Thomas Masaryk in his friendly relations with Israel and with the Jewish population of his country. Although popular antisemitism has not disappeared, particularly in Slovakia, it is significantly — as in the pre-1939 era — less evident than in most neighbouring East European states, where the ghosts of the past are once more resurgent.

13
■ ■ ■

Poland: Antisemitism without Jews

In 1939, on the eve of the German invasion, Poland contained the largest Jewish community in Europe, numbering around 3,460,000 persons. As a result of the devastating Nazi Holocaust the Jewish population had fallen to 250,000 in 1945, many of them having returned from the USSR, where they spent the war years after Poland's eastern territories were annexed by the Soviet Union. Before the war Jews had already suffered from an increasingly hysterical and nationalistic Polish antisemitism which led to the deaths of hundreds of Jews in the late 1930s, to economic boycotts, government discrimination and open calls from most Polish political parties for the mass emigration of Jews.[1] The nationalist doctrine of 'Poland for the Poles' was exceedingly popular in a newly independent state with many national minorities (Ukrainians, Byelorussians, Germans, etc.) and an immensely creative Jewish community that represented over 10 per cent of the total population.

An intensely chauvinist, xenophobic antisemitism was particularly central to the ideology of Poland's largest opposition movement, the National Democrats (Endeks), and it also exerted an influence on the authoritarian, post-Pilsudski regime which came to power after 1935.[2] The National Democrats believed the Jews were fundamentally unassimilable and intransigent enemies of the Polish national cause. After the Soviet invasion of 1920 they were also charged by Endeks with supporting Bolshevism and being bent on destroying the traditional social order. This myth of 'Jewish

Communism' (*Zydo-Komuna*) which has never really died in Poland, would have a devastating effect on Polish-Jewish relations for the next seventy years.

At the same time Jews were also attacked for having a disproportionate influence in Poland's economic and intellectual life, and the drastic reduction of the Jewish role in the Polish economy was even declared a government aim in the mid-1930s.[3] There was a certain plausibility to these demands in so far as Jews constituted (as in most other East European countries) a very high proportion of all doctors, lawyers, educators, journalists and publishers; in commerce they were ubiquitous and in the largest Polish cities like Warsaw, Lodz, Vilna, Lwow and Cracow they formed between a quarter and a third of the entire population.[4] Moreover, the distinctiveness of their religion, customs, speech, dress and culture in a predominantly agrarian and intensely Catholic society inevitably provided a constant source of tension, conflict and pressure for assimilation.

The very influential and deeply conservative Catholic Church was a particularly active promoter of pre-war antisemitism. Although opposing Nazi racial doctrines, it condemned the Jews as 'atheists', revolutionaries and subverters of Catholic morality. The Primate of the Church, Cardinal Hłond, even declared publicly in 1936 that 'the Jews are committing frauds and dealing in white slavery'.[5] They were widely seen by the Catholic hierarchy as a threat to the Polish tradition and national spirit. In the Polish countryside, too, the peasantry tended towards a more instinctive antisemitism, influenced by the priests and by its own folk superstitions, including an atavistic belief in ritual murder that has not disappeared to this day.

But such religious prejudice, cultural estrangement or nationalistic persecution, while vividly remembered by Jews, was overshadowed for most Poles by the devastating blows inflicted by the Nazis during the Second World War, in which Poland itself suffered three million dead, lost her independence and eventually fell, after 1945, under Soviet domination. The Jewish historian Emmanuel Ringelblum, who witnessed the Holocaust in Poland, paid tribute to the magnanimity of those common Polish people who made great sacrifices to save Jews during the war, but was on the whole deeply disappointed by the passivity of most Poles (including the underground resistance) in the face of Nazi atrocities against Jews. Their apathy and long-standing hostility seemed, if anything, to intensify during the course of the war.[6] Some Poles even rejoiced openly that Hitler appeared to be solving the 'Jewish Question' for them, albeit in a brutally Germanic fashion; some unfairly blamed the Jews for their lack of resistance to the Germans or else, like the more simple-minded peasants in the countryside, imagined that this was a divine punishment for the Jews having killed Christ. On the other hand there is no basis to the widespread legend that Poles 'collaborated' in the 'Final Solution' or that the Nazis placed the death-camps in Poland because it was considered such an antisemitic country.

If 'collaboration' was impossible in the light of the German determination to enslave the Poles and physically liquidate their élites, there was nonetheless considerable approval among Polish nationalists and fascists for Hitler's Jewish policy.[7] Moreover, during the war itself, Poles materially benefited from the liquidation of Jewish businesses, property and homes by the Nazis – a fact which drove a wedge between Poles and Jews after 1944 when Jews in their thousands returned from the East to reclaim what had previously belonged to them. The already embittered relationship was made worse by Polish claims that Jews in Eastern Poland had welcomed the Soviet invaders in 1939 with open arms;[8] that they were disproportionately represented in the Soviet security policy; and that the Jewish 'Muscovites' (Polish Communists who had spent the war years in the USSR) had returned to Polish soil with the Red Army in 1944–5 in order to dance on Poland's grave.

Between 1944 and 1947 tens of thousands of Poles were killed in the civil war being fought over the future of the country, among them some 1,500 Jews who fell victim to specifically antisemitic assaults. Lucjan Dobroszycki writes: 'Jews were killed when they came to ask for the return of their houses, workshops, farms, and other property. They were assaulted when they tried to open stores or workshops. Bombs were placed in orphanages and other Jewish public buildings. Jews were shot by unknown snipers and in full view of witnesses. Jews were attacked in their homes and forcibly removed from buses and trains.'[9] Some of these physical attacks were carried out by the anti-Communist underground, convinced that Jews were betraying Poland and the Poles to the hated Soviet occupation forces.

Amidst the general brutalisation engendered by the Nazi occupation and its immediate, post-war aftermath, human life – and especially that of the massacred Jews – had become cheap. The full-scale pogrom of July 1946 which erupted in Kielce (a town notorious for its pre-war antisemitism), during which about forty Jews were killed and more than seventy-five wounded, revealed the extreme physical vulnerability of the remnants of Polish Jewry which had survived the Holocaust. Some saw the pogrom, (which had been sparked off by a blood libel,) as a spontaneous eruption of anti-Jewish feeling which was part of the general hysterical atmosphere in post-war Poland. The right-wing elements and some prominent Catholic bishops blamed it on 'Jewish provocation'; others, like Poland's deputy premier Mikolajczyk, accused the Communists of a deliberate 'provocation' in order to discredit their non-Communist rivals as fascist antisemites in the eyes of Western opinion; while the Communists themselves declared that the pogrom was the work of ultra-nationalistic extremists.[10] Whatever the real causes, about 100,000 Jews emigrated from Poland in the following year, and another 50,000 would leave between 1948 and 1950. It was already apparent to most of them that despite, or perhaps as a result of, the Holocaust, antisemitism had become even more violent in Poland than it was before 1939.

Those Jews who nevertheless remained in Poland, did for the most part have a genuine commitment to the building of a new classless, Communist society.[11] In the period after 1948 some, like Jakob Berman, Hilary Minc or Roman Zambrowski, rose to top positions in the Party, the security services and in economic planning. They were probably considered more reliable agents by Moscow than Polish Communists like Gomulka, who were suspected of nationalist 'deviations'. By the same token these 'Muscovites' were especially hated by the Polish population, not only as Jews but for serving an alien Communist system of quasi-colonial servitude imposed by the Soviet Union. During the Polish October of 1956 the 'Jewish' Stalinists were a convenient scapegoat for popular wrath, and on a visit to Warsaw the Russian Communist leader Nikita Khrushchev encouraged his Polish comrades to purge them as a means of restoring the popularity of the Party.[12]

With the restoration of Gomulka to power after 1957, a more openly nationalistic ideology became a prominent feature of Communist propaganda. It stressed the 'Polishness' of Poland, which in the post-war era, as a result of the German massacres and territorial changes, had in any case lost its old multi-ethnic character, becoming mono-cultural and virtually homogeneous. Although antisemitism had traditionally been viewed by Communists as a reactionary petty-bourgeois ideology, or else as a by-product of fascism, it now became clandestinely incorporated into the neo-Stalinist variant of Polish chauvinism – above all as a political lever in internal party struggles. From the early 1960s Jews (who by this time numbered a little over 30,000 in a population of over thirty million people) were being slowly removed from their remaining high positions in the party and state administration as well as from the civilian and military security apparatus.[13] Senior officials of Jewish origin were under surveillance, and a full card index for Polish Jewry was already being prepared. Plans for a complete purge of Jews from *all* positions of influence were in place even before the Six Day War of 1967 and the student riots of early 1968 which provided the necessary pretext to implement this policy.

The antisemitic campaign that was unleashed in 1967–8 under the official banner of 'anti-Zionism' had little in common with the agitation in pre-war Poland, which had at least been related to some kind of sociological reality – namely, the existence of a three-million-strong national minority with its own distinct culture on Polish soil.[14] The witch-hunt of 1968, which forced two-thirds of Poland's remaining Jews into emigration, was about the manipulation of myths in the service of a battle for power between two warring Communist Party factions – those of Gomulka and of his challenger General Moczar. The latter appealed to a traditional Polish chauvinism, to anti-Russian sentiment and to an antisemitism that attracted young party careerists, seeking to move up the apparatus, as well as members of the Veterans' Association (Zbowid) which was Moczar's political base. His supporters proposed an even more nationalist Communism than that of Gomulka, purged of 'Jewish' cosmopolitanism and of Marxist 'revisionism' – an allegedly Jewish or 'Judaising' vice of reformist intellectuals.

Gomulka, as Party leader, countered Moczar's campaign by adopting his own more moderate brand of antisemitism, singling out Polish Jews in a speech of 19 June 1967 as instigators of an anti-Soviet campaign, agents of Western imperialism and propagators of an aggressive brand of 'Zionism'.[15] (Polish Communist Jews were for the most part ideologically anti-Zionist, but many Polish Gentiles did indeed welcome the decisive Israeli victory over the Arabs as a defeat for the Soviet Union.) The Polish Army was made *Judenrein*, the Foreign Ministry and other government departments, the universities, the press and party schools were purged of the dangerous 'Zionist fifth column'. Jews who had been thoroughly assimilated and lifelong Communists were accused of being 'ideologically alien to Polish culture', cosmopolitan 'national nihilists' or Jewish nationalists loyal to Israel rather than Poland. At the same time 'international Zionism' was blamed for having incited Polish student youth to the anti-government protests of March 1968. The role which a few Jewish students did play in the meetings and demonstrations was singled out at every opportunity by the government media and public prosecutors to demonstrate that there was an organised Zionist conspiracy against Poland. All the attention was focused on them as ringleaders, they were systematically described as of 'Jewish origin' or 'Jewish nationality' and their real Jewish names were consistently put in brackets after their Polish-sounding names (a familiar tactic from the Soviet 'anti-cosmopolitan' campaign twenty years earlier).[16]

In addition to 'Zionism' they were also accused of the old Communist heresies of 'Trotskyism' and Social-Democratic 'revisionism' – vices to which Polish Communist Party theorist Andrzej Werblan considered Jews especially prone. The time had come, Werblan stated in a notorious essay of 1968, to correct the ethnic imbalance in cadre policy. This, he declared, was not antisemitism because 'no society can tolerate excessive participation of a national minority in the élite of power, particularly in the organs of national defence, security, propaganda and representation abroad, coming from an outside cosmopolitan background'.[17]

Such contorted ideological rationalisations were merely a thin masquerade for the forced exodus of Jews from Poland. They were followed by a more far-reaching campaign of vilification against Zionism and world Jewry in general, falsely tainted with having 'collaborated' with the Nazis and also with West German 'revanchists' against Poland, and accused of systematically seeking to blacken its good name.[18] The campaign, originally initiated by Moczar (and supported by the PAX organisation of the pre-war Polish Catholic fascist Buleslaw Piasecki), appeared to have swiftly achieved its aim of a 'Final Solution' of the Jewish problem in Poland.

Gomulka's speech of June 1967, which picked up Moczar's challenge, set in motion the final exodus of the remnants of the great Jewish community which had lived on Polish soil for almost a millennium. After such a tragic *dénouement* what possible further uses could antisemitism serve in a country where after 1968 there were only about 5,000 surviving Jews, most of them sick and elderly? Could the virtual disappearance of a once vibrant Jewish community, which now represented only 0.02 per cent of the country's population, still generate new witchhunts?

The first signs that political antisemitism could renew itself came in 1980–1 as part of a Communist campaign to discredit the increasingly powerfuly trade-union movement Solidarity and its ally, the dissident organisation KOR. Antisemitic articles appeared in the official Communist press charging that 'cosmopolitan' KOR activists had a dominant influence in Solidarity and that they serve 'Jewish' interests. Party newspapers misleadingly suggested that a Solidarity activist like Karol Modzelewski was a Jew masquerading as a Catholic, and antisemitic pamphlets, probably encouraged by the regime, caricatured one of the leading Solidarity advisers, Bronislaw Gieremek, with a large nose and Hassidic side-curls. Other labour activists like Jacek Kuron and Jan Josef Lipski, both Catholics and founders of KOR, were accused by the Communist Party press of having 'Zionist links', a familiar codeword from the 1968 antisemitic campaign. Outside the government, too, the anti-Jewish Grunwald Patriotic Association sprang to life again as a rallying-point against Solidarity while the Catholic Church remained noticeably silent in the face of the government campaign. Even within Solidarity itself, in the final weeks before martial law was imposed, factions within the Warsaw branch were falsely accusing left-wing labour leaders in their own movement of being Jewish.[19]

Ten years later, after the collapse of Communism in Poland, the wheel has come full circle. In the Polish elections of 1990

Lech Walesa, Solidarity's working-class hero, in an unrestrained, often vulgar but ultimately successful campaign for the presidency, helped to stir up atavistic feelings, including antisemitism and hatred of intellectuals. His former ally, the liberal Catholic Prime Minister, Tadeusz Mazowiecki – one of the first intellectuals to support Solidarity – found himself smeared by Walesa's supporters as a crypto-Jew who was soft on Communism.[20] Mazowiecki's government was allegedly controlled by Jews rather than 'real Poles', a theme that went down well with an electorate embittered by economic chaos, poverty, unemployment and the soured promise of its present experiment in democracy.[21] In the power vacuum of a volatile post-Communist Eastern Europe, and noticeably in Poland, old hatreds were rising to the foreground, especially antisemitism.

As in the Soviet Union, Hungary and Rumania, people once more recalled that the Communist Parties in their Stalinist phase had seemed to be full of Jews, a convenient peg on which to hang all the failures of their society and economy.[22] The return of the old slogan 'Judeo-Communism' reflected the depths of hatred for a discredited regime, the new politics of resentment, xenophobia and a renewed emphasis on the identity of nation and religion. Not only the issues but also the style and language of the 1930s seem to be making a comeback as a popular alternative to the earnest efforts at creating a liberal market economy and democratising the political system. The endemic weakness of the Polish economy and the persistence of antidemocratic sentiments in the Polish nation, along with the long tradition of denigrating or blaming minorities, has further favoured the re-emergence of an antisemitism, paranoically directed at 'hidden' Jews in the government responsible for the crisis.

Even before the 1990 electoral campaign, the controversy over the Carmelite monastery in Auschwitz had helped to reactivate a whole cluster of anti-Jewish stereotypes and animosities still buried in the Polish national consciousness.

Despite the fraternal Catholic-Jewish dialogues inspired by *Nostra Aetate* (the Vatican Council's historic declaration on Judaism in 1965) it transpires that little of the new thinking has percolated through to the masses. Many Polish peasants still believe in the medieval blood libel – namely that Jews actually use Christian blood for the baking of *matzos*.[23] Many young children are still taught that 'the Jews killed Christ'. Even university students, though more open and curious about Judaism than in the past, still tend to think in a stereotypical manner about 'Jewish traits', unable to test them through contact with real, living persons.

The ignorance about Judaism and Jewish history is, of course, a particularly fertile breeding-ground for antisemitism, as is the quasi-automatic identification in Poland of '*Polak-katolik*' ('the Pole is a Catholic').[24] This identification, so strongly made in the pre-war period by the leader of the rabidly antisemitic National Democrats, Roman Dmowski, is today upheld by one of his most illustrious post-war disciples, the Primate of Poland, Cardinal Jozef Glemp. The Cardinal's antisemitic homily in Czestochowa on 26 August 1989 warned Jews not to 'talk to us from the position of a people raised above all others' and not to 'dictate conditions that are impossible to fulfil'.[25] Rather demagogically claiming that 'a squad of seven Jews from New York launched attacks on the convent at Oswiecim [Auschwitz]' which supposedly threatened the lives of the nuns, he then addressed world Jewry: 'Your power lies in the mass media that are easily at your disposal in many countries. Let them not serve to spread anti-Polish feeling.'[26] Glemp presented antisemitism as a legitimate form of self-defence and even proclaimed that it was a natural response to Jewish 'anti-Polonism'. His posture was that of a ruler defending his Catholic nation against unprovoked foreign attacks.

One of Glemp's closest advisers, Professor Maciej Giertych, whose conscious aim is to rebuild the pre-war National Democratic movement with the full backing of the Catholic

9a *above left* Late nineteenth-century cartoon by Caran d'Ache depicting the consequences of the French Revolution. The Jews have replaced the aristocracy as oppressors of the peasantry.

9b *above right* A hundred years after the French Revolution, this election poster for the antisemitic candidate Adolphe Willette calls on voters to rise up against 'Jewish tyranny'.

9c Alfred Dreyfus stands before the court martial at Rennes in 1899.

10a The five sons of Mayer Amschel Rothschild (*clockwise from the top*): Amschel (Frankfurt), Salomon (Vienna), James (Paris), Karl (Naples), Nathan (London).

10b 'The Jewish danger', from the 1934 French edition of *The Protocols of the Elders of Zion*, symbolises the spectre of global Jewish domination.

11a Antisemitic electoral poster from 1920 alluding to the danger of racial pollution.

11b Public humiliation in Hamburg on charges of *Rassenschande* (racial defilement), as laid down in the 1935 Nuremberg Laws. On the woman's board: 'I am the filthiest woman here. I let only Jews call me dear.'

12a 'The Jewish children and teacher are expelled from school.' From a children's book published by *Der Stürmer* in 1938.

12b (From the same book.) The sign reads: 'One-way street – the Jews are our misfortune.' The accompanying text reads: 'In the far south lies the country which was once the birthland of the Jews. That's where they should go.'

12c 'Jews are not wanted here.'

13a Nazi pickets outside a Jewish shop
during the economic boycott campaign of 1933.

13b The wrecked and pillaged windows of a Jewish shop
in the Friedrichstrasse, Berlin after the *Kristallnacht* pogrom
of November 1938. Passers-by appear to be enjoying the sight.

14a President Reagan visits Bitburg cemetery, where members of the Waffen SS were buried, in May 1985. This visit, made at the insistence of Chancellor Kohl, aroused intense controversy.

14b German neo-Nazis carrying posters of Nazi leader Rudolf Hess, 18 August 1990.

15a The Ku Klux Klan are still active in the United States in promoting their creed of white supremacy, racism and antisemitism.

15b A British Movement supporter during the November 1980 demonstration in London, his arm tattooed with various Nazi slogans, including 'Perish Judah'.

16a Hoveniersstraat in Antwerp after the 1981 bomb attack on the synagogue which killed two people. This was one of a series of terrorist actions against Jewish targets throughout Europe during the last decade.

16b In September 1987 the leader of the Front National in France, Le Pen, called the gas chambers 'merely a detail in the history of the Second World War'.

Church, was very supportive of this stand, calling his speech 'very sensible and very correct' in an interview with me in Warsaw in October 1990.[27] Giertych suggested that it was the international media and the 'Jewish press' in particular which deliberately and artificially whipped up antisemitism in Poland, where it does not in fact exist! This was nothing but a concerted campaign by Jews with 'a great influence in the world's media', directed against Poland in order, so he believes, to whitewash German war crimes.

Professor Giertych, it might be noted, is now editor of the monthly *Slowo Narodowy*, which combats Socialism, Communism, the German menace, Western materialism, 'cosmopolitanism' and all those values alien to Catholic Poland and its national culture – which naturally includes the pernicious influence of international Jewry. Along with other radical right groupings like the Polish Catholic-Social Union, the Pax Movement and the National Front, they reflect that 'natiocentric' tradition in Poland which has always combined antisemitism with chauvinism, xenophobia, authoritarianism and an archaic form of Catholicism. The great vacuum left by the death of Communism may heighten their appeal, especially among the marginalised youth who in Poland, as elsewhere in Europe, are a natural source of recruitment for populist right-wing movements.

Antisemitism itself has, however, really never been marginalised in post-war Poland, as the slogans, graffiti, murmurings and insinuations during the most recent electoral campaign so shockingly revealed. Walesa's hints about 'true Poles' and deeply equivocal statements saying that he has nothing against Jews (but 'why do some of them hide under Gentile names'?) – along with the implication that the allegedly Jewish origins of a political rival must be considered significant – are signs of a deep disorientation and definitive proof that actual Jews are not necessary for antisemitism to thrive.

The problem, as it was put to me in Warsaw by the Polish

journalist Konstanty Gebert (who deliberately writes under the Jewish-sounding pen-name of David Warszawski), is that antisemitism was never truly discredited in Poland. One reason for its seeming legitimacy is that Poles have seen their own extraordinary suffering during the war as having been on a par with that of the Jews, and as having continued for forty years under a tyrannical system of Communism. In other words, they feel themselves to be as victimised as the Jews, and for them Auschwitz is no less important a symbol, representing as it does Polish national and religious martyrdom. Indeed, Poles for a long time tended to posthumously 'Polonise' the Jewish victims of the death camps (grouping the three million Jews massacred in Poland in the general category of Polish victims). Not recognising the exceptional character of Nazi treatment of the Jews has enabled many Poles to avoid confronting questions about their own responsibility during this tragic period and obfuscates the need to critically re-examine Polish antisemitic traditions.

As a result antisemitism has often been considered to be a *legitimate* opinion, a viewpoint that is tolerated and rarely subjected to firm moral rejection or to serious political resistance.[28] This ambivalence has been as true of the Solidarity movement (though in its earlier period it did repudiate antisemitism as a political programme) as it is of the Catholic Church, while the Communists never hesitated to manipulate antisemitism for their own needs. The rather grotesque (if partly understandable) reverse side of that particular coin was the massive popular hostility to the Jews, engendered by their involvement in Stalinism and the post-war Communist regime.

There are, of course, those who would argue that Poles absorbed antisemitism with the teachings of the Church and that the myth of the Christ-killers is the main reason for its persistence.[29] The Polish Catholic Church is certainly wedded to more archaic, conservative and antimodernist concepts than its counterparts in the West. Moreover, with a Polish

Pope in Rome and the highest number of churches and proportion of practising Catholics of any country in Europe, the influence of the Church cannot be underestimated.[30] No doubt its post-war failure to take a clear stand in condemning antisemitism outright has contributed to the respectability which anti-Jewish stereotypes still enjoy.[31] When the Mother Superior of the embattled Carmelite Sisters of Auschwitz could recently tell a Polish-American weekly that Jews had no right to 'special treatment' at the camp; that they believe themselves to be a 'chosen' race; and that 'Polish Communist Jews' ran the government after 1945 'with the specific intention to introduce atheism into Poland', there is no doubt that she exemplifies a popular strain of Christian antisemitism in the country.[32] More seriously, such statements are an unwitting indictment of the Polish Catholic Church. They would be inconceivable without its public refusal to acknowledge its own role as a catalyst in igniting traditional Polish antisemitism and its singular failure to re-educate the Polish people at grassroots level.[33]

It would, however, be misleading and unfair to place all the blame on the Catholic Church, which is responsible neither for the folk superstitions of the Polish peasantry nor for the nationalist and political antisemitism which has been a fairly continuous feature of Poland's history in the twentieth century. Moreover, such an indictment would ignore the fact that there has been in recent years a Catholic-Jewish dialogue involving liberal Catholic intellectuals and priests who do not agree with Cardinal Glemp's vision and who reject the antisemitic past without ignoring it. Despite their prestige, the influence of such intellectuals is probably rather limited, but this does not mean that the prospect of a genuinely democratic, pluralist Poland without antisemitism is forever doomed.

Attitudes towards Jews in contemporary Poland are not, of course, based on real experience but more on mythological images, whether positive or negative – themselves the outcome of history, religion, folk superstition, parental structures and political manipulation. In contrast to pre-war antisemitism, it has no direct connection – be it rational or perverse – with the presence of a coherent Jewish community.

Contemporary Polish antisemitism expresses a deeper existential uncertainty – that of disorientated, lost and confused individuals in a society now undergoing rapid social change, dislocation and doubts about its own identity. There is a climate of fear as well as hope, bitterness as well as opportunity opened up by the fall of Communism. Antisemitism represents in this context a morbidly defensive reaction to perceived threats and 'conspiracies', whether real or imaginary, as well as a desperate response to unsatisfied needs and to economic adversity.[34] In such a climate of prejudice and anxiety about the future there has been a nearly automatic response in modern Polish society – 'the Jews are to blame' – even when there are barely any Jews to be found.[35]

14

■ ■ ■

The Soviet Disunion

There was no other state on the European continent which officially pursued such repressive anti-Jewish policies in the nineteenth century as the Tsarist Russian Empire. For as long as they could, the Russian Tsars had sought to keep Jews out of the lands which they ruled, but the partitions of Poland at the end of the eighteenth century brought nearly half a million Jews under their sway. By 1897 this number had increased to 5,189,400 (4.13 per cent of the total Russian population), and by 1914 about half of world Jewry was concentrated in the gigantic, sprawling land-mass controlled by the Tsars. Most of them were confined by law to the 'Pale of Settlement' (a territory of approximately a million square kilometres which stretched from the Baltic to the Black Sea), where they lived in poverty and deprivation and were subjected to endless, humiliating decrees purportedly designed to 'protect' the local population from the spectre of 'economic exploitation'.

Russian antisemitism was in its origins a combination of simple primitive hatred for the Jews as 'aliens' and of Christian orthodox religious prejudice which regarded the Jewish people as deicides. Such prejudice remained alive and virulent both at the state level (Tsarist absolutism derived its legitimacy from a Byzantine Caesaropapist version of Christianity) and among the millions of superstitious and illiterate Russian peasants.[1] The Orthodox Christian idea was in many ways the *spiritus movens* of Tsardom, one of the most important criteria of Russianness and the most basic part of the nation's spiritual essence. Polish Catholics, Baltic Lutherans and even more the

171

Jews, with their ancient loyalties, distinct customs, religion and languages, stood outside the fold. Moreover, very few Jews chose to convert, and even then the distinction between converts and 'real' Christians was generally maintained. By the end of the nineteenth century, however, the older, more traditional Judeophobia was becoming transformed into a set of distinctly modern myths which viewed the Jews as engaged in an international conspiracy to subvert the very foundations of Holy Russia.

The Tsarist regime, by constantly imposing economic disabilities on the Jews and driving them into insecure middleman occupations which involved direct, often unpleasant contact with the poorer peasants, itself contributed to the exacerbation of popular Judeophobia. When pogroms occurred in 1881 in about 160 cities and villages of Russia, the government did not intervene to stop the murder and pillage. Instead, a year later, it enacted further anti-Jewish economic legislation (the notorious May Laws). Jews were made to feel even more isolated by the fact that the Narodniki (populist revolutionaries) had welcomed the 1881 pogroms as a rising of the peasantry against Jewish petty-bourgeois 'exploitation', which supposedly heralded the coming social revolution. Despite this acute disappointment, many young Jews continued to join the Russian revolutionary movement in the hope that it would succeed in overthrowing the backward, oppressive Tsarist regime and lead to a Western-style parliamentary social democracy.

The involvement of Jews in Russian radicalism gave a convenient pretext to conservative antisemites within the government like Konstantin Pobedonostsev (Director of the Holy Synod) and the Minister of the Interior Count von Pleve to divert popular discontent away from the regime and against Jewry by means of pogroms.[2] It was widely believed that von Pleve had encouraged the brutal Kishinev pogrom of 1903, or was at least morally responsible for it. The increased strength of the revolutionary movement in 1905 and the threat which

172

it posed intensified the antisemitic propaganda fostered by the government. Tsar Nicholas II subsidised the monarchist, antisemitic organisation the Union of the Russian People, and the proto-fascist gangs of Black Hundreds, who sought to rally the masses against liberals and revolutionaries by spearheading pogrom agitation.[3] It was in the context of the 1905 revolution that *The Protocols of the Elders of Zion* was first published under secret police auspices by the press of the Tsar, although he personally believed the work to be a fraud.

The pogroms of 1905 and the Beilis ritual-murder trial in Kiev (1911), in which the government put its full weight behind the frame-up of an innocent Jewish artisan, confirmed the unique position of Russia as by far the most reactionary monarchy in Europe in its treatment of Jews. As the historian Hans Rogger has pointed out, although Russia's official anti-Jewish policy was not based on the pseudo-scientific racial ideas already fashionable in the West, 'it came as close to racism as it is possible to be without an explicit theory'.[4]

Russian antisemites – monarchist, Christian, illiberal and anti-Western – were indeed hostile not only to the Jewish religion but also to Jewry as an ethnic group, a 'racial' and 'nationalistic cult', to use the terminology of the Slavophile ideologue Ivan Aksakov.[5] They believed that the passion for acquisition and money-grubbing were innate characteristics of the 'Semites', and that Jews represented a particularly harmful and dangerous group in Russian society which had to be isolated from the rest of the population. Such half-formed racist arguments helped to justify the refusal of the Tsarist regime to grant the Jews emancipation and civic rights.[6] Jewish numbers, power and economic prowess would, so the argument ran, overwhelm the still backward Russian *moujiks* and intensify popular anger even further, if they were ever fully emancipated.

With the coming to power of the Bolshevik Party in November 1917 and the ensuing Civil War, pre-war anti-semitism assumed an unprecedentedly violent character as the counter-revolutionary White Armies carried out murderous pogroms, especially in the Ukraine. The troops of Petliura, Denikin and Kolchak, fed on the modern myth of a Judeo-Masonic conspiracy against Russia and persuaded that the Revolution was the work of Antichrist, massacred over 100,000 Jews – perhaps the worst disaster in modern Jewish history before the Holocaust. The Whites distributed the Tsarist forgery of *The Protocols of the Elders of Zion* as part of their propaganda against the Bolsheviks, whose armies were commanded by Leon Trotsky, a brilliant Russified Jew who, together with Lenin, had masterminded the Communist *coup d'état* in Petrograd.[7]

Lenin, the new head of the Soviet government, had already written in 1914 that 'no other nationality in Russia is so oppressed and persecuted as the Jews'.[8] As a Marxist he sincerely believed that antisemitism, like all forms of ethnic prejudice, was an outgrowth of class conflict which would eventually disappear in a classless society. It was essentially a feature of reactionary feudal and capitalist regimes, exploited for the benefit of the ruling classes to sow division in the masses and deflect them from supporting the radical cause. Lenin realised, moreover, that antisemitism was being turned against the Bolshevik regime by its most dangerous opponents – the White counter-revolutionaries – who took advantage of the fact that a number of the top Russian Communist leaders were of Jewish origin. Hence, for pragmatic as well as ideological reasons, he fiercely attacked antisemitism in statements and speeches during the Civil War, and as early as 27 July 1918 the Soviet government defined instigators of pogroms as 'enemies of the Revolution' who had to be outlawed.[9] Stringent legislation, backed up by education and propaganda, was employed to suppress antisemitism in the 1920s, though such feelings continued to persist, especially during the New Economic Policy.

Popular antisemitism was stimulated mainly by the large influx of Jews from the former Pale of Settlement to industrial and administrative centres, where they now competed for jobs; by the new agricultural settlements of Jews on land in southern Russia and the Crimea; and by the prominent role which the more literate, urbanised Jews came to play in the apparatus of the Communist Party, of the state and in the emerging, new Soviet culture. Jews were to be found occupying leading government posts, as top Party Commissars, as heads of the security services, in the universities and in other areas of public life which, less than a decade earlier, had been hermetically sealed to them.[10]

There were, however, other features of Soviet policy which were spiritually harmful to Jewish life. Synagogues were being closed down as part of the atheistic campaign directed against all religions but especially against the Russian Orthodox Church. In the early 1920s, Hebrew was outlawed as a 'counter-revolutionary' language; Jewish political movements, including Zionism and the Bund (Jewish Workers' Movement), were prohibited; an independent, autonomous Jewish culture (which in pre-revolutionary Russia had been especially rich and diverse) was gradually crushed. In its place came a flattened 'proletarian' socialist culture in the Yiddish language – ideologically neutralised and in conformity with the official party line.

Nevertheless, until the mid-1930s there was no hint of public anti-Jewish propaganda, no acts of violence or discrimination against Jews, no teaching of contempt such as had been the norm before 1917.[11] Stalin's Great Purges of 1936–7 signalled the beginning of a change for the worse, not only because they rooted out all opposition to his totalitarian rule but because the government initiated a systematic liquidation of Jewish institutions and of those who were in charge of Jewish affairs. The Jewish Section of the Communist Party (*Yevsektsia*) had already been disbanded in 1931, but it had been unpopular among many Jews for its suppression of the Jewish religion, Hebrew culture and Zionism. During the Great Purges, however, organised Jewish life was almost completely paralysed. Hundreds of Jewish schools were closed, departments for Yiddish language and culture at the universities of Kiev and Minsk were shut down, most Jewish papers ceased to appear and special courts where Yiddish could be used by the Jewish population stopped functioning.[12] Moreover, during the years that the Nazi–Soviet pact was in operation (1939–41) the Soviet press ceased to report on the anti-Jewish persecution in Germany, or on the murder of Jews in Poland after the Second World War broke out. The Soviet regime did nothing to alert its Jewish population to the facts of Nazi genocide and indeed discouraged, criticised and even punished those who after the war sought to emphasise the special suffering of the Jewish people.

During the war with Nazi Germany it is true that the position of the Jews did improve as Stalin saw the utility of winning the support of Jewish public opinion in the West (especially in America and Britain) for the Soviet cause. A Jewish Anti-Fascist Committee was established, which was chaired by the Director of the Jewish State Theatre in Moscow, Solomon Mikhoels (he would be murdered on Stalin's orders by the Soviet secret police in 1948). Jews were briefly permitted to re-establish their links with other Jewish communities in the Western world and even with Palestinian Jewry.[13] Despite the consistent anti-Zionism in Communist ideology and practice, overtures were made to Zionist leaders in Palestine which would eventually culminate in Stalin's support for the creation of a Jewish State in Palestine.[14] But such measures were taken solely for reasons of *Realpolitik* and did not change Soviet hostility to Zionism or Stalin's growing suspicion of Jews, which after 1945 seems to have developed into a paranoic hostility.

The blackest years of Soviet Jewry, between 1948 and 1953, began with a two-pronged campaign against the sins of bourgeois Jewish nationalism and of 'rootless cosmopolitanism' – two deviations that seem mutually contradictory yet expressed the same ingrained, deeply-rooted suspicion of

Jews that had revived in the Soviet Union during the war years.[15] At a popular level the intensive Nazi antisemitic propaganda had undoubtedly left its mark on sectors of the Soviet population, especially in the Ukraine, Byelorussia and the Baltic States, who had collaborated with the German invaders in massacring Jews. The Soviet government itself was now more willing to exploit this antisemitism from below in the service of reinforcing its rule.

With the onset of the Cold War, as Stalin concentrated on hermetically sealing the USSR off from any Westernising influences and openly encouraged a cult of Great Russian nationalism, the Jews appeared as a useful tool and also a convenient scapegoat for his policies. In the satellite countries of Eastern Europe, like Hungary, Poland, Rumania, Czechoslovakia, East Germany and Bulgaria, which had come under Communist rule, Jewish Stalinists were trusted allies in the first stage of 'Sovietisation', for their loyalties to Moscow had already been amply demonstrated. But Stalin did not hesitate to sacrifice them in show-trials like that of Rudolf Slansky in Czechoslovakia (1951–2) in which leading Communists of Jewish origin were branded as 'crypto-Zionist' traitors to the cause of socialism. One reason for encouraging this antisemitic agitation among the masses may have been to deflect East European hatred of Russian domination.

In the USSR itself, the Jewish cultural institutions which had been revived during the war were rapidly liquidated in 1948. Virtually all of the most prominent Soviet Yiddish writers and many Jewish artists were arrested and sent to prison or to Siberian concentration camps. In 1952, the cream of this Soviet Yiddish intelligentsia (including famous authors like Perez Markish, Dovid Bergelsen and Itzik Feffer) were secretly executed and others were allowed to die in prison.[16] Stalin's pretext for this crime was that a proposal made after the war by leaders of the Jewish Anti-Fascist Committee for Jewish settlement in the Crimea, was in reality a plot to create a pro-Western base on Soviet soil serving the 'imperialist' enemies of the USSR.[17]

The 'Doctors Plot' of 1953 in which nine prominent physicians (six of them Jews) were accused of seeking to poison the Soviet leadership under instructions from Western intelligence agencies and from the American Joint Distribution Committee (a Jewish philanthropic organisation) escalated antisemitism to new and unprecedented heights in the USSR.[18] Virtually all Jews came under suspicion, Jewish employees were dismissed from various institutions, Jews in the streets were sometimes assaulted, as were Jewish children in schools. Only Stalin's death a few weeks after the announcement of the 'plot' may have averted a pogrom and the planned deportation of most Soviet Jews to Siberia, which appears to have been the Soviet dictator's goal.

Stalin's successors retracted the accusations concerning the 'doctor murderers' as a secret police fabrication, but they did not initiate any campaign against popular antisemitism. In Khrushchev's famous secret report to the Twentieth Party Congress (1956) he denounced Stalin's many crimes but omitted those against the Jews from the list. This was not surprising in view of Khrushchev's own prejudices against Jews and his defence of Stalin's policy in the notorious Crimea affair. Khrushchev's criticism of the Russian poet Yevgeny Yevtushenko for having evoked the spectre of antisemitism in his famous poem 'Babi Yar' (1961) – which had commemorated the war-time German masscre of Jews in Kiev – indicated his personal feelings only too clearly. It was under his rule that Jews were being singled out for having committed 'economic crimes' and executed in disproportionate numbers. Atheistic campaigns were now revived with new intensity and Judaism presented as an extremely negative religious, cultural and historical phenomenon. One of the worst examples was the openly antisemitic book by the Ukrainian 'scholar' Trofim Kychko, *Judaism without Embellishment* (1963), published by the Ukrainian Academy of Sciences. It was also Khrushchev who initiated the Soviet military alliance with Nasser and the Arab world as a part of a more aggressive Third-World 'anti-imperialist' strategy which brought in its wake constant denunciations of Israel and Zionism that adversely affected the image of Jews in the USSR.[19]

It must be emphasised that by the 1960s Jews had been almost completely eliminated from the diplomatic and foreign service, from leading positions in the Army and from any prominence in top Communist Party posts, and they were noticeably underrepresented in such institutions as the Supreme Soviet or the Soviet of Nationalities. Their representation was much higher among members of the Soviet academic and professional élite (i.e. among physicians, scientists, academicians, journalists and artists), but it was significantly lower than in the 1930s. Moreover, the number of Jewish students at the universities has been steadily falling in the post-war period, clearly the result of an unofficial but fairly systematic policy of *numerus clausus*. This discriminatory government policy undoubtedly reflects the deep suspicion of the Communist Party and the security services concerning the loyalties of Jews (e.g. their possible links with the West and with the State of Israel) and their different mental outlook and nonconformity to the totalitarian mould, as well as representing a concession to popular resentments and frustrations.

The Six Day War of 1967, in which Israel decisively defeated the Arab States (armed and supported by the Soviet Union), provoked an *official* anti-Jewish campaign which has lasted for two decades and has been unprecedented even by Soviet standards for its longevity and virulence.[20] Although the target was ostensibly the State of Israel and its so-called 'racist' or 'Nazi' policies towards Arabs, the style, techniques and motifs of this verbal and visual propaganda were unmistakeably antisemitic in their underlying meaning. Judaism was presented, for example, as a criminal, religious tradition from ancient times, educating its followers in racial superiority and hatred of other peoples. At a 1971 debate in the United Nations Security Council on the Middle East, the Soviet Ambassador Yakov Malik declared, for example, that Zionism is 'fascist' and 'racist' because it is purportedly based on a doctrine of chosenness (there is no such idea in Zionism but it is central to Judaism).

> The chosen people: is that not racism? What is the difference between Zionism and fascism, if the essence of the ideology is racism, hatred towards other peoples? The chosen people. The people elected by God. Where in the second half of the twentieth century does one hear anyone advocating this criminally absurd theory of the superiority of one race and one people over others. . . . Try to prove that you are the chosen people and the others are nobodies.[21]

As the context makes clear, the Soviet attempt to link Zionism with racial chosenness evokes not only German fascist strivings for hegemony but also the Protocols myth of a Jewish plan for world domination. This was also a central motif in books by 'anti-Zionist' ideologues of the Brezhnev years like Vladimir Begun, whose *Creeping Counter-Revolution* (1974) specifically denounced the 'chauvinistic idea of the God-chosenness (*bogoizbrannost*) of the Jewish people, the propaganda of messianism and the idea of ruling over the peoples of the world'.[22] For Begun, 'Zionist gangsterism' is rooted in the Torah – 'an unsurpassed textbook of bloodthirstiness, hypocrisy, treason, perfidy and moral degeneracy' and in the Judaic division of the world into Jews who are 'chosen' and non-Jews who are 'despised by God'.

Begun also advanced the idea that Jewish capitalists and businessmen stood behind the mad monk Rasputin, who had dominated the Tsarist court in its closing years. This was part of his general re-evaluation of the position of Jews under Tsarism, a theme adopted by other Soviet 'anti-Zionists' of the 1970s. Like the well-known critic Dmitri Zhukov, Begun stressed that the real power of the Jewish bourgeoisie was far greater than its formal civil rights (a thesis already to be found in the young Marx) – hence, even under Tsarism it was becoming part of the ruling caste. Russian popular anti-semitism of this period could therefore be best understood (and justified) as part of the class-struggle of the oppressed masses against their Jewish capitalist oppressors.[23] Begun, Ivanov, Zhukov, Kichko, Skurlatov, Yevseyev and other imitators emphasised that, in the twentieth century, Zionism (with its notions of 'racial exclusivity') had become the official ideology of Jewish banking capital in its drive for world domination. No perfidy was too base for these 'Fascists under the blue star of David' (Yevseyev's phrase), including 'collaboration with Hitler' and helping the Nazis burn hundreds of thousands of Jewish 'workers' and poor people in order to achieve their political goals.[24]

Reviving an old antisemitic canard, Yevseyev claimed, for example, that at the centre of the 'Zionist' operation stood some 500 of the 'most influential and most mighty bankers and businessmen from dozens of small and large capitalist countries of all continents'; in addition to this financial monopoly (according to Yevseyev's purely fictitious statistics) no less than '80 per cent of the local and international information agencies "belong to the Zionists"'.[25] It is obvious that in this genre of Soviet hack literature, massively diffused in the 1970s and early 1980s, the conspiracy theories that informed Henry Ford's *The International Jew* or *The Protocols of the Elders of Zion* fifty years earlier had merely been updated, replacing the term 'International Jewry' with the myth of 'World Zionism'.[26] This was simply old antisemitic wine in new anti-Zionist bottles!

Nor is it a coincidence that such veterans from the official Brezhnevite anti-Zionist campaigns as Yevseyev, Begun, Valery Emelianov or Alexandr Z. Romanenko – author of the racist diatribe *The Class Essence of Zionism* (1986) – have been among the post popular lecturers of the ultra-nationalist Pamyat organisation.[27] For their overtly antisemitic works, published in large runs (and probably filtered through the

KGB), helped to form the mass consciousness that shaped the popular Jew-baiting rhetoric of the late 1980s in a disintegrating Soviet society.[28] They could flourish the more easily given the total lack of information about Jews from other officially permitted sources. Even for several generations of Soviet Jews, this antisemitic literature was all that was available concerning Jewish history, religion or culture – let alone the history of Zionism or of Israel.[29] As a result, a wildly distorted picture of the Jewish people as a historical phenomenon has emerged, in which terms like Judaism, Zionism, the 'Jewish bourgeoisie' and Israel are used interchangeably to create an undifferentiated malevolent stereotype. The Jews were turned into a group lacking any identity of its own, any historical continuity, any link with Palestine or even with the revolutionary movements of modern times in Europe or in the Russian Empire – except that of a negative, parasitic or reactionary presence. Conspiracy theories and pure slander replaced any serious scholarly research or objective portrayal of the place of Jews in Soviet society, in world culture or in international affairs.

Thus, semi-official propaganda has reinforced the suspicion and hostility towards Jews deriving from religious, social and ethnic stereotypes, creating an overall image of Jewish disloyalty, subversion and sinister plotting. Official discrimination and popular prejudice nourished by class and national tensions in Soviet society were further strengthened by a kind of pseudo-intellectual antisemitism that has come to the foreground in recent years. In this widely diffused literature disseminated in historical novels, science fiction, essays and pamphlets, it is the Jews who are held responsible for undermining the basis of Russian society – destroying its cultural cohesion, causing its military and economic failures, the collapse of Tsarism, the cruelties of the Russian Revolution, the Gulag labour-camp system and the Stalinist terror. Expanding on the theories of nineteenth-century conservative Slavophiles, this contemporary literature has assigned a completely Manichean role to the Jews – that of embodying evil throughout history and more specifically of being the hereditary enemies of the Russian people.[30]

Since the coming to power of Gorbachev in 1985 the main standard-bearers of chauvinist antisemitism have been the xenophobic Great Russian organisations that have flourished under *glasnost*. The most active and well-known of these organisations is Pamyat, which has some support in the government, the Communist Party and the Soviet cultural establishment as well as among the masses.[31] It controls the Movement for the Restoration of Monuments of Russian Culture, the Russian Republic Culture Fund and a number of environmental movements. There are active supporters of Pamyat in the Union of Russian Artists and the Society Against Alcoholism, and very vocal antisemites in the highly influential Union of Writers of the Russian Republic.[32] Other ultra-nationalist organisations aligned to the world-view of Pamyat are the Patriot Society, Otchestvo (Fatherland) based in Novosibirsk, and Rossy, centred in Leningrad. The most important publications which espouse antisemitism as an integral part of their nationalist ideology are *Nash Sovremenik* (Our Contemporary), the journal of the Union of Writers of the Russian Republic, and the Komsomol literary monthly, *Molodaya Gvardiya*, but the newspaper *Sovietskaya Rossiya* and the weekly *Nedelya* have also participated in the campaign.

Among the most prominent publicists and agitators of Pamyat are the journalist and photographer Dmitri Vasiliev and Igor Sichev, while veteran 'anti-Zionist' authors like Romanenko and Emelianov are among its leading ideologues. More disturbing, perhaps, is the intellectual basis of the new antisemitism provided by such a prominent mathematician and former dissident intellectual as Igor Shafarevich or by leading writers like Valentin Rasputin, Valentin Pikul and Vasily Belov.[33] Thus, alongside the uniformed thugs of Pamyat with their black-shirted youthful cohorts, there is also a more respectable New Right with supporters in high places among government officials, KGB personnel, writers, artists, scientists and planners.

Their ideology is rooted in the bitter disappointment with Communism, in the general crisis of Soviet society and in their anger at alleged discrimination against ethnic Russians.[34] They are in favour of patriotism, law and order, and traditional values blended with ecological concerns to preserve the Russian cultural heritage.[35] What they claim to hate are the destructive influences of 'liberals' in Soviet life, the fads and trends imported from the West, the cosmopolitan intellectuals and so-called 'Russophobes' – those émigrés, dissidents and above all Jews who are quite falsely said to denigrate Russian history and mock the backwardness of Russian culture. Shafarevich's tract, entitled *Russophobia* (1989), can be taken as the Bible of this anti-Western, anti-Socialist and antisemitic gospel, driven by intellectual paranoia and an apocalyptic vision of the spiritual crisis confronting Soviet society.

One of his key notions is that a small group of people (*maly narod*), motivated by a rabid fear and hatred of everything Russian, are conducting an internal struggle against 'the Big People' (*bolshoy narod*), to ruin their self-respect and depict them as a nation of power-worshipping slaves. According to Shafarevich, 'Russophobic literature is under the strong influence of Jewish nationalist sentiments'. Among the Russophobes whom he mentions (not all of them Jews) are Galich and Vysotsky, Amalrik, Grossman and Tarkovsky, Bialik and Babel. Similar efforts at domination by this small Jewish nation can be found, he argues, in the influence of Freud, the fame of the composer Schoenberg, Kafka, or the poets Heinrich Heine and Joseph Brodsky. The aim of the 'small nation', writes Shafarevich, is 'the ultimate destruction of the religious and national foundations of our life, and given the first opportunity, the ruthlessly purposive subversion of our national destiny, resulting in a new and terminal catastrophe, after which probably nothing will be left of our people'.[36]

Shafarevich regards the mere discussion of antisemitism as proof that a powerful Jewish lobby exists and that Jewish issues have 'acquired an incomprehensible power over people's minds', overshadowing the problems of Russians, Ukrainians, Estonians, Crimean Tartars, etc. 'Jewish national emotions,' he complained in *Nash Sovremennik*, 'are the fever of the whole country and the whole world. They are a negative influence on disarmament, trade agreements and international relations of scientists. They provoke demonstrations and strikes and emerge in almost every conversation.'[37]

It must be stressed that such vulgar ideological myths about foreign and internal Russophobes (Jews, dissidents, liberals, democrats and émigré intellectuals) enjoy increasing popularity among the Soviet intelligentsia. Hundreds of openly antisemitic articles have appeared in papers like *Nash Sovremennik* (whose circulation has increased two-fold and is close to a million), *Molodaya Gvardiya*, *Literaturnaya Rossia* and other strongholds of the nationalist current.[38] They have revived the old Stalinist concept of 'rootless cosmopolitans' (a euphemism for Jews) and repeatedly identify Jewry in the words of Anatoly Buylov at a recent meeting of the Russian Writers' Union, as 'the only nationality with an interest in dissension among us'.[39] Jewish 'cosmopolitanism' is contrasted with *pochvennichestvo* (being rooted in one's native soil) as best expressed in the works of nationalist writers like Viktor Astafev, Vasily Belov, Stanislav Kunyayev, Iury Kuznetsov or Valentin Rasputin.[40] An émigré Russian Jewish poet like the Nobel Prizewinner Joseph Brodsky can by this criterion never be a true Russian even if he writes in the Russian language; the songs of Aleksandr Galich are deplored as 'amoral belletrisation' divorced from the blood of the nation; the 'genetic memory' and 'national traits' of Jews and Russians are totally different, according to the critic Vladimir Bondarenko;[41] in Stanislav Kunyayev's absurdly simplistic view the aesthetic 'impoverishment' of Jewish culture is the result of the extreme rootlessness induced by 2,000 years of Diasporic existence.[42]

Hence, the cosmopolitan Jews naturally encourage the obnoxious and destabilising foreign fads from the West which have acquired an enormously harmful influence over indigenous Russian culture. The impact of the Western-style consumer society, of Western rock music, beauty contests, sex education, defence of homosexuality, pornography in the Soviet cinema, theatre and arts, of rising crime and drug abuse are all classic symptoms for Slavophiles, nationalists and 'village prose' writers of the decadence of Soviet society.[43] For a conservative historian like Apollon Kuzmin, only a fundamentally alien social element like the Jews would have had an interest in introducing such Western models into the USSR. The current policy of cultural liberalisation, the 'pluralism' of tastes, viewpoints and predilections which characterise *perestroika* are clearly anathema to the New Right and all too easily blamed on urban, intellectual and 'rootless' Jews.

The anti-*perestroika* alliance of the late 1980s has included neo-Stalinists as well as radical Slavophiles and conservative nationalists in its ranks. In *Sovetskaya Rossiya* (March 1988) the college teacher Nina Andreyeva articulated the neo-Stalinist critique of *perestroika*, whose chief political sponsor has been Yegor Ligachev, at the time Gorbachev's most dangerous rival in the Communist Party Politburo. Her essay, rabidly antisemitic in its depiction of Trotsky and of the Jews as a 'counterrevolutionary' nation, was also intended to rehabilitate Stalin and Stalinism for having transformed Russia into a superpower.[44] These and other similar critiques of liberalisation argued that *perestroika* was undermining the Russian State simply by allowing freedom of expression and ideological *rapprochement* with the bourgeois West. The most antisemitic element in this critique has been the attempt to shift the blame for the Soviet Gulag, the forced collectivisation and the terror from Stalin to his 'Jewish' lieutenants like Lazar Kaganovich, or back to Trotsky and other Bolsheviks of Jewish origin prominent in the 1920s.

Thus, for Stanislav Kunyayev it was Trotsky (always called

Leib Bronstein to emphasise his Jewishness) who invented the
Gulag camp system shortly after the Revolution, as well as the
Communist terror and the idea of breakneck industrialisation.
Kunyayev carefully selects all senior NKVD officers with
Jewish-sounding names to reinforce his claim that they had
organised the Gulag system.[45] The only non-Jew attacked in
this indictment is Nikolai Bukharin, whom the nationalists still
hate for having initiated a drive against Russian national
culture. But it is above all the Jewish intelligentsia which is
seen as instigating in the 1920s and 1930s the assault on the
ancient cultural traditions of the fatherland. These 'enemies of
the people' deliberately set out to destroy the soul, body and
memory of the nation, of Russian culture and of the Russian
people as a whole. They were responsible, according to the
editor of *Molodaya Gvardiya*, Anatoly Ivanov, the radical
Slavophile critic Vadim Kozhinov and other New Right
intellectuals, for terrorising the Russian peasantry during the
drive towards collectivisation and for blowing up Moscow's
churches in the 1930s.[46]

The ideology of the Russian New Right is of course reminiscent in many ways of the German *völkisch* antisemitism in
the Weimar period or of pre-war French integral nationalism.
There is the same illiberalism, preoccupation with cultural
decadence, apocalyptic mood and sense that the Russian
people have become strangers in their own home, threatened
both biologically and culturally with extinction. What cements
this ideology together is once again the same bogeyman, the
image of the omnipotent and ubiquitous Jew – a crafty and
immensely malevolent enemy. He has many disguises –
liberal, freemason, Social-Democrat, Stalinist, Trotskyite,
fascist or Zionist – but he embodies everything that is today
defined as Western, modernist, cosmopolitan and above all
non-Russian. This was exactly the kind of ideological mind-set
out of which Nazism developed in Weimar Germany, as a
simplistic answer to the spiritual, economic and political crisis
of modernity.[47]

The seeming collapse of Stalinist Socialism in the USSR which brought this congealed intellectual débris to the surface has also been a fertile breeding-ground for the racist anti-semitism of the gutter. Threats of pogroms, anti-Jewish rallies in public, street scuffles, graffiti with signs like 'Death to the Yids!' and harassment of Jewish children in schools have become commonplace. In January 1990 Pamyat thugs beat their way into the Moscow Writers' Club armed with mega-phones and knuckledusters and began to shout: 'You dirty Jewish mongrels, you're not writers! Get out to Israel! Now we are masters of the country and neither the Party, nor KGB, or the militia are going to help you! Next time we'll come with machine-guns!' Hurling abuse at the writers (most of them not even Jews) and laying about them, the gang went on an unrestrained rampage.[48] When the militia eventually arrived after a long delay it dealt very courteously with the Pamyat people, as if they were old friends, and seemed indifferent to the damage done – raising once more the question of official complicity. Admittedly, Konstantin Smirnov-Ostashvili, the Pamyat activist who led this escapade, was recently convicted at the Moscow city court of insulting Jews and promoting ethnic hatred – the first and only time that the Gorbachev government has acted firmly in response to the resurgence of Russian antisemitism. Smirnov-Ostashvili, it should be said, holds Jews 'responsible for the mass genocide of the Russian people', denies that the Jewish Holocaust took place, sympa-thises with Muslim fundamentalists and American neo-Nazis and wants a Russo–German alliance to eliminate the 'dark forces' of Zionism from the world.[49]

Despite his imprisonment, it must be recognised that the Russian nationalist antisemites have protectors at various levels of the Communist Party and the KGB. As I heard personally from the former KGB General Oleg Kalugin, towards the end of 1990 in Moscow, on the basis of his intimate knowledge, 'some people in the top echelons of the KGB and the Communist Party were antisemitic at the core of their thinking'; a considerable number of KGB officers have always regarded Jews as 'potential enemies of the State' and spies for the CIA; he personally knew of 'people in the top echelons of Pamyat who have dealings with the KGB on a daily basis'; and many of his former colleagues in the KGB suspect Jews of being behind the radical, progressive forces in the USSR today.[50] This might help to explain why the Communist Party has permitted Pamyat meetings on its premises, extended official approval for public marches and the use of public halls and generally avoided criminal indictments of antisemitic organisations, even though incitement of racial or religious enmity is forbidden in the USSR.

The Soviet President Mikhail Gorbachev has also failed to denounce publicly the growing tide of antisemitism in his country. Indeed, he even appointed a Russian writer sympathetic to Pamyat, Valentin Rasputin, to his new Presidential Council. Although no serious person imagines that Gorbachev is himself an antisemite, the tolerance of the authorities towards movements that openly style themselves as heirs to the Russian Black Hundred tradition is troubling. There has been, for example, no response to several appeals by leading Jewish activists to Gorbachev to curb the threatening propaganda that has helped to generate the largest mass exodus in the history of Soviet Jewry since the 1917 Revoluton. There has been no educational campaign against antisemitism, no sustained judicial interventions, no demonstrations in the streets against the black-shirted fascists; no unequivocal or authoritative statement by the President pointing to the dangers which antisemitism might represent to the general well-being of Soviet society, let alone reassurances concerning the physical menace to Jews themselves.[51]

The present economic chaos, the inter-ethnic violence and the possible disintegration of the Soviet Union as a result of the calls for secession and full national independence by a growing number of Republics can only add to the sense of demoralisation of the Jewish minority. As one of their leading spokesmen, Mikhail Chlenov, put it to me in Moscow, they feel that the social crisis is 'reminiscent of the situation in Germany during the 1920s which was so propitious for the growth of Nazism'.[52] Antisemitism, as Soviet Jewish activists emphasise, now exists at all levels of society, from the establishment down to the street, among the educated and the uneducated, in the bureaucracy, the intelligentsia and the working class. It is a product of *glasnost* and at the same time a weapon against *perestroika* whose increasingly palpable shortcomings merely feed the resentment and anger of its victims among the Soviet population at large.[53] As so often in the past – whether in Russia or in other societies in deep spiritual, economic and political crisis – antisemitic mythology displaces and ventilates all the bottled-up hatreds against the most vulnerable and time-honoured scapegoat.[54]

Thus far, there have been no antisemitic pogroms in the European parts of the Soviet Union, though in the more volatile southern Republics – in Baku, in Sungeit, Nagarno-Karabakh and Uzbekistan – there has been violence against Armenians, Turkic Muslims and other minority groups which bodes ill for the Jews.[55] They have the feeling that the Soviet government is either unwilling, unable or not interested in containing these inter-ethnic conflicts, which may even serve to perpetuate Communist rule for a time. The lack of government response to the incendiary rhetoric of the antisemites suggests to the Jewish population that no real protection will be forthcoming should *mass* violence against them also be unleashed. For example, a Leningrad Jewish activist, Avram Dyomin, recently told me:

These antisemitic organisations expound their propaganda very actively at factories, in the new technical schools; they disseminate their literature among the people there. As a rule, the authorities' attitude towards them is one of approval; either they do not remark upon their activities or in several cases they even help. Several times recently, Jews have been subjected to serious attacks on the street, and there have even been several murders with antisemitic motives, and as a rule the police try not to make investigations into these cases.[56]

With the disastrous state of the Soviet economy and a long tradition of both state and popular antisemitism to contend with, the outlook for Soviet Jewry is grimmer than ever before. Uncertainty, anxiety, even panic have been the response, although thus far the antisemites have not been effectively organised on a political platform or achieved any striking electoral successes. Indeed, outside of the Russian Republic and some disturbing trends in Soviet Central Asia, there has been little overt violence, even in such traditionally antisemitic regions as the Ukraine. Nevertheless, the Jews have been made to feel that they are unwanted strangers in the Soviet Union, for whom there is no future.[57] They are being blamed by reactionary forces for all the worst catastrophes in Russian history, and being made the scapegoat for a Communist experiment that after seven decades and untold suffering is ending in disaster.

Part 3

■ ■ ■

■

Between Moses
and Mohammed

15

■ ■ ■

Jews in Islamic Lands

Although Jews and Muslims have coexisted continuously since the emergence of Islam in the seventh century of the Christian era, sometimes at peace and at other times in bitter conflict, generalisations about antisemitism in Islamic lands are notoriously difficult to make. Partly this is due to the sheer size, ethnic heterogeneity and religious variety of the Muslim world and the Jews within it, often so disparate in their demographic structure, cultural background and level of development. But it is also a function of the relative lack of objective research into the field itself. Myths have grown up which either grossly exaggerate the hospitable, idyllic and harmonious nature of Jewish–Muslim relations over the centuries or, at the other extreme, present Islam as being relentlessly persecutory and unredeemably oppressive in its treatment of Jews.[1] The matter is complicated by the contrast between theory and practice, between anti-Jewish stereotypes and actual anti-Jewish behaviour in different periods of Islamic history. The Jewish condition in the age of Mohammed and the early Muslim conquests (620 to 750), in the relatively flourishing period until around 1200, in the later Middle Ages, under the Ottoman ascendency, during the period of Western colonialism and finally in the later twentieth century has, after all, been far from uniform.

At times, tolerance towards Jews prevailed and they made real intellectual advances, enjoyed economic prosperity and occasionally even some political influence. But more often, their existence from northern Africa to Iran was punctuated by misery, humiliation and persecution.[2] Admittedly, under Muslim rule, Jews before the modern era usually found greater toleration than under Christianity and were spared the regular massacres and frequent expulsions which were their curse in Christendom. There were indeed towns and cities under Muslim rule in the Mediterranean and the Near East with Jewish communities that had known more than two thousand years of continuous Jewish settlement; this, despite a constant danger of anti-Jewish discrimination and popular violence, sometimes sporadic but at other times more persistent and sustained.

In the Moroccan city of Fez, for example, more than 6,000 Jews were massacred in 1033; in the Muslim part of Spain, between 1010 and 1013 hundreds of Jews were killed (mainly in Cordoba), and in Granada during the Muslim riots of 1066 the entire Jewish community of approximately four thousand people was massacred.[3] This was a disaster, as serious as that which overtook the Rhineland Jews thirty years later during the First Crusade, yet it has rarely received much scholarly attention. In Kairouan (Tunisia) the Jews were persecuted and forced to leave in 1016, returning later only to be expelled again.[4] In Tunis in 1145 they were forced to convert or to leave, and during the following decade there were fierce anti-Jewish persecutions throughout the country.[5] A similar pattern of events occurred in Morocco after the massacre of Jews in Marrakesh in 1232. Indeed, in the Islamic world from Spain to the Arabian peninsula the looting and killing of Jews, along with punitive taxation, confinement to ghettos, the enforced wearing of distinguishing marks on clothes (an innovation in which Islam preceded medieval Christendom), and other humiliations, were rife. It was such eleventh- and twelfth-century tribulations which led the greatest of medieval Jewish philosophers, Maimonedes, to lament in his *Epistle to Yemen*: '. . . it is on account of our many sins that God has hurled us amidst this nation of hostile Ishmael. . . . Never has a nation risen more injurious to us than this people; nor one which has come to degrade us and decimate us and make hating us their chief intent.'[6]

On the other side of the coin, it must, however, be recognised that the period from Saadya Gaon (born in AD 882) to the death of Maimonedes in AD 1204, also marks a Golden Age of medieval Jewish creativity nurtured in a receptive Islamic environment. To this era belongs the poetry of Judah Halevi (died 1141), Samuel Hanagid, Solomon Ibn Gabirol, and Moses Ibn Ezra; the renowned Bible commentaries of Abraham Ibn Ezra; and Maimonedes's own masterpieces, *Mishneh Torah* and *Guide of the Perplexed*. These and other Sephardic Jews participated fully in the cultural renaissance inspired by medieval Islam, often composing their philosophical works and *halachic* treatises in a form of Judeo-Arabic (Arabic in Hebrew letters), though poetic composition was more often in Hebrew. Arabic was indeed the *lingua franca* of the day, in which Jews conducted their business, carried on correspondence and studied classical Jewish sources.[7] Not until the nineteenth century in Germany and Austria would Jews once more develop a symbiotic relationship of such significance with a surrounding culture.

Jews also participated actively in the economic life of the larger, Arabic-speaking society, even though in theory they did not enjoy the same rights and privileges as their Muslim neighbours. From the beginning of the ninth century under the Muslim caliphate, a stratum of wealthy court Jews emerged, first in Baghdad, then in Egypt and Muslim Spain.[8] Their opulence, ostentatious life-style and position of authority aroused the xenophobic hatred of the masses. The Caliph Al-Ma'mun (813–833) had already acted against the rise in Jewish economic status, and under his successors popular resentment of Jews in senior administrative positions also increased. But it was not until the end of the tenth century and the beginning of the eleventh that really systematic anti-Jewish propaganda was produced, especially in Egypt, which resulted in hatred and violence towards the Jews by the Sunni masses. This poisonous propaganda in the time of Yaqub Ibn Killis (a Jewish vizier who had converted to Islam) depicted Jews as treacherous exploiters and oppressors of the Muslims, condemning them as the true rulers of Egypt. Such hatred, based on envy of the socio-economic success of the Jews, became widespread in many sections of the population.[9] It continued in Spain, using similar motifs of contrasting the wealth and authority achieved by the Jews with the poverty of the Muslim masses. Already at the end of the tenth century, intense envy and hostility had been directed against prominent Jewish courtiers like Hasdai Ibn Shaprut, Jacob Ibn Jau, Samuel Ha-Nagid and Jehoseph ben Samuel Ha-Nagid.[10] The assassination of the last-named, as a religious duty, was demanded by Abu Ishaq of Elvira in a long poem which denounced Jews for selfishly exploiting Granada's wealth, abusing the trust of Muslims, mocking their faith and learning their secrets in order to betray them.[11] Such polemics were particularly directed against the financial success and influence of the Jews, tending to decrease once their position in the royal courts of Muslim Spain had been eroded.

Nevertheless, one can find in the Arabic sources for the twelfth and thirteenth centuries, for example in the works of 'Abd al-Rahim al-Dimashqi, examples of how the envy of Jewish success continued to inspire venomous accusations.[12] The Jews might seem outwardly submissive, he suggested, but their religion required them to hate Muslims and, where possible, to poison their food or cause them harmful illnesses. In such literature, the Jews (and to some extent Christians also) are presented as enemies of Islam and their degradation is seen as desirable. But Christians were sometimes regarded more favourably, for they had wielded power in Byzantium (itself a source of some of the anti-Jewish traditions and discriminatory legislation in Islam) and elsewhere, and they were thought to engage in more respectable occupations and also to assimilate more easily.

In order to understand the religious roots of such feelings

one must go back to the dawn of Islam in seventh-century Arabia and the relationship of the prophet Mohammed with both Judaism and Christianity. Mohammed saw himself as the last of a series of prophets sent by God to bring his revelation to mankind. He regarded the Torah as revealed to Moses, the Psalms as given to David and the Gospels as 'given' to Jesus as valid written revelations to be believed by all Muslims. At the same time, he went back to Abraham (in Muslim tradition neither Jew nor Christian but the father of the Arabs) as the protagonist of a pure, undiluted monotheism which had been revived in the final and perfect faith of Islam. The earlier revelations of the Old and New Testaments had been authentic but they had been corrupted by their unworthy custodians and were now superseded by the Koran, the literal word of God as mediated to Mohammed through the angel Gabriel.[13]

The Koran contains echoes of Mohammed's conflicts and polemics with the Jews after his emigration from Mecca to Medina in 622 (the *Hijra*) where he encountered resistance from the various Jewish clans and three major Jewish tribes. Two of these tribes he expelled from Medina and the third, the Qurayza, he exterminated. This conflict, in which he emerged victorious, no doubt explains the harsh passages in the Koran, in which Mohammed brands the Jews as enemies of Islam or depicts them as possessing a malevolent, rebellious spirit.[14] There are verses in the Koran which speak of their abasement and poverty, of the Jews being 'laden with God's anger' for their disobedience and 'because they had disbelieved the signs of God and slain the prophets unrightfully' (Sura 2:61/58). According to another verse, 'the unbelievers of the Children of Israel' were cursed both by David and by Jesus (Sura 5:78/82), and the penalty for those who suffer God's wrath forever is to become apes and swine or worshippers of idols (Sura 5:60/65). The curse was related to their disbelief in God's signs, in the miracles performed by the prophets, in the Book of God given to them and in the prophecy of Jesus. They had rejected Mohammed, even though they knew him to be a prophet, because he was not a Jew and out of jealousy of the Arabs. Such actions were supposedly consistent with the deceitful, treacherous and vile nature of the Jews, whom another verse described as 'they whose hearts God desired not to purify; for them is degradation in this world' and a 'mighty chastisement' in the world to come. (Sura 5:41/45) Muslim commentary and exegesis interpreted these words to mean that Jews would never walk in the straight path, for God Himself had made their hearts that way and wanted to lead them astray. Many verses accuse them of 'falsehood' (Sura 3:71), of distortion (4:46) and of being 'corrupters of Scripture' (3.63), along with such other vices as cowardice and greed. The Koran explicitly declares that 'the strongest in enmity against those who believe are the Jews and the idolaters'. (Sura 5:85).[15]

The main archetype fostered by this Koranic portrayal is that Jews have rejected Allah's truth and always persecuted His prophets, including Mohammed who had been given the perfected version of their own revelation. Indeed, driven by their perfidious nature, they had acted with conspiratorial malevolence towards the Prophet, allying themselves with his enemies. This notion, a commonplace in the *hadith*, *sira* and early Islamic literature, even included a standard story of Mohammed's painful, protracted death from poisoning by a Jewish woman called Zaynab and the attribution of sectarian civil strife in Islam to a putative Jew, 'Abd Allah b. Saba, allegedly the founder of the heterodox Shi'ite sect. The existence of such mythological archetypes (probably reflecting the conflict betweem Islam and the Jews in Medina) were constructed 'as part of Islam's portrayal of the "proper" world order where malevolent, conspiratorial Jews were finally humbled under Muslim rule.' Once the 'Jewish threat' had been tamed and domesticated by early Islam, Jews generally became objects of contempt (and often of legal or social discrimination) rather than hatred.[16]

Since Jews and Christians did after all possess authentic revelations and scriptures, under Muslim law they were

accorded a certain tolerance within the framework of discrimination. As 'Peoples of the Book' (*Ahl al-Kitab*), their
religions were officially recognised and a special status was
evolved for them which combined subjection with protection.[17] As *dhimmis* ('protected peoples') they were in a more
honourable category than pagans and were permitted, on
payment of the poll-tax (*jizya*) to practice their religious rites
even in the *dar al-Islam* ('the house of Islam') and to have their
own communal organisations.[18] But they were also subject to
certain disabilities designed to emphasise their inferior status
and to underline the superiority of Islam. Thus they could not
bear arms, they could not ride horses, they were required to
wear distinctive clothing (the yellow badge has its origins in
Baghdad, not in medieval Europe), and they were forbidden –
at least in theory – to build new places of worship. Here is the
description by the author Bat Ye'or, based on a profusion of
documents relating to the status of the *dhimmis* as elaborated
by Muslim jurists from the inception of Islam until the
twentieth century:

> *Dhimmis* were often considered impure and had to be
> segregated from the Muslim community. Entry into
> holy Muslim towns, mosques, public baths, as well as
> certain streets was forbidden them. Their turbans –
> when they were permitted to wear them – their
> costumes, belts, shoes, the appearance of their wives
> and their servants had to be different from those of
> Muslims in order to distinguish and humiliate them; for
> the *dhimmis* could never be allowed to forget that they
> were inferior beings. The humble donkey was generally
> the sole beast of burden permitted them and then only
> outside the town and on condition that they would, as
> a sign of respect, dismount on sight of any Muslim and
> mount again only after their superior was out of sight.
> Even their saddles had to be ugly and uncomfortable
> and often they were forced to mount side-saddle. In the

street, *dhimmis* were obliged to walk on the left, or impure, side of a Muslim. Their gait had to be rapid and their eyes lowered. Their graves had to be level with the ground so that anyone could walk on them, and in desert lands it was assumed that the elements would quickly obliterate their remains. These were the more common rules which in some regions prevailed into the twentieth century; but there were other no less vexing obligations applicable to the *dhimmis* and to them alone.[19]

One might of course argue that the position of *dhimmis* (Jews and Christians) under Islam was better than anything which existed in pre-modern Christendom, however remote either may be from the standards of twentieth-century democracies with their concepts of human rights, equality before the law and social justice. The *dhimmi* status did not, for example, preclude Jews from owning land, practising various crafts or even participating as equals in a burgeoning imperial economy. Commercial life under Islamic rule did not carry the same stigma as in medieval Christendom, nor were Jews restricted to usury, with all the accompanying negative stereotypes in European society. They were not associated with the Devil, with ritual murder (it was Orthodox Christians under Muslim rule who would introduce this charge during the nineteenth century) with well-poisoning or with other medieval Christian superstitions. Above all, they did not carry the theological odium of being Christ-killers. Indeed, according to the Koran, Jesus had never actually been crucified (he had been saved by God and a likeness killed in his place), while Mohammed had won his battle against the Jewish tribes. This helps to explain why the Koranic image of the Jew – while still predominantly negative, as we have seen – lacked the diabolical quality which it acquired in medieval Christianity.[20]

The more relaxed theological attitude of Islam at the peak of its civilisation is reflected also in the absence of that vast anti-Jewish polemical literature by means of which medieval

Christian theologians sought to refute Judaism and convert Jews to Christianity. Until the twentieth century, Muslim theologians, not feeling the constant Christian compulsion to justify their 'usurpation' of Judaism and replacement of the Old by the 'New' Israel, did not engage in frequent polemics against Judaism. It was more often Jews who converted to Islam, like Samau'al al-Magribi in the middle of the twelfth century, who felt obliged to demonstrate why Judaism was so contemptible that it ought to be degraded or repressed.[21] Medieval Muslims, unlike their co-religionists today or their Christian counterparts centuries ago, were on the whole sufficiently self-confident not to be fearful of Jews as participants in a deadly plot to destroy them. The Jews, to be sure, were often viewed as devious and treacherous schemers but they were considered far too weak, cowardly and ineffectual to be really dangerous. This would only begin to change with the decline of Muslim military power over the last two hundred years and the loss of many central Islamic lands to foreign colonial rule, which eroded the traditional sense of Islamic hegemony and made Islam much more suspicious of minorities.

In the pre-modern era, however, Islamic Jews continued to enjoy certain advantages over their co-religionists living under Christian rule. Whereas, by the end of the eleventh century, Jews were virtually the only non-Christians left in Christendom, in medieval Islamic civilisation with its Christians, Jews and Zoroastrians (not to mention the diverse non-Arab ethnic groups), pluralism was more deeply ingrained. Muslim discrimination was directed at the *dhimmis* as a whole and not just against the Jews in particular. The latter might be regarded socially and religiously as inferiors, but they were not rigidly set apart in the way that this happened in the more corporate, hierarchically organised Christian societies. Nor could Jews be seriously regarded as 'alien' to a region where their ancestors had often lived for generations before the Islamic conquests.[22]

Forced conversions of Jews to Islam were also comparatively rare and the religious hostility, while real enough,
lacked the sharp edge of Christianity, with its whole theology
of rejection and insistence on the *collective guilt* of the Jews for
having murdered God in the flesh. Nevertheless, scorn and
contempt for Judaism (and Christianity) were well anchored
in Muslim tradition and were frequently brought into play
when *dhimmis* rose to positions of authority at various times, in
apparent contravention of the regulations governing Jews and
Christians. The original decrees, which were called the 'Pact of
'Umar' (in honour of the eighth-century Caliph 'Umar I), were
after all intended to degrade the *ahl ad-dhimma* or 'protected
peoples', while permitting them to exercise their religion in
return for paying tribute and accepting certain humiliations.
They had not originally been designed to permit Spanish, Iraqi
or Turkish Jews to make brilliant careers in the courts of
Caliphs, Sultans and Princes, thereby seeming to mock the
whole system of discrimination formulated by the Prophet and
the Muslim jurists.

Clearly, the discriminatory legislation was not rigorously
applied by Muslim rulers when it conflicted with their own
economic or political interests. The ruling authorities, where
they lacked an independent tribal or military base for their
rule, might have recourse to Christians or Jews. Moreover, in
an age of Islamic expansion, prosperity, population growth,
mobility and intellectual openness such as prevailed between
the ninth and twelfth centuries, the *dhimmi* status might be
honoured more in the breach than otherwise. But this did not
mean that the *dhimmi* status was purely theoretical.[23] For in
this same period, as we have seen, there were the fierce
Almohad persecutions of the twelfth century in North Africa
and Muslim Spain, the attacks on Egyptian Jewry by the
Fatimid Caliph al-Hakim and the diatribes of Abu Ishaq against
the Jews of Spain. The exercise of conspicuous power by a Jew
(or Christian) could easily arouse the Muslim masses and
ignite demands by religious reformers to restore the *dhimmis* to

their proper place. The demand for anything approaching Jewish economic or political equality (indeed any divergence from the norm of humiliation and abasement) was perceived as a provocation, a breach of the Pact of 'Umar, a sign of haughtiness and arrogance which could be punishable by death.[24]

The restrictions on *dhimmis* were most rigorously enforced on the periphery of the Muslim world, in countries like Iran, Yemen and Morocco, where one finds conditions of physical insecurity, marginalisation and submission in their pristine forms, well into the modern period. A British traveller to Morocco in the 1820s observed: 'The Moroccans think that they have a natural right to mistreat Jews and Christians.'[25] The reports of virtually all travellers to Morocco from the end of the seventeenth century concur that Jews lived in abject fear of Muslims and were subject to continuous humiliation, degradation, contempt and oppression.[26] In periods of anarchy and insecurity, the *mellahs* of Moroccan Jewry were easy targets for looting, rape and killing, as in Meknes in 1728, Demnat in 1875 and 1884, Sefrou (1890), Taza and Settat (1903). In the sixteen years preceding 1880, more than 500 Jews were murdered in Morocco, often in broad daylight in the main streets. Even in a coastal port like Casablanca, in 1907 30 Jews were killed and 200 women, girls and boys abducted, raped and then ransomed. While in Fez, on 18 April 1912, at the start of French rule, Muslim riots led to the killing of 60 Jews and the sacking of the Jewish quarter in the city.[27]

In neighbouring Algeria, where under Turkish rule before 1830 Jews had to wear a black skullcap, grey cloak and hood, 40 Jews were murdered in 1805. At the end of the century there would be rampant anti-Jewish violence throughout Algeria, though this would be the work of French and European settlers rather than Muslim Arabs. Thirty years earlier, on the Tunisian island of Djerba in 1864, Arab bands pillaged the Jewish communities, burned and looted synagogues and raped the women.[28] In Tunis itself, in 1869 18

Jews were murdered in the space of a few months by Muslims.[29] In Libya, too, there was violence (hundreds of Jews had been murdered in 1785), and harsh anti-Jewish measures were carried out in 1860. In neighbouring Tripolitania, the synagogues were plundered in 1897 throughout the country and several Jews were killed. In Egypt Jews were attacked in anti-foreign riots in 1882, as they would be again in 1919, 1921 and 1924. More ominously, they would be accused in Alexandria in 1844, 1881 and 1902 of using human blood for ritual purposes.

The 'blood libels' which abounded in the Muslim Ottoman Empire, especially during the nineteenth century, were not in fact supported by the Ottoman state, which was generally tolerant of Jews and discriminated against them less than it did against Christians. They originated among the Greek Christian population, leading to pogroms in Smyrna (1872) and Constantinople (1874).[30] The charges stemmed from traditional Christian superstitions and economic rivalry with the Jews, who were dangerous competitors in trade and commerce. The 'blood libels' were sometimes supported by the consuls of Catholic countries like France, as in the notorious Damascus Affair of 1840.[31] This necessitated the intervention of prominent Western Jews like Moses Montefiore and Adolphe Crémieux, who rallied European opinion against this dangerous myth and persuaded the Ottoman Sultans to issue *firmans* unequivocally condemning the blood libels.[32] But the calumny, initiated by Near Eastern Christians, nonetheless spread, with instances recorded in Beirut (1824), Antioch (1826), Hamma (1829), Tripoli (1834), Damascus (1848), Aleppo (1853) and Damanhur (1877) to name only a few.[33] The native Christians (Greek Orthodox, Catholic, Maronite, Armenian, etc.) who helped to pioneer the ideology of modern secular Arab nationalism, also brought classical European antisemitic notions to the Arab world, which undoubtedly infected the Muslims.[34] A calumny, essentially alien to the Islamic tradition, has in the twentieth century been fully integrated into Muslim perceptions of Jews even at the highest level.

A good example can be found in the remarks of King Feisal of Saudi Arabia, which appeared in the 1970s in the Arabic weekly *al-Musawwar*, stating that Jews

> have a certain day on which they mix the blood of non-Jews into their bread and eat it. It happened that two years ago, while I was in Paris on a visit, the police discovered five murdered children. Their blood had been drained and it turned out that some Jews had murdered them in order to take their blood and mix it with the bread that they eat on this day. This shows you what is the extent of their hatred and malice toward non-Jewish peoples.[35]

Another more recent and no less chilling illustration can be found in the book *The Matzah of Zion*, written by the Syrian Defence Minister Mustafa Tlas and published in Arabic in 1983. In this hate-filled work, Tlas accepted as literally true the charges in the Damascus blood libel of 1840, in which eight Jews were falsely accused of murdering a Capuchin monk and his servant, and of using the victims' blood to bake *matzot*. Tlas, a lawyer and respected author who had presented his doctoral thesis at the Sorbonne, claimed through his book 'to throw light on some secrets of the Jewish religion based on the conduct of Jews and their fanaticism'.[36] He relates that the people of Damascus learned their lesson in the 1840s: 'From that moment on every mother warned her child: Do not stray far from home. The Jew may come by and put you in his sack to kill you and suck your blood for the Matzah of Zion.' Further on, Tlas describes the religious beliefs of Jews as being based on a 'black hatred of all humanity and all religions' and suggests that 'Zionist racism' is 'just an extension of Talmudic teachings including their crimes and deviations'.[37]

It is indeed ironic that Christian *dhimmis*, so long the object of Muslim discrimination, should have heavily contributed to the dissemination of such archetypal antisemitism in the Arab world, though it may be psychologically understandable as a form of 'identification with the aggressor'. For antisemitic rhetoric that points to the Jews as a common enemy of the Arabs may indeed have served as an illusory way for Arabised Christians to escape from their minority status and low political status within Islam. For Muslims, too, there may be benefits in adopting traditional Christian accusations like the blood libel against the Jews. For this can provide a common link with Western antisemitic discourse that Muslim anti-Judaism based on the Koran alone cannot hope to elicit. Moreover, on the internal Arab front, it might on occasion help to cement Muslim–Christian unity against the Jews and Zionism.

During the period of Western colonial rule, however, the Christian minorities (and to a lesser extent the Jews) undoubtedly sympathised with both British and French domination of the Middle East, to which they owed their liberation from the traditional *dhimmi* servitude. For a while, the minorities flourished under this protection, though in the case of the Jews, who were fewer, poorer and less influential than their Christian rivals, this proved to be a mixed blessing. The fact that Jews in North Africa or the Levant came to be seen as the allies of foreign colonial powers was bound to add a new layer of resentment to the traditional Muslim attitudes of hostility and contempt. The rise of secular Arab nationalism and Islamic fundamentalism strengthened the xenophobic suspicion of all minorities, with Christian Armenians and Assyrians, as well as Muslim Kurds, being massacred during the course of this century.[38] But Jews were especially subject to hostility against the background of the growing struggle between the Zionists and the Arabs in Palestine after 1918. From the 1920s onwards, a much more virulent anti-Jewish propaganda became influential, with many Muslims coming to see the Jews not merely as a weak, religious minority but as a national-Zionist 'fifth column'. Although some Arab leaders claimed that they genuinely distinguished between Zionists and Jews, this distinction was barely tenable for the Arab masses. The net result would be a further undermining of the ever more vulnerable position of the Jewish minorities in the Muslim Arab world.

The rise of Arab nationalism, the radicalisation of the Muslim masses, the effects of economic crisis, social unrest and political instability, allied to the results of decolonisation and of Zionism, would eventually lead to the uprooting of Jews in Islamic lands.[39] The whole historic process was accompanied by riots and pogroms against virtually every Jewish community in the Arab countries. In Morocco in June 1948, 43 Jews were killed during Muslim riots and over 150 wounded in Djerada. In 1952, unstable political conditions led to anti-Jewish mob violence by Muslims, followed two years later by pillaging of Jewish property and the destruction of some Jewish schools. This was repeated in 1955 with several Jews also killed in Safi and Oued Zem. In February 1957 exit visas for Jews were abolished, with the result that they could no longer legally leave the country, and a year later the number of Jewish officials in the Moroccan government decreased. By 1974 only 20,000 Jews remained in Morocco, compared with the 285,000 who had lived there in 1948 – the majority having emigrated to Israel.[40] In Algeria, before the Second World War, antisemitism had traditionally been a preserve of the French settlers, though in 1934 25 Jews had been killed during Muslim attacks in Constantine.[41] From the beginning of the Algerian war of liberation against the French, however, Jews suffered, with their shops sacked in Oran in 1956 and an Arab boycott slowly forcing them out of businesses and the professions. In 1960, in Algiers, during anti-French riots, the Great Synagogue was desecrated and destroyed.[42] A year later, the Algerian provisional government opposed Jewish emigration to Israel and in 1962 it deprived Jews of many economic rights. Following Israel's victory in the 1967 war against the Arab states, synagogues were desecrated. By the mid-1970s there were only 500 Jews left in Algeria, as against the 140,000 still present in 1948. The majority emigrated to France, along with the rest of the European settler population.

In Tunisia, the Jewish population of 110,000 in 1948 had fallen to a mere 2,000 by 1975. Before the war, Jews had already been attacked by an Arab mob in Sfax (July 1932), protesting at the Jews of Europe going to Palestine. Under the brief wartime German occupation, over 4,000 Jews in Tunisia had been arrested in November 1942 and some were even deported to concentration camps in Europe. The antisemitic propaganda in Arabic, broadcast from Berlin, had a considerable impact in the country (as it did in Morocco, Egypt, Iraq and other Arab countries), leading some Arabs to point out Jews to the occupying German forces. After independence from France in 1956 the treatment of Jews deteriorated, even though the nation's leader, Habib Bourguiba, was a secular, pro-Western statesman who took a relatively moderate position on the Palestinian question and was anything but an antisemite. There was a clamp-down on Jewish community councils in the late 1950s and rabbinical tribunals were abolished. In 1964 the regime imposed serious restrictions on Jewish economic activity. On 5 June 1967, during the Six Day War, the Great Synagogue of Tunis was burned and scrolls of the Law destroyed in anti-Jewish riots, which Bourguiba himself publicly condemned. But as the Tunisian-born writer Albert Memmi (who in the 1950s had been an ardent supporter of the Arab nationalist movement) noted in 1975, 'We should have liked to be Arab Jews. If we abandoned the idea, it is because over the centuries the Muslim Arabs systematically prevented its realisation by their contempt and cruelty.'[43]

A Libyan Jewish writer, Maurice Roumani, in the same year made some similar observations about his native country, where the Jewish population fell to twenty, from its 1948 figure of 38,000. He wrote that in Libya 'the man in the street was intolerant of the mere existence of the Jew in his country'.[44] In 1938 Libyan Jews had already been subjected to Italian 'racial' laws, despite their close identification with the Italian rulers of the colony. During the war the situation of Libyan Jews became worse, for German occupation led to the sacking of the Jewish quarter of Benghazi and the deportation across the desert of about 20,000 Jews, with many dying *en route*.[45] The presence of a British military administration failed to prevent savage anti-Jewish riots in Tripoli on 5 November 1945, in which more than a hundred Jews were massacred.[46] The pogrom was carefully planned and occurred against the background of the anniversary of the Balfour Declaration and stories of violence in Palestine. In Tripoli, three years later, Arab mobs attempted to repeat the performance but found the *hara* (Jewish quarter) well prepared by the Haganah. This time the attackers were repulsed with 12 Jews and 4 Arabs killed, but many Jewish houses were destroyed. Before independence in 1951 the majority of Libyan Jews emigrated to Israel. Those who stayed had their right to vote removed in 1963 and were forbidden to hold office. During the Six Day War about 100 Jews in Benghazi and another 18 in Tripoli were killed; synagogues, shops and homes were looted and burned; and there was widespread destruction of Jewish property.[47] In July 1970, the new Libyan ruler, Colonel Muammar Qaddafi, one of the most ferocious enemies of Israel, announced the seizure of all Jewish property without compensation.[48]

In Egypt a more complex situation prevailed, for Jews in the inter-war years occupied a secure and respected position in society and had considerable influence on the Egyptian economy. They were only one among many minorities, outnumbered by the Christian Copts, rivalled by the Greeks in economic and cultural influence, to a lesser extent even by the Italians, Syrians and Armenians. There was little hostility to Egyptian Jews until the Arab revolt in Palestine (1936–9), and whatever resentment there was appeared to come from the Christian minorities. Moreover, they were to a certain extent protected by the European powers, especially the British and

French. Nevertheless, Egyptian Jewry by the late 1930s had become an internal enemy to committed Muslim nationalists.[49] They were neither Muslim, nor were most of them familiar with the Arabic language and culture. Indeed, many Jews were not of Egyptian origin and held foreign nationality, which was not unusual for minorities in inter-war Egypt. Their activities in the Egyptian nationalist, and above all the communist movements, tended to be viewed with suspicion. Their association with Zionism (usually exaggerated) became a particular source of hostility as the Palestine Question assumed greater importance for Egyptian public opinion. The powerful Muslim Brotherhood was able to mobilise classic anti-Jewish themes against them, especially in militant Islamic circles, by adapting Koranic sources to the needs of the anti-Zionist struggle.[50] Aḥmad Ḥusayn's proto- fascist Miṣr al-Fatāt (Young Egypt) movement, with its paramilitary Green Shirts, was even more openly antisemitic, as part of its militant Egyptian nationalism.[51]

As a result of this agitation there were serious anti-Jewish riots in many Egyptian towns in 1938–9 against the background of the Palestine Question.[52] On 'Balfour Day' (2 November 1945) violence again escalated with the looting of shops and wrecking of synagogues. There were 10 Jews killed and some 350 injured. During the first Arab–Israeli war, Jewish casualties and damage to homes by rioting Muslims was again extensive. In June–July 1948 over 50 Jews were killed, some of them suffering savage mutilations. On 22 September 1948, 20 Jews died and 61 were injured following an explosion in the Jewish quarter of Cairo.

The Suez war of 1956 brought new and more serious tribulations to Egyptian Jewry, with 4,000 being summarily expelled after they had been compelled to abandon all property rights and financial claims. During May–June 1967 all Jews in official employment were dismissed, 500 Jews were arrested and some were brutally tortured. By the mid-1970s only 350 Jews remained out of the once thriving Jewish community which had still numbered 75,000 in 1948. The persecutions of 1948, 1956 and 1967, which forced the Jews into exile to avoid the threat of prison and torture, had brought to a tragic end the long history of Egyptian Jewry. Their fate belied the claims of the Egyptian dictator Gamal Abdul Nasser that he was only 'anti-Zionist', for even Egyptian Jews who guarded a low profile and wanted nothing to do with Israel suffered from the mass arrests and were accused of being 'traitors'.[53] Moreover, the rabid antisemitism still prevalent today, in an Egypt 'without Jews', more than a decade after the Peace Treaty with Israel, suggests that, as in Europe, negative stereotypes can flourish even more successfully when the Jewish communities who were once their concrete object have vanished from the scene.

Syrian Jewry before the First World War had enjoyed the benevolent protection of the Turkish authorities from the various blood libels, spread mainly by local Christians. For most of the French mandate period, there were only isolated and sporadic incidents against Jews, except during the Druze revolt against French rule in 1925. But in 1938, with the Palestine question causing great agitation in Syria, attacks against Jews became more frequent and serious.[54] Following independence in 1945, passports were refused for travel to Palestine, the Jewish quarter in Damascus was raided and in June the director of the Alliance Israélite school was murdered. On 2 December 1947, in Aleppo, the masses ran amok in the Jewish quarter, burning most of the synagogues, breaking into 60 shops and 150 houses and setting them ablaze.[55] In February 1948 and again in August 1949, bombs were placed in the Damascus Jewish quarter, leading to scores of deaths and many wounded. In July 1949 13 Jews were murdered in Damascus and the local synagogue was damaged.[56]

The Six Day War brought new trials and tribulations, with 57 Jews killed by Syrian mobs in Kamishliye during anti-Jewish riots. Since that time draconian restrictions have been enforced on Syrian Jews, completely forbidding them to emigrate, virtually confining them to their places of residence and stamping their identity cards with the word '*Musawi* (Mosaic, a Jew). They are frequently subject to curfews and forbidden to have radios, telephones or postal contact with the outside world. The property of the few Jews who managed to leave Syria illegally was confiscated and the remaining relatives were mistreated by the Syrian police. At an international conference in Paris in 1971 two Syrian Jews who had escaped testified that the secret police supervised all Jewish gatherings, including synagogue services, and that local Jews were subjected to unemployment, poverty, arrests and sometimes even to torture. In the Jewish quarter of Damascus, the remaining 3–4,000 Jews are often maltreated by their Palestinian refugee neighbours, their life is very hard and they have for decades been hostages of the brutal Assad regime.[57]

In neighbouring Iraq, there are today only a few dozen Jews left out of a community which in 1948 had still numbered 135,000. The historical record since the country gained independence from Great Britain in 1932 has been a grim one for a Jewish community whose origins dated back almost three millennia. Under the British mandate Iraqi Jews enjoyed full equality with Muslims, freedom and a feeling of security. They were accepted into the civil service as officials and judges and enjoyed representation in the Iraqi parliament. A Jew even held the office of Finance Minister between 1920 and 1925. Until 1934 there was no government discrimination against Jews or attacks by the Muslim populace, though Zionist activity was forbidden after 1929.

The situation deteriorated with the rise of Nazism in Germany (the German envoy Dr Fritz Grobba helped to disseminate Nazi propaganda with growing success) and with the growing influence of exiled Syrians and Palestinians in the administration, political parties and the school system. In September 1934 dozens of non-Muslims were dismissed from government service and the following year secret instructions were given by the Ministry of Education to limit the number of Jews in secondary schools and institutions of higher learning. Many Jews were prevented from travelling to Palestine. Following the disturbances there, which began in 1936, Iraqi Jews were accused of 'dual loyalties' and some responded by dissociating themselves from Zionism or even claiming to be fervent adherents of the Pan-Arab idea. But in 1936 ten Jews were killed by Arab rioters in Baghdad and Basra. Again, in July 1937 there were violent anti-Jewish demonstrations in Baghdad, incited mainly by Syrians and Palestinians.[58]

Shortly after the outbreak of the Second World War, a new coterie of Arab exiles from Palestine, led by the Mufti of Jerusalem, Haj Amin al-Husseini, arrived in Baghdad, a development which reinforced anti-British feelings and hatred of the Jews. Axis radio propaganda and pro-Nazi sympathies in the Iraqi army and among influential student leaders impressed by the German example also helped to poison the atmosphere. On 18 April 1941 Rashīd Ālī al-Gailānī formed his second Cabinet, which included individuals known for their Nazi connections and their anti-Jewish attitudes like Yunus al-Sab'āwī.[59] With the collapse of the pro-German regime, following the reconquest of Iraq by Britain, a terrible pogrom (known in Arabic as *Farhūd*) was perpetrated by Muslims in Baghdad against the Jewish community on 1–2 June 1941. Several hundred Jews were slaughtered, many more wounded and Jewish property worth more than a million English pounds was looted. The British Army, at the gates of the city, did not intervene and showed no inclination to appear as the protector of the Jews by searching for the perpetrators of the bloodshed.[60]

Anti-Jewish propaganda continued in Iraq during the war years, with Arabs welcoming German military successes and with leaflets circulating which promised further massacres against Iraqi Jews in the future. In July 1946 there were anti-Jewish riots in which hundreds of Jews were wounded and much property destroyed. In 1947 the political climate deteriorated still further, with the UN resolution on the partition of Palestine. In August 1948 Zionism was officially declared a crime by the Iraqi government and many Jews were imprisoned, some of them even hanged – all were accused of supplying arms to the 'Zionists'. They included a Jewish millionaire, Shafiq 'Adas, whose contacts in high places did not save him from the unyielding hatred of the anti-Jewish Defence Minister, Ṣādiq al-Baṣṣām. By this time Iraqi Jews began escaping by the hundreds to Israel via Iran. On 4 March 1950 the Iraqi government finally legalised this haphazard exodus. An official decree confiscated all the property of Jews leaving for Israel, and appointed a special custodian to sell it by public auction. All bank accounts of emigrants were seized by the state. By the end of 1951, the vast majority of Iraqi Jews (113,545) had flown to Israel, leaving only a very small number behind.[61]

Immediately after the Six Day War of 1967, scores of Jewish merchants were arrested on the pretext of having smuggled money out of the state. Then, at the end of 1968, more Jews were imprisoned, this time accused of spying for Israel by the Iraqi Ba'ath regime. Nine of them were sentenced to death for alledged 'Zionist' activity and publicly hanged on 27 January 1969 to the shouts of jubilant crowds. The last remnants of Iraqi Jewry were now being held up as scapegoats for the Arab military disaster of 1967, as the 'fifth column', the local agents of imperialism and Zionism. This new outbreak of anti-semitism (1967–70) gave rise to a series of new discriminatory measures, including the imposition of quotas on Jews at Iraqi universities, the cancelling of jobs and contracts, the freezing of Jewish property transactions and liquid assets.[62]

But it was the gruesome spectacle of the January 1969 show-trials (comparable in their more modest way to the Moscow trials of the 1930s) and the public hangings which followed them which pointed the way to the totalitarian future. For the mass participation in the hanging of the 'Zionist' spies in Liberation Square was crucially important to the legitimation of Ba'athism. It proved, as Tariq 'Aziz (currently the Iraqi Foreign Minister) would assert in 1972, that the Ba'ath regime had the will and capability to eradicate *all* 'conspiracies' and 'espionage networks'. Referring to the 1969 hangings, he denied that they were 'barbaric' or 'primitive': 'That event was a monument of confidence staged by the revolution in the most important square in Baghdad to prove to the people that what had been impossible in the past was now a fact that could speak for itself.'[63] The monstrous regime of Saddam Hussein, built on terror, fear and the ubiquitous secret police, has had many occasions since then to demonstrate to the masses the concreteness of so-called 'imperialist-Zionist plots' against the 'freedom-loving' Iraqi Republic. His repeated threats to incinerate Israel with chemical weapons and his historic identification with Nebuchadnezzar, the pagan Babylonian destroyer of the First Temple, have been macabre reminders of the myth-making destructiveness of totalitarian politics.

The demise of the once prosperous Iranian Jewish community as a result of the Islamic Revolution of 1979 has been an equally tragic example of the fate of contemporary Jews in Muslim lands. The legal status of Persian Jewry before 1906 had been governed by traditional Muslim law, leaving them without any rights as citizens and their residency dependent on payment of the poll-tax. In the Sharī'a courts which controlled the judicial system, the evidence of a Jew against a Muslim was considered invalid and a Muslim was not put to death for the murder of a Jew, even if two Muslim witnesses had given testimony against him. Religious functionaries, who had great influence on the masses in this devout Shī'īte country, were consistently hostile to the Jews and adhered to a stringent theory about the ritual impurity of non-Muslims which did not exist in Sunni Muslim countries. The humiliation, persecution and suffering of the Persian Jews induced constant intervention by foreign states and Western Jewry to ease their degraded *dhimmi* status. Constitutional equality was eventually achieved in 1906, but during the next four years Jews were assaulted in Shīrāz, while there was also looting and murder in Hamadhān, Darab and Kermanshāh. In 1910, 12 Jews were killed and some 50 wounded in Shīrāz.[64]

The military dictatorship instituted by Riza Shah Pahlavi after 1925 brought the Iranian Jews equality with Muslims in many spheres, though non-Shī'ite Muslims could still not serve as government ministers or elect any but their own representatives to parliament. The humiliating poll-tax was abolished and the impurity practices prohibited, though they were never successfully uprooted among religious Shī'ite Muslims; even today they regard Jews as unclean and would not eat fruit handled by them or use a glass from which they have drunk. But Riza Shah's determination to modernise the country by introducing secular laws, civil marriage and other measures that reduced the power of the Muslim clergy undoubtedly helped to improve the status of the Iranian Jews.[65] This policy was continued by his son, under whose regime the Jews became fully acculturated, were concentrated in Teheran and transformed into an economically thriving community. Hatred of Jews diminished, though never entirely disappeared, being periodically encouraged by the more fanatical religious and nationalist elements.

The most formidable of all the opponents of the Shah was the Ayatollah Khomeini, who constantly denounced the attempts of the Pahlavi dynasty to circumvent Islam, its links to the United States and Israel, the cult of materialism in Iranian society and its growing loss of spiritual identity. As early as 1962 one can find an antisemitic discourse in Khomeini's speeches and writings, linked to his obsession with foreign conspiracies and internal decadence. He warned Iranians that 'the independence of the country and its economy are about to be taken over by Zionists, who in Iran appear as the party of Baha'is, and if this deadly silence of Muslims continues, they will soon take over the entire economy of the country and drive it to complete bankruptcy.

Iranian television is a Jewish spy base, the government sees this and approves of it.'[66] Khomeini consistently linked foreign cultural products with materialistic intoxication by the West and with the poisonous corruption of Muslim religious values. Israel, Zionism and the Jews of Iran played a crucial role in this 'sinister influence' of Western cultural and economic imperialism, aided and abetted by the Shah's regime.[67]

'Israel, the universally recognised enemy of Islam and the Muslims . . . has with the assistance of the despicable government of Iran', so he declared in 1971, 'penetrated all the economic, military, and political affairs of the country.' In Khomeini's eyes, Israel was a 'cancerous growth in the Middle East', sowing dissension among Muslims and plotting, with the help of America, 'satanic' conspiracies against the Islamic Revolution.[68] But his anti-Israelism was often but a thin veneer for a virulent anti-Judaism, returning to the Koranic sources of the Islamic faith. As he put it in his 'Program for the Establishment of an Islamic Government' (1970),

> We see today that the Jews (may God curse them) have
> meddled with the text of the Koran and have made
> certain changes in the Korans they have printed in the
> occupied territories. It is our duty to prevent this
> treacherous interference. . . . We must protest and
> make the people aware that the Jews and their foreign
> backers are opposed to the very foundations of Islam
> and wish to establish Jewish domination throughout
> the world. Since they are a cunning and resourceful
> group of people, I fear that – God forbid! – they may
> one day achieve this goal, and that the apathy shown
> by some of us may allow a Jew to rule over us one day.
> May God never let us see such a day.[69]

With Khomeini's Islamic revolution, the wheel came full circle for the remnants of Jewry in Islamic lands. A government was established for whom Islamic archetypes of the Jews (reinforced by specific Shī'ite phobias) from seventh-century Arabia were valid for the conduct of politics in the late twentieth century. The strategems of Israel were merely a continuation of the 'anti-Islamic propaganda' which the Jews had allegedly engaged in during and since the days of the Prophet. The Koranic teachings and the books of the *hadith* were eternally valid for society, the economy and political life. The *jizya* would have to be restored for the *ahl ad-dhimma* ('protected peoples'), along with all other rules of the Muslim religious law. The secular rulers of Muslim countries, out of touch with the believers and with God's ordinances, would have to be overthrown. Because of their incompetence and heresy, 'a handful of wretched Jews' (agents of America, Britain and other foreign powers) had occupied Muslim lands and Holy Places, trampling on the sacred rights of the faithful.[70]

This extremist, radical ideology, which has functioned with the full backing of the state for over a decade in Iran, has of course greatly strengthened antisemitism. The 15,000 Jews left in the country (just before the Revolution there were 80,000) are discriminated against, persecuted, physically insecure and deprived of any cultural or spiritual future. They have to keep a low profile, dissimulate their real beliefs, behave as if they were Muslims who identify with the cause of the Ayatollahs. They are always exposed to the risk that the government may claim that they are 'Zionists', since many have relatives in Israel and may desire to correspond with them. Some ten or eleven Jews have already been executed in Iran on charges of being 'Zionist spies'. Such allegations, however spurious, reinforce the familiar image of the Jew as plotting against Islam, which is the standard refrain of Iranian propaganda.[71] Jews in Iran, as a matter of government policy, have at times been forced to identify with the antisemitism and anti-Zionism of the regime, and to demonstrate in favour of the future liberation of Jerusalem by the Muslims.

This degrading spectacle is a sad conclusion to the history of what was once the largest Jewish Diaspora community in Asia – one whose origins go back over two millennia. But it is a faithful reflection of the meaning of the *dhimmi* status, of the renewed and obsessive Muslim concern with Jews and Judaism in the contemporary world and the inability of Islam to transcend obsolete stereotypes from a bygone era.

16
· · ·

Conspiracies and Holy Wars

During the past forty years a vast anti-Jewish literature has appeared in Arab and Islamic countries using theological, racial and demonological motifs as well as the more familiar forms of political anti-Zionism and anti-Israelism. Some of this literature is obviously European or Western in origin – texts translated into Arabic like Hitler's *Mein Kampf*, Henry Ford's *International Jew* or *The Protocols of the Elders of Zion*. It seems at first sight to have no more basis in local Middle Eastern tradition than the anti-Jewish cartoons and caricatures which have so frequently appeared in the Arabic press and remind one of German or Russian antisemitic stereotypes. But a more careful analysis suggests that Muslim writers, even when they exploit Western antisemitic images and concepts, usually manage to link these imported notions in a natural, even an organic manner, with ideas from within their own cultural tradition.[1]

Foremost in this synthesis has been the wedding together of archetypes fixed in the consciousness of early Islam with the theories of a 'world Jewish conspiracy' adapted from modern European antisemitism. This kind of fusion is evident in contemporary Islamic fundamentalist literature produced not only in the core-lands of the Arab world but also on the periphery, from the Maghreb and Sudan to Iran, Pakistan and Malaysia.[2] Indeed, physical isolation from the Arab–Israeli conflict sometimes seems to give Islamic perceptions of the Jews as a threat and an evil force in world affairs a more deadly quality of abstraction, altogether divorced from reality. Such attitudes are actively encouraged and spread into the Muslim diaspora in Asia, Africa and Europe by government financing coming particularly from Iran, Saudi Arabia and Libya. They are reinforced by the ritual presentation of anti-Jewish and anti-Zionist propaganda at Islamic conferences and international meetings attended by government representatives and Muslim notables.

The alleged historical misdeeds of Jews against Islam, the revival of the blood libel by Muslims, the denunciations of the Talmud and the demonic image of a ruthless, oppressive Israel which dominate these diatribes are mixed together in a highly combustible, dehumanised stereotype of the Jewish and Zionist enemy. This kind of literature is extremely popular today among Arab youth in Cairo, Jordan and in the territories occupied by Israel after the 1967 war, where it is promulgated by fundamentalist groups like Hamas and the Islamic Jihad.[3] Indeed, wherever Islamic movements appear to be on the ascendant, the use of antisemitic symbols comes into the foreground as part of a cultural and religious confrontation with the Jews that transcends mundane politics. There is no serious differentiation between the Jews, Judaism, world Jewry and Israel, for they are all seen as part of a global conspiracy to create an alien body in the heart of the Muslim world, to violate the rights of the Palestinians and steal away a Muslim Arab land. For the fundamentalists there can be no compromise over Palestine since a Muslim land in the heart of *dar al-Islam* (the abode of Islam) can only be ruled by a Muslim authority.[4] The 'usurpation' of this holy land is perceived not only as an act of brutal aggression by Israel but as an assault on the morality and civilisation of Islam which the West actively encouraged out of a mixture of imperialist motives or to purge its own sense of guilt for the persecution of Jews.

In the fundamentalist world-view there can be no separation of politics and religion. The Arab–Israeli conflict is not simply territorial and political, it has the theological and even metaphysical dimension of a clash between Islam and the

Jews, between two fundamentally opposed conceptions of the world.[5] The archetypal notions about Jews, like all other beliefs and doctrines laid down in the Holy Koran, have an unalterable quality, they are binding on all believing Muslims as eternal verities which must guide their actions. As long as the Jews conformed to their assigned role as *dhimmis*, they could be tolerated, even if they had been cursed by God and were suspected of plotting against the believers.[6] The latent hostility and hatred was attenuated in the past not only by social, economic and cultural interaction between Jews and Muslims, but above all by a *political* order which guaranteed Islamic superiority. But once this military and political domination was undermined in the modern era, first by Christian European powers and then by Israel, essential aspects of Arab–Muslim identity were thrown into question. For the eclipse of Islam threatened one of its central myths, that Allah had promised victory in *this* world to the followers of Mohammed.

Fundamentalism can be seen in part as a way of grappling with the tremendous shock induced by this painful encounter with modernity, in the form of a conquering, more technologically advanced Western civilisation. It seeks to restore Muslim greatness by countering the decline in religious belief which it holds to be at the root of Islam's problems in the modern world. The emergence of Israel in 1948 at the very moment when the process of de-colonisation had suggested to many Arabs that history might again be reverting to its proper course, dealt a traumatic blow to these hopes and to Muslim self-esteem in general. For not only did Israel establish a sovereign Jewish state in a part of the Arab homeland, not only has it consistently defeated Muslim Arab armies on the battlefield and occupied the third holiest sanctuary in Islam; it is a state which represents to many Muslim minds a group of people destined by Allah only for suffering and humiliation, entitled at most to be a protected minority under Islamic rule. Its very existence created a new 'Jewish question' for Islam, the acuteness of which was unprecedented and which has aroused such anxiety, precisely because it seems to threaten their self-conception, their worth, their identity and their dignity as Muslims and Arabs. It was bad enough to be defeated by the powerful forces of Western imperialism, but to be humiliated by what had been traditionally perceived by Muslims as a small, weak and defenceless minority, the Jews, calls into doubt fundamental claims about Islam's 'spiritual' superiority and finality.

Fundamentalist antisemitism must be regarded at the psychological level as a somewhat desperate attempt to rationalise and explain away this failure which has been for many Muslims a truly wrenching dislocation of Allah's plans for His chosen people. For this purpose it is not enough simply to proclaim the immutable character of Koranic doctrines about the Jews as the great enemy of Islam from its inception, or to emphasise their innate wickedness, perfidy, hypocrisy and ungodliness. It is also necessary to demonstrate how Jews in the modern world have been responsible for Islam's civilisational crisis, how they are linked to pernicious Western domination, to the failures of secular Arab regimes and to the undermining of religion and traditional values.[7] What was only implicit in the ancient Islamic sources had itself, ironically enough, to be 'modernised' by appropriate borrowings from the armoury of Western antisemitism to demonstrate to Muslims that they were combating a Satanic evil in the form of Zionism. A good example of this synthesis can be found in the writings of the leading Egyptian fundamentalist, Sayyid Qutb (executed by Nasser in 1966), especially his essay 'Our Struggle With the Jews', first published in the early 1950s.[8]

In this essay, the Jews emerge as a metaphor and symbol for the danger of Western domination and immorality, as well as a continuing threat in their own right to the integrity of Islam which they compulsively seek to destroy. By nature they had always been resolved to sow confusion and corruption in the hearts of believers, to undermine the Creed by encouraging

225

sectarian rifts and by allying themselves with Islam's enemies. In the twentieth century they had deliberately encouraged secularism and modernity in Egypt, by means of which they successfully poisoned the Muslim Arab intelligentsia, alienating it from its own traditions. It was the Jews who had disseminated 'the doctrine of atheistic materialism' (Marx), of 'animalistic sexuality' (Freud), of rationalistic sociology (Durkheim), and who had encouraged the destruction of the family and immutable religious truth.[9] Their devilish, misanthropic and essentially subversive nature had led them to construct the modern Western ideologies which were sapping the authentic spirituality of Islam. The monstrous spectre of heresy had reached its apex with the Satanic evil of Zionism and Israel, which openly aimed at the subjugation of Allah's Chosen, the righteous Muslims. It was the same diabolical Jewish–Zionist conspiracy that had created secular nationalist regimes in the Arab world, whose Westernising policies made them 'traitors' to their people and destroyers of Islam from *within*.[10] For Qutb's fundamentalist followers in Egypt, Syria and other parts of the Muslim world, the proof of his theses would come with President Sadat's visit to Jerusalem and the Egyptian Peace Treaty with Israel in 1979. This was a vividly dramatic demonstration that heretical, pseudo-Muslim rulers were truly 'agents' of Israel, that their illusory peace would provide an open door to the Jews to smuggle into Egypt the products of a poisonous 'racist-imperialist' Western culture.

For the fundamentalist Muslim Brotherhood in Egypt there was no greater danger than that of 'normalisation' with Israel, invariably defined as a fanatical, racist state and, through its Jewish–American connection, as a direct threat to the family life, morals and culture of Egyptian Muslims. Ever since the 1930s the Brotherhood, under the leadership of Hasan al-Banna, had advocated a *jihad* (Holy War) in defence of Egypt, Arabism and Islam against the British and the Jews.[11] They had been the most militant fighters in Egypt during the 1940s on behalf of the Palestinian cause against the 'Jewish crusaders' (*al-salibiyya al-yahudiyya*) who were seeking to conquer Muslim lands and subvert Muslim society. After the Second World War the Muslim Brothers had attacked the Jewish quarter in Cairo and led an antisemitic campaign against Egyptian Jewry. Increasingly, they also denounced America with its 'Zionist-dominated' press, radio and films for undermining everything Muslim and 'Eastern' as part of a sinister campaign to secure Palestine for the Jews.[12] Nor did they hesitate to depict President Nasser (after he had allied himself with the Soviet Union) as the agent of an international Jewish plot. How else could one explain the disasters he had brought upon Egypt? Such Arab nationalist leaders, however anti-Western or anti-Israel they might be in their rhetoric, were easy prey in their eyes for outside 'Jewish' influences, and fated to surrender to Zionism and the West. The seeds of Sadat's 'betrayal' were already there in Nasser's misrule and his ruthless suppression of the Brotherhood.[13]

For the fundamentalists, the peace with Israel was and still remains nothing less than a poison threatening the life-blood of Islam, a symptom of its profound malaise, weakness and decadence. In the articles of Umar al-Tilmisani (spiritual leader of the Muslim Brothers in Egypt and chief editor of their monthly *al-Da'wa*) this intensely hostile view found a most trenchant expression in the early 1980s. 'Normalisation of relations with Israel,' he wrote, 'is the most dangerous cancer eating away at all the life-cells in our bodies.'[14] Israel, he further declared, was the snake-like head of the international anti-Islamic forces, and its embassy in Egypt was the command centre for destroying the economy, the values and customs of the nation. The Jews would bring with them 'all manner of moral evils such as cabarets, drinking of liquor and white slavery'; they would 'exploit all the writers who will sell their faith and honour', encourage economic exploitation and the taking of interest, and 'institute ways of deceitful propaganda'. Their best weapon, according to al-Tilmisani, 'as they spread their poison among the youth' was their spurious claim 'to be fighting backwardness which they allege is due to Islam; while they also in fact fight all varieties of Islamic tradition.'[15]

In the anti-Jewish polemics of *al-Da'wa* (The Mission), one can find, therefore, many of the stereotypes of European antisemitism in an Islamic costume. Of all the myriad enemies of Islam (the crusading West, Communism, secularism), Jewry represents the ultimate abomination, evil in its purest ontological form. The French scholar Gilles Kepel, summarising *al-Da'wa*'s definition of the Jew, puts it thus: 'The race is corrupt at the root, full of duplicity, and the Muslims have everything to lose in seeking to deal with them: they must be exterminated.'[16] 'Israel's behaviour is understood solely in terms of this negative essence, influenced by *The Protocols of the Elders of Zion*, no less than by a selective interpretation of Koranic verses.[17] Hence, Holy War must be remorselessly waged against the Jewish State until the Dome of the Rock and the Al-Aqsa Mosque in Jerusalem, and the entire country in which it stands, is brought again under Islamic rule. Sadat's visit in 1979 to a Jerusalem still occupied by the Jewish 'infidels' was therefore the ultimate act of betrayal and his assassination by Muslim militants could only be welcomed.

A similar synthesis of Islamic and Western antisemitism can be found in the works of the former Rector of Cairo's al-Azhar University (the major seat of Islamic learning in the Muslim world), Abd al-Halim Mahmoud, who died in 1978. His book *al-Jihad wa an-Nasr* (Holy War and Victory), published in Cairo four years earlier, connects in classical fashion Jewish treachery against Mohammed with the Jewish-Zionist conspiracy to undermine the Arab states and ultimately to control the world. The struggle for Islamic Truth and Justice was presented here as nothing less than a struggle against a Satanic conspiracy.

> Among Satan's friends – indeed his best friends in our age – are the Jews. They have laid down a plan for undermining humanity, religiously and ethically. They

have begun to work to implement this plan with their money and their propaganda. They have falsified knowledge, exploited the pens of writers and bought minds in their quest for the ruination of humanity. Thus they proceed from this to seizing power . . . domination, mastery, and gaining full control.[18]

This unrestrained antisemitic rhetoric recalls the venomous diatribes against the Jews and Israel at the Fourth Conference of the Academy of Islamic Research, held in Cairo in 1968 at Nasser's behest to discuss the fundamentals of the Middle East conflict. Theologians and Muslim notables from all over the Arab world had on that occasion called for a *jihad* to destroy Israel as the culmination of the historical and cultural depravity of the Jews, their baseness viewed as being congenital and immutable in nature. Contemporay Jewry was not and had never constituted a true people or nation but was merely a riff-raff which had always provoked the hatred and persecution of the peoples with which they came into contact. Their repugnant qualities, depicted in the Bible as well as the Holy Koran, had been transmitted unchanged down into modern times through their own cultural inheritance.[19] As Kamal Ahmad Own (Vice-Principal of the Tanta Institute) put it, what had happened in Palestine was the logical result of the 'scenes of bloodshed, sex perversion and the violation of the Prophets' to be found in the Old Testament. The wickedness of the Jews was 'incurable' unless they were completely subdued by force, for it derived from their own Holy Book and the Talmud, which 'are full to the brim with such horrible deeds, evils and crimes that make us feel they deserved all the disasters and the afflictions that befell them'.[20] Modern civilisation had only 'increased their hypocrisy, their power, their wealth and their penetration into the social life of nations from behind the scenes'.

The Syrian delegate Muhammad Azzah Darwaza also emphasised the innate wickedness and evil of the Jews from the days of the Prophet to their 'merciless' treatment of Arabs and Muslims in Palestine. 'The Jews followed the attitudes of their ancestors towards the Prophet and the Muslims. The Jews kept on sticking to their corrupt demoralised instinct and their vicious wicked prejudice. They committed their treacherous oppressive atrocities in Palestine . . . atrocities so terrific that they curdle one's blood.'[21]

Professor Abdul Sattar El Sayed, the Mufti of Tursos (Syria) was even more bellicose, comparing the Jews to 'germs of a malignant disease where only one germ is sufficient to eliminate an entire nation'. The Arabs were no different from other peoples in regarding the Jews as 'a pest which humanity had to tolerate and live with like other calamities of life and other diseases'.[22] As the Koran had revealed, they were 'a plague like Satan who was expelled by God', but despite their apparent support from Western imperialism, they were weaker than the Devil and inferior to him 'in the face of the faithful who adhere to religion'.

The Lebanese Sheikh Nadim al-Jisr was equally confident that Muslims would inevitably regain their ascendency over the illegitimate artificial and 'deformed' Jewish state, quoting extensively from the *hadiths* in which the Prophet was said to have predicted a final battle to annihilate the Jews.[23] Mohammed, so it was reported on the authority of Abu Huraira, had stated: 'The Hour [i.e. salvation] would not come, until you fight against the Jews; and the stone would say, "O Muslim! There is a Jew behind me: come and kill him".'[24]

The Mufti of the Lebanese Republic, Hassan Khaled, fully agreed with the consensus of opinion that 'the Jews were the most atrocious enemies to Islam and the Muslims' in the Age of the Prophet, as they had once more become through the deeds of contemporary Zionism. Hence the need for a *jihad* to rescue a decadent and dissolute Islamic society which had 'become an easy prey to the dogs of humanity' (the Jews), and to restore the usurped, desecrated Holy Land.[25]

The scholars of al-Azhar did in fact reluctantly change their position in 1979 at President Sadat's strenuous bidding, claiming that the Egyptian-Israeli peace treaty was 'founded on Islamic rules, because it arises from a position of strength, after the holy war and victory Egypt achieved on 10th Ramadan, 1393' (October 1973). But Mohammed's truce with the Jews, which provided their precedent, was itself only a temporary expedient and even the subservient scholars of al-Azhar were far from accepting either the Jewish claim to nationhood or legitimate historical roots for a Jewish state in Palestine.[26] Moreover, in the 1980s, with the growing popularity of fundamentalist preachers, writers and militants in Egypt, even such modest accommodations as that of al-Azhar seemed to lack any deeper Muslim legitimacy. For radical Islam, 'palace *ulema*' appointed by the government could only reflect the timidity, servility and pseudo-religiosity of a corrupt Establishment. Thus, even tactical and conditional acceptance of Israel was seen as a complete contradiction to Islam and a negation of Egypt's Islamic Arab identity, at least among Muslim activists.[27]

In this aggressive stance, the Muslim Brotherhood felt strengthened by the Islamic revolutionaries in Iran whose intransigent hatred of the Jews and Zionism corresponded to their own. In the occupied West Bank and Gaza, too, Ayatollah Khomeini's message of extirpating the 'cancer' of Israel with a surgical knife and returning to Jerusalem under the banner of *jihad* enthused the radicalised Muslim youth.[28] The reconquest of Al Kuds (the Arabic name for Jerusalem) was indeed a powerful rallying-cry of the Islamic revolution, until it got bogged down in the marshlands of the Shatt al-Arab and an interminable Gulf War with Iraq. Like Khomeini, the erratic Libyan leader, Colonel Qaddafi, was no less committed to the liberation of Jerusalem in the name of his Islamic socialist and Pan-Arab ideals, never losing an opportunity to preach the destruction of Israel as the highest priority of Islam. It should, however, be noted that, except for the medieval Islamic struggle against the Crusaders and the post-1967 Muslim campaign against the 'Judaisation' of Jerusalem of the Israelis, the city had never been spiritually unique or historically pre-eminent in Islam like Mecca and, secondarily, Medina have been. Indeed, during the nineteen years between 1948 and 1967, when its Muslim holy places were under Jordanian rule, Jerusalem's sanctity was not particularly emphasised.[29]

Of all the Muslim leaders who bitterly deplored the fall of Jerusalem to the 'infidels' in 1967, pride of place must go to the Saudi monarch, King Feisal, the guardian of Islam's holiest sites in the Arabian peninsula. In 1974 Feisal, speaking in the name of the Islamic world, had told the Vatican that under Islam 'Jews had never been allowed in Palestine and particularly in Jerusalem' and that Jews had no holy places in the city.[30] This was manifestly untrue but consistent with the Saudi rulers' *absolute exclusion* of Jews from their own Kingdom. The Saudis had preceded any other Muslim or Arab country in their open promotion of a virulent antisemitism, even before the Second World War. A good example of this attitude can be found in the remarks by King Abd al Aziz ibn Sa'ud to a semi-official British visitor to Riyadh, Colonel Dickson, in the autumn of 1937. King Sa'ud deplored the 'strange hypnotic influence which the Jews, a race accursed by God according to His Holy Book, and destined to final destruction and eternal damnation', appeared to exercise over the British government and people.[31] The final fate of the Jews had been fixed by the unalterable words of God in the Koran, which he recommended to the British government for perusal.

Ibn Sa'ud also appealed to what he clearly believed to be the core of the antisemitism animating Christians: 'Our hatred for the Jews dates from God's condemnation of them for their persecution and rejection of Isa [Jesus Christ], and their subsequent rejection later of His chosen Prophet.'[32] It was beyond his understanding how Britain, 'the first Christian power in the world', could wish to reward 'these very same Jews who maltreated your Isa'; how, he wondered, could they risk Arab friendship for 'an accursed and stiffnecked race which has always bitten the hand of everyone who has helped it since the world began'.[33] The Jews were unquestionably the enemies of Arabia and of England, they were determined to sow discord between them and then to seize 'the whole of Palestine, Transjordan and their old stronghold Medina – the land they went to when driven out of Palestine and dispersed after the Romans destroyed Jerusalem'. Hence King Sa'ud's total opposition to any partition of Palestine, which would merely be the first step towards a vast expansion of Jewish power. Quoting a well-known *hadith*, he informed the British visitor to his court: 'Verily the word of God teaches us, and we implicitly believe it, that for a Muslim to kill a Jew, or for him to be killed by a Jew, ensures him an immediate entry into Heaven and into the august presence of God Almighty.'[34]

King Feisal was in the same tradition as his father, and also a firm believer that Zionism and Communism were two aspects of the same international Jewish conspiracy. He was known for his custom of giving a free copy of *The Protocols of The Elders of Zion* (for which the Arab world is still the biggest market today) to visiting officials and delegations, including even the former American Secretary of State, Henry Kissinger.[35] The Saudis, the Iranians and Libyans (not to mention Pakistan, which is a leading centre for the publication of this scurrilous literature) have done everything to disseminate the notion of a world conspiracy to make Israel and the Jews appear in the most sinister light possible. The astonishing wealth and power of the Saudis, in particular after the 1973 oil crisis, has insured that these antisemitic calumnies now carry more weight, given the priority which many Western governments place on good relations with the oil-producing states.[36]

The Saudis have also surreptitiously helped to finance antisemitic Holocaust denial literature in the West, such as *Anti-Zion* (originally entitled *The Jews on Trial*) and *The Six Million Reconsidered*, written by an American neo-Nazi, William Grimstad, registered as a Saudi agent with the US Department of Justice since 1977.[37] These publications were mailed to all members of the United States Senate and British Parliament by the World Muslim Congress in 1981 and early 1982. This latter organisation, with its headquarters in Pakistan, had been under the presidency of a notorious antisemite and collaborator with Nazi Germany, Haj Amin al-Husseini (ex-Mufti of Jerusalem) until 1974. Its officers and members had been thoroughly inculcated in a *Protocols*-like vision of world Jewry and the 'Zionist scourge' during the twenty-three years of Haj Amin's stewardship.[38] For example, the World Muslim Congress in August 1981 would declare that not only was a settlement with Israel 'treason against Muslims' but that the Zionists aimed at 'controlling the world and if not possible . . . annihilating the entire human race'.[39] In December 1984 the President of the World Muslim Congress, Dr Ma'ruf al-Dawalibi, provided another more archaic example of outspoken antisemitism in his 'learned' exegesis of the Talmud. Speaking to the UN Centre for Human Rights' Seminar on the Encouragement of Understanding, Tolerance and Respect in Matters Relating to Freedom of Religion and Belief (sic!), he declared: 'The Talmud says that "if a Jew does not drink every year the blood of a non-Jewish man, then he will be damned for eternity".'[40] According to this Muslim authority, the Talmud maintains that 'the whole world is the property of Israel and the wealth, the blood, and the souls of non-Israelis . . . are theirs'.[41] This demented belief, he claimed, was the real source of discrimination and oppression against the Jews!

The constant use by Muslims of antisemitic motifs derived from the European Christian tradition like the blood libel, the *Protocols* and distorted caricatures of the Talmud is indeed striking. Canon August Rohling's scurrilous *Der Talmudjude* first appeared in Arabic as early as 1899 (it had been published two decades earlier in Central Europe). But in more recent years there have been many more works of purely Arab provenance alleging that the Talmud permits Jews to lie, cheat and steal from Gentiles, to violate their women with impunity, shed their blood and in general to treat them as if they were

234

animals in human form. The Arabist Norman Stillman has pointed to the ubiquity of the blood libel even in seemingly scholarly tomes by Muslim writers like 'Alī 'Abd al-Wāhid Wāfī, Muhammad Sabrī, Hasan Zāzā, Mustafā al-Sa'danī and the prominent Egyptian woman writer 'Ā'isha 'Abd al-Rahmān (pen-name, Bint al-Shāti') — a literature that, *inter alia*, treats the draining of children's blood at Passover as a recognised Jewish ritual.[42] Another Egyptian author, Kaṁil Sa'fān in his book *al-Yahud Ta'rīkhan wa-Aqīdatan* (*Jews — History and Doctrine*), published in 1981, also accepted the accusations of ritual murder in the Damascus Affair of 1840 and maintained that many other cases went unnoticed through the manipulation of the Jews. At the same time an introduction to his book stressed in classic antisemitic language the danger of the invisible Jewish 'penetration' and 'infiltration' of Western countries in order to pursue their secret, conspiratorial designs.[43]

The adoption of blood-libel myths and notions of secret Jewish cabals controlling the world have been popular in the Arab world since the 1950s (Nasser's regime published and disseminated many such works) and gained wide exposure through the Arab press, radio broadcasts and school textbooks as well as cartoons and caricatures. By the early 1960s this Muslim and Arab antisemitism had become throughly pervasive. It was at this time that great efforts were made by Arab states to dissuade the Vatican from exculpating the Jews from collective guilt for Jesus's death. The landmark document of the Second Vatican Council (28 October 1965), *Nostra Aetate*, which repudiated the charge of deicide against the Jewish people caused visible consternation in the Arab-Muslim world, although the accusation itself has no basis in Islamic tradition and is entirely Christian in provenance. Yet not only the Fathers of the Eastern Church (concerned about the fate of Catholics and other Christian minorities in the Middle East), but also Muslim dignitaries and Arab diplomats insistently sought to maintain the Christ-killer accusation intact.[44] They even alleged that its removal was a result of 'Zionist' influence over the Catholic Church and a political victory for Israel. The Council of the World Muslim League in Mecca charged that Vatican II was 'antagonistic toward Islam and the Arabs'; it was asserted that this was 'a purely political move aimed at securing the Christian world's support for the Zionist concept and its devilish and wicked designs against Islam, the Arabs, and the whole human race'.[45]

In short, *Nostra Aetate* was presented as a Jewish plot, a view echoed many years later by one of Egypt's leading journalists and authors, Anīs Mansour, himself a Muslim. Mansour (at one time a leading adviser of President Sadat) wrote in 1979 that it was Jewish money which had corruptly bought exoneration from the Crucifixion charge. For two thousand years Jews had been deservedly accursed by Christians, but, worried by the anger of American Jewry and fearful for their capital invested abroad, the Vatican had abjectly surrendered to a people 'who have killed tens of prophets, who butchered little children in Europe, and in Palestine as well, who poisoned Christian kings, who spread the plague'. Mansour's conclusion was that the Vatican 'has sold Christ once again to the Jews, but for a high price, the money and indignation of the Arabs'.[46] What is so remarkable in this antisemitic diatribe is the transparent way that a Muslim intellectual bases his views on Christian myths alien to his own tradition, in order to uphold traditional Christian vilification of the Jews.

Nevertheless, it must be emphasised that Muslim anti-semitism does not make purely arbitrary borrowings from Christian and modern secular European varieties of Judeo-phobia. Furthermore, the perceptions of Jews as a treacherous, conspiratorial and potentially evil force have their autonomous roots in Islamic theological thought and have been greatly reinforced by the revival of radical Islam and of the notion of *jihad* in face of a powerful Jewish state in the Middle East. The very existence of Israel is a sign to many Muslims that 'the forces of darkness and immorality, of wickedness and apostasy' have gained a temporary ascendency in the world.[47] This has been particularly true for radical fundamentalists who challenged the regimes of Sadat in Egypt and of Assad in Syria during the early 1980s.[48] They felt that they alone sprang from the native soil of Islam and expressed the passions of the submerged popular masses. Unlike the liberals, secularists, Communists or Arab nationalists (whose ideologies were essentially European) they expressed something authentically Middle Eastern.[49] The contemporary problems of internal decay, cultural Westernisation, imperialism and Zionism had only one solution – the Islamisation of the whole Middle East. Not for nothing did the killers of Sadat (members of a radical Jihad group) chant in unison at their sentencing: 'Our state is Islamic, Islamic. Not Jewish, not Zionist. We are neither of the Eastern bloc, nor of the Western bloc, we are one hundred per cent Islamic.'

Some of these radical Muslims were undoubtedly more concerned about first purging their own countries of 'godlessness' before turning to the Zionist enemy of Israel. Their outlook was a natural response to the persecution and repression they had suffered at the hands of secular nationalist regimes, who had miserably failed the trial by fire of the Six Day War. The trauma of defeat in that war had destroyed much of the magic of Pan-Arabism and left an ideological vacuum quickly filled by the revival of Islam. For the post-1967 generation this fact did not diminish but rather reinforced their hatred of Israel and Zionism. The Israeli invasion of Lebanon in the summer of 1982 further added to the traditional Islamic vituperation against Jews, the demonic dimension of powerful, ruthless and barbarian foes – who have been depicted as the 'new Mongols'.[50] For Sunni Arab radicals, as for the pro-Iranian Shi'ite factions in Lebanon (the Hizbollah, Islamic Amal and Islamic Jihad) the humiliation of a Jewish army laying siege for the first time to an Arab capital (Beirut), was yet another reason for radicalisation. This in turn favoured a new brand of Islamic antisemitism, reiterating many of the traditional themes, yet harnessed to the cause of a Khomeini-style revolution throughout the Middle East.

The effects of this *jihad* have been felt all through the 1980s and right up until the present day. Fundamentalist Islam, which has always distinguished between *Dar al-Harb* (the abode of war) and *Dar al-Islam* (the abode of Islam), makes it theoretically inconceivable in Muslim law that there should be *silm* (peace) between it and a territory in its midst governed by non-Muslims. In the case of Jews, peace is even less conceivable, as long as they hold Palestine and are seen to be displacing or dispossessing its Arab and Muslim population. The *intifada* in the occupied territories has strengthened this traditional Muslim view, especially in the Gaza strip and to some extent in the West Bank, where the influence of Islamic fundamentalist radicalism has steadily grown. The opposition to Israel's very existence is much more intransigent in Hamas (the Islamic Resistance) than it is today among secular Palestinian nationalists. For the ideologues of the Islamic Resistance, Israel is the spearhead of 'satanic' forces aiming to create a Zionist empire from the Nile to the Euphrates. For them there can be no compromise in any form with the 'illegal' usurpation of Palestine, no negotiation, no peaceful compromise but only unswerving loyalty to the commandment of *jihad*.

With this intransigent ideology goes an equally unyielding antisemitism that reinforces the chilling calls for Israel's extinction. In the classic traditions of *The Protocols of the Elders of Zion*, 'world Zionism' and the 'warmongering Jews' are accused of having caused the First and Second World Wars, 'through which they made huge financial gains by trading in armaments, and paved the way for the establishment of their state.' Both the capitalist West and the Communist East were willing accomplices in this conspiracy against Islam and Palestine. The Jews, we are told, had been 'behind the French Revolution, the Communist Revolution and most of the revolutions we heard and hear about', according to article 22 of the Hamas Covenant of August 1988. 'With their money they formed secret societies,' the Covenant adds, 'such as Freemasons, Rotary Clubs, the Lions and others in different parts of the world for the purpose of sabotaging societies and achieving Zionist interests.'[51]

This world-conspiracy idea has long served to compensate Muslims for the unpalatable reality of repeated defeats at Israel's hands. It has sought to make Israel's existence and its goals appear sinister in the eyes of Arabs, Muslims and sympathetic outsiders in the Third World. It perpetually links Zionism with European, Western or Communist imperialism as a deceptively powerful, omnipotent force which would otherwise dissolve without sustenance from outside. Above all, the antisemitic conspiracy theory serves to mobilise the destructive passions in the Muslim and Arab population, in order to reinforce the will to fight for Islam. In the words of Hamas in one of the opening sentences in its official Covenant: 'Israel will exist and continue to exist until Islam will obliterate it, just as it obliterated others before it.'[52]

17
...

The Question of Palestine

The seeds of the modern Arab–Jewish conflict in Palestine began to develop under Turkish rule in the closing decades before the First World War with the emergence of the first Zionist settlements. Already in 1891 some Arab notables had sent a petition to the Ottoman capital, Istanbul, demanding the prohibition of Jewish immigration and land purchase. In Haifa, Jaffa, Beirut and Damascus, anti-Zionist newspapers were published by Arabs between 1908 and 1914, though this opposition did not become really intense until after the Balfour Declaration of the British government in November 1917, promising to establish a Jewish National Home in Palestine.[1]

In the period before the First World War, Arab anti-Zionism was based on a mixture of Ottoman loyalism, local patriotism and Arab nationalism. Zionism was primarily viewed as a nationalist 'separatist' movement within the Ottoman Empire which was also dangerous to local Palestinians. Some Arabs, mainly Christian merchants prominent in the commercial sphere, feared unwelcome economic competition. They rationalised their apprehensions by claiming that Jews were unscrupulous in business and used sharp practices which would undermine the position of local Palestinian merchants.[2] Such economic antisemitism was reinforced, especially among French-speaking Catholics, by motifs which derived from the clerical and nationalist anti-Dreyfusard agitation in France, which found an echo in the Levant, including Palestine.[3]

Muslims, on the other hand, were more concerned about preserving unchanged the 1,300-year-old historic tradition of

Palestine as a Muslim land and the fundamental concept of Islam's superiority over other religions. Before the First World War they had already become alarmed by the emergence of a new Jewish society in Palestine which challenged such assumptions by its activities, behaviour, life-style and attitudes. The Second *Aliyah* (ascent) of Jewish settlers from Russia, many of them imbued with secular, revolutionary and socialist ideals, clashed sharply with the more traditional Muslim society. They had rapidly broken out of the boundaries of the old *yishuv* (settlement) and begun to work the land as part of their socialist ideology; they refused to be marginalised or accept a subordinate status; they had created their own political organisations and self-defence units. The *kibbutzim* and the communal life-style which they established seemed to many Muslims to be a mixture of communism, anarchy, licence and sexual promiscuity.[4]

In the 1920s and 1930s this led logically enough to an antisemitic and anti-Bolshevik discourse among Palestinian Muslims, facilitated by the radical ethos of the Third *Aliyah* from Russia and the founding of a Communist Party in Palestine, staffed overwhelmingly by Jews. In their appeals to the British Mandatory Government, Palestinian notables deplored the fact that the new immigrants were spreading 'Bolshevik' principles which provoked disorder, bloodshed and ruin throughout the country. It was necessary 'to expel this deviant revolutionary group from Palestine so that this holy land, the cradle of religion and peace, need not become a fount of immorality and a source of that flame which could ignite the entire East and cause the end of all civilisation whether Eastern or Western'.[5] The charge of 'immorality' was particularly instructive, for the sight of Jewish women dressed in shorts, enjoying relative sexual and political freedom and near equal status with men in the new immigrant society was profoundly unsettling to the mores of a Muslim culture. It seemed to herald nothing less than the overturning of family life, social order and religion. These and other differences in

241

customs, culture and values undoubtedly intensified Palestinian resistance to Jewish immigration as a source of future disaster to their traditional way of life.

The Arab identification of Zionism with Communism, while not wholly implausible in the 1920s (though the Comintern had already denounced Zionism as an agent of British imperialism), had assumed a manifestly antisemitic character from the outset. The Palestinian Arab leaders repeatedly asserted that anarchism and revolution were inherent in the Jewish 'character', which was to sow dissension, subversion and ruin everywhere. The Jews were blamed for the Russian and German Revolutions and for seeking to overthrow established dynastic Empires, and accused of aiming to destroy both Christianity and Islam. Antisemitism in Eastern Europe after 1918, it was suggested, was a natural response to their activities and it would inevitably be provoked in Palestine by their mass immigration, as it had been in other countries.[6]

This argumentation was obviously borrowed from European Christian sources and from *The Protocols of the Elders of Zion*, which emphasised that Communism was part of a plot for Jewish world domination. Its use by Palestinian Arabs showed that Westernisation was making some inroads, not least through the adoption of European antisemitic ideologies and their translation into the language of Arab nationalism. But it was above all the anti-Zionist awakening among the Palestinians after the First World War which favoured this discourse, though it was not intrinsic to its central arguments.

Palestinian arguments against Zionism focused above all on the need to preserve the Arab and Muslim character of Palestine. Initially, the Wilsonian principle of the right of all nations to self-determination, which in 1918 seemed sacrosanct, was particularly emphasised. It was pointed out that at the time of the Balfour Declaration 90 per cent of the population in Palestine were Arabs, most of them Muslims; that Palestine was a holy land to hundreds of millions of Muslims (and Christians) who were far more numerous than the 15 million Jews throughout the world; that Jerusalem was the third holiest city of Islam, containing the mosques of Al-Aqsa and the Dome of the Rock. Moreover, the Arabs had lived in Palestine uninterruptedly since the Muslim conquest of the seventh century – an argument of historic continuity which Palestinian nationalists dubiously extended back even to the Canaanites, who were claimed as ancestors of the Arab population. On the other hand, the Jews were deemed not to be a nation at all, but merely a *religious* group whose rights as a minority were already guaranteed in their lands of residence. They had never lived continuously in Palestine, they had left few traces of their presence, and their claim to 'historic rights' was seen as an anachronistic attempt to turn the clock back.[7]

None of these standard arguments were anti-Jewish or required antisemitic motifs in order to make them appear persuasive. Indeed, initially the Arab national movement distinguished clearly between the indigenous Jewish population, whom it regarded as 'brothers' and foreign Zionist immigrants, whom it rejected. The Palestine Arabs were aware that some of the native Sephardic Jews, and also the ultra-orthodox from the Jerusalem Jewish community, were in fact anti-Zionist; that both groups resented the pre-eminence of secular Ashkenazi Zionists over the *yishuv* after 1918 and the threat which this posed to the traditional Jewish way of life. But the 'tolerance' of Palestinian nationalism for these anti-Zionist Jews was predicated on the assumption that they would, at the very least, continue the low profile and self-effacing attitude of *dhimmis* who sought no role in administrative or public life; that they would accept absorption as culturally Arabised Jews or even identify themselves with Arab national aspirations in Palestine.[8]

This proved exceedingly difficult, if not impossible, given that the Arab masses made no practical distinction between indigenous Jews and Zionists. In the Arab demonstrations of February/March 1920 slogans like 'Palestine is our land and the Jews our dogs' abounded. In April 1920 Arab mobs in

Jerusalem headed straight for the Jewish Quarter of the Old City, and it was the traditional Jews of the 'old *yishuv*' who suffered most.[9] This pattern was repeated, much more tragically, during the pogroms of 1929 in Hebron and Safed in which around 100 orthodox Jews of the old community were murdered.

These massacres were a direct result of the deliberate religious inflammation of the Muslim masses in Palestine by the Grand Mufti of Jerusalem, Haj Amin al-Husseini. Since the early 1920s he had sought to rouse the believers by claiming that the Jews intended to take over the Temple Mount area (*al Haram al-Sharīf*) in order to rebuild Solomon's Temple on the ruins of the great mosques. He had called on Muslim leaders throughout the world to rally to the defence of the holy places of Islam against the 'perfidious' Zionist designs. Undoubtedly this tactic to stir up the national movement came to fruition in the 1929 pogroms, which were presented as an 'anti-imperialist' uprising and a glorious page in Palestinian Arab history. By showing that Zionism threatened the religious as well as the national status quo in Palestine, he had created the basis for a more popular national movement in the 1930s and succeeded in bringing the Palestinian cause into the forefront of Pan-Islamic and Pan-Arab concerns.[10] By couching the struggle against Zionism in the idiom of populist Islam, both Haj Amin and the martyred leader of the 1930s, Sheikh 'Izz al-Dīn al-Qassām, could reach out to the majority of the Palestinian population who were not yet receptive to the slogans of secular Arab nationalism.[11] The effects of this agitation were visible in the marked rise in national consciousness and in the sense of an emerging Palestinian identity during the 1936–9 Revolt against British Mandatory rule and expanding Zionist settlement.

In the 1930s, the latent antisemitic element in Palestinian anti-Zionism grew even stronger with the rise of German National Socialism. Hitler was widely admired in the Arab world for having reversed the Versailles Treaty and humiliated both Britain and France, the two dominant imperialist powers who had carved up the Middle East after 1918.[12] He was seen as a strong nationalist leader, who in contrast to the Italian Fascists had no obvious ambitions to expand in the Mediterranean area at the possible expense of the Arabs.[13] The antisemitism of the Nazis strengthened this feeling of identification among many Arabs, despite the fact that it was provoking a mass *aliyah* of German and Eastern European Jews to Palestine in the 1930s. This influx, one of the main causes of the Arab Revolt in Palestine, was of course detrimental to the Palestinians and should, rationally speaking, have caused resentment towards Hitler and the Nazis. Moreover, Nazi doctrines of 'Aryan' racial superiority and the fact that the Arabs were despised as 'Semites' themselves, might have provided cause for serious reflection.[14] Yet, almost immediately after Hitler's accession to power, Haj Amin contacted the German consul in Jerusalem, proposing an alliance with the Nazis and a joint boycott against the Jews. The Arabs clearly realised that German antisemitism was above all anti-Jewish and evidently rejoiced that a great European power was putting the Jews in their place. Although Nazi officials were more than lukewarm about the value of Arab support and considered the goodwill of the British Empire as far more important to them (at least until 1939), Haj Amin persisted in courting them throughout the 1930s.[15]

After escaping from Palestine to Syria, then to Iraq, from there to Italy and finally to Berlin, he became extremely active in pro-Axis propaganda, also organising Muslim SS troops from Bosnia and collaborating with German Intelligence against the Allies. In his talks with Hitler on 28 November 1941 he thanked the Führer of the Greater German Reich for the 'unequivocal support' he had shown for the Palestinian Arabs in public speeches. The Arabs, Haj Amin declared, were 'natural allies of Germany, as could be seen by their mutual enemies: the British, the Jews, and the communists'; they were 'deeply convinced that Germany would win the war', welcomed its sympathy for Arab liberation and its support for 'the elimination of the national Jewish homeland'; he, the Mufti in the name of the Arabs, was ready to form an Arab legion, to engage in sabotage and to encourage political destabilisation in order to ensure a German victory. Although Hitler did not give Haj Amin the *public* commitment he had wanted, he did promise that when the time was ripe he would do so and that 'thereafter, Germany's only remaining objective would be limited to the annihilation of the Jews living under British protection in Arab lands'.[16]

Haj Amin did everything he could to make sure that the Nazis would keep their promise and he also wrote in the summer of 1943 to the Foreign Ministers of the lesser Axis Powers (Italy, Hungary, Rumania, Bulgaria) urging them not to permit Jews to leave for Palestine. His letter of 28 June 1943 to the Hungarian Foreign Minister warns him of 'the hope which the Jews have never relinquished, namely, the domination of the whole world through this important strategic centre, Palestine'.[17] Allowing them to escape from Hungary or the Balkans to Palestine would not solve the 'Jewish question', would greatly strengthen their 'dangerous influence' and damage the Arabs. It was indispensable, Haj Amin insisted, that they be sent to countries 'where they would find themselves under active control, for example, in Poland, in order thereby to protect oneself from their menace and avoid the consequent damage'.[18] It is reasonable to assume that Haj Amin, who was in contact with Himmler and Eichmann, knew precisely what 'active control' meant in Poland in the summer of 1943, namely the extermination of Jews.[19]

It is significant in this context that Palestinians and other Arabs have rarely if ever criticised the Mufti's complicity in the Holocaust. After the war the main reaction in the Arab press, *belles-lettres* and political propaganda was silence.[20] The post-war struggle for Palestine was strictly divorced from the Jewish tragedy in Europe, though it had a decisive impact on the Jews themselves and, to a lesser extent, on world opinion. The

17 A poster of Trotsky used by White Army opponents
of Bolshevism during the Russian Civil War, 1919.
Anti-Asiatic racism also figures here.

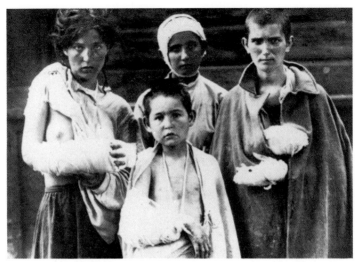

18a Pogrom victims in
Kiev, 1917.

18b The lightning,
spelling GPU (now
KGB), is shown striking
'counter-revolutionary
vermin' during the
Moscow show trials of
the late 1930s.

19a In January 1953 nine Kremlin doctors, most of them Jewish, were arrested as agents of Western intelligence, accused of plotting to poison the Soviet leadership. A wave of antisemitic hysteria swept through the USSR. 'The Doctors' Plot' was fabricated by Stalin as a prelude to his planned purging of the Jews from Soviet society.

19b In this cartoon from *Trud*, 18 January 1972, Judaism, the driving force behind anti-Communism and anti-Sovietism, is drawn by a crippled dollar.

19c A young supporter with an anti-Jewish poster, Moscow, 1990.

20a This wooden cross was erected in 1989 by Carmelite nuns just outside the walls of Auschwitz. The intrusion of this Christian symbol at the death-camp provoked Jewish protests, international controversy and renewed antisemitism in Poland.

20b Poland's only rabbi, Menachem Joskowitz, stands in front of the vandalised Jewish State Theatre in Warsaw. The graffiti relate to the controversy over the Carmelite nuns in Auschwitz.

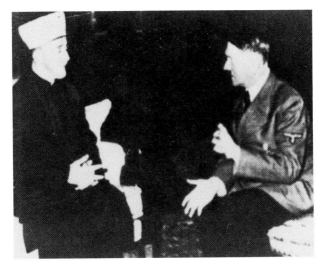

21a The meeting in Berlin between the Grand Mufti of Jerusalem, Haj Amin, and Adolf Hitler on 28 November 1941, in which they discussed 'the Jewish Question'.

21b Antisemitic books displayed outside one of Cairo's main bookshops, September 1986. The Arab edition of *Mein Kampf*, seen in the foreground, was circulated by the PLO in 1982.

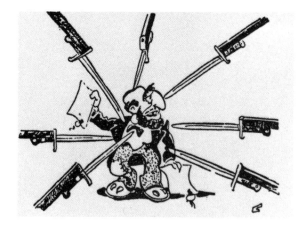

22a An Egyptian cartoon depicting the Arab response to the UN resolution of November 1947, which paved the way for the creation of the state of Israel.

22b 'Instructions for the use of the Star of David.' This cartoon appeared during the June war of 1967 in Baghdad and Cairo.

22c By September 1987 the Israelis were regularly portrayed as Nazis. In this cartoon about the closure of the PLO Washington office the Israeli Prime Minister, Itzhak Shamir, is shown dictating American policy.

23a The jacket of Syrian defence minister Mustafa Tlas's book *The Matzah of Zion*, published in Damascus in 1983. In this book he treats Jewish ritual murder as a documented fact.

23b Kurt Waldheim's election to the Austrian presidency in 1986 was celebrated by *Filastin-el-thaura* (the journal of the Abu Nidal faction of the PLO). The text reads: 'Waldheim's victory is a powerful slap in the face for the Zionist movement and its racist state.'

24 A Hassidic Jew contemplates tombstones
in the Mount of Olives cemetery,
desecrated by Arab vandals.

standard response, when pressed, was to maintain that since the Arabs had no responsibility for European antisemitism they should not be made to pay the price of accepting a Jewish state in Palestine. Sometimes it was claimed that the Jews exaggerated the Holocaust out of all proportion for their own propaganda purposes; other Arabs suggested that the Jews had simply received what they deserved at the hands of the Germans.

One must remember that in the 1950s and 1960s Hitler had remained a rather popular figure in the Arab world, not least among Palestinians, who, feeling embittered at their defeat by Israel, looked back with some sympathy at a leader who had inflicted such suffering on the Jews. Perverse responses in the Arab world to the Eichmann trial in Jerusalem (1961), which treated the Nazi mass murderer as a 'martyr' and congratulated him for having 'conferred a real blessing on humanity' by liquidating six million Jews, were not at all uncommon.[21] The first leader of the PLO (Palestine Liberation Organisation), Ahmad Shukeiry, who had declared on the eve of the Six Day War with Israel that hardly a Jew would survive to be repatriated to Europe, might well have identified with this kind of thinking. It was also Shukeiry who first articulated the view, enshrined ever since in article 22 of the Palestinian National Covenant, that Zionism is itself not only fanatical, racist and imperialist, but 'its methods are those of the Fascists and the Nazis'. The proposition that Zionism is a form of Nazism or even more dangerous than its supposed German 'model' is one that has proved immensely popular ever since in pro-Palestinian propaganda, despite its transparent hyperbole.

The Palestinian National Covenant, first formulated over twenty years ago and never officially repudiated, provides an insight into mainstream Palestinian ideology as it finally emerged in the late 1960s. Its basic premise is the total repudiation of Israel's existence as an independent Jewish state – this demand that it *cease to exist* is implied in nearly half of its thirty-three articles.[22] The *whole of Palestine* must be restored to the Palestinians because only thus can they recover their full self-determination. Jews may only reside in 'liberated' Palestine if they actually lived there before the 'beginning of the Zionist invasion' (1917), which would effectively exclude nearly all Israelis.[23] Armed struggle is deemed the only way of liberating Palestine – a view still held by the extremist radical factions of the PLO led by George Habash, Nayef Hawatmeh and Ahmad Jibril. The mainstream leader of the PLO, Yasser Arafat, has however sought for the past decade to combine diplomacy with armed struggle, and at the end of 1988 the Palestine National Council in Algiers finally appeared to offer a conditional recognition of Israel. The resolutions were equivocal since they supported the Palestinian struggle for independence by means which included violence against Israeli civilians; they accepted the 1947 partition resolution calling for an Arab Palestinian State, but ignored the part that laid the legal foundation for a Jewish State; they called for the West Bank and Gaza to be handed to the PLO without direct negotiation, without removing the ambiguity about whether pre-1967 Israel is still considered 'occupied Palestine'.

Nevertheless, this was a great advance over previous Palestinian positions, including the favourite formula of the 1970s which had advocated a 'secular, democratic state' in all of Palestine after Israel had first been 'de-Zionised' and in effect, dismantled. Following much soul-searching, the PLO appeared to have accepted the principle of a *two-state* solution (one Jewish, one Arab state alongside each other) after over forty years of unrelenting opposition to the very existence of Israel. On the other hand, there is no sign that the PLO or the Palestinians have abandoned their basic view of Zionism as an 'illegitimate', racist, colonialist and imperialist movement. PLO propaganda still regularly refers to 'usurped' or 'occupied' Palestine, to the racist 'Zionist entity', to Zionist 'genocide' against Palestinians and to the Nazi-like state of Israel. Yasser Arafat, who ten years ago declared his solidarity with

Ayatollah Khomeini's *jihad* to liberate Jerusalem,[24] now stands at the right-hand of Saddam Hussein, whose bellicose threats to incinerate Israel have turned him into a reincarnated Saladin for countless Palestinians. Alongside him in Baghdad are all the bloodstained Palestinian terrorist leaders like Abul Abbas, Abu Nidal, George Habash and Nayef Hawatmeh, who have shown many times in the past their readiness to attack Israeli and Jewish civilian targets as part of their unceasing war against Zionism.

The radicalisation among the Palestinians and the PLO in the past two years is undoubtedly linked to internal developments in Israel itself. The influx of Soviet Jews, fleeing Russian antisemitism, is rapidly tilting the demographic balance inside the Jewish state in Israel's favour. It is raising fears that the occupied territories will eventually be flooded with Soviet immigrants, thereby dooming any hope of a West Bank Palestinian state. Once more, as in the 1930s, Palestinian Arabs are alarmed that they may pay the price of European anti-semitic intolerance and be displaced to make way for Jewish immigrants. Some of them even see in this mass influx a 'conspiracy' between the Soviet Unon, the United States and Israel at their expense. Many Palestinians also regard Muslim autonomy on the Temple Mount as under threat from nationalist and fundamentalist Jews. The *Haram as-Sharīf* has always been viewed as a symbolic cornerstone of their independence, and since the days of the Grand Mufti it has been a powerful rallying-cry for the Palestinian national movement. This is more true than ever in the middle of the *intifada* and at a time when the influence of Islamic funda-mentalists in the occupied territories has never been greater. Once more the mendacious slogans that Israel is planning to seize the Muslim holy places fill the air, as do calls for the 'slaughter of the Jews' issuing from the mosques and from fanatical fundamentalist preachers.[25]

Antisemitism has returned with a vengeance as the inevit-able corollary of this Islamic fundamentalism, while its mirror-image, a growing Israeli hatred and racist stereotyping of Palestinian Arabs, threatens to make mutual accommodation impossible.[26] Palestinian intellectuals will insist, of course, that there is no anti-Jewish element in their nationalist position, and for the more enlightened and Westernised spokesmen among them, this is undoubtedly true. They see Palestinian reactions in purely *political* terms as a concrete response to a repressive Israeli state that is occupying Arab lands. For such Palestinians, the victims have become the victimisers, it is the Israeli Jews who are 'racist' and they are the objects of racism, dehumanisation and ruthless oppression.[27] Their struggle for Palestinian national identity and human rights under occupation has nothing in common with European traditions of antisemitism. It is not governed by hatred of Jews, though it does embrace a total repudiation of Zionism as a political ideology and practice which excludes and discriminates against them, has dispossessed their people and negates their very existence. Their anti-Zionism is the other side of their affirmation of Palestinian national identity, a rejection of Israelis not as Jews but as conquerors and settlers. Some Palestinian intellectuals like Edward Said and Hisham Sharabi have even gone so far as to say that it is one of the great misfortunes of the Palestinian people that they have had the Jews as their adversaries, a people themselves so badly wronged by others.[28]

However, the clear distinctions made between Zionists and Jews by some Palestinians during the past twenty years are by no means universally shared or even popular at a street level. For the ordinary Palestinian, Zionism *is* personified by the Jews whom he encounters in oppressive institutionalised roles and as the embodiment of a semi-colonial power structure. He does not necessarily differentiate between hawks and doves within this Israeli political system, between Judaism and Zionism, between Diaspora Jews and Israel. What he has to confront are Jews who have come from all over the world to settle in Palestine and who thereby seem to be crowding him out from his own homeland. It is easier to see them as representatives of an international 'Zionist conspiracy' than as settlers who merely happen to be Jews. Ethnocentrism and religious arrogance on both sides are now too strong to permit subtle distinctions between Zionists and Jews among the masses. The atavistic hatred between the sons of Isaac and of Ishmael, between the followers of Moses and Mohammed, threatens to drown out the still, small voice of reason.

18

▪ ▪ ▪

Arabism, Semitism and Antisemitism

The disarming claim is frequently made in the Arab world that, since Arabs are 'Semites', they cannot by definition be regarded as antisemites. Moreover, it is also suggested that before the advent of Zionism, Arab and Jewish 'Semites' cohabited together in idyllic harmony or, to use Yasser Arafat's words, 'we lived together on our land without discrimination and with love and peace'. The myth of the common 'racial' bond between Jews and Arabs (ironically enough, sometimes echoed in early Zionist writings) is itself contradicted by other Arab claims, such as those recently reiterated by President Assad of Syria, that Jews are in fact descendants of Turkish Khazars and not 'Semites' at all.

The concept of 'Semite' is in any case fictional if it is being applied to members of a so-called Semitic race. In its origins in the late eighteenth century it referred solely to a family of related languages which included Hebrew, Arabic and Aramaic.[1] Developed by European writers like Christian Lassen, Count Gobineau and Ernest Renan in the mid-nineteenth century as a counterpoint to the equally spurious 'Aryan' myth, 'Semitism' was finally incorporated into the pseudo-scientific concept of anti-Semitism by the German journalist Wilhelm Marr in 1879. The concept was never at any time intended to refer to Arabs but simply to provide a racial and political euphemism to replace traditional Christian Jew-hatred in Europe, which in the late nineteenth century seemed unappealing to atheists or anticlericals. European and Western antisemites always understood themselves to be solely and exclusively *anti-Jewish*, which has never prevented some of them from sympathising with the Arab branch of the 'Semitic' linguistic family. This was the case even with Hitler and the Nazis, who welcomed the Palestinian Arab leader Haj Amin al-Husseini to wartime Berlin as an honoured guest and ally, even as they were embarking on the mass murder of European Jewry.

Nor is there much basis in the Arab news media, journals, literature or everyday life for the distinction between Jews and Zionists that is often made by Arab intellectuals who deny the very premise of 'Semitic' antisemitism. For as we have already seen, the term Jews (*Yahūd*) is often mixed up or used interchangeably with Zionists (*Sahyūniyyūn*), Israelis or the Children of Israel (*Banū Isrā'īl*).[2] Moreover, the scale and extent of the antisemitic literature in the Middle East, much but not all of it government-sponsored, is such as to swamp that minority of Arabs who make a genuine distinction between their attitudes to Jews and their rejection of Zionism. This literature can no longer, after forty years or more of systematic defamation of Jews, be treated as a 'foreign import' designed solely to serve the *political* struggle against Israel. It is no less significant as a religious, cultural and national instrument for the affirmation of Arab-Islamic identity, whose resonance among both the intellectuals and the masses suggests that it speaks to deeper needs in the Arab psyche as well as reflecting an ongoing crisis in Arab society as a whole.

This is not to deny that the term 'antisemitism' has a European origin and a specific historical and cultural tradition which is distinct from that of the Muslim Arabs. But when *The Protocols of the Elders of Zion* are published in repeated editions in Arabic, throughout the Arab world, they cease to be simply a European product and begin to enter the mainstream of Arab thought.[3] Their appeal is all the greater because the spectre of a powerful, satanic conspiracy helps to alleviate the trauma and humiliation of successive Arab defeats at the hands of the Jews and of the West.[4] We have already noted the passion of the ultra-conservative Saudi monarch, King Feisal, for this *Protocols* forgery, but even a sophisticated Arab radical leader like President Nasser recommended it warmly in 1958 to a visiting Indian journalist: 'It is very important that you should read it. I will give you a copy. It proves beyond the shadow of a doubt that three hundred Zionists, each of whom knows all the others, govern the fate of the European Continent.'[5] The *Protocols* mythology, like the belief of so many Arabs in an imaginary map on the walls of the Israeli Parliament (showing a Greater Israel from the Nile to the Euphrates) did not therefore begin with Israel's conquest of the West Bank and Gaza (1967), with the invasion of Lebanon (1982) or with the present Palestinian revolt. Rather it was the pre-existent receptivity to such myths which turned them into self-fulfilling prophecies whose 'truth' about Jewish plans for world domination was allegedly being revealed or confirmed by current events. The stereotypes are of course activated and given a more intense meaning for many Arabs precisely because they have to confront in Israel a concrete and efficient enemy with the military, technological and political capacity to inflict punishment or damage upon them. Wherever Israel has exercised this capacity, as in the bombardment of Beirut in 1982 or the more recent killings of unarmed Palestinians in the occupied territories, the feelings of hatred and enmity aroused will naturally favour the resort to stereotypical thinking.

But if the policies and behaviour of Israeli Jews can and have become an exacerbating factor in the equation, they do not explain the irrational beliefs held by many Arabs about a Jewish drive to global domination, about their 'control' of the world economy, their corruption of morals and inherently evil character. These purely antisemitic notions are not a necessary and ineluctable outcome of anti-Zionist thinking or of the war against Israel, yet their widespread popularity in the Arab world cannot be denied. The denigration of Israel and Zionism continually slides over into a vilification of Jews and what one prominent Egyptian scholar defined as the 'arrogant, oppressive spirit' of Judaism. The late President Sadat (who in the early 1950s had eulogised Hitler in the Egyptian press) could declare on Mohammed's birthday anniversary (25 April 1972) that 'the most magnificent thing which the Prophet did was to drive the Jews from the entire Arabian peninsula'; and promise his people 'the removal of Israeli arrogance and lack of restraint so that they shall again be as described in the Koran, living as they are fated to live, in degradation and impoverishment'.[6] Sadat made peace with Israel seven years later, but the Egyptian intelligentsia after the Peace Treaty appears to have scaled new heights of anti-Jewish invective.

This is how Rivka Yadlin, who has made a close study of the subject, begins her book on anti-Zionism and anti-Judaism in present-day Egypt.

> Egyptian writing of the 1980s is permeated with the evil spirit of antisemitism. Such would be the initial and spontaneous feeling of anyone leafing through the Egyptian press or glancing at the titles of books offered for sale at Cairo's pavement stalls. Israel, in political cartoons, is depicted by hooked-nosed and hunch-backed figures with wispy beards and skull caps or black hats, reminiscent of *Der Stürmer* caricatures. Headlines in monthly magazines call for the destruction of the Jewish state. Books and articles return time and time again to the story of Mohammed's betrayal by the Jews.[7]

A random selection of quotes taken from Egyptian sources in the past year (which could be duplicated *ad nauseam* from all over the Arab world) may give an idea of the tenor of this increasingly rampant antisemitism. Thus, in February 1989, in the pro-government Egyptian weekly *October*, one reads: 'It has now become clear that perhaps Hitler did have justification for gassing the Jews. Because if the Jews were allowed freedom of action they would have eaten the others.' In June

1989, Jamal E-Din Muhammad Musa, lecturer at Ein-Shams University, wrote: 'Jews are deliberately flooding Egypt with drugs and have made contact with the International Mafia in order to bring down the Egyptian society.' In the same month, Atef Amer, Councillor at the Egyptian Ministry of Education, wrote a poem about Israel's Prime Minister, Itzhak Shamir: 'The ugly son of an ape . . . remember how you were tortured in the past by your hangman Hitler . . . son of hatred, your nation is hated because it sells dignity and its God. Your tail was cut . . . remember that you are the snake and that once your head is cut off, many will find peace.'[8] In September 1989 a professor of Political Science at Cairo University, Dr Hamid Rabee, claimed in *Al-Wafd* that 'Jews are governed by three enemies: self-hatred, fear and provocative behaviour. Zionist leaders have brought drugs, terror and sexual anarchy to America and western Europe.'[9] This theme was echoed at a Drugs symposium held in Jordan in October 1989, where Dr Majad Abu Rahiya quoted the *Protocols* as advising Jews to distribute drugs in order to blind other people. Such wildly irrational and bigoted views have become more common in Amman, where the Muslim Brotherhood, controlling one-third of the seats in the lower house of the Jordanian Parliament and with five members of the Cabinet, have emerged as the most powerful political organisation in the country. The rise of Islamic fundamentalism in Jordan, the growing ferment among its majority Palestinian population and their fervent support for Saddam Hussein's bloodcurdling threats and missile strikes against Israel have all intensifed the climate of hatred.

But one does well to remember that there is nothing new in Arab antisemitism, even in 'moderate' Jordan. Ten years ago, on 15 December 1980, Hazem Nuseibah, Jordan's Permanent Representative at the United Nations, told the General Assembly that

the Zionists are the richest people in the world and
control much of its destiny. People like Lord Rothschild

every day, in ironclad secrecy, decide and flash round the world how high the price of gold should be each particular day. And there is Mr Oppenheimer of South Africa, who holds 15 million blacks in bondage in order to exploit and monopolise the diamonds, the uranium, and other precious resources which rightfully belong to the struggling African people of South Africa and Namibia.[10]

One can see here just how discredited European antisemitic theories about a 'Jewish cabal' controlling and exploiting the rest of humanity are being exported by the Arabs back to the West and also being beamed at the Third World in order to defame Zionism and the Jewish people. An even better illustration of recycling Western antisemitism for the sake of the Arab war against Israel was given by the Libyan representative at the United Nations on 8 December 1983:

It is high time for the United Nations and the United States, in particular, to realise that the Jewish Zionists here in the United States attempt to destroy Americans. Look around New York. Who are the owners of pornographic film operations and houses? Is it not the Jews who are exploiting the American people and trying to debase them? If we succeed in eliminating that entity, we shall by the same token save the American and European peoples.[11]

Such antisemitic diatribes against Zionism in an international forum, when used by Arabs, aim to find common ground with a Western Christian audience. In a Middle Eastern context, it would be more common to vilify Jews and Israel as expressions of Western culture. Sexual permissiveness, 'promiscuity', 'immorality' and the position of women – all extremely sensitive issues in Arab Muslim society – are often taken by Arabs of an antisemitic persuasion as issues which Jews and Westerners exploit to weaken the moral foundation of their society. They regard Israel as a prime example of a people leading a sexually free life-style which, if imitated, would lead to moral degeneration in the Muslim world. Not only religious but even radical Egyptian writers who justified the unprovoked killing by an Egyptian soldier of Israeli tourists at Ras Burqa in the Sinai in 1985, referred to bare-breasted Israeli women as having somehow 'provoked' the murders. Israel, Zionism and the Jews, it is constantly suggested, deliberately seek to destroy Islam as a religion, to achieve 'normalisation' with Egypt through sex, to promote white slavery, pornography and American television series (*Dallas*, *Love Boat*, *Dynasty*) that corrupt morals, as part of their cultural assault on the Arabs.[12] Even prominent writers in Egypt and other parts of the Arab world have on occasion made allegations of the kind that Jews become obstetricians in order to perform abortions and thus wipe out the Gentile population; or that they are deliberately trying to introduce Aids into Arab countries like Egypt through drugs and sexual immorality.[13] None of these delirious notions are original – they have their origins in Western and Christian fantasies about Jewish sexual licentiousness – but in Arab societies they are liable to have a particularly heavy emotional charge.

Undoubtedly, such falsehoods reinforce the overall image of the Jews as inhuman, evil, corrupt and intent on infiltrating and exploiting all the weaknesses of the society they are supposedly seeking to undermine. Such stereotypes, reminiscent of European antisemitic literature, had already begun to penetrate the Arab world in the 1920s and 1930s, especially as a result of Nazi propaganda and influence. After 1948 they were deliberately utilised by Arab governments and by all those many forces in the Arab world interested in mobilising the semi-literate masses against a common enemy, the Jewish state. This goal was the more easily achieved since the very existence of Israel was perceived by most Arabs as an aggression, a great injustice to the Palestinians and a threat to their own security. The sense of tangible, concrete grievance was emotionally reinforced by the denigration of Jews in general as representing something alien, exclusive and inimical to the ambitions and goals of Arab nationalism. The Jewish state, in particular, was depicted in this Arab national discourse as an implantation of Western colonialism into the Middle East, created in order to frustrate Arab unity. Both Nasserism and Syrian as well as Iraqi Ba'athism were and are still thoroughly imbued with this conspiratorial notion of Zionism as an insidious 'imperialist' plot against the Arabs.

The pan-Arab vision envisaged the eventual unity of the whole Arab nation into a single, large and powerful Arab state stretching from Morocco on the Atlantic ocean to Iraq on the Persian Gulf.[14] The presence of any non Arabic-speaking, non-Muslim sovereign state at the very heart of the Arab lands would in any case have been anathema. That Jews, traditionally a despised and unmartial minority in the Arab midst, should have attained such elevated *political* status turned something already unpalatable into a pan-Arab disaster of unprecedented magnitude. Already in 1943, the Arab nationalist thinker, Mahmoud Azat Darwaza, had warned that the Jews were 'concentrating in the very place which links the Arab countries of Asia with those of Africa. They are a racial and geographical obstruction between the Arab countries, and this forces the Arabs, who surround them on all sides, to continue to fight them and to tighten the siege around them until this new phenomenon will be destroyed.[15] In the early 1960s, the heyday of Nasserism, Arab broadcasts and writings would endlessly elaborate on this idea of Israel as a negation of Arab unity, the Arab homeland, Arab civilisation and the whole philosophy of life embraced by Arab nationalism.[16] Yehoshafat Harkabi, who made the first systematic study of Arab attitudes to Israel during that period, considered that the antisemitism which invariably accompanied this nationalist world-view was essentially ideological and political, directed primarily against Israel. Because of their hatred of Israel, most Arab political and intellectual élites felt no inhibitions about denigrating the culture and history of the Jews. Since they desired and openly called for the physical elimination of Israel, they felt that they had to portray it as uniquely despicable and radically depraved in order to justify their extremist goals. This led to a systematic dehumanisastion of the Zionist 'enemy' and reinforced an antisemitism which portrayed the baseness of the Jews as deeply embedded in their religion, their history and culture. As Harkabi has put it: 'If the Jews are depraved, then their state, their creation, is also inherently debased; and conversely, the depravity of Israel is transferred to the Jews. Thus a cycle is formed: reinforced depravity from the Jews to Israel and from Israel to the Jews.'[17]

Harkabi and others have pointed out that it is this nexus which constitutes the originality of Arab antisemitism, and today it has extended beyond the Middle East. A political antisemitism based on total opposition to Israel and under-cutting its moral right to exist has spread from the Arab world to Europe, America, the Third World and the non-Arab Muslim world. It singles out Israel as a *criminal* state, based on violence, terror, racism and unending aggression, which are inherent in its very nature. It is not the specific policies, details or failings of the Jewish state which are examined, but rather the *negative essence* at the heart of Zionism which precludes the existence of any positive and redeeming characteristics.[18] Thus Zionism will rarely if ever be viewed by radical Arab nationalists as an authentic and legitimate expression of Jewish nationalism. Instead it may at best be regarded as a narrow, particularistic, tribalist and racially exclusive form of Judaism which has become a malignant wound in the body of Arabism. No matter what it does, the fact that it *exists* constitutes an infringement of the nationalist vision of Pan-Arab and Muslim destiny, a judgement shared equally by Assad, Saddam Hussein and Qaddafi, like Nasser before them.

The existence of Israel constitutes, therefore, the negation of Arabism, the dismemberment of an Arab and Islamic land, its usurpation by Jews. In Arab literature, the Zionist conquest of Palestine is presented as a catalogue of crimes and horrendous atrocities (sometimes invented, sometimes grotesquely magnified) which either explicitly or by implication demonstrate the cruelty and callousness of Jews, their devilish cunning and ruthlessness. Against this background the destruction of the Jewish state and the 'liberation of Palestine' appear as sacred goals of Arab nationalism, the supreme legitimising cause for any pretender seeking to unify the Arab nation.[19] It is no accident that a secular nationalist like Saddam Hussein, despite his call to *jihad* against Israel and the West, has revived the image of the pre-Islamic Babylonian conqueror Nebuchadnezzer, who had liberated Palestine over 500 years before Christ and exiled the Jews in chains to Babylon. Nebuchadnezzer had a rather poor reputation in early Islamic literature but having been refurbished as a symbol of Iraqi imperial ambitions, Pan-Arabism and the destruction of Israel, he could serve the needs of a modern dictator.[20]

It is true, however, that Arab nationalism after 1967, in its discourse for Western consumption, did try and modify the tone of its demands. Following in the wake of the PLO and the Palestinians, it began to emphasise issues of human rights and the withdrawal of Israel from occupied territories rather than the final goal of liquidating the Jewish state. The maligning of Jews did not cease at any time but could now more easily be blamed on Israeli behaviour and actions. A greater awareness developed among some Arab leaders and intellectuals that open antisemitism and talk of 'throwing the Jews into the sea' might be counter-productive to the Arab cause in the West. The new policy, adopted in the late 1970s primarily by Sadat's Egypt, spoke of the *containment* rather than the destruction of Israel, as a way of weakening it and gradually stripping it of its Zionist identity, so that it could be absorbed into the region.[21] Zionism, with its premise of Jewish statehood and its reminder of past colonial subjugation by the West, was still considered irreconcilable with Arab nationalism; but a de-Zionised Israel, 'an Arabised Jewish nation among the united Arab states' (a formula put forward in 1975 by Butros Ghali, Egyptian Minister of State for Foreign Affairs), could conceivably be integrated.[22]

This more 'moderate' pan-Arab vision looked forward to the peaceful dissolution of Israel, its domestication in stages. Anti-Jewishness, which alienated the Western world, had to be explicitly rejected and the attack directed against Israeli expansionism and Zionist 'political thought'. As the Egyptian Deputy Prime Minister, Dr Mustapha Khalil, phrased it in Tel Aviv in December 1980, Egypt was recognising the Jewish religious and cultural community in Palestine, not its political sovereignty. 'When we speak of the Jews, we never regard them as constituting a national entity through their religion. A Jew can be an Egyptian Jew, a German Jew, or a French Jew . . . we always regard the Jewish religion as strictly a religion and not the mark, the symbol of a national entity.'[23] Full peace, it was implied both here and in moderate pan-Arab thinking in general, would eventually involve the self-dissolution of Israel as a nation-state, the ultimate disappearance of Zionism and the return of the Jews to their historic status as a 'tolerated' religion in the Muslim Arab world.

Although pan-Arabism, whether in its moderate or extremist forms, declined somewhat in the 1980s, it never completely disappeared as a focus of ideological identification. Its fundamental view of Zionism as an existential threat to the Arab nation and to its historical destiny continues to colour the view of many intellectuals in Egypt and elsewhere in the Arab world. Today, as in the past, Zionism is rejected because of its core-value, namely the right to a sovereign Jewish political existence in Palestine. For Pan-Arab nationalists, as much as for Muslim fundamentalists or for the PLO, the struggle with Zionism was traditionally seen as a zero-sum game, namely: Who will destroy whom? In this *total* conflict, Zionism is not held by militant pan-Arabists (who oppose the present

Egyptian regime and its policy) to be something separate from Judaism, but rather as deriving from it. In this 'secular' literature, the continuity in Jewish goals, strategy and tactics over thousands of years is particularly stressed, often in an antisemitic way, as Rivka Yadlin has shown.[24] The bottom line of these polemics is that contemporary Zionism is inherent in Judaism, which in turn is responsible for the 'abominable' traits in the behaviour of Israel. The most disturbing aspect of such insistent anti-Judaism is that its main foothold should be amongst *intellectuals* in Egypt, who after the Peace Treaty seem to have taken the lead in disseminating unmistakeably anti-Jewish opinions.

The situation is even worse under repressive, authoritarian Arab regimes like Syria, Iraq or Libya, which nominally espouse some blend of Arab nationalism and revolutionary socialism while permitting no legal opposition at all. In such countries, propaganda against Israel, Zionism and the Jews can expect to command quasi-automatic ideological support, as indeed it does in the more theocratic Islamic regimes. The resulting antisemitism is government-inspired and any voices raised against it would have great difficulty in making themselves heard. Even exiled Arab intellectuals in the democratic West do not find it easy to break ranks against the cumulative impact of this torrent of vituperation. The eminent Orientalist, Bernard Lewis, has noted in this connection:

> The volume of antisemitic books and articles published, the size and number of editions and impressions, the eminence and authority of those who write, publish and sponsor them, their place in school and college curricula, their role in the mass media, would all seem to suggest that classical antisemitism is an essential part of Arab intellectual life at the present time – almost as much as it was in Nazi Germany, and considerably more than in late nineteenth- and early twentieth-century France, where the clamour of the anti-

Dreyfusards was answered by at least equally powerful voices in defense of reason and tolerance.[25]

Lewis nuances this sombre verdict with the point that despite the quantity of this published and broadcast anti-semitism, the visceral, deep and intimate hatred 'characteristic of the classic antisemite in Central and Eastern Europe' is comparatively rare in the Arab world. The antisemitism appears to be ideological and political, literary and intellectual more than it is truly an expression of popular attitudes. Nor does its articulation necessarily preclude normal, at times friendly, relations with Jews, and sometimes even with Israelis. Thus, in spite of the vehemence or seeming ubiquity of Arab and Muslim antisemitism, it is 'still something that comes from above, from the leadership, rather than from below, from the society – a political and polemical weapon.'[26] If this assumption is correct, a resolution of the Arab–Israeli conflict and of the Palestinian question might yet prevent an irrever-sible poisoning of Arab society and culture by European-style antisemitism.

But such an optimistic outcome, while devoutly to be wished, seems for the moment improbable and unlikely to reduce Arab or Muslim susceptibility to antisemitism in the immediate future. The new antisemitism of the 'Semites' has, after all, powerful local and Islamic roots which once activated are not easy to switch off. One may doubt that the pattern of prejudice which already exists is any less visceral than its European and Western counterparts;[27] especially since it is grounded in a fundamental dogma of Islam and Arabism, that Jews are a minority whose inferior political status (and its accompanying humiliations) is religiously and culturally pre-destined. Moreover, while it is true that Arab antisemitism is historically newer (and in that sense more superficial) than its Christian European antecedents, since 1945 it has rapidly made up the lost ground.[28] Indeed its attitudes to Israel, Judaism and the Jews seem to have acquired precisely that deeply obsessional quality which arises whenever the 'Jewish Question' is held to be central to the religious, national and cultural identity of a particular human group.

This is not of course to deny that the origins of the Arab–Israeli conflict have their roots in a clash of two national movements over the same territory as much as in the history of prejudice and the persecution of minorities. Racial anti-semitism, for example, has nothing directly to do with the Arab–Israeli conflict or with the Palestinian question, except in so far as it has inadvertently served to strengthen the Zionist movement. Arab hostility to Israel can no doubt be explained or justified without recourse to antisemitic stereotypes, though, as we have seen, the temptation for Arabs to fall back on such simplistic devices is a constant and growing one. It is, however, undeniable that an anti-Jewish Arab ideology has crystallised and acquired its own momentum over the course of the last few decades, one that has distorted and blackened the image of the Jew in ways that were historically un-precedented for the Islamic world.[29] Inevitably, this ideology has been able to feed on feelings of anger and hostility towards Israel, intensified by its questionable treatment of the Palestinians. The anti-Jewish ideology has been constantly disseminated through books, newspapers, caricatures, radio and television media which have reached a mass audience. Among Palestinian children and adolescents, who have known nothing but Israeli occupation of the territories, daily events doubtless have the effect of seeming to confirm some of their fears and deeply ingrained stereotypes. The harsh reality of conflict thereby fans the flames of hatred and prejudice, leading to a dehumanisation of the 'enemy' by both Arabs and Israelis.

Since the Lebanese war of 1982 this has led on the Arab side to the return of the idea that Israel embodies a powerful demonic drive for domination which is explained in terms of Old Testament savagery, cruelty and the unrestrained use of force. Superimposed on this archaic image of Biblical chosenness and 'Jewish' arrogance is the modern myth of a 'Nazi-like' Israel wreaking racist vengeance on the Arabs, torturing prisoners, raping women and imposing its colonialist will on the whole Middle East. This demonisation of Israel and of the Jews has admittedly been more prominent in fundamentalist Islamic than in Arab nationalist propaganda, which even in the most rigidly anti-Zionist regimes is usually less permeated with anti-Jewish themes. The degree of commitment of the secular nationalist regimes to the Arab–Israeli conflict may indeed be questionable, whatever lip-service they have paid over the years to the Palestinian cause. For it must be increasingly apparent to the more sober, rational Arab leaders and intellectual élites that the core problems of Middle Eastern underdevelopment, political corruption and the societal failure to engage modernity on level terms have had little to do with Western colonial exploitation or with Israel. Neither the West nor the establishment of the Jewish state can indefinitely be made a scapegoat for the endemic violence of inter-Arab politics, its instability, irrationality, insecurity and constant relapse into terrorism. Neither Zionism nor imperialism can adequately explain the chronic inability of the Arab world to capitalise on its oil wealth and other resources to achieve economic development, pluralist democracy and social stability.[30]

In the shadow of the bitter Gulf war it is, however, highly unlikely that reason or common sense will prevail in the Middle East. Popular myths about the Western betrayal of Palestine and about a sinister Jewish conspiracy to subvert Arabism and Islam will probably continue to flourish, whatever the new international order that may emerge in the region. For at the heart of the Middle Eastern problem for most Arabs is their emotional refusal to accept Israel and the right of the Jews to exercise any sovereignty in a Muslim domain. Neither in Arab nationalism nor in Islam can national independence and equality for Jews be tolerated.[31] For Palestinians, too, who have eagerly hailed a cruel, brutal oppressor like Saddam Hussein as their hero and liberator, 'peace' and 'justice' seem to mean little more than a demand for the complete Arabisation of the Jewish state. None of these propositions are in themselves anti-Jewish in a classical European sense of the term, but they echo an anachronistic 'teaching of contempt', which, if it is not corrected, can only lead the Middle East further down the road to self-destruction.

Notes

Chapter 1

1. Shaye D. Cohen, '"Anti-Semitism" in Antiquity: The Problem of Definition', in David Berger (ed.) *History and Hate: The Dimensions of Anti-Semitism* (Philadelphia, 1986), pp. 43–7
2. Salo W. Baron, *A Social and Religious History of the Jews*, Vol. 1 (New York, 1952), p. 194. The late Menahem Stern's massive three-volume collection of sources, *Greek and Latin Authors on Jews and Judaism* (Jerusalem, 1974–1984) is indispensable
3. The view of Jewish Sages, responding to antisemitism in the Hellenistic-Roman world, was however more varied and complex. See the remarks of Moshe David Herr in Shmuel Almog (ed.) *Antisemitism Through the Ages* (Oxford, 1988), pp. 27–32
4. Hannah Arendt, *Antisemitism* (New York, 1968), p. 7
5. On Apion, whose work provoked an apologetic treatise by the Jewish historian Josephus, see John Gager, *The Origins of Anti-Semitism: Attitudes toward Judaism in Pagan and Christian Antiquity* (Oxford/New York, 1985), pp. 45–7
6. Louis H. Feldman, 'Antisemitism in the Ancient World', in D. Berger (ed.), p. 31, Gager, *op. cit.*, p. 40. For texts and discussion, see Stern, Vol. 1, *op. cit.*, pp. 181–4
7. Feldman, *op. cit.*, pp. 22–3
8. Gager, *op. cit.*, pp. 39–66
9. Menahem Stern on the attitude of the Roman authorities to the Jews, in Almog (ed.), *op. cit.*, pp. 13–25
10. *Ibid.*, p. 22
11. Gager, *op. cit.*, pp. 56–7
12. Book 5 of Tacitus's *Histories*. 'Sed adversus omnes alios hostile odium. Separati epulis, discreti cubilibus, proiectissima ad libidinem gens; concubitu alienarum abstinent; inter so nihil illicitum.' My thanks to my colleague, Professor Moshe David Herr of the Hebrew University, for this reference

13. H. Levy, 'Tacitus on the Origin and Manners of the Jews' (in Hebrew), *Zion*, 8 (1943), pp. 17–26
14. Quoted in Gager, *op. cit.*, pp. 85–6
15. *Ibid.*, pp. 65–6
16. M. A. Adler, 'The Emperor Julian and the Jews', *Jewish Quarterly Review*, 5 (1893), pp. 591–651
17. Feldman, *op. cit.*, pp. 30–6
18. Edward H. Flannery, *The Anguish of the Jews* (New York, 1985), pp. 15–19
19. Rosemary Ruether, *Faith and Fratricide: The Theological Roots of Anti-Semitism* (New York, 1971), p. 181 emphasises the extent to which Christian self-affirmation, unlike its pagan forerunners, depended on the negation of Judaism

Chapter 2

1. Moritz Güdemann to Kamilla Theimer, 19 December 1907, Central Archives of the History of the Jewish People (Jerusalem) A/W 731.5
2. Hyman Maccoby, *The Sacred Executioner: Human Sacrifice and the Legacy of Guilt* (London, 1987), p. 134
3. *I Thessalonians 2*: 15–16
4. On Paul's polemics against Jews, see Gager, *op. cit.*, pp. 193–264
5. Rosemary Ruether, *op. cit.*, p. 113
6. *Ibid.* Also Maccoby, *op. cit.*, p. 146
7. Homily 1, *Against the Jews*, in W. A. Meeks and R. L. Wilken *Jews and Christians in Antioch in the First Four Centuries of the Common Era* (Missoula, Mont., 1978), p. 97.
8. Maccoby, *op. cit.*, p. 19
9. Joshua Trachtenberg, *The Devil and the Jews: The Medieval Conception of the Jew and its Relation to Modern Antisemitism* (New Haven, 1943)
10. Friedrich Heer, *God's First Love* (London, 1967) and Flannery, *op. cit.*, p. 50
11. For the doctrinal background, see Marcel Simon, *Verus Israël. Etude sur les relations entre Chrétiens et Juifs dans l'Empire Romain* (Paris, 1948); F. Lovsky, *Antisémitisme et Mystère d'Israël* (Paris, 1955); Jules Isaac, *Genèse de l'Antisémitisme* (Paris, 1956); and A. T. Davies (ed.) *Antisemitism and the Foundations of Christianity* (New York, 1979)
12. Maccoby, *op. cit.*, p. 151
13. Flannery, *op. cit.*, pp. 56–7
14. *Ibid.*, p. 75. Also Bernhard Blumenkranz, *Juifs et Chrétiens dans le monde occidental* (Paris, 1960)
15. Isaac, *op. cit.*, p. 272

16. *Ibid.*, p. 279. Flannery, *op. cit.*, p. 84 observed that in the intensity of his vituperation, 'Agobard has few equals in anti-Judaic literature'
17. See the remarks of Jeremy Cohen, in Berger (ed.), *History and Hate*, pp. 67–71
18. Solomon Grayzel, *A History of the Jews* (Philadelphia, 1960), pp. 339–58
19. Gavin Langmuir, *History, Religion and Antisemitism* (Berkeley/Los Angeles 1990), p. 261–2
20. Interview with Professor Langmuir, Stanford University, May 1990. On the phenomenon of religious doubt in this context see Langmuir, *op. cit.*, pp. 232 ff
21. Text in S. Grayzel, *The Church and the Jews in the XIIIth Century* (Philadelphia, 1933)
22. See Kenneth R. Stow, 'Hatred of the Jews or Love of the Church? Papal Policy toward the Jews in the Middle Ages', in Almog (ed. *Antisemitism through the Ages*, pp. 71–89
23. Flannery, *op. cit.*, pp. 104–6
24. Robert Chazan, 'Medieval Anti-Semitism', in Berger (ed.) *History and Hate*, pp. 49 ff
25. Archie Baron, 'Hidden Exodus', *The Listener*, 1 November 1990
26. Flannery, *op. cit.*, p. 90

Chapter 3

1. Gavin I. Langmuir, 'Medieval Antisemitism', in Henry Friedlander and Sybil Milton (eds.) *The Holocaust: Ideology, Bureaucracy and Genocide* (New York, 1980), p. 32
2. Robert Bonfil, 'The Devil and the Jews in the Christian Consciousness of the Middle Ages', in Almog (ed.) *Antisemitism through the Ages* pp. 91–8
3. See Norman Cohn, *The Pursuit of the Millennium: Revolutionary Millenarianism and Mystical Anarchists of the Middle Ages* (New York, 1970), pp. 75–9. According to the legend, Antichrist would be born in Babylon through the impregnation of a Jewish prostitute by Satan himself and would later proceed to Palestine. See Maccoby, *op. cit.*, pp. 172–5
4. Gavin I. Langmuir, 'Historiographic Crucifixion', in *Les Juifs au Regard de l'Histoire. Mélanges en l'honneur de Bernard Blumenkranz* (Paris, 1985), pp. 109–27 provides a detailed analysis of this first medieval accusation of ritual murder against Jews
5. Maccoby, *op. cit.*, pp. 154 ff
6. *Ibid.*

7. Langmuir, 'Medieval Antisemitism', p. 33
8. See Marie Despina, 'Les accusations de profanation d'hosties portées contre les juifs', *Rencontre*, 22/23 (1971), pp. 150–73, pp. 180–96
9. Léon Poliakov, *The History of Antisemitism*, Vol. 1 (London, 1974), pp. 107–22
10. Mordechai Breuer, 'The "Black Death" and Antisemitism', in Almog (ed.), *Antisemitism through the Ages* pp. 144–49
11. *Ibid.*, p. 150
12. Kenneth R. Stow, *op. cit.*, pp. 81–5
13. Heiko A. Oberman, 'The Stubborn Jews: Timing the Escalation of Antisemitism in late Medieval Europe', *Leo Baeck Institute Yearbook* (henceforth *LBIYB*), 1989, pp. XV ff
14. Jeremy Cohen, *The Friars and the Jews: The Evolution of Medieval Anti-Judaism* (Ithaca, 1982)
15. Flannery, *op. cit.*, p. 115
16. *Ibid.*, pp. 116–17
17. Y. Baer, *History of the Jews in Christian Spain*, Vol. 2 (Philadelphia, 1961), pp. 95–9 and his *Die Juden in christlichen Spanien: Urkunden und Regesten*, Vol. 2 (Berlin, 1936), pp. 210–18, 231–2
18. Michael Glatzer, 'Pablo de Santa Maria on the Events of 1391', in: Almog (ed.) *Antisemitism through the Ages*, p. 135
19. E. Vacandard, 'La question du meurtre rituelle chez les Juifs', *Etude de critique et d'histoire religieuse* (Paris, 1912), pp. 341–2. Cecil Roth, *History of the Marranos* (New York, 1959)
20. Joseph Kaplan, 'Jews and Judaism in the Political and Social Thought of Spain in the 16th and 17th centuries', in Almog (ed.) *Antisemitism through the Ages*, pp. 156–59
21. Quoted by Oberman, *op. cit.*, p. XVI
22. *Ibid.*, p. XXI ff
23. *Ibid.*, p. XVII
24. I. Brandt (ed.) *Luther's Works*, Vol. XLV (Philadelphia, 1962), pp. 200–1
25. Martin Luther, 'Von den Juden und Ihren Lügen, *Luthers Reforma-tions-Schriften*, Vol. XX (St Louis: Concordia, 1890), pp. 1861–2026. Karl H. Rengstorf/Siegfried von Kortzfleisch (ed.) *Kirche und Synagoge: Handbuch zur Geschichte von Christen und Juden, Darstellung mit Quellen*, Vol. 1 (Stuttgart, 1968), pp. 419 ff
26. Heiko A. Oberman, *The Roots of Antisemitism in the Age of Renaissance and Reformation* (Philadelphia, 1984), p. 117
27. Quoted in Salo Baron, *A Social and Religious History of the Jews*, Vol. XIII, p. 218

28. Haim Hillel Ben-Sasson, 'The Reformation in Contemporary Jewish Eyes', in *Proceedings of the Israel Academy of Sciences and Humanities*, IV, 12 (Jerusalem, 1971), pp. 241–326

29. For a comparison between Luther and Calvin's view of the Jews, see Alice L. Eckardt, 'The Reformation and the Jews', *Shofar*, Vol. 7, No. 4 (Summer 1989), pp. 23–47

30. Richard Gutteridge, *Open Thy Mouth for the Dumb: The German Evangelical Church and the Jews, 1879–1959* (Oxford, 1976)

Chapter 4

1. S. Ettinger, 'The Secular Roots of Modern Antisemitism', in O. D. Kulka and P. Mendes-Flohr (eds), *Judaism and Christianity under the Impact of National Socialism* (Jerusalem, 1987), p. 43

2. S. Ettinger, 'Jews and Judaism as seen by the English Deists of the 18th Century', *Zion*, XXIX (1964), in Hebrew

3. Arthur Hertzberg, *The French Enlightenment and the Jews* (New York, 1968), p. 313

4. Voltaire, 'Lettres' (14 December 1773) and 'Sermon des Cinquantes' in *Oeuvres Complètes de Voltaire* (Paris, 1785), Vol. LXII, p. 279; XXXII, p. 381

5. Voltaire, 'Juifs', *Dictionnaire Philosophique, ibid.*, XLI, p. 152

6. Voltaire, *ibid.*, XLI, pp. 136–82; *Essai sur les Moeurs, ibid.*, XVII, pp. 530–4

7. O. D. Kulka, 'Critique of Judaism in European Thought: On the Historical Meaning of Modern Antisemitism', *The Jerusalem Quarterly* (Fall 1989), No. 52, pp. 126–44

8. Jules Michelet, *La Bible de l'Humanité* (Paris, 1864), pp. 374 ff. See also G. Monod, 'Michelet et les juifs', *Revue des Etudes Juives*, 53 (1907), pp. 1–25

9. E. Renan, *History of the People of Israel*, Vol. 1 (Boston, 1905), p. 97

10. E. Renan, *Histoire générale et système comparé des langues sémitiques* (Paris, 1855), pp. 468 ff

11. *Ibid.*, pp. 16–18

12. *Ibid.*, p. 4

13. S. Almog, 'The Racial Motif in Renan's Attitude to Jews and Judaism', in *Zion*, 32 (1967), pp. 175–200, in Hebrew

14. *Ni Dieu, Ni Maître*, 21 November 1880, 6 November 1881

15. Albert Regnard, *Aryens et Sémites: Le Bilan du Judaisme et du Christianisme* (Paris, 1890)

16. Gustave Tridon, *Du Molochisme Juif: Etudes critiques et philosophiques* (Brussels, 1884), pp. 127–30

17. Edouard Drumont, *La Fin d'un Monde* (Paris, 1889), p. 185
18. See A. Toussenel, *Les Juifs: Rois de l'Epoque: Histoire de la féodalite financière* (Paris, 1845); L. Poliakov, *A. History of Antisemitism* (Paris, 1975) Vol. 111, pp. 377 ff; Z. Sternhell, *La Droite Révolutionnaire 1885–1914: Les Origines Françaises du Fascisme* (Paris, 1978), pp. 384–400
19. S. Ettinger, 'The Young Hegelians – A Source of Modern Anti-Semitism', *The Jerusalem Quarterly*, 28, (1983), p. 82 and Robert S. Wistrich, 'Antisemitism as a "Radical" Ideology in the 19th Century', *The Jerusalem Quarterly*, 28, (1983), pp. 88 ff
20. Ettinger, 'The Young Hegelians', p. 73
21. Nathan Rotenstreich, 'For and Against Emancipation: the Bruno Bauer Controversy', *LBIYB* (1959), IV, pp. 3–36
22 Bruno Bauer, *Die Judenfrage* (Brunswick, 1843)
23. G. F. Daumer, *Der Feuer-und Molochdienst der alten Hebräer als urvaterlicher, legaler, orthodoxer Cultus der Nation* (Brunswick, 1842)
24. 'On the Jewish Question', in Karl Marx, *Early Writings* (London, 1975), pp. 238 ff
25. *Ibid.*
26. Robert S. Wistrich, *Revolutionary Jews from Marx to Trotsky* (London/New York, 1976)
27. Hannah Arendt, *Antisemitism*, p. 27
28. Karl Marx, 'On the Jewish Question', p. 237
29. *Ibid.*
30. *Ibid.*
31. For Bauer's racial antisemitism, see his *Das Judentum in der Fremde* (Berlin, 1863)
32. Ernst Nolte, *Three Faces of Fascism* (London, 1965), p. 332 notes that 'every significant ideology of the nineteenth century had its own brand of antisemitism'

Chapter 5

1. Eleanore Sterling, *Judenhass: Die Anfänge der politischen Antisemitismus in Deutschland (1815–1850)*, (Frankfurt a.M, 1969)
2. O. D. Kulka, 'Richard Wagner und die Anfänge des modernen Antisemitismus', *Bulletin des Leo Baeck Instituts*, 4, (1961), pp. 281–300 on the connection between Wagner's political radicalism and racial antisemitism. See also Hartmut Zelinski *Richard Wagner – ein deutsches Thema. Eine Dokumentation zur Wirkungsgeschichte Richard Wagners, 1876–1976* (Vienna/Berlin, 1983)
3. R. Wagner, *Das Judenthum in der Musik* (Leipzig, 1869), pp. 10–12

4. *Ibid.*, pp. 31–2

5. Letter to Ludwig II, 22.XI.1881. Quoted in J. Katz, *The Darker Side of Genius: Richard Wagner's Antisemitism* (London, 1986), p. 115. Katz's book is useful but unfortunately fails to grasp the passion and depth of Wagner's hostility to Jews. On this point, see Margaret Brearley, 'Hitler and Wagner: the Leader, the Master and the Jews', *Patterns of Prejudice*, Vol. 22, No. 2 (1988), pp. 3–21

6. Paul W. Massing, *Rehearsal for Destruction: A Study of Political Antisemitism in Imperial Germany* (New York, 1949); P. G. J. Pulzer, *The Rise of Political Antisemitism in Germany and Austria* (London, 1988, revised ed.)

7. See the informative but otherwise disappointing biography by Moshe Zimmermann, *Wilhelm Marr: The Patriarch of Antisemitism* (New York, 1986)

8. Adolf Stoecker, *Christlich-Sozial: Reden und Aufsätze* (Berlin, 1890, 2nd ed.); Hans Engelmann, *Kirche am Abgrund: Adolf Stoecker und seine antijüdische Bewegung* (Berlin, 1984), pp. 120–72

9. U. Tal. *Christians and Jews in Germany: Religion, Politics and Ideology in the Second Reich, 1870–1914* (Ithaca/London 1975); Birgitta Magge, *Rhetorik des Hasses: Eugen Dühring und die Genese seines antisemitischen Wortschatzes* (Neuss, 1977)

10. Fritz Stern deals with de Lagarde in *The Politics of Cultural Despair: A Study of the Rise of German Ideology* (Berkeley, 1961)

11. For Treitschke's articles and the response which they drew, see W. Boehlich (ed.) *Der Berliner Antisemitismusstreit* (Frankfurt a.M, 1965)

12. Werner Sombart, *Die Zukunft der Juden* (Leipzig, 1912), p. 52; Paul Mendes-Flohr, 'Werner Sombart's "The Jews and Modern Capitalism": An Analysis of Its Ideological Premises', *LBIYB*, XXI (1976), pp. 87–107. Also Geoffrey C. Field, *Evangelist of Race: The Germanic Vision of Houston S. Chamberlain* (New York, 1981)

13. *Basic Writings of Nietzsche*. Translated and edited with commentaries by Walter Kaufmann (1968), appendix, p. 798

14. *Ibid.*, p. 594

15. *Ibid.*, p. 377

16. *Ibid.* Nietzsche does, of course, also criticise the Jews, whose historic legacy he denounced as being responsible for 'the slave-revolt in morals'. This aspect of Nietzsche's approach to Judaism was as distorted as later efforts to turn him into a spiritual godfather of German Nazism

17. Robert S. Wistrich, *Socialism and the Jews: The Dilemmas of Assimilation in Germany and Austria-Hungary* (London/Toronto, 1982)

18. Hans Jürgen Pühle, *Agrarische Interessenpolitik und preussischer Konservatismus im wilhelminischen Reich* (Hanover, 1966)
19. Werner Jochmann, 'Struktur und Funktion des deutschen Antisemitismus', in W. E. Mosse and A. Paucker (eds.) *Juden im Wilhelminischen Deutschland 1890–1914* (Tübingen, 1976), pp. 389–477
20. Robert S. Wistrich, *The Jews of Vienna in the Age of Franz Joseph* (London, 1989)
21. On the Rohling affair, I. A. Hellwing, *Der konfessionelle Antisemitismus im 19. Jahrhundert in Österreich* (Vienna, 1972)
22. Robert S. Wistrich, 'Karl Lueger and the Ambiguities of Viennese Antisemitism', *Jewish Social Studies* (1983), 45, pp. 251–62
23. Richard S. Geehr, *Karl Lueger: Mayor of Fin de Siècle Vienna* (Detroit, 1990), p. 293
24. *Ibid.*, p. 200
25. Wistrich, *op. cit.*, pp. 258–61
26. Robert S. Wistrich, 'Georg von Schoenerer and the Genesis of Modern Austrian Antisemitism', *The Wiener Library Bulletin* (1976), Vol. XXIX. New Series, Nos. 39/40, pp. 21–9

Chapter 6

1. Werner Maser (ed.) *Hitler's Letters and Notes* (New York, 1974), p. 215
2. 'Warum sind wir Antisemiten? Rede auf einer NSDAP Versammlung', in Eberhard Jäckel/Axel Kuhn (eds.) *Hitler: Sämtliche Aufzeichnungen 1905–1924* (Stuttgart, 1980), pp. 176–7. Also the speech of 6 April 1920, *ibid.*, pp. 119–20
3. John Toland, *Adolf Hitler* (New York, 1977), p. 157
4. On Nazism as a 'political faith', see the inaugural lecture of Uriel Tal, 7 June 1978, at the dedication of the Jacob and Shoshana Schreiber Chair of Contemporary Jewish History, Tel Aviv University
5. Robert Wistrich, *Hitler's Apocalypse* (London, 1985), p. 139
6. Adolf Hitler, *Mein Kampf* (Boston, 1943), p. 65
7. Dietrich Eckart, *Der Bolschevismus von Moses bis Lenin: Zwiegespräch zwischen Adolf Hitler und mir* (Munich, 1924), pp. 35–6
8. H. R. Trevor-Roper (ed.), *Hitler's Table Talk, 1941–1944* (London, 1973), p. 79
9. Wistrich, *Hitler's Apocalypse*, pp. 145–6
10. H. R. Trevor-Roper (ed.), *op. cit.*, p. 722
11. E. Fackenheim, *The Jewish Return into History: Reflections in the Age of Auschwitz and a New Jerusalem* (New York, 1978), p. 76

12. Jerry Z. Müller, 'Communism, Anti-Semitism and the Jews', *Commentary* (August 1988), pp. 30–3

13. Speech of 28 July 1922, in Norman H. Baynes (ed.) *The Speeches of Adolf Hitler* (London, 1942), Vol. 1, p. 29. Also 'The Stock Exchange Revolution of 1918', *ibid.*, pp. 42 ff

14. Andreas Hillgruber, 'Die "Endlösung" und das Deutsche Ostimperium als Kernstück des Rassenideologischen Programms des National-sozialismus', *Vierteljahrshefte für Zeitgeschichte*, 20 (1972), pp. 133–55

15. Saul Friedländer, 'Some Aspects of the Historical Significance of the Holocaust', *The Jerusalem Quarterly* (Fall 1976), p. 51

16. Yisrael Gutman, 'On the Character of Nazi Antisemitism', in Almog (ed.) *Antisemitism through the Ages*, pp. 349–80

17. See R. Bytwerk's article in *The Wiener Library Bulletin* (1976), Vol. XXIX, new series, Nos. 39/40, pp. 41–6

18. 'Memorandum by Adolf Hitler on the Tasks of a Four-Year Plan' (Obersalzberg, August 1936), *Documents on German Foreign Policy, 1918–1945*, Series C. Vol. 5, No. 490, p. 855

19. Peter Loewenberg, 'The Kristallnacht as a Public Degradation Ritual', *LBIYB* (1987), pp. 309–23

20. *Ibid.*, p. 315

21. *Ibid.*, p. 317

22. *Ibid.*, p. 319

23. Norman H. Baynes (ed.) *The Speeches of Adolf Hitler*, I, pp. 740–1

24. See Paul Hilberg, 'German Railroads, Jewish Souls', *Transaction, Social Science and Modern Society* (1976), pp. 60–74; Friedlander/ Milton (eds.), *The Holocaust*

25. Ian Kershaw, *Popular Opinion and Political Dissent: Bavaria 1933–1945*, (Oxford, 1983), p. 275

26. Jeremy Noakes and Geoffrey Pridham (eds.) *Documents on Nazism, 1919–1945* (London, 1974), p. 493

27. *Ibid.*, pp. 492–3

28. *Ibid.*

29. Alfred Baeumler, *Alfred Rosenberg und der Mythos des 20 Jahrhunderts* (Munich, 1943), pp. 19 ff

30. Uriel Tal, 'On the Study of the Holocaust and Genocide', *Yad Vashem Studies*, Vol. XIII (Jerusalem, 1979), pp. 7–46

31. Robert Wistrich, *Hitler's Apocalypse*, p. 135

Chapter 7

1. David Bankier, 'The Germans and the Holocaust', *The Jewish Quarterly* (Autumn 1990), pp. 7–11

2. Elizabeth Noelle and Erich Peter Neumann (eds.) *The Germans: Public Opinion Polls 1947–1966* (Westport, Conn. 1981). The surveys were carried out by the Institut für Demoskopie, Allensbach

3. *Ibid.*, pp. 185–92, 202, 206, 219, 311–16, 333

4. Tom Bower, *The Pledge Betrayed: America, Britain and the De-Nazification of Postwar Germany* (New York, 1982), pp. 229–30

5. Hanns Werner Schwarze, *The GDR Today* (London, 1973). Also Kurt Southeimer and Wilhelm Bleek, *The Government and Politics of East Germany* (New York, 1975)

6. Gareth Winrow, 'East Germany, Israel and the Reparations Issue', *Soviet Jewish Affairs*, Vol. 20, No. 1 (1990), pp. 31–44

7. Eleanore Sterling, 'Judenfreunde – Judenfeinde: Fragwürdiger Philosemitismus in der Bundesrepublik', *Die Zeit*, 10 December 1965. Also the article by Frank Stern, 'From Overt Philosemitism to Discreet Antisemitism and Beyond', in Almog (ed.), *Antisemitism through the Ages*, pp. 385–402

8. See the introduction by Anson Rabinbach to the volume he edited with Jack Zipes, *Germans and Jews since the Holocaust: The Changing Situation in West Germany* (New York/London, 1986), pp. 3–22

9. See my chapter on the Fassbinder Controversy, in Robert S. Wistrich, *Between Redemption and Perdition* (London/New York, 1990), pp. 121–32

10. Quoted by Micha Brumlik, 'Fear of the Father Figure: Judeophobic Tendencies in the New Social Movements in West Germany', *Patterns of Prejudice*, Vol. 21, No. 4 (1987), p. 34

11. 'Philosemiten sind Antisemiten' (interview with Fassbinder), *Die Zeit*, Hamburg, 9 April 1976

12. W. R. Fassbinder, *Der Müll, die Stadt und der Tod* (Frankfurt am Main, 1981), Scene 10

13. Quoted in Wistrich, *Between Redemption and Perdition*, p. 125

14. See Henryk M. Broder, *Der ewige Antisemit* (Frankfurt a.M., 1986), pp. 7–12. Also the article by Vera Ebels-Dolanová, 'On "The Rich Jew" of Fassbinder: An Essay on Literary Antisemitism', *Patterns of Prejudice*, Vol. 23, No. 4 (1989), pp. 3–16

15. Stern, *op. cit.*, p. 385

16. For a critical view of the apologetic tendencies in current German historiography, see Jürgen Habermas, 'Eine Art Schadensabwicklung', *Die Zeit*, 11 July 1986

17. Wistrich, *Between Redemption and Perdition*, p. 126

18. Quoted by Stern, *op. cit.*, p. 387

19. Werner Bergmann, 'Sind die Deutschen antisemitisch? Meinungsumfragen von 1946–1987 in der Bundesrepublik Deutschland', in

W. Bergmann and Rainer Erb (eds.) *Antisemitismus in der politischen Kultur nach 1945* (Opladen, 1990), pp. 108–30

20. Bernd Marin, 'Ein historisch neuartiger "Antisemitismus ohne Antisemiten"?', *Geschichte und Gesellschaft*, 5, (1979), pp. 545–69; Alphons Silbermann, *Sind wir Antisemiten? Ausmass und Wirkung eines sozialen Vorurteils in der Bundesrepublik Deutschland* (Cologne, 1982); W. Bergmann, 'Public Beliefs about Anti-Jewish Attitudes in West Germany', *Patterns of Prejudice*, Vol. 22, No. 3, (1983), pp. 15–21

21. 'Mit Gestrigen in die Zukunft? Umfrage über Hitler, die NS-Zeit und die Folgen', *Der Spiegel*, 15/1989, pp. 150–63

22. *Ibid.* See also 'Le Nazisme à visage humain', *Passages*, 15, (March 1989), p. 31

23. Uwe Backes, 'The West German Republikaner: Profile of a Nationalist, Populist Party of Protest', *Patterns of Prejudice*, Vol. 24, No. 1 (1990), pp. 3–18

24. 'Les vieux ennemis de la liberté', *Le Nouvel Observateur* (1–7 February 1990), p. 50

25. *Newsweek*, 7 May 1990, p. 24

26. *Ibid.*, p. 21, 'A New Life on Top of the Ruins'

27. Peter Pulzer, 'Erasing the Past: German Historians Debate the Holocaust', *Patterns of Prejudice*, Vol. 21, No. 3 (1987), pp. 4–13

Chapter 8

1. F. L. Carsten, *Fascist Movements in Austria: From Schönerer to Hitler* (London, 1977), pp. 75–6

2. John Haag, 'Blood on the Ringstrasse: Vienna's students 1918–1933', *The Wiener Library Bulletin*, Vol. XXIX, new series, Nos. 39/40, (1976), pp. 29–33

3. Carsten, *op. cit.*, p. 90

4. J. Moser, 'Von der antisemitischen Bewegung zum Holocaust', in Klaus Lohrmann (ed.), *1,000 Jahre österreichisches Judentum* (Eisenstadt, 1982), p. 265

5. Bruce F. Pauley, 'Political Antisemitism in interwar Vienna', in I. Oxaal *et al.* (eds.), *Jews, Antisemitism and Culture in Vienna* (London/New York, 1987), p. 159–60

6. *Ibid.*, p. 162

7. Gerhard Botz, *Wien vom 'Anschluss' zum Krieg* (Vienna/Munich, 1978), pp. 406–8, 463

8. Quoted in the catalogue of the Anschluss Exhibition under the auspices of the Yad Vashem Committee of the UK (London, 1988)

9. Quoted in Gerhard Botz, 'From the Anschluss to the Holocaust' in Oxaal *et al.*, *op. cit.*, p. 202–3

10. *Ibid.*

11. George E. Berkley, *Vienna and its Jews: The Tragedy of Success 1880s– 1980s* (Cambridge, Mass. 1989)

12. Robert Knight (ed.) *'Ich bin dafür, die Sache in die Länge zu ziehen': Die Wortprotokolle der österreichischen Bundesregierung von 1945 bis 1952 über die Entschadigung der Juden* (Frankfurt a.M., 1988)

13. John Bunzl, 'Zur Geschichte des Antisemitismus in Österreich', in J. Bunzl and B. Marin (eds.), *Antisemitismus in Österreich* (Innsbruck, 1983)

14. Anton Pelinka, 'The Great Austrian Taboo: the Repression of the Civil War', *New German Critique*, No. 43 (Winter 1988), pp. 69–82

15. Bruce F. Pauley, *Hitler and the Forgotten Nazis: A History of Austrian National Socialism* (Chapel Hill, 1978), pp. 148–51, 219–21

16. Heinz Fischer (ed.) *Einer im Vordergrund: Taras Borodajkewycz: Eine Dokumentation* (Vienna, 1966)

17. Martin van Amerongen, *Kreisky und seine unbewältigte Vergangenheit* (Graz, 1977), pp. 96–107

18. Robert Wistrich, 'The strange case of Bruno Kreisky', *Encounter* (May, 1979), pp. 78–86

19. Richard Mitten, 'Die Kreisky-Peter-Wiesenthal "Affäre,"' in *Wir sind alle Unschuldige Täter! Studien zum antisemitischen Diskurs im Nachkriegsösterreich* (Wien, 1989), pp. 295–322

20. Hilde Weiss, 'Antisemitische Vorurteile in Österreich nach 1945. Ergebnisse empirischer Forschungen', in Julius H. Schoeps and Alphons Silbermann (eds.) *Antisemitismus nach dem Holocaust* (Cologne, 1986), pp. 53–70

21. *Neue Kronen-Zeitung*, 8 March 1986

22. *Wiener Zeitung*, 6 March 1986, *Salzburger Nachrichten*, 8 March 1986

23. *Wiener Zeitung*, 29 March 1986

24. *Kleine Zeitung*, 27 March 1986. Richard Mitten, 'Reflections on the "Waldheim Affair"', ms. to be published in Robert S. Wistrich, *Austrians and Jews in the Twentieth Century*, (London, 1992)

25. Interview of Kurt Waldheim with Claire Trean, *Le Monde*, 3 May 1986

26. Interviews with Ruth Wodak in Jerusalem and Vienna, 1990. Also Ruth Wodak, 'Turning the Tables: Antisemitic Discourse in Postwar Austria' (1990), unpublished ms

27. 'Antisemitic Attitudes in Austrian Society, 1973–1989', study published by the Institute for Conflict Research, Vienna, July 1989.

Chapter 9

1. Bernard Glassman, *Anti-Semitic Stereotypes without Jews: Images of the Jews in England 1290–1700* (Detroit, 1973), pp. 14–50
2. *Ibid.*, pp. 56–8. See the article by Lucien Wolf, 'Jews in Elizabethan England', *Transactions of the Jewish Historical Society of England*, 11 (1928), pp. 1–91
3. G. K. Hunter, 'The Theology of Marlowe's The Jew of Malta', *Journal of the Warburg and Courtauld Institutes*, 27, (1969), pp. 211–40; Hyam Maccoby, 'The Figure of Shylock', *Midstream* 16 (February, 1970), pp. 50–9
4. For the literary and cultural aspects, Harold Fisch, *Jerusalem and Albion: The Hebraic Factor in Seventeenth-Century Literature* (New York, 1964)
5. Chaim Bermant, *The Cousinhood* (London, 1971)
6. W. D. Rubinstein, *The Left, the Right and the Jews* (London/Canberra, 1982), pp. 12–15
7. B. Gainer, *The Alien Invasion* (London, 1972); Lloyd Gartner, *The Jewish Immigrant in England, 1870–1914* (London, 1960)
8. William J. Fishman, *East End Jewish Radicals, 1875–1914* (London, 1975)
9. On antisemitism in British socialist circles, see John A. Garrard, *The English and Immigration: A Comparative Study of the Jewish Influx, 1880–1910* (London, 1971)
10. *Justice* (London), 21 January 1893, 25 April 1896, 7 October 1899. *Justice* was the organ of the Marxist Social-Democratic Federation in Great Britain. During the late 1890s it carried on an antisemitic campaign against what it called 'imperialist Judaism' in South Africa
11. In a speech in the House of Commons on 6 February 1900 Labour leader John Burns declared that wherever he looked, 'there is the financial Jew, operating, directing, inspiring the agonies that have led to this war'. Quoted in the important article by Claire Hirshfield, 'The British Left and the "Jewish Conspiracy": A Case Study of Modern Anti-Semitism', *Jewish Social Studies* (Spring 1981), p. 105
12. *Ibid.*, pp. 106–7
13. Colin Holmes, *Anti-Semitism in British Society, 1876–1939* (New York, 1979) emphasises the strength of the indigenous tradition of British hostility to Jews as aliens who were intent on remaining separate and who represented values which were allegedly a threat to the British way of life
14. 'T. S. Eliot and the Jews: A Row over anti-Semitism mars his centenary', *Newsweek*, 22 August 1988

15. Stephen Wilson, 'Prejudice in Poetry', *Encounter* (July/August 1989), pp. 46–50

16. Shmuel Almog, 'Antisemitism as a Dynamic Phenomenon: The "Jewish Question" in England at the End of the First World War', *Patterns of Prejudice*, Vol. 21, No. 4 (1987), pp. 3–18

17. The *Protocols* were compiled by Russian antisemites in the Parisian office of the Tsarist Okhrana (secret police) at the end of the 19th century. They were printed on a government press in 1905 – as part of a book by a Russian Orthodox mystic, Sergei Nilus, which claimed that they were extracts from the First Zionist Congress in Basel of 1897. The *Protocols* contain lectures by so-called 'Elders of Zion' outlining a secret plan for subjugating the Gentiles and establishing a Jewish world state. In pre-1914 Russia they were used as a weapon against the liberal constitutional movement without much effect, and then again by anti-Bolshevik Whites during the Russian Civil War with much more devastating results. They spread to the West through German and other translations after 1919, achieving their greatest impact in Germany. They were exposed in 1921 by a London *Times* correspondent who showed that they were plagiarised from a French satire of the 1860s, a German novel of the same period by Herrmann Goedsche and other sources. Despite these proofs and the many absurdities in the *Protocols*, their influence has been enormous, demonstrating the deep irrationality in modern antisemitism and the need to believe in a diabolical world conspiracy by occult forces (Jews, freemasons etc.) seeking global power. The best account is in Norman Cohn, *Warrant for Genocide: The Myth of the Jewish World Conspiracy and the Protocols of the Elders of Zion* (London, 1967). For the impact of the *Protocols* in Britain, see Gisela Lebzelter, *Political Antisemitism in England 1918– 1939* (London, 1978)

18. Almog, 'Antisemitism as a Dynamic Phenomenon', p. 14

19. Lord Sydenham, 'The Jewish World Problem', *Nineteenth Century*, November 1921, 'Die-Hard Anti-Semites', *Jewish Guardian*, 6 January 1922

20. Gisela Lebzelter, 'Henry Hamilton Beamish and the Britons: Champions of Anti-Semitism', in K. Lunn and R. C. Thurlow (eds.) *British Fascism: Essays on the Radical Right in Interwar Britain* (New York, 1980)

21. Robert M. Gorman, 'Racial Antisemitism in England: the legacy of Arnold Leese', *The Wiener Library Bulletin*, 43–44 (1977), p. 68

22. Robert J. Benewick, *The Fascist Movement in Britain* (London, 1972); also Robert Skidelsky, *Oswald Mosley* (New York, 1975)

23. Richard Thurlow, *Fascism in Britain: A History 1918–1945* (Oxford, 1987)
24. Tony Kushner, *The Persistence of Prejudice: Anti-Semitism in British Society during the Second World War* (Manchester, 1989)
25. Bernard Wasserstein, *Britain and the Jews of Europe 1939–1945* (Oxford, 1979), pp. 93–4, 112–19
26. *Ibid.*, pp. 345–57
27. Harold Nicolson, *Diaries and Letters 1939–45*, ed. Nigel Nicolson (New York, 1967), p. 469
28. W. D. Rubinstein, *The Left, the Right and the Jews*, pp. 152 ff
29. M. Billig, *Fascists: A Social Psychological View of the National Front* (London, 1978)
30. Bernard Levin, 'So that's what became of Europe's missing Jews', *The Times*, 14 May 1990
31. 'Jews divided over cemetery attacks', *Guardian*, 23 May 1990; 'A time to cry out, or a time to lie low?', *Independent*, 28 May 1990; 'Are the racists loose in our streets again?', *Sunday Telegraph*, 3 June 1990; 'Children targets of anti-semitism', *Independent*, 10 December 1990; 'JFS goes public on race attacks', *Jewish Chronicle*, 14 December 1990
32. Gill Seidel, *The Holocaust Denial: Antisemitism, Racism and the New Right* (London, 1986)

Chapter 10

1. W. D. Rubinstein, *op. cit.*, pp. 136 ff
2. Jonathan Sarna, 'American Anti-Semitism', in D. Berger (ed.) *History and Hate*, pp. 115–26
3. Ralph L. Kolodny, 'Catholics and Father Coughlin: Misremembering the Past', *Patterns of Prejudice*, Vol. 19, No. 4 (1985), pp. 15–25
4. *Ibid.*, p. 24
5. Leo P. Ribuffo, *The Old Christian Right: The Protestant Far Right from the Great Depression to the Cold War* (Philadelphia, 1983)
6. Lloyd P. Gartner, 'The Two Continuities of Antisemitism in the United States', in Almog (ed.), *Antisemitism through the Ages*, pp. 312–14
7. W. D. Rubinstein, *op. cit.*, p. 22
8. Meyer Weinberg, *Because They were Jews. A History of Anti-Semitism* (New York, 1986), pp. 214–15
9. Ernest Samuels, *Henry Adams: The Middle Years* (Cambridge, Mass. 1958), p. 168
10. Leonard Dinnerstein, *The Leo Frank Case* (Athens, Georgia, 1966).

Frank was falsely charged with strangling a teenage Christian girl,
Mary Phagan, in an Atlanta factory which he managed. His death-
sentence was commuted to life imprisonment but several weeks
later he was kidnapped from the state prison and lynched. See also
L. Dinnerstein, *Uneasy at Home: Antisemitism and the American
Experience* (New York, 1987) on the prevalence of antisemitism in
the United States and the historical context of Southern prejudice

11. Weinberg, *op. cit.*, p. 214. The Klan asserted native, white Protestant
supremacy in America and was especially hostile to the immigrant
East European Jews in the 1920s

12. See Robert Singerman, 'The American Career of *The Protocols of the
Elders of Zion'*, *American Jewish History* (September 1981), pp. 48–78

13. Albert Lee, *Henry Ford and the Jews* (New York, 1980), pp. 29–31,
46–51, 69

14. *Ibid.*, p. 46

15. *New York Times*, 7 April 1933

16. Quoted in Melvin J. Urofsky, *We are One! American Jewry and Israel*
(New York, 1978), p. 49

17. David S. Wyman, *The Abandonment of the Jews*: *America and the
Holocaust, 1941–1945* (New York, 1984), p. 8

18. Weinberg, *op. cit.*, pp. 220 ff

19. Leonard Dinnerstein, 'American Jewish Organizational Efforts to
Combat Antisemitism in the United States since 1945' in Michael
Curtis (ed.) *Antisemitism in the Contemporary World* (Boulder,
Colorado, 1986), p. 303

20. *Ibid.*, pp. 304 ff

21. Quoted by Earl Raab, 'American Blacks and Israel' in Robert S.
Wistrich (ed.) *Anti-Zionism and Antisemitism in the Contemporary
World* (London, 1990), p. 159

22. *Ibid.*, pp. 159–60

23. *New York Times*, 17 April 1984, 29 June 1984

24. Raab, *op. cit.*, p. 166

25. Dennis King, 'The Farrakhan Phenomenon: Ideology, Support,
Potential', *Patterns of Prejudice*, Vol. 20, No. 1 (1986), pp. 15–22

26. Jennifer L. Golub, *What Do We Know About Black Anti-Semitism?*
(Working Papers on Contemporary Antisemitism), The American
Jewish Committee, 1990. My thanks to David Singer, Director of
this research project, for bringing these and other materials to my
attention

27. *Ibid.*, pp. 22–4

28. *Ibid.*, p. 15

29. See the Resource Packet, 'The Politics and Background of State

Representative David Duke' (New Orleans, Louisiana, 1990). This very detailed exposure of Duke's neo-Nazi and white suprematist outlook was put out by the Louisiana Coalition against Racism and Nazism

30. Harold E. Quinley and Charles Y. Glock, *Antisemitism in America* (New York, 1979), p. 183 concluded over a decade ago: 'Anti-Semitic attitudes are not nearly as common now as they were in the 1930s and 1940s, and other groups, most notably blacks, have come to bear the main brunt of extremist attacks. Nevertheless, the prevalence of anti-Semitic imagery in the culture at large makes Jews vulnerable to extremist politics. The possibility of future political attacks upon Jews thus cannot be ruled out.' The experience of the 1980s on the whole confirms this prudent assessment

Chapter 11

1. For the antisemitic politics of Drumont see his follow-up works after *La France Juive*, which, though less successful, provide an important insight into fin-de-siècle French society and its attitude to Jews: *La Fin d'un monde* (Paris, 1889), *La Dernière Bataille* (Paris, 1890) and *Le Testament d'un Anti-sémite* (Paris, 1891). Also Michel Winock, *Edouard Drumont et Cie, antisémitisme et fascisme en France* (Paris, 1982)

2. Pierre Sorlin, *'La Croix' et les Juifs 1889–1899* (Paris, 1967) and Stephen Wilson, *Ideology and Experience: Antisemitism in France at the Time of the Dreyfus Affair* (Toronto, 1982), the most comprehensive single study of the subject

3. An outstanding exception to the rule was the liberal Catholic Dreyfusard, Anatole Leroy-Beaulieu, who demonstrated in books like *L'Antisémitisme* (Paris, 1897) and *Les Doctrines de haine: l'antisémitisme, l'antiprotestantisme, l'anticléricalisme* (Paris, 1902) that antisemitism was a profound danger to universalist, humanist principles and to the health of French society as a whole. One should also add that the French Catholic poet and essayist Charles Péguy (a militant Dreyfusard), in his portrait of the Jewish anarchist Bernard Lazare, displayed a degree of empathy with the fate of the Jews rarely achieved in modern European liteature. See Charles Péguy, *Notre Jeunesse* (Paris, 1910)

4. Robert Byrnes, *Antisemitism in Modern France* (New Brunswick, 1950), Pierre Pierrard, *Juifs et Catholiques français: De Drumont à Jules Isaac, 1886–1945* (Paris, 1970)

5. Hannah Arendt, *Antisemitism*, pp. 111–12 quotes Max Régis, calling

upon a cheering Parisian rabble to 'water the tree of freedom with the blood of the Jews'. See also Stephen Wilson, 'The Antisemitic Riots of 1898 in France', *The Historical Journal* XVI, 4, (1973), pp. 789–806

6. Byrnes, *op. cit.*, p. 264; Wilson, *Ideology and Experience*, p. 319

7. Michael R. Marrus, *The Politics of Assimilation: A Study of the French Jewish Community at the time of the Dreyfus Affair* (Oxford, 1971). For the views of the first Jewish Dreyfusard and a radical critic of the 'assimilationist' option, see Nelly Wilson's book, *Bernard Lazare: Antisemitism and the Problem of Jewish Identity in late Nineteenth Century in France* (Cambridge, 1978). For a more contemporary critique, see Shmuel Trigano, *La République et les Juifs* (Paris, 1982)

8. Zeev Sternhell, *Maurice Barrès et le Nationalisme Français* (Paris, 1972)

9. Henry H. Weinberg, 'The Image of the Jew in late Nineteenth-Century French Literature', *Jewish Social Studies*, Vol. XLV, Nos. 3–4 (Summer-Fall, 1983), pp. 241–50

10. *Ibid.*

11. André Gide, *Journals 1889–1949* (London, 1967), pp. 194–6. Also C. Wardi, *Le Juif dans le roman français 1933–1948* (Paris, 1972), pp. 45–51. See also Jeffrey Mehlman, *Legacies of Antisemitism in France* (Minneapolis, 1983)

12. Eugen Weber, *Action Française* (Stanford, 1962) and also his *The Nationalist Revival in France 1905–1914* (Los Angeles, 1968)

13. Henry H. Weinberg, *The Myth of the Jew in France 1967–1982* (New York/London, 1987), pp. 113–15

14. Jean Giraudoux, *Pleins Pouvoirs*, 3rd edition (Paris, 1939), pp. 59–76

15. *Ibid.*

16. Michael R. Marrus and Robert O. Paxton, *Vichy France and the Jews* (New York, 1981)

17. *Ibid.*, pp. 271–9

18. Dominique Schnapper, 'Perceptions of Antisemitism in France' in Curtis (ed.), *op. cit.*,pp. 261–71. In a discussion in Paris in 1989, Schnapper told me that the Vichy racial laws marked the 'death of a certain type of "Israelite",' – of the classical 'assimilationist' Jew in France

19. Paul Webster, 'Shadow over France. The Legacy of Pétain', *Weekend Guardian* (19–20 May 1990), pp. 7–8

20. *Ibid.*, pp. 5–6 which includes an inteview with Le Pen

21. On the background to Holocaust denial literature in France, from Paul Rassinier in the 1950s to the followers of Robert Faurisson in the 1980s, see Gill Seidel, *op. cit.*, pp. 93–111. In 1985 a doctoral

thesis by Henri Roques, which denied the existence of the gas chambers, was accepted at Nantes (it was later cancelled). See 'Les parrains du révisionisme', *L'Express* (6 July 1990). Also interviews with the French 'revisionist' antisemite, Alain Guionnet, conducted in Paris in the summer of 1990 for Thames Television

22. Alfred Fabre-Luce, *Pour en finir avec l'antisémitisme* (Paris, 1979) and the comments of Henry Weinberg, *The Myth of the Jew*, pp. 68–9

23. Jean-Paul Sartre, *Antisemite and Jew* (New York, 1976), p. 71

24. Marrus and Paxton, *op. cit.*, p. 180

25. Meyer Weinberg, *Because They Were Jews*, p. 78

26. Henry Weinberg, *op. cit.*, pp. 31–4

27. Raymond Aron, *De Gaulle, Israël et les Juifs* (Paris, 1968), p. 18

28. Henry Weinberg, *op. cit.*, pp. 45–56

29. Bernard-Henri Levy, *L'Idéologie Française* (Paris, 1981); Annie Kriegel, *Israël est-il coupablé?* (Paris, 1982); Alain Finkielkraut, *La Réprobation d'Israel* (Paris, 1983)

30. Daniel Lindenberg, 'Dérapage de la gauche?', *Les Nouveaux Cahiers*, No. 71, p. 15

31. Robert S. Wistrich, 'The Anti-Zionist Masquerade', *Midstream*, Vol. XXIX, No. 7 (August/September 1983), pp. 8–18

32. Shmuel Trigano, *La République et les Juifs*, p. 33. Interview with Michel Abitbol, Jerusalem, October 1990

33. Henry Weinberg, *op. cit.*, pp. 89–90

34. 'Kristallnacht in Carpentras', *Weekend Guardian* (19–20 May 1990), pp. 4–8, 'Eruption of the Ancient, Ugly Fever', *Time*, 28 May 1990

35. 'Mitterrand joins protest at Jewish grave desecration', *Time*, 28 May 1990. For French Jewry's disillusion with President Mitterrand over his Palestinian policy, Maurice Szafran, 'Mitterrand et les Juifs', *L'Express*, 9 November 1990, p. 9

36. 'L'Incroyable cours de racisme de Mme Stirbois', *L'Evenement du Jeudi*, 17–23 May 1990. Also 'The Extreme Right and Anti-Immigrant Opinion in France', *IJA Research Report*, No. 1 (1990), pp. 1–12

37. Henry Weinberg, *op. cit.*, pp. 126–7

38. David Selbourne, 'French Jews begin to feel like aliens all over again', *Sunday Times*, 3 June 1990. 'In France, at any newspaper kiosk, you can learn . . . that "world pornography is in the hands of the Jews", that "Judaeo-Masonry is up to its old tricks", that "international Jewish capital is buying up the media" and so on'

39. James G. Shields, 'Jean-Marie Le Pen and the new radical right in France', *Patterns of Prejudice*, Vol. 20, No. 1, 1986; 'The French Front National and the downside of respectability', *ibid.*, Vol. 21, No. 1,

1987; Maria Balinska, 'French politics and the 1988 presidential elections', *IJA Research Reports*, No. 3, 1988

40. Maurice Szafran, 'Le dissoudre ou le digérer?', *L'Evenement du Jeudi*, 17–23 May 1990, pp. 13–14. 'Le Pen, c'est la victoire des instincts, et face à cela, les intellectuels sont plutot désarmés'

41. Jean-François Kahn, 'Contre la lèpre antisémite, la déchéance raciste, la haine de l'autre', *L'Evenement du Jeudi*, 17–23 May 1990, pp. 6–7; 'Pas antisémites? Voici ce qu'ils écrivent', *ibid.*, p. 18; Michel Winock, 'Pour une dictionnaire de l'anti-haine', *ibid.*, pp. 22–3; Jerome Garcin, 'Ce qui peut se dire peut se faire', *ibid.*, p. 23

42. *Guardian Weekly*, 17 September 1989

43. *The Times*, 11 May 1990

44. *Jewish Chronicle*, 13 April 1990

45. Interview with Abbé Laguérie, Paris 1990

46. 'France wakes up to demon of antisemitism', *Independent on Sunday*, 20 May 1990, p. 16

Chapter 12

1. François Schlosser, 'L'avant-communisme en Europe centrale et danubienne', *Le Nouvel Observateur*, 1–7 February 1990, pp. 51–2

2. Carol Iancu, *Les Juifs en Roumanie 1866–1919: De l'exclusion à l'émancipation* (Provence, 1978). Also Meyer Weinberg, *op. cit.*, pp. 172–3 for a list of the many anti-Jewish laws passed in Rumania during the 19th century. Between 1900 and 1906 alone, over 70,000 Jews emigrated from Rumania

3. Ezra Mendelsohn, *The Jews of East Central Europe Between the World Wars* (Bloomington, 1987), pp. 186, 188–9

4. Stephen Fischer-Galati, 'Fascism, Communism and the Jewish Question in Rumania', in Bela Vago and George L. Mosse (eds.) *Jews and non-Jews in Eastern Europe 1918–1945* (New York, 1974), pp. 157–76. Also Mendelsohn, *ibid.*, pp. 203–11

5. Meyer Weinberg, *op. cit.*, p. 178. As of 1945, 430,000 Jews still lived in Rumania but many had emigrated to Palestine by 1947. By 1970, there were only about 100,000 Jews left in Rumania

6. *Newsweek*, 7 May 1990, pp. 22–3 for the opinions of the National Peasants Party, which accused Brucan, along with other prominent Jewish Communists of 'organizing the genocide of the Rumanian people' during the postwar years

7. Glen Frankel, '"Saving Jews": Ceaucescu's high price', *International Herald Tribune*, 22 February 1990

8. Peter Hillmore, 'Nasty writing on the wall for Jews', *Observer*, 11

February 1990. Also *Newsweek*, 7 May 1990, p. 23 for the statement by Rabbi Rosen that 'anti-Semitism isn't covert, it is open now'

9. William O. McCagg, *Jewish Nobles and Geniuses in Modern Hungary* (Boulder, Colorado, 1973). John Lukacs, *Budapest 1900: A Historical Portrait of a City and Its Culture* (London, 1989), pp. 95 ff., 101–2

10. On Istóczy, see Nathaniel Katzburg, *Antishemiut B'Hungaria 1867–1914* (Tel Aviv, 1969) and Jacob Katz, *From Prejudice to Destruction: Anti-Semitism, 1700–1933* (Cambridge, Mass, 1980), pp. 237–42, 276–7. The Tisza-Eszlár case was sparked off by the disappearance of a 15-year-old Gentile girl shortly before Passover. Rumours that Jews were responsible were fed by the local Catholic priest and given national prominence by antisemitic propagandists. The ensuing trial led to the acquittal of the Jewish defendants but it provoked antisemitic riots, especially in Bratislava (Pressburg) in September 1882

11. Nathaniel Katzburg, 'Hungarian Jewry in Modern Times: Political and Social Aspects', in Randolph L. Braham (ed.) *Hungarian-Jewish Studies* (New York, 1966), p. 148. On the ideology of the Catholic People's Party, see John Lukacs, *op. cit.*, pp. 132–3

12. Victor Karady-Istvan Kemeny, 'Antisémitisme Universitaire et Concurrence de Classe: La Loi du *numerus clausus* en Hongrie entre les deux Guerres', *Actes de la Recherche en sciences sociales*, 34 (1980), p. 67

13. William O. McCagg, Jr., 'Jews in Revolutions: the Hungarian Experience', *Journal of Social History*, 6 (1972), pp. 78–105

14. Mendelsohn, *op. cit.*, pp. 113–15. Nathaniel Katzburg, 'Hungarian Antisemitism: Ideology and Reality (1920–1943)', in: Almog (ed.), *Antisemitism through the Ages*, pp. 339–47

15. Randolph L. Braham, *The Politics of Genocide: The Holocaust in Hungary*, 1 (New York, 1981), p. 118

16. Paul Lendvai, *Antisemitism without Jews: Communist Eastern Europe* (New York, 1971)

17. Ferenc Feher, ' "The Jewish Question" Reconsidered: Notes on Istvan Bibó's Classic Essay', in A. Rabinbach and J. Zipes (eds.) *Germans and Jews since the Holocaust*, pp. 333–6 on the ambiguous 'philosemitic' attitudes of the Kádár regime in Hungary towards the Jews

18. *Ibid.*, p. 334. See also A. Löwenheim, 'The Jewish Question: The View from Budapest, 1988', *Jews and Jewish Topics in Soviet and East European Publications* (Summer, 1988), pp. 89–95

19. 'Alarm in Hungary', *Jewish Chronicle*, 20 April 1990, p. 3

20. 'Hungarian politician warns of new racism', *ibid.*, 28 September

1990; 'Central and East European Jewry: the impact of Liberalization and Revolution', *IJA Research Report*, Nos. 2 & 3 (1990), pp. 2–6

21. Quoted in Guido Kisch, *In Search of Freedom: A History of American Jews from Czechoslovakia* (London, 1949), pp. 36–7

22. Michael Riff, 'Czech Antisemitism and the Jewish Response before 1914', in Robert S. Wistrich (ed.), *The Wiener Library Bulletin*, 29 (1976), nos. 39/40, pp. 8–19. Also Robert S. Wistrich, *The Jews of Vienna*, pp. 206–7

23. Frantisek Červinka, 'The Hilsner Affair', *LBIYB*, 13, (1968), pp. 142–57. Leopold Hilsner was a Jewish shoemaker's assistant who had been condemned for the 'ritual murder' of a young Christian girl at Polna in 1899. He was sentenced to death, then retried and given life-imprisonment, eventually being amnestied by the Emperor Charles towards the end of the First World War. The case was exploited by Czech and German-Austrian antisemites to considerable effect and greatly disturbed Austrian Jews. The miscarriage of justice was seen by some observers as a mini-Dreyfus Affair, provoking many polemics in the Austro-Hungarian press

24. Thomas G. Masaryk, *Die Notwendigkeit der Revision des Polnaer Prozesses* (Vienna, 1899)

25. Hillel Kieval, *The Making of Czech Jewry* (New York, 1988). Also William O. McCagg, *A History of Habsburg Jews 1670–1918* (Bloomington, 1989)

26. *Neue Freie Presse*, 19 November 1920

27. Mendelsohn, *op. cit.*, pp. 150–1 for the anti-Jewish views of the Slovak leader, Vavro Šrobár, in 1919

28. *Ibid.*, pp. 163–8 for Slovak antisemitism in the 1930s

29. Eugene Loebl, *Sentenced and Tried: The Stalinist Purges in Czechoslovakia* (London, 1969); Artur London, *L'Aveu* (Paris, 1969) and Robert S. Wistrich, *The Left against Zion: Communism, Israel and the Middle East* (London, 1979), pp. 57–64, 72–85, 156–60

30. 'Czechoslovakia: Jewish Legacy and Jewish Present', introduced and annotated by Peter Brod, *Soviet Jewish Affairs*, Vol. 20, No. 1 (1990), pp. 58–68

Chapter 13

1. Celia S. Heller, *On the Edge of Destruction: Jews of Poland between the Two World Wars* (New York, 1977), pp. 121–3; Joseph Marcus, *Social and Political History of the Jews of Poland 1919–1939* (Berlin, 1983), pp. 355–7

2. Jerzy Tomaszewski, *Zarys Dziejów Zydów w Polsce w Latach 1918–1939* (Warsaw, 1990), pp. 57–61
3. Pawel Korzec, *Juifs en Pologne: La Question Juive pendant l'entre-deux-guerres* (Paris, 1980) and his article 'Anti-semitism in Poland as an Intellectual, Social and Political Movement', in Joshua Fishman (ed.) *Studies on Polish Jewry, 1919–1939* (New York, 1974), pp. 12–58
4. Yeshaye Trunk, 'Der ekonomisher antisemitizm in polin tsvishn di tsvei velt-milhomes', *Studies on Polish Jewry*, pp. 3–98
5. Mendelsohn, *op. cit.*, pp. 72–3
6. Emmanuel Ringelblum, *Polish–Jewish Relations during the Second World War* (New York, 1976), p. 53. Yisrael Gutman, *The Jews of Warsaw, 1939–1943: Ghetto, Underground, Revolt* (Bloomington, 1982), p. 252
7. See the passionate protest of the renowned Polish-Jewish poet Julian Tuwim, written in 1944 in New York and republished in *Jewish Currents* (February 1975), pp. 28–30. 'I know for a certainty, from the most reliable sources, that the Polish fascists are grateful to Hitler for having made Poland *judenrein*. The spiritual leader of the world's thugs saved them the dirty work. Otherwise, if in 1940 they had come to power, they themselves would have had to do this work'
8. See the claims of the British historian Norman Davies, who argues that the marked increase in antisemitism in occupied Poland (1939–41) was linked to Jewish 'collaboration' with the Bolsheviks and the Soviet security police in Eastern Poland. These and other assertions sparked an acrimonious debate. 'Poles and Jews: An Exchange', *New York Review of Books*, 9 April 1987, pp. 40–4
9. Lucjan Dobroszycki, 'Restoring Jewish Life in Post-war Poland', *Soviet Jewish Affairs*, 3 (1972), p. 66
10. Michael Chechinski, 'The Kielce Pogrom: Some Unanswered Questions, *Soviet Jewish Affairs*, 5 (1972), p. 57
11. Marcus, *op. cit.*, p. 290 notes that more than a third of the membership of the small, illegal, pre-war Polish Communist Party had been Jewish, even though the Communists scarcely represented either the national or the economic interests of Polish Jewry
12. Anonymous, 'USSR and the Politics of Polish Antisemitism, 1956–68', *Soviet Jewish Affairs* (June 1971), No. 1, pp. 19–38
13. Josef Banas, *The Scapegoats* (London, 1979), p. 73
14. *Ibid.*, p. 197 quotes the assessment of Professor Zygmunt Baumann, a sociologist living in England, who was himself a victim of the 1968 witch-hunt. 'The 1968 anti-Semitic campaign, as distinct from all the pre-war anti-Semitism, is a purely political phenomenon, in

which the Jews are playing the part of a scapegoat to attract the whole accumulated aggressiveness and frustration of the embittered and disillusioned mass'

15. *Ibid.*, p. 87
16. *Ibid.*, pp. 169–70. Jacek Kuron, a non-Jewish radical and today Minister of Labour in the Polish government, was one of those put on trial in 1969. He later recalled: 'During the investigation the interrogating officers tried very hard to find some Jewish name among my ancestors. When they failed to make a Jew out of me, they wanted at least to turn me into a Ukrainian, all in order to be able to denounce me as an alien. During the investigation there were days when I wished to admit I was Jewish, because there are circumstances when every honest man would rather be a Jew'
17. Andrzej Werblan, 'Przyczynek do genezy konfliktu', *Miesiecznik Literacki* (June 1968). See also Adam Ciolkosz, 'Anti-Zionism in Polish Communist Party Politics', in Robert S. Wistrich (ed.) *The Left against Zion*, p. 145
18. Ciolkosz, *op. cit.*, pp. 142, 146–7
19. 'Blaming the Jews – Again', *Newsweek*, 15 February 1982
20. 'Bez maski', *Gazeta Wyborcza* (Warsaw), 22 September 1990, 'Premier Milczał', *ibid.*, 13 November 1990, for examples of the vocal populist antisemitism exploited by Walesa's supporters during the electoral campaign
21. Bernard Lecomte, 'Walesa après Walesa', *L'Express*, 28 September 1990, pp. 49–55. It should, however, be remembered that Walesa had earlier condemned the antisemitic statements of Cardinal Glemp (August 1989) and had personally put up a plaque in Kielce, honouring the victims of the 1946 pogrom
22. Alexandre Adler, 'La marche du temps', *L'Arche*, October 1989, pp. 23–6. Marie-France Calle, 'Pologne: les faux-changements', *ibid.*, p. 27. Yves Cuau, 'Le retour des démons', *L'Express*, 1 June 1990, p. 13
23. Interview in Warsaw with the Polish scholar Alina Cała (October 1990), who conducted a pioneering study of the image of the Jew in Polish peasant culture. Dr Cała emphasised to me that the mass of Polish peasantry still believes in the blood libel. See also Abraham Brumberg, 'The Problem that Won't Go Away: Anti-Semitism in Poland (Again), *Tikkun*, January/February 1990, pp. 31–4
24. Interview with David Warszawski (Konstanty Gebert) in Warsaw, October 1990. See his article, 'The Convent and Solidarity', *Tikkun*, Vol. 4, No. 6 (1989), pp. 30 ff
25. *Ibid.*, p. 31

26. *New York Times*, 30 August 1989. *Guardian*, 31 August 1989
27. Warszawski, 'The Convent and Solidarity', p. 93, describes Giertych as the 'self-avowed heir to the tradition of the nationalistic, anti-Semitic prewar National Democratic party' and his movement as being 'overtly antisemitic'. I formed a similar impression from my own interview with Professor Giertych
28. Interview with David Warszawski, Warsaw
29. See the interview with Claude Lanzmann, 'Anti-Semitism without Jews', *The Jerusalem Post*, 15 September 1989
30. *Ibid.* Lanzmann insists that the Catholic Church has 'remained anti-Jewish to the core, in spite of Vatican II'. He points to the declarations of Pope John Paul II on the 'unfaithfulness of the Jews towards God' and to his Polish background as an explanation of his attitudes. According to Lanzmann, one could say that 'Rome is not in Rome any more, but in Poland, and that the Vatican is in Auschwitz'. This is undoubtedly an exaggeration which ignores the positive results of the Polish–Jewish and the Catholic–Jewish dialogue, but the grain of truth which it contains illustrates how much still needs to be done
31. Karen Adler, 'Controversy over the Carmelite Convent at Auschwitz 1988–89', *IJA Research Report*, No. 7 (1989) sums up the Polish and international reactions to Cardinal Glemp's anti-Jewish homily
32. The Mother Superior's remarks are quoted in Monty Noam Penkower, 'Auschwitz, the Papacy and Poland's "Jewish Problem"', *Midstream* (August/September 1990), pp. 17–18
33. *Ibid.*, p. 17. Penkower notes the ambiguity of the Pope himself, who canonized Father Maximilian Kolbe and Edith Stein, a German Jewess who converted to Catholicism and died in Auschwitz. Father Kolbe also died a martyr's death in Auschwitz, but before the war he was a typical representative of Polish Catholic antisemitism. The bishops whom I interrogated in Poland in October 1990 simply evaded this fact
34. Patricia Clough, 'Anti-Semitism stalks Polish campaign', *Independent*, 24 May 1990
35. Slawomir Majman, 'The Town I Live In', *The Warsaw Voice*, 30 September 1990. Also the observations of Neal Ascherson, 'Breath of Foul Air', *Independent on Sunday*, 11 November 1990

Chapter 14

1. Hans Rogger, 'The Jewish Policy of Late Tsarism: A Reappraisal',

The *Wiener Library Bulletin* (1971), XXV, Nos. 1 and 2, new series, 22/23, pp. 42–50

2. Salo Baron, *The Russian Jew under Tsars and Soviets* (New York, 1964), R. F. Byrnes, *Pobedonostsev* (Bloomington, 1968), pp. 208–9 argues that the Procurator of the Holy Synod opposed pogroms out of fear that they could unleash revolutionary forces

3. Baron, *op. cit.*, p. 67; Norman Cohn, *Warrant for Genocide*, pp. 84, 112

4. Rogger, *op. cit.*, p. 50

5. Stephen Lukashevich, *Ivan Aksakov* (Cambridge, Mass., 1965)

6. S. Ettinger, 'The Historical Roots of Anti-Semitism in the USSR', in Theodore Freedman (ed.), *Anti-Semitism in the Soviet Union: Its Roots and Consequences* (New York, 1984)

7. Robert Wistrich, *Trotsky: Fate of a Revolutionary* (London, 1979)

8. For an example of Lenin's denunciation of Tsarist antisemitism, see his *Collected Works*, Vol. 17 (London, 1960–70), p. 337

9. Lenin, 'Anti-Jewish Pogroms' (1919), *ibid.*, Vol. 29, pp. 252–3

10. Zvi Gitelman, *Jewish Nationality and Soviet Politics* (Princeton, 1972). Also the valuable older work by Solomon Schwarz, *The Jews in the Soviet Union* (Syracuse, 1951)

11. Zvi Gitelman, 'Soviet Antisemitism and its perception by Soviet Jews', in Curtis (ed.), *op. cit.*, pp. 189–90, rightly observes that in the late 1920s the Soviet regime had made a serious attempt to combat anti-Jewish prejudice. 'Never before in Russian history – and never subsequently – has a government made such an effort to uproot and stamp out antisemitism'

12. Schwarz, *op. cit.*, p. 298. William Korey, *The Soviet Cage: Anti-Semitism in Russia* (New York, 1973), pp. 30, 67

13. Shimon Redlich, *Propaganda and Nationalism in Wartime Russia: The Jewish Anti-fascist Committee in the USSR, 1941–1948* (Boulder, Colorado, 1982), pp. 47–51

14. Robert S. Wistrich, 'From Lenin to the Soviet Black Hundreds' in Wistrich (ed.), *The Left against Zion*, pp. 272–300

15. Zvi Gitelman, 'Soviet Antisemitism', pp. 192–3

16. Yehoshua A. Gilboa, *The Black Years of Soviet Jewry* (Boston, 1971)

17. Arieh Tartakower, 'The Jewish Problem in the Soviet Union', *Jewish Social Studies* (October, 1971), pp. 290–1

18. *Ibid.* See also François Fejtö, *Les Juifs et l'antisémitisme dans les pays communistes* (Paris, 1960)

19. Robert S. Wistrich, 'From Lenin to the Soviet Black Hundreds', pp. 272 ff

20. Shmuel Ettinger, 'Soviet Antisemitism after the Six Day War', *Study Circle on World Jewry* (Shazar Library, Jerusalem, 1985), pp. 9–22

21. Quoted by William Korey, 'Soviet Antisemitism at the UN', in *Antisemitism: Threat to Western Civilisation* (Jerusalem, 1988), p. 84
22. V. Begun, *Polzuchaya Kontrrevolutysiya* (Minsk, 1974)
23. Dmitri Zhukov, 'The Ideology and Practice of Violence', *Ogonyok*, 12 October 1984
24. Y. Yevseyev, 'Fashizm pod goluboy zvezdoy', *Komsomolskaya Pravda*, 17 May 1970; Ts. Solodar, *Dikaya polyn* (Moscow, 1977), p. 34; V. A. Semenyuk, *Natsionalisticheskoe bezumie* (Minsk, 1976), pp. 47, 94; D. I. Soyfer, *Sionizm – orudie antikommunizma* (Dnepropetrovsk, 1976), p. 50
25. *Komsomolskaya Pravda*, 4 October 1967
26. See Y. Ivanov, *Ostrozhno! Sionizm!* (Moscow, 1969); L. Korneev, 'Sionizm kak on yest', *Moskovskaya Pravda*, 16 February 1977; 'Samy sionistskii bzyness', *Ogonyok*, 8 July 1978; 'Otravlennoye oruzhiye sionizma', *Krasnaya Zvezda*, 16 November 1977. See also L. Dymerskaya-Tsigelman, 'L. Korneev as a Phenomenon of Soviet Anti-Semitism in the 1970s–1980s', *Jews and Jewish Topics in Soviet and East European Publications* (June 1986), pp. 8–27. I am grateful to Mrs Dymerskaya-Tsigelman for valuable information on contemporary Soviet antisemitism
27. Howard Spier, 'Zionists and Freemasons in Soviet Propaganda', *Patterns of Prejudice*, Vol. 13, No. 1 (January/February 1979), pp. 1–5; On Emelianov's murder of his wife, see Reuben Ainsztein, 'The fall of an anti-semite', *New Statesman*, 11 July 1980, p. 45; S. Lukin, 'A New Variation on an Old Theme', *Soviet Jewish Affairs*, Vol. 11, No. 3 (1981), pp. 58–61; Personal interview with Emelianov in his Moscow flat in October 1990 in which he ranted on obsessively about 'Jewish Nazis' who have run the Soviet Union since Lenin's time with a brief interlude when Stalin partly purged them. Emelianov, whose background is that of an Arabist (his Russian book, *De-Zionisation*, was published in Paris in 1980 with the help of the PLO), struck me as a true paranoid personality, yet he is a popular lecturer in Russian nationalist, antisemitic circles
28. On Romanenko and the antisemitic *Patriot* group which he chairs, see 'What is Patriot?', *Moscow News*, 28 May 1989. Also 'Fighting the Enemy Within', *IJA Research Report*, No. 5 (1989). Major General Kalugin, formerly a top KGB official, told me in an interview in Moscow (September 1990) that Romanenko's antisemitic and anti-Zionist tract had been promoted through KGB channels
29. Interview with N. V. Iukhneva, a leading Soviet ethnographer, who, though not Jewish herself, has been an active supporter of Jewish cultural activity in the USSR (Leningrad, September 1990).

See also the text of her lecture, 'On the growth of aggressive-chauvinistic and anti-Semitic attitudes in contemporary Russian society', printed in *Leningradskii evreiskii almanakh. Evreiskii samizdat*, No. 26 (Jerusalem, 1988)

30. Interview with Sergei Lezov, a Russian classical philologist and scholar of New Testament antisemitism, in Moscow (September 1990). Dr Lezov has been one of the most active non-Jewish Russians in seeking to combat chauvinist antisemitism in the Soviet Union. See also 'Antisemitism in the USSR and Reactions to it', in *Jews and Jewish Topics* (Spring 1989), pp. 5–44

31. For documents relating to the Pamyat association and criticism of it in the Soviet press, see *ibid.* (Summer 1988), pp. 30–88. Also '"Pamyat": An Appeal to the Russian People' introduced and annotated by Howard Spier, *Soviet Jewish Affairs*, Vol. 18, No. 1 (1988), pp. 60–70

32. *The Increasing Danger of Anti-Semitism in the Soviet Union*, a status report (Union of Council for Soviet Jews, February 1990). My thanks to Mrs Enid Wurtmann for providing me with this material

33. Josephine Woll, 'Russians and "Russophobes": Antisemitism on the Russian Literary Scene', *Soviet Jewish Affairs*, Vol. 19, No. 3 (1989), pp. 3–21; Andrei Sinyavsky, 'Russophobia', *Partisan Review* (1990), 3, pp. 339–44; Walter Laqueur, 'From Russia with Hate', *The New Republic*, 5 February 1990, pp. 21–5

34. John B. Dunlop, *The New Russian Nationalism* (New York, 1985), pp. 39 ff; Alexander Yanov, *The Russian Challenge and the Year 2000* (New York, 1987)

35. Peter Duncan, 'The Phenomenon of Russian Nationalism Today', *Nationalism in the USSR* (Amsterdam, 1989), pp. 52–7

36. Quoted in the *International Herald Tribune*, 13 April 1990. For a discussion of Shafarevich, see Laqueur, *op. cit.*, and Sinyavsky, *op. cit.*, pp. 340 ff

37. 'New Soviet anti-Semitism sees Jews as "little People"', *The Jerusalem Post*, 13 April 1980

38. For an illuminating analysis of this literature, see Yitzhak M. Brudny, 'The Heralds of Opposition to *Perestroyka*', *Soviet Economy* (1989), 5, pp. 162–200

39. J. Woll, *op. cit.*, p. 6

40. *Ibid.*, pp. 10–19. See, for example, Stanislav Kunyayev, 'Two ends of a stick', *Nash Sovremennik*, no. 6 (1989), pp. 158–61

41. Vladimir Bondarenko, 'Discovering Kinship', *V mire knig*, no. 7 (1989), p. 12

42. Kunyayev, *op. cit.*, p. 161

43. Brudny, *op. cit.*, p. 170
44. Nina Andreyeva, 'I Cannot Give up Principles', *Sovetskaya Rossiya*, 13 March 1988. Andreyeva is a chemistry teacher at the Leningrad Technological Institute
45. Brudny, *op. cit.*, p. 184
46. *Ibid.*, pp. 179 ff. See also L. Dymerskaya-Tsigelman, 'Anti-Semitism and Opposition to it at the Present Stage of the Ideological Struggle in the USSR', *Jews and Jewish Topics* (Summer 1988), pp. 3–27. A. Kuz'min, 'To Which Temple are We seeking the Path?', *Nash Sovremennik*, No. 3, 1988, p. 157, describes Leon Trotsky as preparing a 'Moloch to whom entire peoples were being sacrificed. And in the first instance, the peoples of Russia'
47. Laqueur, 'From Russia with Hate'
48. See the account of this incident by Vitaly Vitalyev, 'Seeds of a racist disaster', *Guardian*, 20 February 1990
49. Interview with Smirnov-Ostashvili, Moscow, May 1990
50. Interview with Oleg Kalugin, Moscow, September 1990
51. Interview with Mikhail Chlenov, Co-Chairman of VAAD (The Confederation of Jewish Organisations and Communities in the USSR), Moscow, September 1990
52. *Ibid.*
53. *Independent*, 13 March 1990, p. 10; 'Survey in Moscow sees a high level of Anti-Jewish Feeling', *New York Times*, 30 March 1990; 'When Free Speech means talking pogroms', *Independent*, 4 April 1990; 'Terrorised Soviet Jews find German haven', *Sunday Telegraph*, 27 May 1990
54. Robert J. Brym, '*Perestoyka*, Public Opinion and *Pamyat*', *Soviet Jewish Affairs*, Vol. 19, No. 3 (1989), pp. 24–32
55. Interviews in Tashkent, November 1990 confirmed a disturbing rise in antisemitism in the Muslim Republics of the USSR
56. Interview with Avram Dyomin, Leningrad, September 1990
57. Interview with Sergei Lezov, Moscow, September 1990

Chapter 15

1. Bernard Lewis, *The Jews of Islam* (London, 1984), pp. 1–66 for a nuanced summary of the position of non-Muslims in the classical Islamic order. Also Mark R. Cohen, 'Islam and the Jews: Myth, Counter-Myth, History', *The Jewish Quarterly* (1986), 33, pp. 125–37
2. Bat Ye'or, *The Dhimmi: Jews and Christians under Islam* (London/Toronto, 1985)

3. Eliyahu Ashtor, *Qorot ha-Yehudim bi-Sfarad ha-Muslimit* (The Jews of Muslim Spain), Jerusalem, 1966, in Hebrew, pp. 116–17. See also 'The Fall of the Jewish Vizier of Granada' (1066) in Norman A. Stillman (ed.), *The Jews of Arab Lands: A History and Source Book* (Philadelphia, 1979), pp. 217–25

4. Through most of the tenth and eleventh centuries, the Jewish community of Kairouan was the major intellectual centre of Jewry outside of Iraq

5. Between 1147 and 1160 the Almohads (fanatical Berbers from the Atlas Mountains of Morocco) conquered the Maghreb and much of Muslim Spain, which resulted in widespread massacres and the forced conversion of Jews. H. Z. Hirschberg, *A History of the Jews in North Africa*, 1 (Leiden, 1974), pp. 123–39

6. Moses Maimonedes, *Iggeret Teman* (Epistle to Yemen), ed. Abraham S. Halkin (New York, 1952), p. 94. The text is also reproduced in Stillman, *op. cit.* pp. 233–46. In this translation Maimonedes refers to 'the nation of Ishmael, who persecute us severely, and who devise ways to harm us and debase us', *ibid.*, p. 241

7. Lewis, *The Jews of Islam*, pp. 67–106; S. D. Goitein, *Jews and Arabs: Their Contacts through the Ages*, 3rd rev. ed. (New York, 1974), pp. 125–211

8. Walter J. Fischel, *Jews in the Economic and Political Life of Medieval Islam* (New York, 1969); S. D. Goitein, *A Mediterranean Society: The Jewish Communities of the Arab World as Portrayed in the Documents of the Cairo Genizah*, 4 vols (Berkeley and Los Angeles, 1967–1983)

9. Avraham Grossman, 'The Economic and Social Background of Hostile Attitudes Towards the Jews in the Ninth and Tenth Century Muslim Caliphate', in Almog (ed.), *Antisemitism through the Ages*, pp. 171–87

10. *Ibid.*, p. 179. E. Ashtor, *The Jews of Moslem Spain*, Vol. 1 (Philadelphia, 1973), pp. 181–2, 186–7; M. Pearlmann, 'The Medieval Polemics between Islam and Judaism', in S. D. Goitein (ed.), *Religion in a Religious Age* (Cambridge, Mass., 1974), pp. 103 ff

11. Abu Ishaq, a jurist and secretary to the *qadi* of Granada, made it clear that the *dhimma* pact had been nullified by virtue of Jews exercising power over Muslims:

> Do not consider it a breach of faith to kill them
> the breach of faith would be to let them carry on.
> They have violated our covenant with them
> so how can you be held guilty against the violators?
> How can they have any pact when we are obscure
> and they are prominent?

Quoted from B. Lewis, 'An Anti-Jewish Ode', in his *Islam in History: Ideas, Men and Events in the Middle East* (London, 1973), pp. 158–65. Also reproduced in Stillman, *op. cit.*, pp. 214–16

12. Grossman, *op. cit.*, pp. 180–1

13. G. Vajda, 'Juifs et musulmans selon le hadith', *Journal Historique*, 229 (1937), pp. 57–129

14. Haggai Ben-Shammai, 'Jew-hatred in the Islamic Tradition and the Koranic Exegesis', in Almog (ed.), *op. cit.*, pp. 161–9

15. *Ibid.*, pp. 164–6, Samuel Rosenblatt, 'The Jews and Islam', in Koppel S. Pinson (ed.), *Essays on Antisemitism* (New York, 1942); Jane S. Gerber, 'Anti-Semitism and the Muslim World', in Berger (ed.), *History and Hate*, pp. 78–9

16. Ronald L. Nettler, 'Islamic Archetypes of the Jews: Then and Now', in Robert S. Wistrich (ed.), *Anti-Zionism and Antisemitism*, pp. 73–83

17. A. S. Tritton, *The Caliphs and their Non-Muslim Subjects: A Critical Study of the Covenant of 'Umar* (London, 1930); Antoine Fattal, *Le Statut légal des non-musulmans en pays d'Islam* (Beirut, 1958)

18. On the *jizya*, Daniel C. Dennett, *Conversion and the Poll Tax in Early Islam* (Cambridge, Mass., 1950)

19. See the pamphlet by Bat Ye'or, *Oriental Jewry and the Dhimmi Image in Contemporary Arab Nationalism* (Geneva, 1979), p. 3 and the many relevant texts in her book, *The Dhimmi* (1985). Also Lewis, *The Jews of Islam*, pp. 34ff

20. Bernard Lewis, *Semites and Antisemites: An Inquiry into Conflict and Prejudice* (New York, 1986)

21. The treatise in question, *Ifham al-Yahud* (Silencing the Jews) was published by M. Pearlmann in a critical edition with an English translation, in the *Proceedings of the American Academy for Jewish Research*, 32 (1964)

22. Mark R. Cohen, 'Islam and the Jews', p. 132

23. Gerber, *op. cit.*, p. 84

24. *Ibid.*

25. Quoted in Shalom Bar-Asher, 'Antisemitism and Economic Influence: the Jews of Morocco (1672–1822)', in Almog (ed.), *Antisemitism through the Ages*, pp. 195–212

26. *Ibid.* Also Norman Stillman, 'Muslims and Jews in Morocco: Perceptions, Images, Stereotypes', *Proceedings of the Seminar on Muslim–Jewish Relations in North Africa* (New York, 1975), pp. 13–27 and Stillman (ed.), *The Jews of Arab Lands*, pp. 303–4, 306–17, 367–73

27. David Littman, 'Jews under Muslim Rule in the late 19th Century', in Robert S. Wistrich (ed.), *The Wiener Library Bulletin*, 27 (1975), pp. 65–76 and 'Jews under Muslim Rule II: Morocco 1903–1912',

ibid., 29 (1976), pp. 1–19 for extensive eye-witness accounts drawn from materials in the archives of the Alliance Israélite Universelle (AIU), relating to North Africa

28. David Littman, *ibid.* (1975), p. 67 quotes a letter from Solomon Garsin of the Tunis Alliance Committee to the President of the Paris Alliance (28 October 1864) describing the 'terryifying tale of atrocities in all its horror, which these unfortunate people have undergone'

29. *Ibid.*, pp. 67–8. Another letter from the Tunis Alliance Committee to Adolphe Crémieux in Paris (14 February 1869).

30. Jacob Barnai, '"Blood Libels" in the Ottoman Empire of the Fifteenth to the Nineteenth Centuries', Almog (ed.), *Antisemitism through the Ages*, pp. 189 ff

31. For documentation on the Damascus Affair, see Stillman (ed.), *The Jews of Arab Lands*, pp. 393–402

32. *Ibid.*

33. Jacob M. Landau, 'Ritual Murder Accusations and Persecutions of Jews in 19th Century Egypt', *Sefunot* 5 (1961), pp. 417–60, in Hebrew. Also Jane S. Gerber, *op. cit.*, p. 87

34. Stillman (ed.), *The Jews of Arab Lands*, p. 107, observes: 'The beginnings of anti-Semitism in the Arab world may be seen as part of the struggle of one partially emancipated minority – the Christians – to protect itself against the economic competition of another partially emancipated but less assimilated minority – the Jews.' This is true in so far as one is talking about *modern* antisemitism, but, as we have seen, anti-Jewish attitudes in the broader sense existed from the beginning of Islam – usually dormant but potentially inflammable at any time

35. 'Fu'ad al-Sayyid, 'al-Malik Faysal Yatahaddath 'an', *al-Musawwar*, No. 24, 4 August 1972, p. 13

36. See the documentation in the Paris newspaper, *Le Matin*, 19 August 1986, under the headline, 'Le Juif pourrait prendre ton sang pour faire son pain sioniste'. Interview of Mustafa Tlas in *Der Spiegel*, 22 September 1986. I am also grateful to the Simon Wiesenthal Center in Los Angeles and its director, Gerald Margolis, for access to their files relating to this affair

37. See *Response* (Bulletin of the Simon Wiesenthal Center), August 1986

38. Ronald L. Nettler, *Islam and the Minorities* (Jerusalem, 1979). This booklet was produced by the Israel Academic Committee on the Middle East

39. See Gudrun Krämer, *The Jews in Modern Egypt 1914–1952* (London, 1989)

40. André Chouraqui, *Between East and West: A History of the Jews of North Africa* (Philadelphia, 1968)

41. *Ibid.*, p. 153

42. Terence Prittie and Bernard Dineen, *The Double Exodus: A Study of Arab and Jewish Refugees in the Middle East* (London, n.d.), pamphlet, p. 22

43. Albert Memmi, *Jews and Arabs* (Chicago, 1975), pp. 30 ff

44. Maurice Roumani, *The Case of the Jews from Arab Countries: A Neglected Issue* (Jerusalem, 1975). On the modern history of Libyan Jewry, see Renzo de Felice, *Ebrei in un paese arabo: Gli ebrei nella Libia contemporanea tra colonialismo, nazionalismo arabo e Sionismo (1835–1970)* (Bologna, 1978)

45. Prittie, *op. cit.*, pp. 22–3

46. *New York Times*, 7 November 1945. Also the account of Ben Segal, who was in Tripoli in 1945–6 in charge of Arab education in the British Military Administration and witnessed the pogrom. *The Jewish Quarterly* (Winter 1990–1), pp. 67–8

47. Roumani, *op. cit.*, p. 21; Prittie, *op. cit.*, p. 23

48. *New York Times*, 22 July 1970

49. Hayyim J. Cohen, *The Jews of the Middle East (1860–1972)* (Jerusalem, 1973), pp. 48–9

50. G. Krämer, *op. cit.*, pp. 141–2

51. James P. Jankowski, 'Egyptian Responses to the Palestine Problem in the Inter-War Period', *International Journal of Middle East Studies*, 12 (1980), pp. 1–38. My thanks to Professor Jankowski for drawing my attention to relevant materials in our discussions several years ago in Jerusalem

52. G. Krämer, *op. cit.*, pp. 146–54

53. Yahudiya Masriya, *Les Juifs en Egypte* (Geneva, 1971), pp. 45–65. In the annexe to her book (pp. 66–9) there is a list of former German Nazis who not only found refuge in Nasser's Egypt but also found new employment in the Arab struggle against Zionism and 'International Jewry'. Also Hayyim Cohen *op. cit.*, pp. 49–52; Joan Peters, *From Time Immemorial: The Origins of the Arab–Jewish Conflict over Palestine* (London, 1984), pp. 48–50; and Krämer, *op. cit.*, pp. 162, 205–21

54. Cohen, *op. cit.*, pp. 45–6

55. *Ibid.*, p. 46

56. *New York Times*, 7 August 1949

57. See Joan Peters, *op. cit.*, pp. 109–15, 119–27 for interviews with Jewish refugees from Syria

58. Nissim Rejwan, *The Jews of Iraq: 3000 Years of History and Culture* (London, 1985), pp. 217–30

59. Harold P. Luks, 'Iraqi Jews during World War II', in Robert S. Wistrich (ed.), *The Wiener Library Bulletin* (1977), Vol. XXX, new series, nos. 39/40, pp. 30–8

60. Elie Kedourie, *Arabic Political Memoirs and Other Studies* (London, 1974); Cohen, *op. cit.*, pp. 29–31; Rejwan, *op. cit.*, pp. 220–3

61. Luks, *op. cit.*, p. 38; Rejwan, *op. cit.*, pp. 233–48

62. Samir al-Khalil, *Republic of Fear: The Inside Story of Saddam's Iraq* (New York, 1989), pp. 48–58

63. *Ibid.*

64. Cohen, *op. cit.*, p. 58

65. *Ibid.*, pp. 59–60

66. *Islam and Revolution: Writings and Declarations of Imam Khomeini* (Berkeley, 1981), pp. 177–8

67. Emmanuel Sivan, 'Radical Islam and the Arab–Israeli Conflict', in Curtis (ed.), *op. cit.*, pp. 61 ff

68. *Islam and Revolution*, pp. 195–7, 275 ff, 301 ff

69. *Ibid.*, p. 127. 'Program for the Establishment of an Islamic Government' (1970 lectures)

70. *Ibid.*, pp. 195–6. 'Messages to the Pilgrims', 6 February 1971

71. The Iranian regime has disseminated openly antisemitic writings based on the *Protocols*. See the publication of the Iranian Embassy in London, *Imam* (February 1984), pp. 14–15; (April 1984), pp. 14–15; (May 1984), pp. 12, 21

Chapter 16

1. R. L. Nettler, 'Islamic Archetypes of the Jews', pp. 63 ff

2. Emmanuel Sivan, 'Islamic Fundamentalism, Antisemitism and Anti-Zionism, in Wistrich (ed.), *Anti-Zionism and Antisemitism*, p. 74

3. Interview with Ehud Ya'ari, Arab affairs specialist of Israel Television, by Rex Bloomstein, in Jerusalem (October 1990)

4. Gil Carl Alroy, *Behind the Middle East Conflict: The Real Impasse between Arab and Jew* (New York, 1975), pp. 176–201, and Bernard Lewis, 'The Return of Islam', *Commentary* (January 1976), pp. 39–49

5. Farhang Rajaee, *Islamic Values and World View: Khomeini on Man, the State and International Politics*, Vol. XIII (1983), pp. 26–31, 77

6. Ismail R. al Faruqi, 'Islam and Zionism', in John Esposito (ed.), *Voices of Resurgent Islam* (New York, 1983), pp. 261–7

7. Emmanuel Sivan, *Radical Islam: Medieval Theology and Modern Politics* (New Haven/London, 1985), pp. 47 ff

8. The essay has been translated into English with a commentary and

notes by Ronald L. Nettler, *Past Trials and Present Tribulations: A Muslim Fundamentalist's View of the Jews* (Oxford, 1987). I am indebted to Ronald Nettler for sharing with me in many conversations in Jerusalem and Oxford some of the fruits of his research into Muslim fundamentalism

9. Qutb, in Nettler, *Past Trials and Present Tribulations*, p. 83
10. *Ibid.*, pp. 47–51
11. Richard P. Mitchell, *The Society of the Muslim Brothers* (London, 1969), pp. 55–7, 63–4, 76. Gabriel R. Warburg and Uri M. Kupferschmidt, *Islam, Nationalism and Radicalism in Egypt and the Sudan* (New York, 1983); Krämer, *op. cit.*, pp. 151, 160–2
12. Mitchell, *op. cit.*, p. 228
13. Sivan, *Radical Islam*, pp. 16–20
14. Quoted in R. L. Nettler, 'Islam vs. Israel', *Commentary* (December 1984), p. 27
15. *Ibid.*, p. 28
16. Gilles Kepel, *The Prophet and Pharaoh: Muslim Extremism in Egypt* (London, 1985), p. 112
17. *Ibid.*, pp. 110 ff
18. *Al Jihad wa an-Nasr* (Cairo, 1974), pp. 150–3. See the comments of Ronald Nettler, 'Muslim Scholars on the Peace with Israel', *Midstream*, Vol. XXVI, No. 9 (November 1980), pp. 15–19
19. D. F. Green (ed.), *Arab Theologians on Jews and Israel: Extracts from the proceedings of the Fourth Conference of the Academy of Islamic Research* (Geneva, 1976), p. 9
20. *Ibid.*, p. 24
21. *Ibid.*, p. 36
22. *Ibid.*, p. 42
23. *Ibid.*, pp. 49–50
24. *Ibid.*, p. 51
25. *Ibid.*, p. 65
26. Nettler, 'Muslim Scholars', pp. 16, 19–20
27. Israel Altman, 'Islamic Movements in Egypt', *The Jerusalem Quarterly*, No. 10 (Winter 1979), pp. 87–105. Sivan, *Radical Islam*, pp. 52 ff
28. Wilhelm Dietl, *Holy War* (New York, 1984), p. 264 quotes Khomeini, saying: 'We regard the existence of Israel in the Near East as a cancer that cannot be cured by medication but must be operated on with a surgical knife. Israel is an illegitimate child of the imperialist powers, an American settlement'
29. Hava Lazarus-Yafeh, 'The sanctity of Jerusalem in Islam', in John Oesterreicher and M. Sinai (eds.), *Jerusalem* (New York, 1974), pp. 222–3

30. See *Proche-Orient chrétien*, Vol. 24 (1974), pp. 203–4
31. Foreign Office File 371/20822 E 7201/22/31. The text is reproduced and commented on by Elie Kedourie, *Islam and the Modern World and Other Studies* (London, 1980), p. 71
32. *Ibid.*
33. *Ibid.*, p. 72
34. *Ibid.*
35. During a visit of the French Foreign Minister to Jeddah in January 1974, King Feisal presented an anthology of antisemitic writings as well as copies of the *Protocols* to accompanying French journalists. See *Ha-aretz* (Tel Aviv), 29 January 1974
36. Daniel Pipes, 'The Politics of Muslim Anti-Semitism', in *Commentary*, Vol. 72, No. 2 (August 1981), pp. 39–46
37. On Grimstad and the Saudi connection, Gill Seidel, *The Holocaust Denial*, pp. 82–3
38. Martin Kramer, 'Israel in the Muslim–Christian Dialogue', *IJA Research Report* (November 1986), Nos. 11 and 12, pp. 17–18
39. *Muslim World* (Karachi), 22 August 1981
40. M. Kramer, *op. cit.*, pp. 19–20
41. *Ibid.* According to the *New Republic* (Washington), 4 February and 4 March 1985, Dawalibi appears to have been a German agent in occupied Paris during the Second World War, where he headed a pro-Nazi union of Syrian students
42. Stillman, 'Antisemitism in the Contemporary Arab World', in Curtis (ed.), *op. cit.*, pp. 70–85
43. R. Yadlin, 'Arab Antisemitism in Peacetime', in *ibid,.*, p. 87
44. Y. Harkabi, *Arab Attitudes to Israel* (Jerusalem, 1971), pp. 288–92
45. Statement of the Constituent Council of the Muslim World League, *Majallat Rabitat al-'Alam al-Islami* (Mecca), Vol. 2, No. 7 (January/February 1965), pp. 14–16. Quoted in M. Kramer, *op. cit.*, p. 4
46. Anis Mansour, *al-Ha'it Wal-Dumu* (Cairo, 1979), pp. 64, 99
47. Yvonne Yazbeck Haddad, *Contemporary Islam and the Challenge of History* (Albany, 1982), p. 34
48. Ronald Nettler, 'Les Frères Musulmans, L'Egypte et Israël', *Politique Internationale* (Paris), No. 17 (Fall 1982), pp. 134–43
49. Bernard Lewis, *The Middle East and the West* (London, 1963), p. 114
50. Sivan, 'Islamic Fundamentalism', p. 82
51. Translated from the *Covenant of the Islamic Resistance Movement* (Hamas), 18 August 1988
52. *Ibid.* See Robert S. Wistrich, *Between Redemption and Perdition* (London, 1990), pp. 257–8

Chapter 17

1. N. Mandel, 'Turks, Arabs and Jewish Immigration into Palestine 1882–1914', in A. Hourani (ed.), *St. Antony's Papers, No. 17 – Middle Eastern Affairs*, No. 4 (London, 1965), pp. 77–108
2. Y. Porath, *The Emergence of the Palestinian–Arab National Movement 1918–1929* (London, 1974), p. 56
3. Stillman, 'Antisemitism in the Arab World', in Curtis (ed.), *op. cit.*, pp. 76–7
4. Porath, *op. cit.*, pp. 57–9
5. *Ibid.*, p. 57
6. *Ibid.*, p. 59
7. Yehoshua Porath, 'Anti-Zionist and Anti-Jewish Ideology in the Arab Nationalist Movement in Palestine', in Almog (ed.), *Antisemitism through the Ages*, pp. 221–2
8. Joan Peters, *From Time Immemorial*, pp. 172–217
9. Porath, *The Emergence of the Palestinian–Arab National Movement*, p. 62
10. Nels Johnson, *Islam and the Politics of Meaning in Palestinian Nationalism* (London, 1982), pp. 16 ff
11. *Ibid.*, p. 32
12. Sylvia G. Haim, 'Arabic Anti-Semitic Literature', *Jewish Social Studies*, Vol. 17, No. 4 (1965), pp. 307–312. Also the anthology *Arab Nationalism* (Berkeley/Los Angeles, 1976), pp. 67–8, edited by the same author
13. Haim Shamir, 'The Middle East in the Nazi Conception', in Jehuda L. Wallach (ed.), *Germany and the Middle East* (Tel Aviv, 1975), pp. 167–74
14. L. Hirszowicz, *The Third Reich and the Arab East* (London, 1966), p. 263
15. Francis Nicosia, 'Arab Nationalism and National Socialist Germany, 1933–1939: Ideological and Strategic Incompatibility', *International Journal of Middle East Studies*, 12 (1980), pp. 351–72
16. Robert S. Wistrich, *Hitler's Apocalypse*, pp. 166–70; Gerald Fleming, *Hitler and the Final Solution* (London, 1985), pp. 101–5 and Joan Peters, *op. cit.*, pp. 436–7, who reproduces the Mufti's own account of his meeting with Hitler
17. Peters, *ibid.*, p. 372 for the full text of the Mufti's letter to the Hungarian Foreign Minister
18. *Ibid.*
19. Joseph Schechtman, *The Mufti and the Führer: The Rise and Fall of Haj Amin el-Husseini* (New York, 1965), pp. 139–40, 147–52, 160

20. Y. Porath, 'Anti-Zionist and Anti-Jewish Ideology', p. 225
21. Y. Harkabi, *op. cit.*, p. 279
22. Y. Harkabi, *The Palestinian Covenant and Its Meaning* (London, 1980)
23. Jillian Becker, *The PLO: The Rise and Fall of the Palestine Liberation Organization* (London, 1984), pp. 81–3
24. On 12 February 1979, Arafat sent the following message to the Ayatollah Khomeini: 'I pray Allah to guide your steps along the path of faith and *jihad* . . . until we arrive at the walls of Jerusalem.' Bat Ye'or, 'Holy War or Peace?', *Jewish Chronicle*, 28 May 1982. Palestinian Nationalists appear to have the gift of always choosing the wrong ally. During the 1930s and early 1940s they tied themselves to German Nazis and Italian Fascists, in the 1950s and '60s to Nasser's Pan-Arabism, in the 1970s to the coattails of the Soviet Union, then to Khomeini and now to Saddam Hussein, until recently the arch-enemy of the Islamic Revolution
25. Jon Immanuel, 'A Clash of Perceptions', *The Jerusalem Post International Edition*, 27 October 1990
26. '10,000 gorges hurlent leur haine du juif. On lui promet l'expulsion de la terre arabe, la mort, l'extermination.' Thus opens the description of recent Palestinian demonstrations in Amman, 'Jordanie: Palestine d'abord', *L'Express*, 25 January 1991. The rejoicing of West Bank and Gaza Palestinians at Iraqi missiles raining down on innocent Israeli civilians in Tel Aviv has been widely noted in the world press
27. David K. Shipler, *Arab and Jew: Wounded Spirits in a Promised Land* (London, 1987), pp. 265–88 discusses Israeli stereotyping of Arabs and racist attitudes towards Palestinians which have undoubtedly grown in recent years
28. Transcripts of interviews by Rex Bloomstein in 1990 with Hisham Sharabi in Washington DC, with Sadeq al-Azm at Princeton, with Faisal al-Husseini and Dr Hanan Ashrawi in Jerusalem

Chapter 18

1. Bernard Lewis, 'Semites and Anti-Semites: Race in the Arab–Israeli Conflict', *Survey* (Spring 1971), Vol. 17, No. 2, pp. 170–84
2. N. Stillman, 'Antisemitism in the Arab World', pp. 70–1
3. Y. Harkabi, *Arab Attitudes*, p. 518 lists no less than nine separate editions of the *Protocols*, published in the Arab and Muslim world between 1951 and 1970. The flow has continued since then
4. Misbahul Islam Faruqi (ed.), *Jewish Conspiracy and the Muslim World* (Karachi, February 1967). 'Ali Akbar, *Israel and the Prophecies of the*

Holy Qu'ran (5th rev. ed., Cardiff, 1971). Such works treat the *Protocols* as a 'Zionist manifesto for world conquest', depicting international Jewry as an omnipotent, occult force which holds even the superpowers to ransom

5. Moshe Ma'oz, 'The Image of the Jew in Official Arab Literature and Communication Media', in Moshe Davis (ed.), *World Jewry and the State of Israel* (New York, 1977), pp. 33–51

6. Y. Harkabi, 'On Arab Antisemitism Once More', in Almog (ed.), *Antisemitism through the Ages*, p. 236

7. Rivka Yadlin, *An Arrogant Oppressive Spirit: Anti-Zionism as Anti-Judaism in Egypt* (Oxford, 1989), p. 1

8. All quotations from the Simon Wiesenthal Archives, Los Angeles, which I visited in September 1990

9. On Hamid Rabee, an antisemitic Pan-Arabist author, see Yadlin, *op. cit.*, pp. 28–39

10. Quoted by Daniel Pipes, 'The Politics of Muslim Anti-Semitism', p. 39

11. United Nations General Assembly, Thirty-Ninth Session, No. A/38/PV.88, pp. 19–20

12. Yadlin, *op. cit.*, pp. 94–5, 98–9, 118

13. Interview of Rex Bloomstein with Ehud Ya'ari, Jerusalem, October 1990

14. Although Arabism tried to identify what constitutes Arab identity through history, language and culture, the only social cohesion on which it seems able to build in practice is that which has been instilled by Islam. See Elie Kedourie 'Where Arabism and Zionism Differ', *Commentary*, Vol. 81, No. 6 (June 1986), p. 33

15. Quoted in Shipler, *op. cit.*, p. 257

16. *Ibid.*

17. Y. Harkabi, 'On Arab Antisemitism', p. 229

18. Yadlin, *op. cit.*, pp. 3–5

19. R. Israeli, 'Anti-Jewish Attitudes in the Arabic Media, 1975–1981', *IJA Research Report*, No. 15 (September 1983)

20. Amatzia Baram, 'Mesopotamian Identity in Ba'athi Iraq', *Middle Eastern Studies* (1983), Vol. 19, pp. 445, 455 shows that already in the 1970s Nebuchadnezzar was celebrated by the Iraqi Ba'athist regime for having conquered Palestine from the Jews and brought them back in chains from 'the land of the Arabs'

21. Rivka Yadlin and Amatzia Baram, 'Egypt's Changing Attitude Towards Israel', *The Jerusalem Quarterly*, No. 7 (Spring 1978), pp. 68–87

22. Quoted by Ronald Nettler, 'The Ambivalence of Camp David

Rhetoric: The Arab Idea of "Peace with Israel"', *Encounter* (June/July 1982), p. 104

23. *News Views* (Jerusalem), 1 February 1981, p. 19
24. Yadlin, *op. cit.*, pp. 95–6
25. Bernard Lewis, 'The New Antisemitism', *New York Review*, 10 April 1986, p. 33
26. *Ibid.*, p. 34
27. Ernest Gellner, 'Prejudicial Encounters', *Times Literary Supplement*, 22 August 1986, p. 903
28. Conor Cruise O'Brien, 'Keen pupils of our own prejudice', *The Times*, 8 September 1990
29. Moshe Ma'oz, 'The Image of the Jew in Official Arab Literature'
30. After the 'catastrophes' of 1948 and 1967, the 1973 October war against Israel was interpreted by much of the Arab world as a 'victory' and the apparent impact of the oil weapon strengthened dreams of beckoning glory and settling scores with the West. The illusions and disappointments behind this hubris are sensitively analysed by Fouad Ajami, *The Arab Predicament: Arab Political Thought and Practice since 1967* (Cambridge, 1981). They help one to better understand the continued need of the Arab world to find scapegoats for its divisions and failures today
31. For a characteristic example of the *either-or* mentality towards the existence of a Jewish state (whatever its boundaries) in the Middle East, see the interview with the former President of the Algerian Republic, Ahmed Ben-Bella, 'Tous contre Israël', *Politique Internationale*, No. 16 (Summer 1982), pp. 106–7. 'Je le répète: nous n'accepterons jamais ce corps étranger dans notre region. Israël est un véritable cancer gréffé sur le monde arabe.' Ben-Bella, once the spokesman of Pan-Arabism and revolutionary Third World radicalism, is today a militant fundamentalist. For the millions in the Arab world who still think like him the mere existence of Israel means the demise of Arabism and of Islam

Glossary

aliyah: In Hebrew the term means 'immigration' or 'ascent'. It is generally used to describe the five waves of Jewish immigration to Palestine between 1882 and 1939. Today it denotes the act of emigration from the Diaspora (q.v.) to the state of Israel. In Zionist ideology it has the additional connotation of self-fulfilment and rising to a higher plane of actively participating in the rebuilding of the Jewish state.

Antichrist: The enemy of Christ and of all Christians, a figure embodying absolute evil, whose coming is interpreted as heralding the Last Days. Antichrist is a kind of counter-Messiah in Christian popular legend, who would be crowned in Jerusalem and restore the Jewish Temple. He would attract many followers (especially among the Jews) but was ultimately to be defeated in a terrible battle which was expected to be the prelude to the Second Coming of Christ and a future era of peace and glory. The legend of Antichrist haunted the theological and popular imagination during the Middle Ages and at the time of the Crusades contributed to the millennial fervour that led to the massacre of Jews. During the Protestant Reformation the idea of the Antichrist was extended to the Pope in Rome and the Muslim Turks who were threatening Christendom from without.

Ashkenazi: A term originally used to designate the Jews of Germany (*Ashkenaz* in Hebrew) and since the sixteenth century the Jews of Central and Eastern Europe. It also generally includes most of the Jews in the United States (descended in the main from Russian and East European Jewry) and has today come to embrace all non-Sephardic (q.v.) Jews. The Ashkenazic Jews of Russia and Eastern Europe developed a distinct civilisation, mode of thinking, customs, liturgy, ceremonials and a rich literature in the Yiddish language. Before the modern era they resisted secularism and assimilation more than their Sephardic co-religionists, but this changed in the nineteenth and twentieth centuries. Except for Israel and France, the

309

Ashkenazim constitute by far the largest segment in the major communities of world Jewry today.

Ba'ath: In Arabic the term means 'renaissance' or 'resurrection'. Ba'athism is a quasi-secular form of Arab nationalism whose motto has always been 'one Arab nation with an eternal mission'. The Arab nation, according to Ba'athi ideologists, was characterised by unique and special virtues which were the result of its successive rebirths. Ba'athism sees itself as revolutionary, socialist pan-Arab and anti-imperialist. The Ba'ath party was founded in Damascus by a Christian, Michel Aflaq, in 1940. Since the 1960s it has held power in both Syria and Iraq, two regimes which share a common ideology and also a bitter rivalry for the leadership of the Arab national cause. The 'liberation of Palestine' has always been a central rallying-cry for Ba'athists in Syria and Iraq.

Balfour Declaration: This Declaration, made by the British Government on 2 November 1917 at a crucial moment during the First World War, was the beginning of a formal British commitment to create in Palestine 'a national home for the Jewish people'. His Majesty's Government promised to use 'their best endeavours to facilitate the achievement of this object'. The Declaration was issued in the name of the British Foreign Secretary, Lord Balfour, and designed to win the support of world Jewry for the Allied cause. At the same time Balfour saw it as a compensation for the wrong which Christendom had inflicted upon the Jewish people for centuries. It gave the Zionist movement international legitimacy and paved the way for the British Mandate in Palestine, approved by the League of Nations, in order to establish a Jewish national home. For the Arab world (and especially the Palestine Arabs) the Balfour Declaration has usually been seen as a disaster and the date of its declaration as a day of mourning, often sparking demonstrations, protests and even riots for the last seventy years.

blood libel: A Christian antisemitic myth dating from the twelfth century which asserted that Jews are required by their religion to murder Christian children and use their blood to bake *matzot* (Passover bread). Throughout the Middle Ages and into the modern era, blood libels have abounded in the Christian world, frequently provoking persecutions and massacres of Jews. Even in the late nineteenth century there were notorious blood libel cases in Tisza-Eslár (Hungary), in Polna (Czechoslovakia) and Poland. As late as 1911 the Russian government sought to exploit popular antisemitism by putting on trial a poor Jewish artisan in Kiev, Mendel Beilis, who was eventually acquitted. German Nazi publications like *Der Stürmer* also used the blood libel to whip up antisemitism. In the Arab world, the blood libel was spread in the nineteenth century largely by Greek Christians. In the last twenty years it has been widely promoted by Muslims and fully incorporated into the antisemitic literature that is currently enjoying some popularity in the Arab world.

Crusades: From the French world *croix*, meaning 'Cross'. The Crusaders were Soldiers of the Cross, who went to the Holy Land to wage a Holy War, beginning in 1095. Their aim was to liberate the Church of the Holy Sepulchre in Jerusalem (the site where Christ was believed to have been crucified) from the 'infidel' Muslims. On their way to Palestine the Crusader mobs indulged themselves in the mass slaughter of Jews in the Rhineland cities of Mainz, Worms and Cologne, where entire Jewish communities were destroyed. The ecclesiastical authorities sought in vain to protect the Jews, whom they had themselves denounced for centuries as 'infidels' and Christ-killers. The religious fervour of the Crusades, with their unprecedented violence against Jews, firmly embedded antisemitism at a popular level in the Western psyche.

Damascus Affair: The most famous blood libel (q.v.) to have occurred in the Ottoman Empire during the nineteenth century and one which was to have far-reaching international implications. It began with the disappearance of a Capuchin monk, Father Tomaso, and his servant in Damascus on 5 February 1840. His fellow monks, encouraged by the French consul Ratti-Menton, declared that he had been killed by Jews for ritual purposes. Many Damascus Jews were arrested and tortured (one communal leader died under questioning, another Jew confessed under torture and one even converted to Islam) while the French consul encouraged an antisemitic press campaign in France against the Damascus Jews and international Jewry in general. The affair provoked outrage in Europe and the vigorous intervention of several other European states, especially the British government. A delegation of Western Jewish notables led by Adolphe Crémieux was despatched to the Middle East and succeeded in persuading the Ottoman Sultan to intervene and issue an edict (*firman*), denouncing the blood libel as a baseless fabrication. Nevertheless, there are still books published in Arabic today which treat the Damascus Affair as proof that Jewish ritual murder is a historical fact.

Dar al-Islam: In Arabic this means the 'Abode' or 'House' of Islam and refers to all territory under Muslim rule. In Islamic law it is usually juxtaposed with *Dar al-Harb* (the 'House of War'), the non-Muslim world beyond the frontiers of Islam. In Muslim legal theory there is a perpetual state of war between *Dar al-Islam* and *Dar al-Harb*, until such time as the non-Muslim world submits to the supremacy of Islam, the only 'true' religion. This state of war may be temporarily suspended by truces, especially when the Muslim side is weaker. The implications of a literal interpretation of this legal theory for Islam's relations with the West and with Israel are obvious.

dhimmi: From the Arabic *dhimma*, a pact between the dominant Muslim state and non-Muslim minorities (especially Jews, Christians, Zoroastrians, Buddhists, etc.) which defines their legal status under Islamic law. The status of the *dhimmi* was that of a 'protected minority', permitted to exercise their religion freely in return for payment of the poll-tax and provided they recognised the supremacy of Islam. The status of the *dhimmi* involved many humiliating restrictions and disabilities, of a social and symbolic as well as an economic character, including the kinds of clothes *dhimmis* might wear and the beasts they could ride. They were not allowed to bear arms; they were required to refrain from noise and display in their ceremonies, and to show deference at all times to Muslims. Churches and synagogues were not to be higher than mosques and no new ones were, in theory, to be built. This *dhimmi* condition is quaintly referred to as an example of Muslim 'tolerance' and still advocated today by some fundamentalists as a desirable arrangement in an Islamic state.

Diaspora: The dispersion of the Jews in the lands outside Israel. Already in pagan Antiquity the Jews suffered exile (in Hebrew: *galut*) but did not assimilate to the surrounding nations, retaining their sense of a special vocation and being a chosen people, covenanted with God. Five centuries before the Christian era they had been exiled to Babylon and by the first century they constituted more than 10 per cent of the population in the Roman Empire. In the Diaspora they have clung to their separate religious beliefs, customs and laws for more than two thousand years, despite periods of cultural symbiosis or attempts at assimilation and integration. Undoubtedly this stubborn particularism has been a factor in the persistence of anti-semitism, though it would be simplistic to see it as a prime cause. In the traditional Jewish self-understanding, diasporic existence is a form of 'exile', of living under 'alien rule', of being uprooted from one's homeland in Zion and hence a state of alienation. In the post-emancipation era, Diaspora acquired a much more positive connotation and was even validated as a Jewish 'Mission' to the Gentiles by Liberal and Reform Judaism.

firman: Edict.

Goyim: In Hebrew, the term refers to all the nations of the world, except Israel, i.e. the 'Gentiles'. The word '*Goy*', (singular of *Goyim*) that is to say any non-Jew, acquired a pejorative association for many Jews as a result of relentless persecution over the centuries at the hands of the Gentile nations. This was especially the case in Eastern Europe, where the gulf between Jews and non-Jews was more persistent and saddled with bitterness. Thus a '*Goy*' was frequently assumed to be an antisemite, unless proof to the contrary was available.

hadith: An Arabic term which refers to the oral tradition by means of which sayings or deeds attributed to the Prophet Mohammed have been handed down to serve as a guide for Muslim believers. The sources were collected together in the ninth century and provide a major source of Islamic law.

Halacha: The legal system of Judaism based on accumulated jurisprudence and decisions of the Sages. *Halacha*, which in Hebrew means 'law', was not so much 'created' by the rabbis as it was a codification and clarification of legal teachings which had to be adapted to changing social conditions. This flexibility protected Rabbinic *Halacha* from degenerating into the sterile fundamentalism advocated by some Orthodox Jewish halachists today.

hijra: Arabic word for the 'migration' of Mohammed from Mecca to Medina in 622. Today, the term has assumed a special meaning for Muslim fundamentalists and radicals who seek to overthrow the existing social order. They see '*hijra*' as opting out of a corrupt society in order to live according to the original teachings of the Prophet and as a central part of their efforts at reform and rebirth.

Haram as-Sharif: In Arabic, the 'Noble Sanctuary', the holiest site of Islam in Palestine, which includes the Dome of the Rock and the Al-Aqsa Mosque. Both mosques are situated on the place known to Jews as the Temple Mount, the site of Solomon's Temple in Jerusalem. The Noble Sanctuary adjoins the Wailing Wall, sacred to Jews as a remnant of the last Temple of the Jewish nation – that which was built by Herod and destroyed by the Roman legions of Titus.

jihad: A Holy War for Islam against the unbelievers. The primary meaning of the term in Arabic is 'striving' or 'struggle' in the cause of God. This is a religious duty prescribed by the faith for every believing Muslim and is closely linked to the concepts of *Dar al-Islam* (q.v.) and *Dar al-Harb* (q.v.) The Islamic *jihad* is potentially, at least, worldwide. From time to time there is a resurgence of the *jihad* in the Muslim world, whether it has been against the Soviet occupation of Afghanistan, against the 'infidel' West or against Israel.

jizya: Arabic for 'ransom'. A poll-tax levied by Muslim rulers against *dhimmi* (q.v.) peoples, mainly Christians or Jews.

Judenrein: German word which became part of the official Nazi jargon that was applied in the so-called 'Final Solution of the Jewish Question'. It means cleansed or 'free' of Jews.

kibbutzim: Voluntary Jewish agricultural collectives in Palestine where there is no private wealth and all property is owned in common. The first Jewish *kibbutz* was established in Deganiah in 1909.

Koran: In Arabic, 'recitation'. The Holy Book of Islam which, according to Muslims, was dictated to Mohammed by God himself. The revelations given to the Prophet (who could not himself write) were collected by his disciples in the middle of the seventh century.

marranos: A term of contempt employed by Spanish and Portuguese Catholics towards Spanish Jews who had adopted the Christian faith under pressure but were still believed to practise Judaism in secret. Many *marrano* families rose to positions of influence and enjoyed high status in Spain before the expulsion (1492) which drove out more than 150,000 Jews from the country. The loss to Spanish life and culture was incalculable. The *marranos* dispersed to Italy, North Africa, Turkey and even Poland. They founded the modern Jewish communities of Amsterdam and London, playing an important role in commerce and international trade.

mellahs: Enclosed Jewish quarters in Moroccan towns, established as a royal protection for the Jewish communities in the fifteenth century against a hostile populace. Though not originally intended as a punishment or humiliation, the *mellahs* did, under later rulers, serve to isolate and penalise the Jews.

midrash: A form of analysis, exposition and exegesis of the Holy Scriptures which reads complex ideas into simple verses and esoteric meanings into every passage of the sacred texts. The sermons of the Rabbis in the Diaspora (q.v.) from the fourth century onwards contain much *midrashic* material – parables, allegories, stories and elaborate interpretation of Biblical texts.

Mishnah: In Hebrew this means to 'repeat one's learning' or 'review'. The *Mishnah*, one of the two basic parts of the Talmud, is the codified core of the Oral Law and had its origin after the return of the Jews to Judea from their Babylonian exile. The compilation, editing and codification of this accumulated body of Oral Law was only completed around AD 200.

Mufti: An official Muslim expert in Islamic jurisprudence. The title was usually granted to a learned Muslim scholar of spotless reputation. This was certainly not the case with Haj Amin al-Husseini, promoted to this position by the British Mandatory Government in Palestine, in the mistaken belief that it might moderate his attitudes.

Muslim Brotherhood: (*Ikhwan al-Muslimim*) A religious and political movement founded in Egypt in 1929. Its ideology has been consistently fundamentalist, anti-Western and anti-Jewish, and its methods frequently terroristic. It forms a powerful opposition movement in many Muslim countries today.

numerus clausus: Laws promulgated in Tsarist Russia and Eastern Europe between the two world wars which sought to limit the number of Jews in universities, in the civil service, the army, the professions and parts of the economy, to their proportion of the population. The call for a *numerus clausus* was the standard refrain of antisemites ever since Jewish emancipation had exposed them to competition from Jews on an equal footing.

Qadi: Muslim magistrate or judge who administers the Islamic law.

pogrom: Russian word meaning 'devastation'. It was used to designate the spontaneous or organised massacres of Jews in late nineteenth- and early twentieth-century Tsarist Russia. The worst pogroms occurred in 1881, 1903 and 1905 and appeared at times to enjoy the tacit support of the authorities. During the Russian Civil War (1918–20), terrible pogroms were also carried out by the counter-revolutionary White armies under Petliura in the Ukraine – the worst massacres of Jews before the Nazi era.

Purim: The Jewish Festival of Lots (the Hebrew word *pur* means 'lot') which celebrates the rescue of the Jews of Persia from Haman's plot to exterminate them. The story is recounted in the Biblical Book of Esther, though its historicity is a matter of conjecture. The figure of 'Haman' has represented the archetypal antisemite, or enemy of the Jewish people, ever since the Middle Ages.

Sephardim: Spanish and Portuguese Jews (*S'pharad* is Spain in Hebrew) and their descendants. In modern times the term has been extended to include all non-Ashkenazi (q.v.) Jews, especially the Jews of the Middle East ('Oriental' Jews) living in Israel. Sephardic Judaism dominated Jewish culture from around AD 600 to the expulsion from Spain at the end of the fifteenth century. Some Sephardic Jews rose to positions of eminence in Spain, Portugal, North Africa and Turkey, as royal advisers, court physicians, financiers, philosophers and poets. They were generally more open to secular knowledge than their Ashkenazi brethren, more aristocratic and ostentatious in their religious services and life-style. In the Middle Ages they wrote mostly in Arabic, but their vernacular has remained Ladino, especially in the Mediterranean Sephardic communities. In the twentieth century the Sephardim came to Zionism later than their Ashkenazi co-religionists, but after 1948 it was Middle Eastern Jews who provided the largest waves of immigration to Israel.

shtetl: A small Jewish city, town or village in the Russian Empire or Eastern Europe with its own distinctive socio-cultural pattern and way of life. The *shtetlach* of Poland, Lithuania, the Ukraine, Rumania, Hungary, Bessarabia, etc. were the bulwarks of traditional Jewish values, piety and Ashkenazic culture before the Holocaust.

Shi'a: The term refers in Arabic to the 'partisans' of Ali, cousin and son-in-law of the Prophet, who should have succeeded him instead of Abu Bakr, the first Caliph. Shi'ites, like Sunni Muslims, uphold the five pillars of Islam but have different devotional and religious practices. They believe, for example, in the Hidden Imam, an Islamic Messiah who will return to inaugurate the Golden Age. They are far more concerned than Sunnis with matters of ritual purity, and contact with non-Muslims (especially Jews) is forbidden to them, nor can they use clothes, food or utensils handled by them. This obsessive concern with ritual pollution is especially evident in Shi'ite Iran, where Jews, as the most important non-Muslim minority, have long suffered from the hostility of the populace.

Sunnis: The Sunnis constitute the overwhelming majority of Muslim believers, except for Iran, Iraq and parts of the Lebanon. A Sunni is a Muslim who follows the *Sunna* ('the way') laid down by the Prophet in everything he said, did or caused to be enacted. In practice, Sunni Muslims were usually more tolerant than Shi'ites in their attitudes to Jews, with expulsions, massacres and forced conversions being comparatively rare occurrences. On the other hand, Sunnis have proved to be receptive in the twentieth century to modern European doctrines of nationalism and Western-style antisemitism, as well as absorbing their own variety of Islamic radicalism.

Talmud: A monumental compendium of sixty-three books containing the body of Jewish civil, ceremonial and traditional law which developed out of the Torah (q.v.) and the oral and written commentaries upon it by the leading rabbis. The name is derived from a Hebrew root meaning 'to study' and 'to teach'. A reservoir of rabbinical thought, the Talmud has no dogmas but is a long, complex explication of the Torah which records all the commentaries, interpretations, disagreements and clashing views that evolved over centuries. For a dispersed people it provided an intellectual cement, a common language, code of law and ethics, indispensable for maintaining the cohesion of the Diaspora (q.v.). Christian antisemites since the Middle Ages have seized on the Talmud as an abomination, a heretical book to be burned, though one must assume that few, if any, of the Jew-baiters have ever read a line of the work they execrate. The Christian myth of the 'Talmud Jew' has gained increasing popularity in the Muslim world in recent years, where it is equally divorced from reality.

Torah: In Hebrew the word means 'teaching' or 'doctrine'. The Torah is the text of the Pentateuch (the Five Books of Moses). The very essence of Judaism as a religion, philosophy and set of values is contained in its pages. The 613 commandments set out in the Torah are binding on observant Jews and regulate the conduct of everyday life in minute detail. The Torah is seen as a priceless gift of God to Israel, to prepare it for its religious vocation as a 'holy people'.

ulema: 'Learned men' who devote themselves to the study of the Holy Law of Islam. Derived from the word *alim* (singular of *ulema*), the function of these learned men is in many ways analogous to that of rabbis in Judaism. Their status is derived from their knowledge and learning. They are in no sense priests, having no sacerdotal or priestly mediating role between God and the faithful. Unlike the Shi'ite mullahs, the *ulema* in the Sunni Muslim world have usually been subservient to the secular authorities.

Yishuv: The Hebrew term for the Jewish community in Palestine before 1948. The Old Yishuv denotes the traditional Jewish communities (Ashkenazi and Sephardi) living in the Holy Land before the First Aliyah (q.v.) of 1882 and the New Yishuv refers to the Zionist settlement on the land that gathered pace in the twentieth century.

Select Bibliography

Akbar, Ali, *Israel and the Prophecies of the Holy Qu'ran* (Cardiff, 1971)

al-Khalil, Samir, *Republic of Fear: The Inside Story of Saddam's Iraq* (New York, 1989)

Almog, Shmuel (ed.), *Antisemitism through the Ages* (Pergamon, Oxford, 1988)

Alroy, Gil Carl, *Behind the Middle East Conflict: The Real Impasse between Arab and Jew* (New York, 1975)

van Amerongen, Martin, *Kreisky und seine unbewältigte Vergangenheit* (Graz, 1977)

Arendt, Hannah, *Antisemitism* (New York, 1968)

Aron, Raymond, *De Gaulle, Israël et les juifs* (Paris, 1968)

Ashtor, Eliyahu, *The Jews of Moslem Spain* (Philadelphia, 1973–1984) (3 Vols.)

Baeumler, Alfred, *Alfred Rosenberg und der Mythos des 20 Jahrhunderts* (Munich, 1943)

Baer, Y., *History of the Jews in Christian Spain*, Vol. II (Philadelphia, 1961)

Banas, Josef, *The Scapegoats* (London, 1979)

Baron, Salo W., *The Russian Jew under Tsars and Soviets* (New York, 1964)

Bauer, Bruno, *Die Judenfrage* (Brunswick, 1843)

——, *Das Judentum in der Fremde* (Berlin, 1863)

Baynes, Norman H. (ed.), *The Speeches of Adolf Hitler* (London, 1942)

Begun, V., *Polzuchaya Kontrrevolutsiya* (Minsk, 1974)

Benewick, R. J., *The Fascist Movement in Britain* (London, 1972)

Berger, David (ed.), *History and Hate: The Dimensions of Anti-Semitism* (Philadelphia, 1986)

Bergmann, Werner and Erb, Rainer, (eds.), *Antisemitismus in der politischen Kultur nach 1945* (Opladen, 1990)

Berkley, George E., *Vienna and its Jews: The Tragedy of Success 1880s–1980s* (Cambridge, Mass, 1989)

Billig, M., *Fascists: A Social Psychological View of the National Front* (London, 1978)

Blumenkranz, Bernhard, *Juifs et Chrétiens dans le monde occidental 430–1096* (Paris, 1960)

Boehlich, W. (ed.), *Der Berliner Antisemitismusstreit* (Frankfurt, 1965)

Botz, Gerhard, *Wien vom Anschluss zum Krieg* (Vienna/Munich, 1978)

Braham, Randolph L., *Hungarian Jewish Studies* (New York, 1966)

Broder, Henryk M., *Der ewige Antisemit* (Frankfurt, 1986)

Bunzl, John and Marin, Bernd (eds.), *Antisemitismus in Österreich* (Innsbruck, 1983)

Byrnes, Robert, *Antisemitism in Modern France* (New Brunswick, 1950)

——, *Pobedonostsev* (Bloomington, 1968)

Carsten, F. L., *Fascist Movements in Austria: From Schönerer to Hitler* (London, 1977)

Cohen, Hayyim J., *The Jews of the Middle East 1860–1972* (Jerusalem, 1973)

Cohen, Jeremy, *The Friars and the Jews: Evolution of Medieval Anti-Judaism* (Ithaca, 1982)

Cohn, Norman, *Pursuit of Millennium: Revolutionary Millenarianism and Mystical Anarchists of the Middle Ages* (New York, 1970)

——, *Warrant for Genocide: The Myth of the Jewish World Conspiracy and the Protocols of the Elders of Zion* (London, 1967)

Curtis, Michael (ed.), *Antisemitism in the Contemporary World* (Boulder, Colorado, 1986)

Daumer, G. F., *Der Feuer und Molochdienst der alten Hebräer als urvaterlicher, legaler orthodoxer Cultus der Nation* (Brunswick, 1842)

Davies, A. T. (ed.), *Antisemitism and the Foundations of Christianity* (New York, 1979)

Davis, Moshe (ed.), *World Jewry and the State of Israel* (New York, 1977)

Dietl, Wilhelm, *Holy War* (New York, 1984)

Dinnerstein, Leonard, *The Leo Frank Case* (Athens, Ga, 1966)

——, *Uneasy at Home: Antisemitism and the American Experience* (New York, 1987)

Drumont, Edouard, *La France Juive* (Paris, 1886)

——, *La Fin d'un monde* (Paris, 1889)

——, *La Dernière Bataille* (Paris, 1890)

——, *Le Testament d'un antisémite* (Paris, 1891)

Duncan, Peter, *Nationalism in the USSR* (Amsterdam, 1989)

Dunlop, John B., *The New Russian Nationalism* (New York, 1985)

Engelmann, Hans, *Kirche am Abgrund: Adolf Stoecker und seine antijüdische Bewegung* (Berlin, 1984)

Eckart, Dietrich, *Der Bolschevismus von Moses bis Lenin: Zwiegespräch zwischen Adolf Hitler und mir* (Munich, 1924)

Esposito, John (ed.), *Voices of Resurgent Islam* (New York, 1983)

Ettinger, Shmuel, *Antisemitism in the Modern Age* (Tel Aviv, 1978) (in Hebrew)

Fabre-Luce, Alfred, *Pour en finir avec l'antisémitisme* (Paris, 1979)

Fackenheim, E., *The Jewish Return into History: Reflections in the Age of Auschwitz and a New Jerusalem* (New York, 1978)

Fassbinder, W. R., *Der Müll, die Stadt und der Tod* (Frankfurt, 1981)

Fattal, Antoine, *Le Statut légal des non-musulmans en pays d'Islam* (Beirut, 1958)

Fejtö, François, *Les Juifs et l'antisémitisme dans les pays communistes* (Paris, 1960)

de Felice, Renzo, *Ebrei in un paese arabo: gli ebrei nella Libia contemporanea tra colonialismo, nazionalismo e sionismo 1835–1970* (Bologna, 1978)

Field, Geoffrey C., *Evangelist of Race: The Germanic Vision of Houston S. Chamberlain* (New York, 1981)

Finkielkraut, Alain, *La Réprobation d'Israël* (Paris, 1983)

Fischel, Walter J., *The Jews in the Economic and Political Life of Medieval Islam* (New York, 1969)

Fischer, Heinz (ed.) *Einer im Vordergrund: Taras Borodajkewicz: Eine Dokumentation* (Vienna, 1966)

Fishman, Joshua (ed.), *Studies on Polish Jewry 1919–1939* (New York, 1974)

Fishman, William J., *East End Jewish Radicals 1875–1914* (London, 1975)

Flannery, Edward H., *The Anguish of the Jews* (New York, 1985)

Fleming, Gerald, *Hitler and the Final Solution* (London, 1985)

Freedman, Theodore (ed.), *Anti-Semitism in the Soviet Union, its Roots and Consequences* (New York, 1984)

Friedlander, Henry and Milton, Sybil (eds.), *The Holocaust: Ideology, Bureaucracy and Genocide* (New York, 1980)

Gager, John, *The Origins of Antisemitism: Attitudes towards Judaism in Pagan and Christian Antiquity* (Oxford / New York, 1985)

Gainer, B., *The Alien Invasion* (London, 1972)

Garrard, John A., *The English and Immigration: A Comparative Study of the Jewish Influx 1880–1910* (London, 1971)

Gartner, Lloyd, *The Jewish Immigrant in England 1870–1914* (London, 1960)

Geehr, R. S., *Karl Lueger: Mayor of Fin de Siècle Vienna* (Detroit, 1990)

Gide, André, *Journals 1889–1949* (London, 1967)

Gilboa, Yehoshua A., *The Black Years of Soviet Jewry* (Boston, 1971)

Giraudoux, Jean, *Pleins Pouvoirs* (Paris, 1939)

Gitelman, Zvi, *Jewish Nationality and Soviet Politics* (Princeton, 1972)

Glassman, Bernard, *Anti-Semitic Stereotypes without Jews: Images of Jews in England 1290–1700* (Detroit, 1973)

Goitein, S. D., *Jews and Arabs: Their Contacts through the Ages* (Third revised ed., New York, 1974)

——, *A Mediterranean Society: The Jewish Communities of the Arab World as Portrayed in the Documents of the Cairo Genizah* (4 Vols.) (Berkeley / Los Angeles, 1983)

—— (ed.), *Religion in a Religious Age* (Cambridge, Mass., 1974)

Grayzel, Solomon, *A History of the Jews* (Philadelphia, 1960)

——, *The Church and the Jews in the Thirteenth Century* (Philadelphia, 1933)

Green, D. F. (ed.), *Arab Theologians on Jews and Israel: Extracts from the Proceedings of the Fourth Conference of the Academy of Islamic Research* (Geneva, 1976)

Gutman, Yisrael, *The Jews of Warsaw 1939–1943: Ghetto, Underground, Revolt* (Bloomington, 1982)

Gutteridge, Richard, *Open Thy Mouth for the Dumb: The German Evangelical Church and the Jews 1879–1959* (Oxford, 1976)

Haim, Sylvia (ed.), *Arab Nationalism* (Berkeley / Los Angeles, 1976)

Harkabi, Y., *Arab Attitudes to Israel* (Jerusalem, 1971)

——, *The Palestinian Covenant and its Meaning* (London, 1980)

Heer, Friedrich, *God's First Love* (London, 1967)

Heller, Celia S., *On the Edge of Destruction: Jews of Poland between the Two World Wars* (New York, 1977)

Hellwing, I. A., *Der konfessionelle Antisemitismus im 19 Jahrhundert im Österreich* (Vienna, 1972)

Hertzberg, Arthur, *The French Enlightenment and the Jews* (New York, 1968)

Hirschberg, H. Z., *A History of the Jews in North Africa*, Vol. I (Leiden, 1974)

Hirszowicz, L., *The Third Reich and the Arab East* (London, 1966)

Hitler, Adolf, *Mein Kampf* (Boston, 1943)

Holmes, Colin, *Anti-Semitism in British Society 1876–1939* (New York, 1979)

Isaac, Jules, *Genèse de l'antisémitisme* (Paris, 1956)

Ivanov, Y., *Ostorozhno! Sionizm!* (Moscow, 1969)

Jäckel, Eberhard and Kuhn, Axel (eds.), *Hitler: Sämtliche Aufzeichnungen 1905–1924* (Stuttgart, 1980)

Johnson, Nels, *Islam and the Politics of Meaning in Palestinian Nationalism* (London, 1982)

Katz, J., *The Darker Side of Genius: Richard Wagner's Antisemitism* (London, 1986)

Katzburg, Nathaniel, *Antishemiut B'Hungaria 1867–1914* (Tel Aviv, 1969)

Kedourie, Elie, *Arabic Political Memoirs and Other Studies* (London, 1974)

——, *Islam and the Modern World, and Other Studies* (London, 1980)

Kepel, Gilles, *The Prophet and Pharoah: Muslim Extremism in Egypt* (London, 1985)

Kershaw, Ian, *Popular Opinion and Political Dissent: Bavaria 1933–1945* (Oxford, 1983)

Khomeini, *Islam and Revolution: Writings and Declarations of Imam Khomeini* (Berkeley, 1981)

Kieval, Hillel, *The Making of Czech Jewry* (New York, 1988)

Kisch, Guido, *In Search of Freedom: A History of American Jews from Czechoslovakia* (London, 1949)

Knight, R. (ed.), *'Ich bin dafür, die Sache in die Länge zu ziehen': Die Wortprotokolle der österreichische Bundesregierung von 1945 bis 1952 über die Entschädigung der Juden* (Frankfurt, 1988)

Korey, William, *The Soviet Cage: Anti-Semitism in Russia* (New York, 1973)

Korzec, Pawel, *Juifs en Pologne: La question juive pendant l'entre-deux-guerres* (Paris, 1980)

Krämer, Gudrun, *The Jews in Modern Egypt 1914–1952* (London, 1989)

Kriegel, Annie, *Israël est-il coupable?* (Paris, 1982)

Kulka, O. D. and Mendes-Flohr, P. (eds.), *Judaism and Christianity under the Impact of National Socialism* (Jerusalem, 1987)

Kushner, Tony, *The Persistence of Prejudice: Antisemitism in British Society during the Second World War* (Manchester, 1989)

Langmuir, Gavin, *History, Religion and Antisemitism* (Berkeley/Los Angeles, 1990)

Lebzelter, Gisela, *Political Antisemitism in England 1918–1939* (London, 1978)

Lee, Albert, *Henry Ford and the Jews* (New York, 1980)

Lendvai, Paul, *Antisemitism without Jews: Communist Eastern Europe* (New York, 1971)

Lenin, Vladimir I., *Collected Works* (London, 1960–1970)

Leroy-Beaulieu, Anatole, *L'Antisémitisme* (Paris, 1897)

——, *Les Doctrines de haine: l'antisémitisme, l'antiprotestantisme, l'anticléricalisme* (Paris, 1902)

Levy, Bernard-Henri, *L'Idéologie Française* (Paris, 1981)

Lewis, B., *Islam in History: Ideas, Men and Events in the Middle East* (London, 1973)

——, *Semites and Antisemites: an Inquiry into Conflict and Prejudice* (New York, 1986)

——, *The Middle East and The West* (London, 1963)

Loebl, Eugen, *Sentenced and Tried: The Stalinist Purges in Czechoslovakia* (London, 1969)

Lohrmann, Klaus (ed.), *1000 Jahre österreichisches Judentum* (Eisenstadt, 1982)

London, Artur, *L'Aveu* (Paris, 1969)

Lovsky, F., *Antisémitisme et mystère d'Israël* (Paris, 1955)

Lukacs, John, *Budapest 1900: A Historical Portrait of a City and its Culture* (London, 1989)

Lukashevich, Stephen, *Ivan Aksakov* (Cambridge, Mass., 1965)

Maccoby, Hyam, *The Sacred Executioner: Human Sacrifice and the Legacy of Guilt* (London, 1987)

Marcus, Joseph, *Social and Political History of the Jews of Poland 1919–1939* (Berlin, 1983)

Marrus, Michael, *The Politics of Assimilation: A Study of the French Jewish Community at the Time of the Dreyfus Affair* (Oxford, 1971)

Marrus, Michael and Paxton, Robert, *Vichy France and the Jews* (New York, 1981)

Masaryk, Thomas G., *Die Notwendigkeit der Revision des Polnaer Prozesses* (Vienna, 1899)

Masriya, Yahudiya, *Les Juifs en Egypte* (Geneva, 1971)

Maser, Werner (ed.), *Hitler's Letters and Notes* (New York, 1974)

Massing, Paul W., *Rehearsal for Destruction: A Study of Political Antisemitism in Imperial Germany* (New York, 1949)

McCagg, William, *Jewish Nobles and Geniuses in Modern Hungary* (Boulder, Colorado, 1973)

——, *A History of Habsburg Jews 1670–1918* (Bloomington, 1989)

Mehlman, Jeffrey, *Legacies of Antisemitism in France* (Minneapolis, 1983)

Memmi, Albert, *Jews and Arabs* (Chicago, 1975)

Mendelsohn, Ezra, *The Jews of Eastern Central Europe Between the World Wars* (Bloomington, 1987)

Michelet, Jules, *La Bible de l'humanité* (Paris, 1864)

Misbahul, Islam Farruqi (ed.), *The Jewish Conspiracy and the Muslim World* (Karachi, 1967)

Mitchell, R. P., *The Society of the Muslim Brothers* (London, 1969)

Mosse, Werner E. and Paucker, Arnold (eds.), *Juden in wilhelminischen Deutschland 1890–1914* (Tübingen, 1976)

Nettler, Ronald L., *Past Trials and Present Tribulations: A Muslim Fundamentalist's View of the Jews* (Oxford, 1987)

Noakes, Jeremy and Pridham Geoffrey (eds.), *Documents on Nazism 1919–1945* (London, 1974)

Nolte, Ernst, *Three Faces of Fascism* (London, 1965)

Oberman, Heiko A., *The Roots of Antisemitism in the Age of Renaissance and Reformation* (Philadelphia, 1984)

Oxaal, I. *et al* (eds.), *Jews, Antisemitism and Culture in Vienna* (London/New York, 1987)

Pauley, B. F., *Hitler and the Forgotten Nazis: A History of Austrian National Socialism* (Chapel Hill, 1978)

Peters, Joan, *From Time Immemorial: The Origins of the Arab–Jewish Conflict over Palestine* (London, 1984)

Pierrard, Pierre, *Juifs et catholiques français: de Drumont à Jules Isaac, 1886–1945* (Paris, 1970)

Pinson, Koppel S. (ed.), *Essays on Antisemitism* (New York, 1942)

Poliakov, Léon, *A History of Antisemitism* (London, 1974)

Porath, Y. *The Emergence of the Palestine–Arab National Movement 1918–1929* (London, 1974)

Pühle, Hans Jürgen *Agrarische Interessenpolitik und preussischer Konservatismus in wilhelminische Reich* (Hanover, 1966)

Pulzer, P. G. J. *The Rise of Political Antisemitism in Germany and Austria* (London, 1988, revised edition)

Rabinbach, Anson and Zipes, Jack (eds.), *Germans and Jews since the Holocaust: The Changing Situation in West Germany* (New York/London, 1986)

Redlich, Shimon, *Propaganda and Nationalism in Wartime Russia: The Jewish Anti-Fascist Committee in the USSR 1941–1948* (Boulder, Colorado, 1982)

Regnard, Albert, *Aryens et Sémites: Le bilan du judaisme et du christianisme* (Paris, 1890)

Rejwan, Nissim, *The Jews of Iraq: 3000 Years of History and Culture* (London, 1985)

Renan, Ernst, *Histoire générale et système comparé des langues sémitiques* (Paris, 1855)

——, *History of the People of Israel*, Vol. I, (Boston, 1905)

Ringelblum, Emmanuel, *Polish–Jewish Relations During the Second World War* (New York, 1976)

Roth, Cecil, *History of the Marranos* (New York, 1959)

Roumani, Maurice, *The Case of the Jews from Arab Countries: A Neglected Issue* (Jerusalem, 1975)

Ruether, Rosemary, *Faith and Fratricide: The Theological Roots of Anti-semitism* (New York, 1971)

Rubinstein, W.D., *The Left, the Right, and the Jews* (London/Canberra, 1982)

Sartre, Jean-Paul, *Antisemite and Jew* (New York, 1976)

Schechtman, Joseph, *The Mufti and the Führer: The Rise and Fall of Haj Amin el-Husseini* (New York, 1965)

Schoeps, Julius and Silbermann, Alphons (eds.), *Antisemitismus nach dem Holocaust* (Cologne, 1986)

Schwarz, Solomon, *The Jews in the Soviet Union* (Syracuse, 1951)

Seidel, Gill, *The Holocaust Denial: Antisemitism, Racism, and the New Right* (London, 1986)

Semenyuk, V. A., *Natsionalisticheskoe bezumie* (Minsk, 1976)

Silbermann, Alphons, *Sind wir Antisemiten? Ausmass und Wirkung eines sozialen Vorurteils in der Bundesrepublik Deutschland* (Cologne, 1982)

Shipler, David K., *Arab and Jew: Wounded Spirits in a Promised Land* (London, 1987)

Simon, Marcel, *Verus Israël: étude sur les relations entre chrétiens et juifs dans l'empire romain* (Paris, 1948)

Sivan, Emmanuel, *Radical Islam: Medieval Theology and Modern Politics* (New Haven/London, 1985)

Skidelsky, Robert, *Oswald Mosley* (New York, 1975)

Solodar, Ts, *Dikaya polyn* (Moscow, 1977)

Sombart, Werner, *Die Zukunft der Juden* (Leipzig, 1912)

Sorlin, Pierre, *'La Croix' et les juifs 1889–1899* (Paris, 1967)

Soyfer, D. I., *Sionizm – orudie anti-kommunizma* (Dnepropetrovsk, 1976)

Sterling, E., *Judenhass: Die Anfänge der Politischen Antisemitismus in Deutschland 1815–1850* (Frankfurt, 1969)

Stern, Fritz, *The Politics of Cultural Despair: A Study of the Rise of German Ideology* (Berkeley, 1961)

Stern, Menahem, *Greek and Latin Authors on Jews and Judaism* 3 Vols. (Jerusalem, 1974–84)

Sternhell, Zeev, *La Droite révolutionnaire 1885–1914: les origines françaises du Fascisme* (Paris, 1978)

——, *Maurice Barrès et le nationalisme français* (Paris, 1972)

Stillman, Norman A., *The Jews of Arab Lands: A History and Source Book* (Philadelphia, 1979)

Stoecker, A., *Christlich-Sozial. Reden un Aufsätze* (Berlin, 1890, second ed.)

Tal, U., *Christians and Jews in Germany: Religion, Politics and Ideology in the Second Reich, 1870–1914* (Ithaca/London, 1975)

Thurlow, Richard, *Fascism in Britain: A History 1918–1945* (Oxford, 1987)

Toland, John, *Adolf Hitler* (New York, 1977)

Tomaszewski, Jerzy, *Zarys Dziejów Zydów w Polsce w Latach 1918–1939* (Warsaw, 1990)

Toussenel, A., *Les Juifs: Rois de l'époque: Histoire de la féodalité financière* (Paris, 1845)

Trachtenberg, Joshua, *The Devil and the Jews: The Medieval Conception of the Jew and its Relation to Modern Antisemitism* (New Haven, 1943)

Trevor-Roper, Hugh (ed.), *Hitler's Table Talk* (London, 1973)

Tridon, Gustave, *Du Molochisme juif: Etudes critiques et philosophiques* (Brussels, 1884)

Trigano, Shmuel, *La République et les juifs* (Paris, 1982)

Tritton, A. S., *The Caliphs and their non-Muslim Subjects: A Critical Study of the Covenant of 'Umar* (London, 1930)

Vago, Bela and Mosse, George (eds.), *Jews and non-Jews in Eastern Europe 1918–1945* (New York, 1974)

Wagner, Richard, *Das Judentum in der Musik* (Leipzig, 1869)

Wallach, Jehuda (ed.) *Germany and the Middle East* (Tel Aviv, 1975)

Wardi, Charlotte, *Le Juif dans le roman français 1933–1948* (Paris, 1972)

Wasserstein, Bernard, *Britain and the Jews of Europe 1939–1945* (Oxford, 1979)

Weber, Eugen, *Action française* (Stanford, 1962)

——, *The Nationalist Revival in France 1905–1914* (Los Angeles, 1968)

Weinberg, Henry H., *The Myth of the Jew in France 1967–1982* (New York/ London, 1987)

Weinberg, Meyer, *Because They Were Jews: A History of Anti-Semitism* (New York, 1986)

Wilson, Nelly, *Bernard Lazare: Antisemitism and the Problem of Jewish Identity in Late Nineteenth-Century France* (Cambridge, 1978)

Wilson, Stephen, *Ideology and Experience: Antisemitism in France at the Time of the Dreyfus Affair* (Toronto, 1982)

Winock, Michel, *Edouard Drumont et Cie: Antisémitisme et Fascisme en France* (Paris, 1982)

Wistrich, Robert, *Trotsky: Fate of a Revolutionary* (London, 1979)

—— (ed.), *The Left Against Zion: Communism, Israel and the Middle East* (London, 1979)

——, *The Jews of Vienna in the Age of Franz Joseph* (London, 1989)

——, *Hitler's Apocalypse* (London, 1985)

——, *Between Redemption and Perdition* (London/New York, 1990)

——, *Revolutionary Jews from Marx to Trotsky* (London/New York, 1976)

——, *Socialism and the Jews: Dilemmas of Assimilation in Germany and Austria-Hungary* (London/Toronto, 1982)

—— (ed.), *Anti-Zionism and Antisemitism in the Contemporary World* (London, 1990)

Yadlin, Rivka, *An Arrogant Oppressive Spirit: Anti-Zionism as Anti-Judaism in Egypt* (Oxford, 1989)

Wyman, David S., *The Abandonment of the Jews: America and the Holocaust 1941–1945* (New York, 1984)

Yanov, Alexander, *The Russian Challenge and the Year 2000* (New York, 1987)

Yazbek, Yvonne Haddad, *Contemporary Islam and the Challenge of History* (Albion, 1982)

Ye'or, Bat, *The Dhimmi: Jews and Christians under Islam* (London/ Toronto, 1985)

Zelinski, H., *Richard Wagner: Ein deutsches Thema: Eine Dokumentation zur Wirkungsgeschichte Richard Wagner 1876–1976* (Vienna/Berlin, 1983)

Zimmerman, M., *Wilhelm Marr: The Patriarch of Antisemitism* (New York, 1986)

Index

Index

Index

Bulgaria, 177, 246
Bund (Jewish Workers' Movement), 175
Burns, John, 105
Butz, Arthur, 112
Buylov, Anatoly, 185

Caeserea, Jewish revenge on Christians at (556), 20
Cain, 18–19
Cairo, 223, 227; Academy of Islamic Research Conference (1968), 229–30; al-Azhar University, 228, 230–1
Cala, Alina, 292n
Caligula, Emperor, 6
Calvinism, 38, 116
Carnegie family, 117
Carol, King of Rumania, 147
Carpentras grave-desecration (1990), 138
Carto, Willis, 124
Casablanca, 205
Casimir IV, King of Poland, 34
Cassel, Sir Ernst, 106
Catholic Conservative Party (OVP), Austria, 92
Catholic People's Party, Hungary, 150
Catholics, xx, 28, 39, 67, 80, 101, 115, 116, 122, 235–6, 293n; Anglo-, 106–7; Austrian, 62, 63, 64, 66, 89, 96; Czech, 155; French, 44, 45, 46, 48, 126, 127, 128, 133, 134, 137, 140, 142, 144; Hungarian, 150; medieval, 33–8; Near Eastern, 206; *Nostra Aetate*, 166, 235–6; Polish, 115, 158, 160, 164–5, 166–7, 168–9, 171; Spanish, 35–7; *see also* Christianity; Protestantism
Ceaucescu, Nicolae, 147, 148, 149
Céline, Louis-Ferdinand, 129, 130, 134, 144
Chabauty, Abbé, 127
Chaeromon, Egyptian priest, 7
Chamberlain, Houston S., xxiv, 56, 60, 69, 118
Chamberlain, Joseph, 105
Charlemagne, Emperor, 21, 22
Chesterton, C. E., 106
Chesterton, G. K., 106
Chlenov, Mikhail, 190
Christian Democratic Youth Union, Germany, 84
Christian Front, USA, 115
Christian Party, USA, 115
Christian-Social Party, Austria, 63, 64, 89
Christian-Social Party, Germany, 58
Christian Social Union, Germany, 84
Christianity, Christians, xviii–xxii, xxv, 7, 10, 11–12, 43, 54, 115, 232, 234, 235–6,

242, 252, 257, 264; Armenian, 206, 208, 211; in Britain, 44, 101, 102; Coptic, 211; Crusades, xix, 18, 22, 23–5, 30, 196, 231, 311; *dhimmi* status, 201–2, 203, 204–5, 207–8, 312, 313; early, 13–28; German and Austrian, 49–60 *passim*, 66, 67, 68, 69; Greek Orthodox, 206, 211; in Islamic lands, 198, 199, 200–2, 203, 204–5, 206, 207–8, 211, 213, 235; Maronite, 206; medieval, xix, 3, 29–42; Russian Orthodox, 115, 171–2, 175; Spanish *conversos/marranos*, 35–6, 314; US, 115, 116, 122; *see also* Catholics; Protestants
Chrysostom, St John, 16–17
Church Fathers, 16–17, 18, 21
CIA (Central Intelligence Agency), 189
cicero, *Pro Flacco*, 8
circumcision, 11, 15, 31
Clemenceau, Georges, 129
Clore, Charles, 111
Codex Theodosianus, 19–20
Codreanu, Corneliu, 146
Cohen family, 103, 111
Cold War, xxii, 177
Comintern, Zionism denounced by, 242
Communism/Communist parties, xxiii, xxv, 233, 238, 242; British, 110; Czech, 155–6; French, 137, 140; Hungarian, 151–2, 153; in Islamic countries, 212; Palestine, 241; Polish, 158, 159, 160, 161–4, 165, 167, 168, 170, 291n; Rumanian, 147, 148; Soviet, xxii, xxiv, 173, 174–91 *passim*
concentration-death camps, 73, 91, 92, 95, 112, 133, 159, 168, 177, 210; Auschwitz, 74, 79, 83, 84, 96, 112, 139, 141, 168, 293n; *see also* Gulag labour camps
Conservative Party, British, 110, 111
Conservative Party, German, Tivoli Programme (1892), 61
Constantine (Algeria), 209
Constantinople (now Istanbul) pogrom (1894), 206
conversos or *marranos* (converted Jews in Spain), 35–6, 314
Coptic Christians, 211
Cordoba, killing of Jews in (1010–13), 196
Corpus Christi, feast of, 32
Coston, Henri, 131
Coughlin, Charles E., 115
Counter-Reformation, 37
Crémieux, Adolphe, 206, 311
Crimea affair, 178

Index

Index

Feisal, King of Saudi Arabia, 207, 232, 233, 254, 304n
Ferdinand and Isabella, King and Queen of Spain, 36
Fellner, Hermann, 84
Ferrer, St Vincente, 35
Feuerbach, Ludwig, 50
Fez (Morocco) massacre of Jews in, 196, 205
'Final Solution' (Nazi extermination of Jews), xxii, 30, 66–77, 78, 79, 91, 133, 159, 314
First World War, 61, 69, 88, 89, 104, 106, 118, 126, 150, 154, 242
Flaccus, Roman governor, 6
Flannery, Edward, 28
Flavia, 9
Flavius Clemens, 9
Forain, Jean, 130
Ford, Henry, 118–19; *The International Jew*, 181, 222
Fourier, Charles, 48, 137
Fourth Lateran Council (1215), 25–6, 32, 33
France, xv, 23, 38, 43–8, 101, 116, 126–44, 211, 213; Algerian War, 209; antisemitic bombings and outrages, 138; Damascus Affair (1840), 206, 207, 235, 311; Dreyfus Affair, 126–7, 128–9, 137, 142; Druze revolt against (1925), 213; grave-desecrations in, 138–9; Libyan independence from (1951), 211; New Right, 127, 134, 139–42, 143; North African Arab and Jewish immigrants, 138, 139, 143, 209–10; Popular Front government (1936), 131; post-1945: 134–44; Syrian independence from (1945), 213; Tunisian independence from (1956), 210; Vichy goverment (1940–44), 131, 132–4, 142
Francis of Assisi, St, 28
Franciscan order, 34
Frank, Leo, lynching of (1916), 118, 283–4n
Frankish Kingdom, 21–2
Franklin family, 103
Franz Joseph, Emperor, 63–4
Free Democrats movement, Hungary, 153
Freedom Party, Austria, 93, 97
French Revolution (1789), xxi, 43–4, 55, 126, 127, 131, 133
Freud, Sigmund, 54, 62, 184, 226
Fries, Jakob, 55
Fritsch, Theodor, 58

Front National, France, 126, 134, 139–42, 143

Gabirol, Solomon Ibn, 197
al-Gailānī, Rashīd Ālī, 215
Galdich, Aleksandr, 184, 185
Gaon, Saadya, 197
Gaulle, President Charles de, 136
Gavrielscu, Valentin, 148
Gaza, Israeli occupation of, 231, 238, 248, 254
Gebert, Konstanty, 168
Germany, xv, 18, 23, 37, 43, 48–53, 55–61, 66–87, 101, 116; Allied de-Nazification of, 79–80; Austrian *Anschluss* (1938), 88, 89–90; East (GDR), 80; Eichmann Trial (1961), 247; fall of France to (1940), 132; Final Solution, xxii, 30, 66–77, 78, 133, 159, 314; 'Hep! Hep!' riots (1819), 55; al-Husseini's collaboration with Hitler, 245–6, 253; invasion of Soviet Union (1941), 72, 75, 94, 176; *Kristallnacht* pogrom, 71, 73, 74; medieval, 32–3; Nazi occupation of Czechoslovakia (1939), 155; Nazi occupation of Poland (1939), 157, 158–9, 160, 168; Nazi-Soviet Pact (1939–41), 176; neo-Nazis and Right-wing, 84, 85–6, 87; New Left, 81–3, 87; occupation of Libya, 211; occupation of Tunisia, 210; post-1945 Federal Republic, 78, 79, 80–6; Reformation, 38–42; Third Reich (Nazi regime), xix, xxii, 30, 52, 53, 66–77, 78, 79, 81, 84, 109, 110, 118, 120, 131, 134, 137, 146, 158, 176, 187, 190, 214, 244–6; unification of (1990), 79, 86–7, 142; Weimar Republic xvii, 54, 69, 81, 187
Gerö, Ernö, 152
Ghali, Butros, 262
ghettos, ghettoisation, 28, 35, 37, 54, 55, 71, 132, 196
Gide, André, 130
Gieremek, Bronislaw, 164
Giertych, Professor Maciej, 166–7, 293n
Giraudoux, Jean, 129, 132
Giscard d'Estaing, Valéry, 138
Glagau, Otto, 57
glasnost, 183, 190
Glemp, Cardinal Jozef, 140, 166–7, 169, 292n
Globke, Hans, 80
Globocnik, Odilo, 91
Gobineau, Artur, Compte de, 47, 57, 126, 130, 252

332

Index

Index

Index

Index

Index

Index